THE MAKING OF VICTORIAN SEXUALITY

Michael Mason is a Senior Lecturer in English at
University College London.

DATE DUE

DEMCO 38-296

P9-EAN-898

R

The Making of
VICTORIAN
SEXUALITY

❧❧❧❧❧❧❧❧❧❧❧❧

MICHAEL MASON

❧❧❧❧❧❧❧❧❧❧❧❧

Oxford   New York

OXFORD UNIVERSITY PRESS

Riverside Community College
Library
4800 Magnolia Avenue
Riverside, California 92506

FEB '98

HQ 18 .G7 M28 1995

Mason, Michael, 1941-

The making of Victorian
sexuality

Oxford OX2 6DP

Bombay
am Delhi
Karachi
Melbourne
ngapore

Taipei Tokyo

and associated companies in
Berlin Ibadan

Oxford is a trade mark of Oxford University Press

First published by Oxford University Press 1994
First issued as an Oxford University Press paperback 1995

© Michael Mason 1994

All rights reserved. No part of this publication may be reproduced,
stored in a retrieval system, or transmitted, in any form or by any means,
without the prior permission in writing of Oxford University Press.
Within the UK, exceptions are allowed in respect of any fair dealing for the
purpose of research or private study, or criticism or review, as permitted
under the Copyright, Designs and Patents Act, 1988, or in the case of
reprographic reproduction in accordance with the terms of the licences
issued by the Copyright Licensing Agency. Enquiries concerning
reproduction outside those terms and in other countries should be
sent to the Rights Department, Oxford University Press,
at the address above.

This book is sold subject to the condition that it shall not, by way
of trade or otherwise, be lent, re-sold, hired out, or otherwise circulated
without the publisher's prior consent in any form of binding or cover
other than that in which it is published and without a similar condition
including this condition being imposed on the subsequent purchaser.

British Library Cataloguing in Publication Data
Data available

Library of Congress Cataloging in Publication Data
Data available
ISBN 0–19–285312–0

3 5 7 9 10 8 6 4 2

Printed in Great Britain
at Biddles Ltd
Guildford and King's Lynn

*For my mother
and in loving memory
of my father*

Contents

❧

Abbreviations

꒰ঌ꒱

BMJ   *British Medical Journal*
EHR   *English Historical Review*
JSSL   *Journal of the [Royal] Statistical Society of London*
PS   *Population Studies*
TNAPSS   *Transactions of the National Association for the Promotion of Social Science*
VPNL   *Victorian Periodicals Newsletter*

Chapter One

꧁ᔑ꧂ᔑ꧁ᔑ꧂ᔑ꧁ᔑ꧂ᔑ꧁ᔑ꧂ᔑ

LOCATING RESPECTABILITY

꧁ᔑ꧂ᔑ꧁ᔑ꧂ᔑ꧁ᔑ꧂ᔑ꧁ᔑ꧂ᔑ

I

The Alien Victorians

THE main reason for this book about the past is a fact about the present. In our culture the Victorian age has a special place: more than any other era it awakens in us our capacities to feel hostile towards a past way of life, to perceive the past as alien, unenlightened, and silly. This is by no means the only feeling we have about the Victorians, but in attracting certain other feelings—including the positive ones of nostalgia, sense of affinity, and even admiration—the Victorian period is like any historical era. What makes it distinctive is the hostility included in the mix of attitudes we have about it.

If we had to identify a point at which the past becomes unequivocally the past most of us would probably locate it near the latter end of Victoria's reign, around 1900. Though we live in the final decade of the twentieth century we are still remarkably capable of feeling united with all the generations back to 1900; after the turn of the last century everyone, so to speak, is family; before the turn of the century lies the other, the irrecoverable, the strange—human beings who are not like us and who are sundered from us by the power of historical processes. 'Twentieth century' still means something like 'modern' in our present usage.

The fact that the Victorians are the first historical people is surely connected with our special hostility towards them. Sooner or later historical consciousness will have to move its frontiers forward, and decide that the past starts well after 1900. Perhaps the advent of the second millennium will dissolve prejudices and enable us to release the Victorians from their long tour of duty, but at the moment it is hard to imagine any part of the last ninety years having the necessary feeling of the alien about it. None the less, it is virtually certain that our own culture will at some time be stigmatized, because it has become the most recent example of the past for some future generation. It is an interesting exercise to try to predict the grounds on which the future will anathematize us. To judge by the Victorian experience, the faults which our descendants detect in our culture will *not* be the faults which we most readily attribute to ourselves.

At the other end of Victoria's reign the element of hostility fades from our sense of the past. We can have a variety of feelings about George IV, Jane Austen, Jeremy Bentham, Thomas Paine, Nelson, the younger Pitt, and William Blake, but there is not mixed up in them that curiously personal disapproval which we tend to feel for any comparable group of Victorians. Admiration for Tennyson is likely to be an ambivalent state of mind in a way that admiration for Keats is not, and so on for many pairs one could construct. In fact, as I shall mention shortly, our modern sense of affinity with the stirring political and cultural developments of the decades around 1800 is such that it must appear as something of a mystery that the derided episode of the 'Victorian' ever managed to insert itself.

'Victorian', as we employ the term in our ordinary usage, is unique among historical labels, or very unusual, in the amount of meaning it can carry beyond the chronological. Such expressions often have a descriptive or judgemental potential when they are used on their own territory (a phenomenon in the Middle Ages may be 'typically medieval'), but very few have this kind of force regardless of the historical framework, and then usually in particular applications. An administration may be 'Byzantine', and an individual may have 'Renaissance' qualities of mind, but a person, or a frame of mind, or a belief, or an institution, or an utterance, from any period, can be 'Victorian'. The primary meaning of the term in this figurative use—that is, what we would suppose was being said if we heard a non-nineteenth-century person being baldly described as 'Victorian' without further explanation—is most interesting. It indicates the essence of our hostile feeling about the period. I would suggest that to hear something baldly referred to as 'Victorian' must convey the idea of moral restrictiveness, a restrictiveness which necessarily and even primarily applies to sex.

It makes good sense if the nub of our hostility to the Victorians is their supposed sexual moralism. Tolerance and candour about sexual matters are for most people key elements in their sense of attachment to our modern culture, features of the moral climate which they are definitely pleased with, not to say smug about—and which make them think the present is an improvement on the past. This may seem a doubtful generalization in view of the existence of a body of opinion which deplores the modern sexual freedoms, but this antagonism has to be compared with the scale of the doubt that exists on other recent developments in our society. There is not unanimous approval of our current arrangements on marriage and divorce, contraception (and abortion in some contexts), non-standard sex between consenting adults, and censorship; but nor is there unanimity as to whether most of our political and social arrangements are in good shape. Perhaps only universal suffrage, of all post-Victorian innovations, would be found to command decisively larger support than the tendency of our modern sexual code (there is thus a considerable irony in the fact that many women suffragists at the end of the nineteenth century were vehemently opposed to any relaxing of sexual standards, and actually urged greater continence). We feel that our age is unusually liberal on sexual questions, and the great majority of us agree with the spirit of this liberalism if not with its letter.

Also important here is the fact that our modern sexual consensus is in its very essence reactive, and impossible even to state without the notion of an ideological enemy being brought into play. Our current sexual positives are not just activity, but liberation, emancipation, freedom; not just hedonism, but disinhibition; not just tolerance, but hostility to taboos and censorship. An anti-sensual code is likely to find itself with a similar requirement for phantom enemies in order to give itself a conceptual skin or solidity, and in fact the Victorian code was conceived just as reactively as ours. There is truth in Michel Foucault's perception that the nineteenth and twentieth centuries are more united by their tremendous interest in sex, than they are divided by the 'repressive' and 'anti-repressive' turns which moral codes have taken in the two periods. For the Victorians, however, the pro-sensual opposition was not located in any particular historical era: they located it most consistently in human personality, in tribal or ancient societies, and in the animal kingdom. We with a remarkable rigour have identified the anti-sensual enemy as residing almost solely in the culture of a hundred years ago.

It is correct to think that the latter twentieth century, in the West, is unusual in its permissiveness about sex. By the same token it is wrong to single out the Victorians as exponents of the opposite philosophy. Indeed, to suppose that there is anything out of the ordinary about the basic framework of sexual orthodoxy in the Victorian period is a blunder of the crudest sort: the Victorians could probably not have discovered a period on the past plausibly to demonize even if they had wished. Attacks on masturbation may seem absurd to twentieth-century Western readers, but we cannot take heart from the notion that only the demented Victorians thought otherwise; our culture is hopelessly outvoted on this question as on many others relating to human sexuality. Male and female masturbation, unconstrained liaisons for both sexes and all kinds of non-marital intercourse for women, and very frequent intercourse within marriage (that is to say, intercourse as often as physiology permits) have been deplored, repressed, and even punished in the majority of known human societies. Of the leading prohibitions in the Victorian sexual code only that on homosexuality is not almost universal among other cultures (and our modern concept of the exclusively homosexual personality is also a cultural rarity: even societies tolerant of homosexuality have generally sought to integrate it into a predominant code of stable heterosexual bonds).[1]

This does not rule out a more sophisticated version of events, to the effect that there were relatively subtle intensifications of sexual reticence and restraint in the Victorian era. But why did these occur? The worst difficulty about our modern stereotype of the Victorian is that it delivers a picture of historical change which is not just abrupt, but perverse. For we perceive the pre-Victorian years—the decades around 1800—as more than just an era in which the 'Victorian' had yet to assert itself. This is the era of revolution and romanticism, which strikes us as positively opposed in spirit to the 'Victorian' in important respects. We tend to look back on it as a congenial episode, even to hail it as a precursor of our own era. Thus the Victorians emerge as oddly bracketed by the 'modern'. The idea of a to-and-fro movement in the sexual culture of the last 200 years (per-

[1] Ford and Beach 1951: 18–19, 75–83, 106–8, 115, 130–2, 156–8; Marshall and Suggs 1971: 212.

haps given a certain air of plausibility by imagery of pendulums of sexual moralism swinging back and forth) is often to be encountered, but there is something unsatisfactorily arbitrary about this way of thinking. It would be pleasing to develop a more continuous and sequential account. My main effort in this study, in fact, is to bring out the extent to which the disparaged sexual moralism of the Victorian years grows directly from aspects of late eighteenth-century and early nineteenth-century culture which are likely to strike us as among the most bold, progressive, and refreshing features of that period.

There are therefore implications for the role of reticence and restraint in our modern sexual culture. It is the chief oddity of our modern sexual code in the West that it has no place for the notion of sexual excess; the very idea tends to strike us as embarrassing and old fashioned. This has made prohibitions on sexual behaviour, of any sort, seem problematic, and possibly indefensible. But we should not be inhibited about inhibitions: at all times and at all places constraints and prohibitions have been woven into the fabric of human sexuality. Indeed, a liberalized sexual code has in some respects sharpened our awareness of the need for sexual repression. The belief that male sexual activity should be confined to moderate inter-course in marriage may have been rejected, for example, but it is widely agreed that this cannot be a charter for 'sexual harrassment', let alone for rape and the sexual abuse of children. Some women feel that it is even immoral for a man to masturbate without the know-ledge or consent of the woman whose body or voice he is using as his sexual stimulus: so masturbation, against the odds, is still on our modern agenda of moral issues. A major implication of the chapters which follow is that we can understand and even see the point of nineteenth-century sexual moralism if we realize that, for many men and women in the period, issues about sexual behaviour presented themselves as they do to modern feminists: as issues to be judged according to a secular, rational, and progressive code rather than in the light of the deliverances of moral and religious authority.

It is, after all, only to be expected that the Victorian version of pro-hibition should be relevant to our own sexual code, more relevant than that of any other era. Not only were the Victorians the heirs to the egalitarian, rational, and progressive tradition of the Enlighten-ment to which we can trace so many of our modern ideals, but we share with them, as with no other previous epoch, the social context in which their sexual culture was set. The Victorians were seeking outlets for their sexual needs in a society very much closer to the urbanized, capitalist, technology-ruled societies of the modern West than any that had gone before. The reader exploring the documents of Victorian sexual culture will encounter many unfamiliar concerns and beliefs, but also the first comment and description concerning such matters as the sex-education of children, urban 'night life'—as we would now term it—and courtship in urban communities, middle-class marriages involving commuting husband and home-based wife, the competing claims of pleasure and procreation in married sex, and the rationale of divorce.

The progressive element in Victorian sexual moralism is not the whole of the story I seek to tell: I have tried to give a broad account of the heterosexual culture of nineteenth-century England up until about 1880 (the evidence about homosexuality in the period being extremely meagre). It seems to me that most studies of the 'Victorian' have been too restricted, ignoring not only the demographic and anecdotal evidence about actual behaviour, but even expressions of attitude outside a narrow band of moralistic discourse. There is an honourable handful of essays and books which have not shunned the challenge of bridging between nineteenth-century attitudes and behaviour. Peter Gay's *The Education of the Senses* (1984) and Françoise Barret-Ducrocq's *Love in the Time of Victoria* (1991) are distinctive and valuable for this reason, one in relation to the middle classes in the West and the other in relation to the English working class. Both these books, however, draw on a more selected body of evidence than I have surveyed here.

I am very conscious of the uncertainties attending both sides of the subject, and of the difficulty of fitting the two together in other than a trivial or far-fetched way. On the one hand are sexual practices, which can be only imperfectly reconstructed from demography and contemporary descriptive evidence. On the other hand are sexual attitudes—but it is usually an uncertain step from a particular surviving statement of an attitude to worthwhile generalizations about attitudes at large. And the sexual culture of a society is a matter of practices and attitudes set side by side: what connections, let alone connections which can now be discerned, do they have with each other? In this study—of which the first third (that is, about two-thirds of the present volume) is about practices, and the rest about attitudes—I try to be as explicit as possible about the character of the evidence I am using at every point, and I discuss the major problems in interpreting it as they arise.

Certain interesting conclusions I believe are none the less secure. In its sexual practices nineteenth-century England emerges as a society which suffered some kind of crisis of confidence, temporarily, over courtship, marriage, and procreative intercourse in its first two or three decades. Thereafter, in the mid-century at least, intercourse within marriage or relationships of concubinage to some extent displaced traditional resort to prostitutes and perhaps other kinds of casual sex. Married and unmarried couples at various levels of society adopted artificial contraceptive methods as early as the 1860s and these practices spread widely and quickly: they may have increased the amount of non-marital intercourse taking place at the end of the period. Certainly the foundations for such a development were there in the considerable freedom and intimacy with which young people of all classes, betrothed or not, were allowed to consort.

In its attitudes to sex this society had a widespread and principled belief that there should be discipline and unobtrusiveness in all sexual activity, though this belief is hard to distinguish from the powerful influence of ideals of gentility in behaviour, particularly among the working class. It is a belief with more strands to it than is commonly recognized: a newly vigorous Nonconformist or low church religious spirit is only a part of it, and an equivocal one at that. It was sustained much more significantly by secularist and progressive opinion, to which the ideals of sexual control and reserve were generally deeply congenial. To this phenomenon must be traced the failure of liberationist ideas to thrive for most of the period, for it was inevitably in the stony soil of progressive thought that they were sown.

Uniting most manifestations of this anti-sensual mentality (with the notable exception of a powerful surviving tradition I have called 'classic moralism') was a belief in the power of environmental conditions over an individual's inner nature—extending even to his or her sex drives. This belief emanated from progressive thought in the Enlightenment, but became extremely widespread in nineteenth-century England and helped to bind together in an anti-sensual coalition otherwise disparate parties (it is an aspect of the complex role of Evangelicalism that it was often in tune with the progressive belief in environmental forces). But the medical understanding of sexuality was not wholly consistent with this theoretical vision of the libido, and in neither lay nor medical circles—despite one of the most popular modern clichés about the period—was there a significant antagonism to, or ignorance about, the sexual response in women. On the contrary, the belief that a woman had to experience orgasm in order to conceive was general among the lay public well into the last decades of the century.

II

A Developing Stigma

The idea of the 'Victorian'—of a disparagingly regarded cultural phase that starts around 1837 and has doctrines of sexual restraint, perhaps hypocritical, as key elements—did not arise before Victoria's death, though it did very quickly establish itself thereafter. It had its first currency in informal and unwritten, or at least unpublished, usage. In 1910 Edward Garnett, introducing his father's biography of the Unitarian Radical W. J. Fox, makes considerable play with the 'Victorian' in the mentality of Fox and his associates. The adjective does have a hostile edge, but only to the extent that Garnett finds the Victorians tending to moral complacency. In general, he claims to admire the 'optimism, and moral idealism' of the period. And it is interesting that his father Richard, who completed his work on the book in 1906, did not avail himself of the opportunity to identify Fox's irregular sexual life (which I discuss in the next volume) as in any sense 'Victorian'.[2] But such usages must have been only just sustainable, even at this early date. A loaded sense of the 'Victorian' was lurking in the wings, in less formal discourse. As soon as men and women start to use the term in a fully judgemental way in published contexts, about five years later, they are also likely to refer to a habit of such use which they allege is widespread—even to the point of defending Victoria's reign against accusations of prudery and so forth. In 1918 Edmund Gosse appealed with some confidence to his readers' experience of the phenomenon: 'for a considerable time past everybody must have noticed, especially in private conversation, a growing tendency to disparagement and even ridicule of all men and things, which can be defined as "Victorian"'.[3]

How long might Gosse's readers have understood this 'consider-

---

[2] Garnett 1910: pp. viii–ix.   [3] Gosse 1918.

able time' to be? For Arthur Quiller Couch, in a lively account of 'the fashion of scorning all things "Victorian"' spreading outwards epidemically over the country from Cambridge, where 'it had raged with something like virulence', 1913 was the important date. But he also says that the 'especial virus' was Samuel Butler's *The Way of All Flesh*, which was first published in 1903 (and, supposedly, 'hung fire' until the edition of 1910). Compton Mackenzie recalled the first issue of *The Way of All Flesh* as 'the most important literary event of my time in Oxford' for the way the 'younger generation' found in the novel 'a point of concentration for their ideas of the Victorian'. This all suggests that the real beginnings of Oxbridge anti-Victorianism dated from earlier than 1913, perhaps considerably earlier. When a 75-year-old memoirist, writing in 1915, complains that 'mid-Victorian' is 'a reproach at the service of every puny whipster of the chair' it is hard to think that he is noticing an undergraduates' craze of about two years' standing. As early as 1914 an American authoress of domestic advice-books, Annie Winsor Allen, had made 'Victorian Hypocrisy' (admittedly, as identified in both Britain and America) the subject of an *Atlantic Monthly* article—and also made it her chief business to confront hostile clichés about the period. 'The worst Victorian hypocrisy, of course,' she says, 'is held to be prudishness'. In that 'of course' there is a strong sense of cliché well-entrenched and widespread.[4]

There does survive occasional evidence of 'Victorian' and its variants circulating as hostile locutions in young people's usage in Britain very early in this century. Already by 1908 the younger generation was accused by an older writer on the Victorian era of expressing in its conversation 'pitying tolerance' and 'indulgent rebuke' towards the period. D. H. Lawrence, in a letter of 1910, says that a female friend 'still judges by mid-Victorian standards' because 'she refuses to see that a man is a male, that kisses are the merest preludes and anticipations'. Lawrence had just read H. G. Wells's novel *Ann Veronica*, published the previous year, a text which contains perhaps the clearest surviving evidence on the point. Wells twice uses the vocabulary of 'Victorian', in dialogue, in disparaging allusion to the

[4] Quiller Couch 1922: 296–7; C. Mackenzie 1933: 143; Whiteing 1915: 259; A. W. Allen 1914. Whiteing specifies the 'mid-Victorian' chiefly because this was the period of his young manhood, but he may also be accurately reporting a transitional step to fully fledged anti-Victorianism, as I shall illustrate shortly. See also *The Times*, 26 Apr. 1912, p. 7: 'our moral ideas . . . seem every day more different from the moral ideas of fifty years ago'.

sexual moralism of the period. Ann Veronica's would-be lover, Ramage, who is a businessman in his late forties, upbraids the heroine: 'I mean to have you! Don't frown me off now. Don't go back into Victorian respectability and pretend you don't know and you can't think and all the rest of it.' And later Ann Veronica, in a fancied conversation with the man she herself loves, reflects that 'the Victorians overdid it a little, I admit. Their idea of maidenly innocence was just a blank white' (the 'I admit' is presumably meant to betoken Ann's conversion to an established view of Victorian sexual values: Wells's heroine is actually entering a qualification—'there *is* innocence . . . One wants to be *clean*'—in a way that the present study will suggest is plausible for a progressive mentality of the period).[5]

By the end of the Great War anti-Victorianism was evidently no longer an invading virus quarantined in 'private conversation', but a settled condition of English intellectual culture. In 1918 'acute disparagement' of the Victorians was noticed as 'the fashion for writers in the press and elsewhere'. Two years earlier the *New Statesman* had carried an attack on the period which is particularly notable for its venom and swagger: 'as an era, it may have been good, but it was good in a wicked way.' By 1918 the *Times Literary Supplement* was voicing an attitude that went strikingly beyond mere detestation of the Victorian age, a sheer sense of alienation from an 'odd and almost incredible epoch': 'Although as a matter of date it is only yesterday that the Victorian Age ended . . . so strangely different a world do we live in now that an air of remoteness has already settled on that recent epoch.'[6]

The growth of anti-Victorianism in the early years of this century was as precipitate as it looks. That is to say, there was scarcely any preparation for it in Victoria's reign itself, and in that sense the 'Victorian' is a very un-Victorian notion. It is perhaps not to be expected that actually hostile views of the period would have been very current before 1901. In the closing years of the reign the two jubilees, of 1887 and 1897, would have deterred disrespectful perceptions (a survival of such an effect may be part of the reason why, by about 1910, men and women were apparently disparaging

[5] Carr 1908; Boulton 1979: 153; H. G. Wells 1909: 203, 243. Neither Lawrence's nor Wells's labelling was strict, however, and they could as readily stigmatize the whole 19th cent. (see Boulton 1979: 124; H. G. Wells 1911: 45). On Lawrence's qualified term 'mid-Victorian' see n. 4.

[6] Bridges 1919: 1; 'The Victorian', *New Statesman*, 10 (1917), 180–1; *TLS* 16 May 1918, p. 230.

Victorian values privately but not publicly). The jubilees, and the Queen's death, did jog writers into pondering 1837 as a moral watershed, however, and the surprising point is that until these promptings the reign simply does not seem to have struck commentators as an interesting unit of moral history, of whatever colour. The historian G. W. E. Russell, for example, published two volumes of *Collections and Recollections* that straddled the end of the reign. In the first (originally serialized in the *Guardian* in 1898) it is the eighteenth/nineteenth-century borderline that marks a revolution in the moral world and an ascent from a '*nadir* of English virtue' in the 1790s. In Russell's second volume, of 1902, the main divide—not without some touches of contradiction—has moved forward to 1837, to suit a new historical model of 'society . . . purged and disciplined by Queen Victoria's sweet influence'.[7] Probably the earliest surviving discussion of moral change in the nineteenth century which puts a firm emphasis on the accession of Victoria is Walter Besant's *Fifty Years Ago* of 1888. Even this is essentially a reflection on the first jubilee, shifted forward by a year. Besant is so determined to supplant 1800 as a moral watershed that he invents a strange and prophetic trope, whereby the eighteenth century lasts until Victoria comes to the throne: 'it cannot be too often repeated that in 1837 we were still in that century'.[8]

The weakness of the notion of the 'Victorian' in the last years of the nineteenth century is strikingly illustrated by its absence from the thinking of the men and women who were trying to liberalize sexual attitudes and practices at the time. These were the individuals temperamentally least likely to be daunted by the shibboleth of respect for the Queen, yet the historical model in question does not appear in their writings, if at all, until rather late, when it is already a commonplace with less bold spirits. Part of the explanation lies with the very seriousness of these writers' attack on contemporary sexual codes. Men such as Grant Allen, Edward Carpenter, and Havelock Ellis

---

[7] G. W. E. Russell 1899: 64, 1908: 8. The diamond jubilee similarly encouraged the novelist Mary Betham-Edwards to put an emphasis on Victoria's reign as a time of moral regeneration: 'one of the greatest changes in the Victorian era is a progressive moral standard' (Betham-Edwards 1898: 110). Algernon West, with a brief to write a magazine piece in 1897 on 'Some Changes in Social Life during the Queen's Reign', supplemented memories of his youth in London in the 1850s with the indirect evidence of the recollections of older individuals to develop a picture of the early part of the reign as a time of powerful 'Puritan restraints' coexisting with great laxity (A. West 1897).

[8] Besant 1888: 265.

were trying to bring about a secular change in this domain and they
thought in large chronological terms and extensive cultural phases:
Christianity, capitalism, civilization, even human history as a whole.
But more gadfly sexual emancipationists in the 1890s, with more
local concerns, do not focus on Victoria and her reign either. And
emancipationists of all types tend to fall in with the prevailing anti-
Victorianism of the Great War years and after.

Grant Allen's epoch of sexual oppression is the grandest. It
stretches back out of historical sight (consequently this reformer is
perhaps the only one in the period whose historical model is not in
some way cyclical, with sexual emancipation understood as a recov-
ery of lost sexual freedoms). For Allen sexual reticence and restraint
are 'taboos' on a particular 'bodily function' and taboos are a 'legacy
of savagery'. We have to return to the plant and animal kingdoms for
the spectacle of sex as Grant Allen would wish the 'new hedonists' to
practise it: bird-song and blossom represent sexuality unabashed.
The feminist Mona Caird took almost as long a view as Allen but in
her version there is at least, at the dawn of history, a time when society was a matriarchal affair with an enlightened sexual code: 'the
greatest evils of modern society had their origin, thousands of years
ago, in the dominant abuse of patriarchal life: the custom of woman-
purchase'.[9]

Edward Carpenter's historical picture included a clearly envisaged
sexual utopia, that of the 'early societies' with their 'worship of Sex
and Life' and their practice of 'group-marriage'. It is not apparent
when this happy epoch is understood to have ended: certainly
Christianity (with its 'monks, mystics, and world-spiting puritans')
deals it a blow, but Carpenter's socialism required that the horrors of
modern sexuality should also be a product of capitalism and thus a
post-feudal phenomenon. Carpenter is a good case of a forthright
emancipationist of the 1890s who later slips into the new rhetoric of
anti-Victorianism, which he then deploys energetically. In 1916, by
grafting on to his existing historical model (though with touches of
hesitation) a notion of growing deterioration, he can achieve this
account:

that strange period of human evolution the Victorian Age, which in some
respects, one now thinks, marked the lowest ebb of modern civilised society:
a period in which . . . commercialism . . . cant in religion, pure materialism in

⁹ G. Allen 1894; Caird 1897: 1.

science . . . the 'impure hush' on matters of sex, class division . . . the cruel barring of women from every natural and useful expression of their lives, were carried to an extremity of folly difficult for us now to realise.[10]

Havelock Ellis's treatment of the historical question was altogether more erudite and nuanced than these simple schemes. But, while it reflected a subtle and richly informed intelligence, it was also affected by this writer's characteristic miscellaneousness of mind and inability to dominate a complex subject. The result is a hazy, even contradictory historical picture. Ellis never, it is true, yields to fashionable anti-Victorianism. When he anticipates a modern cliché in citing the Victorian doctor William Acton and his 'vile aspersion' of female sexual insensibility he brings forward comparisons with ancient Greece and the early Middle Ages to suggest that Acton's is a venerable fallacy. And the distinction he draws between 'modesty' and 'prudery' in the first volume of *Studies in the Psychology of Sex*, published in 1899, allows him a long and a short historical perspective on anti-sensualism. He is nevertheless inconsistent on how the nineteenth century stands in the recent story. He oscillates rather freely between thinking of the period as uniquely prudish, and as the site of burgeoning sexual emancipation. He has an interesting discussion of eighteenth-century English prudery (as evinced, say, in Sterne's 'sudden reticences, the dashes, and the asterisks' and 'the altogether new quality of literary prurience'), but by the time of the sixth volume of the *Studies* (1910) it is the nineteenth century, more orthodoxly, which seems to occupy the role previously attributed to the eighteenth. Indeed Ellis's remarks here about the triumph in the nineteenth century of the 'revolt against nakedness' (though balanced, with his usual insight, by observations on the new positive valuation of nudity), and about other phenomena in the period, amount to an accusation of sexual repressiveness which he levelled at no other epoch.[11]

Writers like Carpenter and Ellis were full-time sexual radicals. There were other writers who joined the emancipationist ranks sporadically in the 1880s and 1890s, on particular issues. The most lively quarrels between reformist and reactionary opinion on sexual questions sprang from literature, and especially from the fiction of the day. These were topical controversies—hinging, for the reformers, on

[10] E. Carpenter 1896: 135–6; 1916: 321–2.
[11] H. H. Ellis 1922; 1932; 1887; 1899: 65; 1910: 99.

the iniquities of Mudie's library or the philistinism of the English middle class—and it is to be expected that jibes and protests about the 'Victorian' would be heard among the shouting if this had formed itself as a sexual-historical category in people's minds. But the Victorian, it seems, is never what the reformers thought they were up against—even if the onset of literary prudery is usually perceived as occurring rather later than it did for Thackeray in his celebrated remark in the preface to *Pendennis* about constraints in force since Fielding's death, or 1754. Sir Richard Burton, introducing the great translation of *Arabian Nights* in 1885, is satirical about those who would like to suppress the erotic material in the tales: he sounds as if he were voicing exactly one of our modern stereotypes about the Victorians ('that most immodest modern modesty which sees covert implication where nothing is implied . . . innocence of the word not of the thought'), but his target is 'Nineteenth Century refinement'. One of the best-known protests against late-Victorian literary prudishness is George Moore's *Literature at Nurse*, his 1885 attack on Mudie's Select Library for refusing to stock *A Mummer's Wife*. Moore's chronology is hazy, to say the least: Mudie has been exercising his stifling influence for 'the last thirty years', but his victim is 'the literature of the nineteenth century'.[12]

The last great quarrel of the century about sex and literature is the one over Hardy's *Jude the Obscure*, published the year before the diamond jubilee. One would comb through the contemporary discussions of this novel in vain for a mention of Victorianism. There are not even many allusions to the nineteenth century. For one commentator on the ground in 1896 the historical context of *Jude* was a calendar of literary emancipation in the period which sounds wholly unfamiliar today:

It is now the better part of a year ago since the collapse of the 'New Woman' fiction began. The success of 'The Woman who Did' [this refers to Grant Allen's novel of that name] was perhaps the last of a series of successes attained . . . by works dealing intimately and unrestrainedly with sexual affairs. It marked a crisis . . . The pendulum bob of the public conscience swung back swiftly and forcibly. From reading books wholly and solely dependent upon sexuality for their interest, the respectable public has got now to rejecting books solely for their recognition of sexuality . . . And the reviewers . . . have changed with the greatest dexterity . . . to a band of public informers against indecorum.

[12] Burton 1885: p. xvii; Moore 1976: 17, 19.

The author of this is not a mere Grub-Streeter, unable or disinclined to lift his head to see beyond the hillocks of recent literary fashion: it is H. G. Wells. In the *Jude* controversy, in fact, only Edmund Gosse put the novel into a perspective with the kind of scale we are accustomed to, but even here the Thackerayan historical markers produce an unfamiliar story:

We have, in such a book as 'Jude the Obscure', traced the full circle of propriety. A hundred and fifty years ago, Fielding and Smollett brought before us pictures, used expressions, described conduct, which appeared to their immediate successors a little more crude than general reading warranted. In Miss Burney's hands and in Miss Austen's, the morals were still further hedged about. Scott was even more daintily reserved. We came at last to Dickens, where the clamorous passions of mankind, the coarser accidents of life, were absolutely ignored, and the whole question of population seemed reduced to the theory of the gooseberry bush. This was the *ne plus ultra* of decency; Thackeray and George Eliot relaxed this intensity of prudishness; once on the turn, the tide turned rapidly, and here is Mr Hardy ready to say every mortal thing that Fielding said, and a good deal more too.[13]

I have already cited Gosse commenting in 1918 on the recent fashion for ridiculing the 'Victorian'. In that essay it is apparent that Gosse had himself come to accept, in some measure, the justness of the new historical bracket and hence a certain forward shift in the chronology of propriety he sketched in the *Jude* review (he had in the meanwhile published *Father and Son*, his account of his own austerely sectarian upbringing in the 1850s and 1860s). By 1918 Gosse is proposing as a unit the period 1840–90, so he does not advance the end-point of his era of prudishness, and he is also very definite that a rigorous sexual moralism is a feature of the early years of Victoria's reign, with substantial foundations in the preceding decades. Gosse points out that Lytton Strachey (whose *Eminent Victorians* is one of the books under review in his article) has tacitly enlarged the category of the 'Victorian' by including Dr Arnold as the subject of one of his studies, since 'the great schoolmaster was hardly a Victorian at all. When he entered the Church George III was on the throne; his accomplishment at Rugby was started under George IV.'

Strachey had said, famously, that we know too much about the Victorians ever to write their history; Gosse seems to be urging that the truly Victorian, and what Strachey was partly recording, is a

---

[13] Lerner and Holmstrom 1968: 120, 135.

remote episode, objectively and subjectively. 'We have passed', he
says, 'in three-quarters of a century, completely out of the atmosphere in which Dr Arnold moved and breathed.' This all serves to
emphasize what is perhaps obvious enough: that Strachey's celebrated formula is tongue-in-cheek, a suitable opening to a work
which never makes an explicit judgement on the Victorians but none
the less delivers an unmistakeable verdict. Despite its first sentence
Eminent Victorians is quite in tune with the *Times Literary
Supplement*'s feeling that Victoria's reign was an 'almost incredible
epoch' and Edward Carpenter's that it was a 'strange period of
human evolution'.

Indeed a certain sense of historical vertigo is something which
does unite the last years of the nineteenth century and the early years
of the twentieth, and it helps to explain why the cliché of the
'Victorian' sprang into being quickly, with so little preparation. The
cliché was indirectly prepared in the 1880s and 1890s in people's
feeling that very great changes, perhaps so great that they beggared
the historical imagination, had occurred in the recent past. It is no
accident that in this period there appear the first compilations of
material from the newspapers and magazines of the past, straight
transcriptions of items illustrating bygone life and manners which are
felt to be entertaining and surprising in themselves. The potential of
such material (now very familiar to us) was first exploited by John
Ashton, in volumes such as *Men, Maidens and Manners a Hundred
Years ago* (1888), *Social England under the Regency* (1890), and
Gossip in the First Decade of Victoria's Reign (1903). Ashton's main
area of quarrying in these collections is the first half of the nineteenth
century. A sense of greatly relaxed moral codes is often to the fore in
the *fin de siècle* perception of headlong change. According to one
commentator on conversational etiquette in 1891 'the *divorcee* desig-
nate . . . especially if . . . she has "broken the record" as regards
numbers of co-respondents, is quite as freely canvassed these days
. . . as a new prima donna would have been discussed a generation
ago'.[14]

Edmund Gosse, in his Hardy review and in his Strachey review, is
in both cases like a man looking into a historical abyss: the only difference is that the bottom of the abyss has, in twenty years, shifted
twenty years. Quiller Couch testifies directly in 1922 to the experi-

[14] Traill 1891.

ence of a movable historical boundary beyond which is the obsolete and absurd: 'what you laugh at as "Victorian", includes a great deal that we laughed at as "Early Victorian" or, later, as "Mid-Victorian"'. The perception of what was historically remote did not, of course, advance smoothly with time. Different writers experienced it differently, or claimed to. If you wished to present yourself as being in the van of a galloping modernity you made out that the very recent past was already scarcely knowable, as Max Beerbohm did in discussing '1880' in 1895: 'the period of 1880 and the few years immediately succeeding' he found 'now so remote from us that much therein is hard for us to understand'.[15]

But until the last years of the nineteenth century most writers interested in these questions continued to locate in its earliest decades an episode of more-or-less extreme, perhaps outlandish, moralism. The Regency years, contrary to later ideas, did not loom large enough, even for writers in their immediate aftermath, to eclipse memories of 'the psalm-loving king, the third George' and his 'divorce-hating queen'. In a sober academic historical survey from the very close of the century (as in the first volume of Russell's *Collections and Recollections*, already cited) the accession of Queen Victoria finds no place as a moral divide. A modern reader might suppose that the following is an account of the Victorian climate: 'It was a serious, self-conscious time, a time when seriousness of purpose told to the full. Finish of manner was at a discount, but an outward moral decorum was expected. "Private indulgences" were suffered so long as the public was not insulted by their exhibition.' But the author is describing the early nineteenth century, and in support of her picture she cites the fact that in 1786 a duke's mistress could be introduced to the Queen, while in 1802 Charles James Fox had to marry his before she could be received in society. In an essay of 1864 which rather strikingly anticipates the vertiginous mood of the 1880s and 1890s the feminist Frances Power Cobbe actually perceives in the third decade of the century a reduction of moral strictness: it is partly by virtue of this new leniency that 'men and women who enjoyed their youthful prime in the first quarter of this century, must have been as little imbued with what we commonly think the Spirit of *our* Age, as any generation in history'.[16]

[15] Quiller Couch 1922: 287; Beerbohm 1895.
[16] 'The Confessions of a Lady of Quality', *London Weekly Magazine*, 1 (1833), 849–53; Bateson 1896; Cobbe 1864.

The first revisions of this model also set in motion Quiller Couch's process of historical slippage: the 'early Victorian' starts to be identified as a period distinguished by moral rigour and severity, from which even moralistic writers can feel alienated. The handful of commentators who, prompted by the Queen's jubilees, emphasized and celebrated 1837 as a moral watershed were also forward-looking in the way they sometimes reserved some disparagement for the first stage of the moral revolution they were otherwise proud of. Walter Besant, for example, is pleased that 'things are vastly improved in the space of two generations . . . there is less of everything that should not be', but he is also moved to something approaching derision by a quotation from Mrs Sandford, writing in 1831 on dependence as an essential female trait: 'Heavens! with what a storm would such a book be now received!'[17] An increasingly explicit distaste for the 1830s and 1840s was certainly a preparatory step, in the first decade or so of this century, towards full-fledged anti-Victorianism (and becomes the nub of the anti-Victorianism of Edmund Gosse, for example). The lawyer and feminist E. S. P. Haynes published in 1904 an essay—anecdotal, contemptuous, rather complacent, and cavalier with facts—that feels modern, as an attack on the Victorians, in everything but its scope, which is specifically the early part of the reign.[18] Annie Winsor Allen's pioneering defence of the Victorians, already cited, takes up the cudgels for them piecemeal: it is chiefly the 'Early' and 'Mid' Victorians who have been misunderstood, criticism of the 'Late' is more just.

But for some reason the process of slippage does come to a halt. By the end of the Great War the stigma of prudish moralism, which had passed from the early nineteenth century, to the early and then mid-Victorian years, comes to rest on the whole Victorian era—and there it has remained until the present. This may mean that a shift which at first seems arbitrary is not entirely so. Is there something objective in the Victorian period which has provided a secure lodging for this freely floating stigma? Is the idea of the 'Victorian', in fact, good history? An important subsidiary point is that the stigma itself has taken several forms, and to that extent different versions of the moral chronology of the nineteenth century may be reconciled with one another. It may be true to say both of the early 1800s and of the early Victorian years that they are high points of prudish moralism if we

---

[17] Besant 1888: 119.   [18] Haynes 1904.

apply the notion in different senses or to different parts of the community in the two periods.

Frances Power Cobbe's essay of 1864, 'The Nineteenth Century', again gives a remarkably early lead here. The central trope of the essay (strangely echoing or foreshadowing several other texts of the period, but especially Gosse's *Father and Son*) is that the pre- and post-Victorian divisions of the century which she can look back on are in a relationship of familial descent: 'There is Nineteenth Century *Père* and Nineteenth Century *Fils*; and they are as different from one another in principles, opinions, manners, and costume as fathers and sons usually contrive to be.' As has been mentioned, in Cobbe's description of this cultural divide there is a major emphasis on a relaxation of strict moralism in the early 1830s. Nevertheless the terms in which she reports this change sometimes imply a continuity between the two phases, with the morality of Nineteenth Century *Fils* just the moralism of Nineteenth Century *Père* spread wider: less obtrusive but also more powerful. Moral life before 1830, she says, had 'a sharper line drawn . . . between the higher and lower kinds of virtue', and, while Wesleyans and Evangelicals were extremely strict, ordinary people 'might then do a good many things, and neglect a great many duties, which in our day would hardly leave them the character "moral" at all'. Since the early 1830s 'religious people are not so strict, and people with no profession of religion by no means so lax, as in the last generation'.

The diffusionist picture offered by this essay, however unconsciously, makes it possibly the earliest example of what has come to be the orthodox account of the connection between the moral culture of early nineteenth-century England and that of the Victorian era. Historians may differ on the significance and mode of influence of particular individuals and groupings in the first decades of the century but there is generally agreement among them that the moralism of the Victorian period is a matter of attitudes originally characteristic of a section or stratum spreading throughout the community from, roughly, the beginning of Victoria's reign. On such a view there will naturally be definite but isolated appearances of this moralism in preceding decades, harbingers of Victorianism such as Frances Power Cobbe, arguably, is representing in her Nineteenth Century *Père*.

This account is in conflict with the perception of most commentators within Victoria's reign: for them a climate of strict moralism had prevailed early in the century and was thoroughly done with by

about 1880. The present study, without intending a wholesale
putting-back of the sexual-historical clock, will suggest that there is
much to be said for the older perception, especially where the end of
Victorianism is concerned. The initial boundary is a more difficult
issue. One writer in the nineteenth century whom I have not yet
cited was quite certain, and almost obsessed by his belief, that a
moral watershed occurred in the neighbourhood of 1800. He also
made a much fuller study of the question than anyone else and
attempted to prove his theory with systematically treated evidence.
His statement of his case is in fact an ideal point of entry into the
whole complicated subject.

III

The First Theory of Nineteenth-Century Respectability

Francis Place (1771–1854) is a major figure in the history of British
working-class politics. His approach to the moral culture of his day
was controlled by political aims and his attention confined to the
lower levels of his society (and, moreover, to those levels mainly as
they could be seen in London). There is none the less a great deal of
intriguing empirical observation in Place's various accounts of manners and morals, whatever political axe he happened to be grinding,
and he was interested in a broad range of working-class and lower-
middle-class grades, from the abjectly poor up to the small businessman. It would be true to say that through Francis Place one may
glimpse something of the moral culture of all social groups in London
in the decades around 1800, with the exception of the professional
and upper middle classes and the gentry. Place addressed himself
deliberately to this subject in the 1820s and 1830s and he consistently argued at this period that, in the groups he was concerned
with, a dramatic increase in moral respectability—including sexual—
had started in the mid-1790s; this was continuing, but by about 1815
had already progressed so far that practices and attitudes standard in
Place's youth were unthinkable.

Place was born just off the Strand and lived entirely at various
addresses in this neighbourhood until his second marriage in 1830.
His father, after a very chequered early career, became the landlord
of a public house on the Strand when Place was 8, and remained

there until 1788. At 14 Place was apprenticed in the leather-breeches trade and in 1791, only about two years after completing his apprenticeship, he married his first wife Elizabeth. Over the next twenty-five years she bore him fifteen children, eight of whom were dead by 1830. Place was scarcely making a living when he married, and he played an important organizing role when the leather-breeches-makers struck for better pay in 1793. The strike was a failure and for eight months after its collapse Place, as a prominent participant, was denied all employment. He and his wife came near to starving, but in this period Place started to enlarge his education by systematic reading, and he continued his self-education for many years thereafter. The great transformation of his character was under way: into the atheist radical, wedded to values of self-improvement, self-discipline, frugality, and decency.

In 1794 Place the political organizer was able to enter a much more important forum. The London Corresponding Society had been founded at the beginning of 1792 by the shoemaker Thomas Hardy as a body which would stimulate and co-ordinate support for parliamentary reform. Its members were almost all artisans or small tradesmen. While the route to more popular government which the Society chiefly advocated was that of progressive reform of the Commons and Lords, Place recalled later that most of the leaders and the ordinary membership were republicans, and a few of them revolutionaries. In May 1794, just before Place joined the Society, Hardy and other leading men were arrested on charges of treason. In this crisis Place threw himself into the affairs of the Society, and in September 1795 was elected chairman of the General Committee. Hardy and the other defendants had been acquitted but fresh legislation was promulgated against political associations at the end of 1795 in the wake of alleged attempts to assassinate the King. Place could not agree with the policies adopted by the Society in this new predicament, and in 1797 he ceased to be a member.

Place had hoped from the outset of his career as a tailor to set up his own shop selling ready-made goods and commissioned clothes produced by his own employees, judging that this was the only way for a breeches-maker like himself to escape into any kind of financial security. After one false start he was able in 1801 to raise enough capital from well-wishers to open a shop, exclusively his, at 16 Charing Cross. Twelve years later this address had become something of a Mecca for radicals and progressives, with its highly profitable shop

on the ground floor and its well-stocked library on the second where
Place the radical, as opposed to Place the tailor, could be visited at
set hours. From this base Place had already organized, with tremendous energy and command of detail, the election to parliament of Sir
Francis Burdett as pro-reform MP for Westminster in 1807. Another
triumph of political mechanics was Place's ten-year campaign to get
the Combination Laws repealed, which achieved its reward in 1824.
Place was extremely active in the struggle for parliamentary reform
and, joining the Chartists in his disappointment at the limitations of
the 1832 Act, was the draftsman of the People's Charter itself.

Place had been able to retire from business by 1817, but in 1827
Elizabeth Place died. Quite quickly Place's personal life, though not
his political, started to diverge astonishingly from its long-established
patterns and principles. Within a few months of Elizabeth's death he
was sexually involved with a widowed Covent Garden actress of
some celebrity, Louisa Chatterley. At first she was his mistress, and
Place was adamant that they should not marry, but in 1830 they did.
By 1833 Place had lost most of his fortune and had to leave Charing
Cross for a smaller house in the West End. He did not lay any blame
for this catastrophe on his new wife. She was, however, no stranger
to financial ruin in her partner: ten years earlier she had lived with a
bank-clerk who was exposed for embezzling money with which to
play the stockmarket on his behalf and hers. In 1851 the Places separated because Francis felt he was being robbed of his remaining
funds by his wife so that she could support her 'rascal' son by her first
marriage. The whole episode was, as his son declared, a 'terrible
falling off from his former rigidly virtuous life' which 'belied all the
moral teaching of which he was an illustration'.[19]

It was, though, consistent with Francis Place's oddly compounded
personality. He was dour, self-absorbed, and pedestrian, stringent
and even harsh with himself and others, but also an impulsive and
affectionate man who had great vitality and a remarkable freshness of
intellect. These qualities in themselves make his *Autobiography*,
mainly written between 1823 and 1835 and unpublished until
recently, a very interesting document. Its main significance, however, is that here Place rehearses most fully the moral transformation
he believed he had witnessed in his society and the causes to which
he attributes it. Place expected that the *Autobiography* would find a

---

[19] Place 1972: 268. Numerals in brackets attached to quotations in the following para-
graphs are likewise page numbers in this volume, the *Autobiography*.

publisher soon after his death as a posthumous memoir. This hope was disappointed, but he did in his own lifetime make known his views on lower-class morality in limited public utterances. In 1829 he wrote a short pamphlet, *Improvement of the Working People*, which he published in 1834 when a Parliamentary Select Committee on Drunkenness was announced. He was duly invited to testify to the committee, and then in the following year to the Select Committee on Education in England and Wales, on further aspects of working-class moral culture.

If the *Autobiography* is set aside, Place's statements on this topic may seem rather modest in scale, but in the context of his career and methods they are a striking evidence of how very important the issue was for him. Apart from *Improvement of the Working People* Place only published one work in his own name, the *Illustration and Proofs of the Principle of Population*. To appear in person before parliamentary committees was also thoroughly out of character for him. Place's whole instinct and aptitude was for making such bodies move in the right direction under his unseen influence. This is not to say that he neglected chances to exert this kind of influence in the case of working-class morals,[20] and it seems probable that the issue of moral change in his society first struck Place when he was organizing witnesses and testimony to go before the Select Committee on the Combination Laws of 1824. For it was in 1823 that he started on the *Autobiography* and also set about compiling as much empirical information in the field of popular morality as he could secure, which survives in several bound volumes in the British Museum.

Though the story Place wished to illuminate now lay some years in the past he did the best he could with the data of the present. He preserved not only new press-cuttings but also those from earlier years which came his way. He wrote down the most accurate versions he could manage of obscene songs he remembered from his youth. He frequently went to check the present character of particular London neighbourhoods against his memory of them. He even took his wife and other ladies, like chemical reagents in human form, into the vicinity of navvies to demonstrate how the latter, in contrast to their former habits, 'now desisted from offensive language' with the approach of respectable females.[21] He was at pains to stir up recollections of a more dissolute past in the minds of the elderly, often

---

[20] PP 1835, vii. 841.   [21] PP 1835, vii. 842.

being struck by how 'improvement has been so gradual and long, that they themselves were scarcely conscious of it' (51). On 5 December 1823, for example, he broached these questions with an acquaintance who had become a wealthy businessman:

On reading some of the preceding sheets, and notes for those which are to follow, his exclamations were vehement and amusing. 'God bless my soul!—why yes!—that's true!—Ah!—Ah!! I had forgotten that!' and then he related a number of similar cases and circumstances, which he said 'were nearly as fresh to him as they were forty years ago'. He could see all these things just as they had occurred (75).

Place's *Autobiography* is another father-and-son text, if not to the extent of Gosse's memoir than at least as much as the autobiography of John Stuart Mill (whose political education, according to one legend, was entrusted to Place by James Mill). Simon Place, Francis's father, dominates the early chapters and his strange traits become a kind of essence of English life in the period of Place's youth. His picture of the one, and by extension of the other, is not simple:

He was a resolute, daring, straightforward sort of a man, governed almost wholly by his passions and animal sensations, both of which were very strong; he was careless of reputation excepting in some particulars in which he seems to have thought he excelled. These were few, mostly relating to sturdiness and dissoluteness: Drinking, Whoring, Gaming, Fishing and Fighting. He was well acquainted with the principal boxers of the day; Slack and Broughton were his companions. Some of these desires and propensities never left him, though most of them became all but extinct with old age. He was always ready in certain cases to advise and to assist others, all who knew him placed the utmost reliance on his word, and as the habit of all ranks then as compared with the habits of each class of men now, were exceedingly dissolute, his conduct was not then obnoxious to the censure of others as such conduct would be now. With all his follies and vices he was much respected. Simon Place was the man to be depended upon in all emergencies good or bad, and he was just as likely to enter into a man's concerns on the wrong as on the right side and to work through them with equal perseverance and vigour. It was enough for him that he was asked to assist anyone who was in difficulty, or who could not help himself. From these causes according to the common acceptation of the term he had many friends (20).

The stress on such positive qualities in the otherwise uncouth Simon as his energy, resoluteness, and loyalty is important. These are among the qualities which may sustain a man in an adequate if rudimentary life, and a society at a sufficient but rudimentary level of development. Simon Place's notions of authority, explicitly said to be those of his society at large, are also minimal and unimproved:

He wished to do his duty towards his children and he thought he did his duty. He had no notion of producing effects by advice, his passions were strong, and too little under control to permit him to produce effects by examples. In his opinion coercion was the only way to eradicate faults, and by its terror to prevent their recurrence. These were common notions, and were carried into practice not only by the heads of families and the teachers of youth generally, but by the government itself and every man in authority under it, in the treatment of prisoners and the drilling of soldiers, who were publicly beaten by the drill sergeants with a cane (62).

Of the traits which recur in these passages two form the keynote of Place's picture of his father: violence, and unexpectedness or incoherence of conduct. Simon Place was astonishingly cruel to his children, but more in the manner of an animal aroused by the sight of an enemy than of a vindictive human being:

If he were coming along a passage or any narrow place such as a door way and was met by either me or my brother he always made a blow at us with his fist, for coming in his way; if we attempted to retreat he would make us come forward and as certainly as we came forward he would knock us down (59).

Once when Francis and a brother and sister were playing truant, peering through a boarding, 'I felt a rope's end at my back, my father was there' (34). Simon Place had certain rules of punishment but, again animal-like, he could be distracted from his prey. Every night he sent for the children's shoes and stockings; 'if they were wet he would come upstairs with a stick, generally the first he could lay his hands on no matter to whom it belonged, and with this he belaboured us until he broke it' (60). However, all was impulse: 'if any circumstance occurred to prevent him coming upstairs at the moment, we should not be molested the next day; he had been prevented from coming up on one or two occasions by being obliged to make punch for . . . customers, and a quarter of an hour's detention was sufficient to save us' (61). Even Simon Place's sexual misdemeanours were marked by a kind of inconsequentiality: 'he used . . . to visit more than one woman who lived at a distance, sometimes staying out all night, without at all intimating any such intention to my mother' (28). In 1785 a woman appeared from nowhere and claimed to be Simon's wife by 'a Fleet marriage some forty years previously' (85).

While in one regard Simon Place is the unregenerate moral soul of the English eighteenth century, in another he is a member of a specific group, a prosperous lower-middle-class individual with appropriate social and even moral aspirations. He wanted Francis to be a lawyer (and, when the latter refused, 'went immediately into his parlour and offered me to anyone who would take me' (71)). He strove to prevent his next son becoming a lighterman on the Thames. The family was delighted when the eldest daughter was courted by 'a sensible respectable man' (92). Simon Place was an admired and efficient publican, organizing his operation in a manner that strangely combined uncouthness and discipline. Midday dinner for the family and staff in the public house was a military affair, starting at exactly a quarter to one and lasting precisely ten minutes. They always dined at the same table in the tap-room, in sight of the drinkers: 'though my father chose to dine in the tap-room, nothing was so offensive to him as anyone looking at him or at the table, and when anyone did so he would show his resentment by a burst of passion vented in sufficiently offensive language' (40).

It is such anomalous combinations in the behaviour of Simon Place and his associates which in Francis's view leave plenty of room for advance towards a true respectability. What 'respectability' this group occasionally exhibits is no more than superficial. The Place family and their circle are towards the upper end of the social spectrum surveyed by Francis, but this simply means that their starting-point in the general rise in moral standards is rather higher than that of socially inferior groups. By 1829, according to Place, this starting-point had been reached and overtaken by the top level of the working class, and what used to be the upper-working-class morality of 1790 had been far surpassed by that of even the bottom groups: 'The very meanest and least informed being much more sober . . . much more orderly and decent . . . than were those who . . . were far above them in respect to the amount of wages they received; whilst the most skilled and best paid are . . . more sober, more moral, and better informed, than were the generality of their employers'.[22]

Sexual morality is no exception to this process of recalibration. Place tells us that the prosperous tradesman's family of his youth was, for example, very lax by later standards where the sexual behaviour of its younger members was concerned, and not just in respect of courtship. Place was apprenticed to a Mr France, who had three daughters. The eldest and youngest were prostitutes (the latter in a superior fashion to the other, being in 'genteel lodgings where she was visited by gentlemen' (71)); the middle daughter was the mistress of a ship's captain, though not faithful to him. A wealthy local trades-man also had three daughters. The eldest settled down with her father's foreman after having several lovers; the second daughter also married a foreman—but in this case her dead husband's, who had been her lover. In such a context it is not surprising that many tradesmen's daughters married 'young men who were as well acquainted with them before marriage as afterwards' (76). And by no means all sexual intercourse between sons and daughters of this class was part of courtship; 'each of my companions', says Place, 'had a sweetheart who was the daughter of some tradesman . . . With these girls I and my companions were as familiar as we could be' (75).

Place himself admits to having an affair with the sister of one of his early employers, and when he meets Elizabeth, who became his first wife, it is evident that he could have sought the same relationship with her: 'I . . . resolved to court her, at first I hardly knew on what terms, but in a little time as a wife' (96). Not unexpectedly, Place's group resorted to ordinary prostitutes. What is more intriguing (though Place says he did not follow his companions here) is the claim that these lower-middle-class youths had a privileged relation-ship with such women: 'most of them were "fine men" to some of the prostitutes who walked Fleet Street, spending their money with them in debauchery and occasionally receiving money from them' (75).

Rather lower down the social scale, generally, were the partici-pants in the 'Cock and Hen Clubs'. Place believed there had been fourteen or fifteen of these clubs along the river between Blackfriars and Scotland Yard in his youth, all vanished by the 1820s (though he admitted that a few still existed in very low neighbourhoods else-where). As their name implies, the business of these clubs was to match up young people for the evening; amidst the drinking and singing and story-telling a simple ritual was performed and 'the boys and girls paired off by degrees till by 12 o'clock none remained' (77). Another place of recreation which especially interested Place was the tea garden, though chiefly because these establishments, which lay on the immediate edge of built-up London and sold both liquor and ordinary refreshments, gave an indication of the extent of lower-class drunkenness. On various occasions Place stressed the improved character of the tea gardens in the thirty or forty years since his youth. Among the activities not to be observed at these places 'for many years' was casual sex: formerly there had been 'dark walks where you might tumble over couples'.[23]

The lowest social stratum of which Place gives a detailed account is that of the street prostitutes. When he moved into 16 Charing Cross there were in the immediate neighbourhood three or perhaps four brothels (his descriptions seem to diverge on this point) directly accessible from the street, and just off it two areas of poor housing, Angel's Court and Johnson's Court, almost entirely occupied by prostitutes. Others plied their trade practically on the street itself: at the Scotland Yard end of Charing Cross there was a wall, used in the daytime to display obscene ballads and pictures but at night by 'horridly ragged, dirty and disgusting' girls who took their clients behind it for twopence. By about 1815 the brothels and courts had been pulled down or improved, and the prostitutes had gone. Indeed prostitutes of the kind formerly to be seen in Johnson's Court and at the Privy Gardens wall 'cannot now be seen in any place', Place judged in June 1824 (213, 227–30).

But it is interesting that he was not confident that prostitution as such had decreased in London. He declined to aver this to the Education Committee in 1834: the main changes were that women from tradesmen's families no longer became prostitutes, while the women who did behaved more decently than formerly. In his materials on 'Manners and Morals' Place records an expedition in September 1824 to a notorious site of prostitution, St Catherine's Lane; he seems not to have been struck by any reduction in the number of prostitutes, but only by a considerable change in their appearance:

When I was an apprentice I went frequently among these girls, that is I went with other lads through the same places I went to see today, and at that time spent many evenings in the dirty public houses frequented by them. At that time, they wore long quartered shoes and large buckles, most of them had clean stockings and shoes, because it was then the fashion to be flashy about the heels, but many had ragged dirty shoes and stockings and some no stockings at all. All now wore stays, many at that time wore no stays, their gowns were low round the neck and open in the front. Those who wore handkerchiefs had them always open in front to expose their breasts, this was a fash-

---

[23] PP 1835, vii. 844.

ion which the best dressed among them followed, but numbers wore no handkerchiefs at all in warm weather, and the breasts of many hung down in a most disgusting manner. Their hair among the generality was straight and 'hung in rat tails' over their eyes, and was filled with lice, at least was inhabited by considerable colonies of these insects (77–8).

This is just some of the material on sexual manners and morals to be found in Place's autobiography and other remains. He reports also on such things as the sale of pornographic prints and books of popular sexual medicine, the jokes and songs which were current in various groups, and the extent of sexual knowledge and discussion among children. He claims that, for the generality of the lower-middle-class and working class, comparisons in all these areas between the facts of 1790 and the facts of 1815 and after would show a massive shift towards greater moral respectability. The material, and the claim, are both extremely striking, and must say something about the 'Victorianizing' of the English nineteenth century. There are several grounds, however, on which one may doubt whether Place's account is of more than marginal interest.

It is necessary to return to two points touched upon earlier: the tendentiousness of Place's activity in this field, and the restricted character of his evidence. There is no question that Place saw his version of recent moral history as a corrective to other views. His interest in the subject arose when he realized that a hostile account of working-class morals was bound up with legislation hostile to the working class, the Combination Laws. He hoped that his unprecedented attempt, in the *Autobiography*, to assemble a piece of 'correctly detailed domestic history' would 'make people more disposed than they are to proceed in the right way by convincing them that instead of mankind growing worse and worse they grow better and better' (91). It has been discovered from the Place manuscripts that he was indignant at the bias in the Drunkenness Committee's proceedings—in their expectations of the evidence, and their receipt and recording of it—towards the view that working-class drinking was becoming aggravated.[24] The author of this study suggests that the support for gin-retailers expressed in Place's own evidence to the committee—odd indeed from this austere, teetotal man—was a product of his dislike for some of the religious witnesses and their belittling judgements on the working class.

[24] Harrison 1968.

If Place could be driven to such a moral position by his political
and intellectual sympathies can he be trusted in the interpretation of
'domestic history'? It must be admitted that his treatment of working-class drinking in *Improvement of the Working People* seems to
embody two different estimates of the extent of recent progress
(depending on whether he is urging the need for working-class education, or its likely utility) and neither is quite consistent with the
historical timetable proposed in the *Autobiography*. And perhaps not
all readers will be satisfied with Place's picture of his father as a barbaric but intermittently 'respectable' man, feeling that the
respectable elements in Simon Place, lower-middle-class Londoner
of the latter eighteenth century, are not adequately accounted for.

What of the limitations of Place's evidence? This has several
aspects. All Place's early knowledge of working-class morals was
drawn from London. Later in life, through direct acquaintance and
indirectly through political contacts, he got to know a good deal
about other regions. The Frenchman Gustave D'Eichthal records
him comparing the debauched condition of the Lancashire cotton
workers, in 1828, with the general moral advance of the English
working class. But Place could only make the intimate comparisons
with a world before 1790, on which so much in the *Autobiography*
turns, where London was concerned. The London of the 1820s, even
in Place's own view, may have been a special case (see Chapter 3).
Moreover Place's London is often a rather restricted affair, and this
can weaken the interest of his observations. It is possible to find
confirmation of the vanishing of specific sites for prostitution and
pornography in the Charing Cross neighbourhood as recorded by
Place, but this was surely mainly due to the creation of Trafalgar
Square in the 1820s and 1830s (in Chapter 3 I shall also discuss prostitution more generally in the area, and recreational sites such as the
Tea Gardens).[25]

Place had no amenities for research in the modern sense. The literary power of the early sections of the *Autobiography*, with their feeling of a cruel, fragmentary, irrational past, may also mean that they
are bad history, for the effect partly depends on the paucity of Place's
information about his ancestors. His exposure to evidence was also
restricted by practical choices he made in his own life and, since he
chose the path of respectability himself, he actually biased the obser-

[25] Ratcliffe and Chaloner 1977: 47; J. Richardson 1855: i. 5–6.

vations he could make in a manner likely to favour his thesis: Place several times stresses in the *Autobiography* that with his first marriage he abandoned his old haunts and associates. And to the extent that his researches were retrospective he may have been seeking an echo in his evidence of his personal history of transition to respectability.

Place has been accused of paying too little attention to the lowest levels of his society, to the truly labouring portion of the working class.[26] Certainly there was a large body of poor unskilled workers in London whom Place does not often refer to, and whose way of life, it is said (though in practice this is an obscure and complicated topic), showed very little sign of increasing respectability. Place was actually well aware of this group, though he does seem to be inconsistent over the question of how much it felt the effects of the new respectability. His most habitual view is perhaps that the truly 'abandoned' are a shrinking proportion of the unskilled working class, but that the remainder have not made as great a moral advance as their skilled brethren, so that by 1829 'the difference between skilled workmen and common labourers is as strongly marked as was the difference between the workman and his employer'.[27]

Place's theory is probably not sound enough to offer more than an agenda for the discussion of nineteenth-century sexual moralism. It should be said that his agenda is a good one, however, not only for the challenging claim, made on the ground, that there was a watershed around 1800, but also because it can remind us that sexual culture, impalpable though it may sometimes seem, is susceptible of factual investigation. Some of Place's observations—on the laxity of tradesmen's wives, for example—would have been hard to quantify usefully even in his own day, but others—on the trade in pornography, for example—concern trends which could be very revealing, if only more information had survived about them. Unfortunately information of this kind *is* rare, but something can be done with demography, social statistics, and contemporary qualitative material to investigate the questions which Place wanted to answer. This will be attempted in the next two chapters.

---

[26] D. J. Rowe 1973.   [27] Place 1834: 6.

IV

Radical Genteelness

There is another aspect to Place's model. He was not content to observe the new respectability, he also sought to explain it. In the *Autobiography* part of this explanation, almost at the level of gut feeling, is offered implicitly in the vision of Simon Place and his generation, so eloquent of a repugnance for the cruel, the animalistic, the impulsive, the irrational, and the disordered. Place also reflects on the causes of the new respectability quite explicitly: the longest passage of this sort deserves to be quoted in full.

Some of the good producing causes are a better regulated Police, and a better description of Police Magistrates. The extension of the Cotton Manufacture which has done all but wonders in respect to the cleanliness and healthiness of women. The rapid increase of wealth and its more general diffusion, subsequent to the Revolutionary War with the North American colonies and their wonderful and perpetual increasing prosperity. The French Revolution which broke up many old absurd notions, and tended greatly to dissipate the pernicious reverence for men of title and estate without regard to personal knowledge or personal worth. The stimulus it gave to serious thought on Government, and the desire for information in every possible direction. The promotion of political societies, which gave rise to reading clubs, the independent notions these encouraged, and the consequent reformation of manners. The introduction of Sunday Schools, and the invaluable mode of teaching employed by Joseph Lancaster, exquisitely adapted for the actually poor. The introduction and establishment of schools on the plan of Dr Bell, and the miscalled National Schools, little as they teach. The desire which the general movement produced in all below the very rich to give their children a much better education than they had themselves received, and the consequent elevation all these matters have produced on the manners and morals of the whole community (14–15).

Some of the items here are physical—the New Police, hygienic clothing, increased prosperity, innovations in schooling—and others are psychological. In both categories, but especially the latter, the modern reader may find inclusions and omissions that do not at all fit with the conventional aetiology of the 'Victorian'. Place's list of psychological factors makes overt what is implied throughout the domestic history sections of the *Autobiography*: that the new standards in the lower classes are an autonomous development, springing from the real aspirations of its members. According to Place they were not, contrary to most later opinion, imposed by another class or group, such as the bourgeoisie, nor by an alien ideology, such as Evangelicalism. Indeed in Place's account there is no ideological element involved—and hence no religious or moral impulses—other than the ideology of working-class advance, which is given a strongly political colouring. The most salient feature of the psychological items in Place's list is that they are 'progressive' and 'advanced'. I draw attention to this vocabulary because it will appear often in this study, and a good deal will hinge on it. It will be used to refer to a wide range of attitudes, and one test which my argument must meet is whether the writers and utterances which I connect under headings such as these can be so connected.

Here at least the relevance of such labels is obvious enough. Place tells us that the new respectability is to a significant extent attributable to the spectacle of the French Revolution and to the experience of English radical political affiliation and activity in response to that event. The Revolution weakened attitudes of deference and stimulated fundamental enquiry about government. The radical political societies continued the process of untrammelled reading and speculation. This is so unfamiliar as an explanation, or even partial explanation, of nineteenth-century respectability that we probably baulk at Place's 'consequent reformation of manners', not finding such a thing 'consequent' on progressive political thinking at all. Though in his public utterances Place was prepared to endorse a less subversive explanation of working-class respectability—as the effect of downwards moral percolation from above, aided by the police[28]—there is no doubting from the evidence of the *Autobiography* that he was convinced of the great significance of 1790s political radicalism in this development. He frequently echoes and amplifies the gist of the sentences quoted above.

What is one to make of Place's repeated claim that the political societies 'promoted an increase of moral conduct' (196)? Is this not very obviously a rationalization, in terms of the author's own experience, of a personal drive towards respectability which he would have exhibited anyway—especially since the London Corresponding Society is given pride of place as 'a great moral cause of the improvement which has since taken place among the People' (200)? The relationship between respectability and the ideology and procedures of working-class radicalism—including such matters as the role of pubs

[28] PP 1835, vii. 845.

for political assembly—will be discussed in the second volume of this study. It seems undeniable that Place overrated the influence of particular institutions, but his account of how the London Corresponding Society worked its moral magic is worth quoting:

The moral effects of the Society were considerable. It induced men to read books, instead of wasting their time in public houses. It taught them to respect themselves, and to desire to educate their children. It elevated them in their own opinions. It taught them the great moral lesson 'to bear and forbear'. The discussions in the divisions, in the Sunday evenings readings, and in the small debating meetings, opened to them views which they had never before taken. They were compelled by these discussions to find reason for their opinions and to tolerate others. It gave a new stimulus to an immense number of men who had been but in too many instances incapable of any but the grossest pursuits, and seeking nothing beyond mere sensual enjoyment (198–9).

This is plausible about the spirit and influence of a lower-class radical organization, and it comes from someone whose experience of this world was probably greater than that of any other man in the period.

Place does make the moral impact of an organization such as the LCS sound somewhat mechanical, the result of limited practical causes in the shape of the society's routines and procedures. For Place, and for other working-class radicals, there was certainly also a connection at a deeper level, a conceptual affinity, between an optimistic commitment to raising the status of ordinary people and the drive towards orderliness, restraint, and decency. But we must not play down his trust in the positive efficacy of sheer practical conditions, for it was shared by an ever-widening sector of English nineteenth-century opinion which soon extended well beyond the working-class radical movement. It is a second odd feature, for the modern reader, of Place's list of 'good producing causes' that he mixes the physical and the psychological or ideological so indiscriminately: cotton garments with anti-authoritarianism, prosperity with raised political awareness. This may strike us as a shallow, and even potentially inhumane, way of regarding the moral life of individuals, but it was optimistic and progressive in its implications—even when it became the orthodoxy of more conservative opinion—because the basic picture is of human nature as indefinitely improvable, given the right environmental conditions. Human beings can be changed morally without their own awareness or consent, by mere physical circumstances. Conversely, lack of awareness and consent is not an obstacle to this process because the human inner self (even that of a Manchester slum-dweller or a Whitechapel prostitute) is wholly upright and good, the soul of Rousseauesque natural man.

Chapter Two

SEX IN THE SOCIETY

I

Can Sexual Moralism be Detected?

I N the next two chapters I consider sexual behaviour in nineteenth-century England and Wales. In this chapter I examine broad patterns in time and space: the most widespread shifts and stabilities in heterosexual marital and extra-marital sexual relations and their procreative outcome. After that the sexual culture of the individual groups composing English society is commented on—with the assumption that in sexual behaviour differences of class are likely to be the most important, though another major distinction, that of town versus country, is not lost sight of. It turns out that the global changes which occur are each sufficiently small to be explicable, perhaps, as changes in the practices of one of the social groups composing nineteenth-century England, and some of the broad movements (most notably birth control) cannot be very helpfully discussed without bringing in questions of class, occupation, and locality. So the two chapters overlap in their implications and approach. There is generally a difference in the kind of evidence used in each, however. Chapter 3 I have called 'Codes and Class' because attitudes and standards receive much more attention here than in the first part of the survey, which is fairly quantitative (though in the discussion of prostitution in the present chapter the question of numbers leads on to more descriptive matters).

There is another profound distinction which I generally treat as being overridden by the influence of class, namely, the distinction of

gender. It may be that there was a much greater difference between
the experiences of women and men in the nineteenth century than I
have been able to detect. It is important to emphasize at this early
point one huge truth about the inquiry which follows: the contemporary written record on which I am largely drawing is in effect the
production of men, with women making a vanishingly small contribution. I hope this fact does not create too great a distortion of women's
role in the sexual culture, as it is covered in the next two chapters.
There is a possibility of more serious distortion in Chapter 4. In
attending to affirmative remarks about women's sexual response, for
example (and certainly before applauding them in reflex fashion), one
must never forget that these are invariably uttered by men. At the
end of the nineteenth century there appears the first group of women
in our history to report on their experience of sex, in the shape of certain of the suffragists. And the first thing which this delegation from
centuries of silence has to say is that the agenda of late nineteenth-
century sexual liberation was self-servingly devised by men, and spurious in its apparent concern for women.

It is not customary for books about the 'Victorian' to include the
weight of evidence about behaviour which I offer here—and certainly not the kind of quantitative material which appears in this
chapter, cursory though it is—but the attempt to survey this evidence needs no apology. The facts are intriguing in themselves, and a
good deal more is known about the sexual behaviour of our nineteenth-century ancestors than is often supposed. The contemporary
descriptive record, as embodied in autobiographies and the writings
of foreign visitors, for example, has not been properly exploited.
Above all, there have been remarkable reconstructions by modern
demographic historians, some on a fine scale, others larger, of various
aspects of nineteenth-century sexual behaviour, and these are not
familiar to non-specialist audiences, or even to all specialists.

But this behavioural story has, potentially, an even larger interest,
above all in view of our modern conviction about the sexual moralism
of the period. Intrinsic to the concept of the 'Victorian', in its commonest versions at least, are various mixes of attitude and behaviour.
There were, allegedly, continuities and discontinuities between the
theory and the practice of sexual moralism—depending on which
aspect of the stereotype of the 'Victorian' is in question. Victorian
middle-class wives, it is orthodox to believe, suffered an actual deprivation of sexual pleasure because of moralistic ignorance about

women's sexual responses. On the other hand, conventional wisdom has it that middle-class husbands were generally cynical disbelievers of the moralistic code they publicly professed, and routinely resorted to prostitutes: so that prostitute levels in Victorian England were exceptionally high.

Francis Place recognized few if any discontinuities in the sexual moralism he detected arising in his society around 1800. People were both less ribald *and* less promiscuous—and so forth. I have suggested that he offers a good agenda of behavioural matters in the researches reported in the *Autobiography*, but I have acknowledged that his claims about such things as marital fidelity and pornography are hard to check. It must also be conceded that Place may have been too ready to take the appearance for the deed. William Cobbett in his *Advice to Young Men*, which is exactly contemporary with Place's *Autobiography*, took a quite different view of 'the refined delicacy of the present age', which was, he believed, all 'modesty in the word and grossness in the thought':

In spite, however, of all this 'refinement of the human mind', which is ever-lastingly dinned in our ears; in spite of the 'small-clothes', and of all the other affected stuff, we have this conclusion, this indubitable proof, of the falling off in real delicacy; namely, that common prostitutes, formerly unknown, now swarm in our towns, and are seldom wanting even in our villages; and where there was one illegitimate child (including those coming before the time) only fifty years ago there are now twenty.[1]

This clash of opinion between two great radical voices of the day actually opens up many of the problems attending the project of link-ing sexual behaviour and sexual beliefs. To start with, it exposes the fact that 'behaviour' is a very broad notion, and includes some ele-ments which are virtually equivalent to beliefs. Certain aspects of demeanour are in effect expressions of attitude—just as likely as ver-bal expressions of attitude to be given the lie by 'behaviour' at another level, one might claim (and Cobbett did claim, offering figures on prostitution and illegitimacy that are in principle thor-oughly checkable). I have divided the coverage of this book into behaviour and belief, because there is an obvious distinction in kind between, say, an essay in the *Edinburgh Review* on Malthusian the-ory, or an Owenite polemic against marriage, and the etiquette of young middle-class couples at dances, or the conversational idioms

---

[1] Cobbett 1980: 225–6.

used to refer to clothing, bodily parts, and so on. But I recognize that the next chapter is about 'codes', that is, about behaviour in a sense closely allied to beliefs about sexual morality.

There are two specific issues about the consistency of nineteenth-century moralism which I therefore postpone discussing until that point, because they have to do with authenticity of demeanour: namely, bourgeois prudery and working-class gentility, and their meaning in terms of sexual practices. But the rest of this difficult topic requires some comment at the outset. It is helpful to refine the categories of 'behaviour' and 'belief' into four narrower notions: sexual activity, demeanour, professed belief, private belief. Will data about the first of these (which I offer predominantly in the present chapter) be likely to reflect the state of the third and fourth, that is, of the professed beliefs of the society, which in turn may or may not correspond to the private beliefs of individuals?

I am aware that some people who subscribe to a concept of the 'Victorian', as it was forged in the early years of this century, would deny that any detectable changes in sexual activity are absolutely required by the hypothesis of an epoch of sexual moralism of the kind proposed. And perhaps all believers in the hypothesis see *some* substantial element of non-detectability (what I called above 'discontinuities' between theory and practice) as central to the phenomenon of the 'Victorian'. Total and partial sceptics alike draw on the same range of arguments. They appeal to the supposed element of hypocrisy in the professed beliefs of Victorians on sexual morality, and perhaps to an important quantitative argument: that the professed moralism of the period was actually only uttered by a minority of people who commanded the organs of opinion. A third reason for doubting that sexual moralism may be detected sometimes accompanies these other reasons: a scepticism that human sexual behaviour is altered by beliefs. My view is that the 'Victorian', in so far as it happened, should have left many traces in the record of sexual activity, and that the reasons for not expecting to find such traces can only have to do with the inadequacy of the record itself. I shall first tackle the three other pessimistic arguments about this which I have just listed. (I postpone discussing the relevant views of the French cultural historian Michel Foucault until the end of the next chapter: his scepticism about the inquiry in question cannot be confronted with the kind of argument which is called for here.)

Is sexual behaviour, in general, influenced by beliefs?

Anthropologists, surveying the practices of societies with a variety of sexual codes, are in no doubt that our sexuality at a surprisingly deep level is culturally controlled: beliefs may affect not simply our sense of how we ought to behave, but also our sense of our physiological possibilities. Frequency of intercourse at different periods of life, in situations where there is not supposed to be any constraint on sexual activity, varies very greatly from culture to culture. In one Ecuadorean tribe, it is reported, a coital rate of twice a week is something that newly married couples will boast of. There is a tribe in the Congo whose members expect to have intercourse more than once a night even when they are 50 or 60 years old. The physical response of both men and women to sexual stimulus is influenced by expectations, to judge by the variation, as between cultures, in the length of time it takes men to ejaculate, and in the ease with which women have orgasms. The latter point is relevant to the English nineteenth century, as is the evidence that doctrines of sexual continence led to reduced marital intercourse in certain Nonconformist groups in Europe and America.[2]

In such groups it also seems that there could be a link between the active conversion of spouses and raised fertility. Is this a case of the emotionalism of the religious experience having an unexpected outcome, or of responsiveness to affirmative sectarian rhetoric about childbearing? Even though beliefs can in principle influence our sexual function it is often the case that a given belief, because of its particular content, will not entail anything clearcut about behaviour. This is an important admonition to bear in mind in thinking about nineteenth-century attitudes. An individual might believe very strongly that sex is a 'lower' function, not to be satisfied just for its own sake if possible, or that a condition of psychological 'purity' on sex is common in children and women (to mention two familiar candidates for an orthodoxy on sex at the period), but there is no obvious behavioural outcome to be expected from such beliefs—or at least not one which there is any chance of detecting. The point is in fact linked to the question of the adequacy of the behavioural record, which I touch on shortly. For instance, marital fertility is an important potential indicator, still available to us today, of the frequency of intercourse in nineteenth-century marriages, but only below a certain threshold. If nineteenth-century doctrines about 'moderate'

---

[2] Marshall and Suggs 1971: 211, 214; Ford and Beach 1951: 78–9, 265–6; W. H. Davenport 1977; Udank 1991.

levels of marital sexual intercourse were interpreted to mean a not austerely infrequent rate of intercourse, above this threshold (and a commonly recommended rate was once or twice a week) the fertility figures would be silent on whether these doctrines were accepted or not.

In reacting against the Victorians' own tendency to link demographic and other data to standards and attitudes we have sometimes failed to notice when a contrary hypothesis, no more secure, is being smuggled in. Victorian interpretations of working-class demeanour and living arrangements, or of bastardy figures, and so forth, are likely to strike us as much too receptive to moral readings. According to modern ideas the rhetoric of most Victorian social comment, however bureaucratic or academic the stable it comes from, is sadly impure in this regard at least until the end of the period covered in this study. But we should probably learn from it, not that preconceptions have been successfully excluded by a more austere rhetoric, but rather the exceptional vitality of uninspected ideas in this field. Sex is a topic about which everyone seems prone to have theories. These may be no more than projections of personal experience or reiterations of some current wisdom, but they are easily turned into axioms for thinking about the past.

For example, until recently it was generally assumed by modern demographic historians that Victorian commentators had been wrong to associate a tendency to higher levels of illegitimacy with a tendency to marry earlier (uniting the two, commonly, as an index of moral laxity). Indeed it was expected that exactly the opposite association would be found. But it is now known that in nineteenth-century England these two demographic measures *were* positively correlated: where individuals tended to have bastards they also tended to marry young, and vice versa.

On reflection, behind the modern expectation that high levels of illegitimacy would accompany high ages of marriage lay some kind of view to the effect that the human tendency to copulate is constant, at least when conditions vary no more than they did between different areas and times in the English nineteenth century. It seems somehow 'natural' to think that if men and women postpone marriage they will have more bastards. But this is just a cliché of our culture, however unwelcome the fact. The assumption it flows from, of an invariant tendency for humans to have sexual intercourse, and the opposite assumption, that this tendency is variable and plastic, will actually themselves be part of the history explored in this book. For views on this question, stated or unstated, are important points of difference between various nineteenth-century positions on sexuality and sexual morals.

Was there, however, a mechanism which served to decouple sexual practices and beliefs specifically in the Victorian period, in the shape of an unusually strong tendency to hypocrisy, or 'cant', to use the idiom of the day? Anthropologists, again, report that a considerable discrepancy between sexual codes and sexual activities is common in human societies. This should be a warning against dismissing the hypothesis of Victorian hypocrisy out of hand: evidently it is rather easy for human groups to do what on the face of it is odd, namely, assent to a code and then disobey it almost as a matter of course.

But the orthodox picture of Victorian hypocrisy is more extreme than this, and truly odd. According to this picture, assent to the public code was a matter of conscious and often reluctant lip-service, with actual behaviour being guided by a fully formed alternative standard. We have been too ready to accept such an account, without enquiring what was the authority that made men and women endorse a set of values which was, allegedly, in such plain conflict with their real code. Human moral systems are made by humans, and there is something preposterous about the degree of self-inflicted moral discomfort which the Victorians are often supposed to have endured. Moreover, sometime in the 1890s, or thereabouts, this strange imperative vanishes for no clear reason. George Eliot and Thackeray, we are told, simply could not, with the best will in the world, be candid about sex in the way they dearly wished. But somehow novelists not more conspicuously courageous or intelligent, such as Grant Allen and George Moore, broke these silken bonds. As a matter of plain fact, sexual hypocrisy in the recorded lives of notable Victorians is rare. It is much more a feature of the biographies of twentieth-century celebrities—which may say something about the origins of our stereotype of the 'Victorian'. Perhaps the nineteenth-century biographical record has been too thoroughly weeded, but it is interesting that when sexual secrets have been disclosed they have often been revelations of non-performance, as in the married lives of Ruskin and Carlyle (and it may be in the extra-marital life of Dickens).

Perhaps the men and women who voiced a moralistic code in the nineteenth century lived by it, but this code had little impact on behaviour because they only composed a small, if salient, minority. This is a line of argument which deserves to be taken very seriously. There were certainly dissenting sexual cultures within Victorian England. There was, for example, evidently a consciously hedonistic culture, prosperous and socially elevated, with its most numerous following in the West End, living by the creed that 'fucking is the great humanizer' (in the words of *My Secret Life*). The heterodox cultures were inaudible, and in a sense suppressed. They did not receive a hearing on equal terms with the orthodox anti-sensualism of the period. They only found expression in raffish weeklies, in lowlife entertainments, in fringe periodicals, and in polemics—such as George Drysdale's *The Elements of Social Science*—which never reached a conventional library or bookshop.

But how disproportionate were the forces of orthodoxy and the forces of heresy? How small a group was succeeding in stifling the views of how large an opposition in the sexual culture of nineteenth-century England? Francis Place would not have admitted that there was any disproportion at all. Sexual moralism was a mass movement, as he observed it, and its tremendous ascendancy in respectable public discourse, right through the century, he would presumably have judged equitable—a fair allotment of party political broadcasting opportunities, so to speak. My own view, too, is that nineteenth-century anti-sensualism had a very broad base. In other words, if I have understood its nature correctly, narrow social origins could not be invoked to explain its lack of visible impact on the nation's sexual practices.

Some subscribers to the hypothesis of the 'Victorian' will not be disquieted by the absence of *any* distinctive features in the record of English sexual behaviour between 1830 and 1900. But I take it that the more common view of the matter is that the 'Victorian' did have some detectable consequences. I have mentioned the question of women's sexual response. What would it mean for the stereotype of the 'Victorian' if it were discovered from a reliable contemporary survey—as was discovered by the Mosher survey late in the century, in America—that middle-class English women usually experienced orgasm in intercourse? Happily for the stereotype, no such survey, quite, was done (but only slightly more indirect evidence, which I bring forward in Chapter 4, suggests that this is indeed what such a survey would have found).

Again, it would be comforting, I take it, for the usual theory of the 'Victorian' if real levels of prostitution could be shown to have risen in the period. This was definitely not the case as far as conventional street-prostitution went; clandestine prostitution is, however, an unknown quantity which can be massaged to suit historical prejudices (see the last section of this chapter). A trickier issue is age of marriage. While everyone would agree that economic and social factors can have a great influence on the age at which men and women get married, the relevant statistics for nineteenth-century England are often cited as also revealing something about attitudes and wishes. They can indeed give some support to a picture of a culture in which young people were blocked, by attitudes, from marrying readily. But the statistical story is annoyingly complicated: I give the relevant sources later in this chapter. Perhaps the behavioural area which it requires the breeziest confidence in the 'Victorian' to ignore is that of birth control. The early onset (that is, in the 1860s) of contraceptive practices, especially in bourgeois and respectable artisan groups which are in some sense the heartland of stereotypical 'Victorianism', is a well-established demographic fact. It has been shunned, it seems to me, by too many students of the period.

I have argued that the record of sexual practices in the nineteenth century should not be silent about the sexual moralism of the period, if that moralism is to conform with history and human nature. And in making out this case I have in fact, by way of correcting a certain stereotype of the 'Victorian', indicated something of what I shall argue this nineteenth-century sexual moralism to have been in reality: namely, a set of sincerely held values which commanded wide assent. But it may also appear, in what I have just said about the problems posed for the standard notion of the 'Victorian' by certain pieces of evidence, that I have cut the ground from under *any* episode of sexual moralism in the period, of whatever sort. Prostitute numbers are not a difficulty in this context (they could be interesting evidence for a climate of genuine sexual restraint, since they appear to decline). But if husbands and wives knew all about the female orgasm, or if age of marriage shows no upward trend, or if couples were successfully arranging to limit their fertility, can the society be said to have been sexually moralistic? Evidently, my version of nineteenth-century sexual moralism will have to cope with these considerations. I believe that the mood, and timing, of this moralism, properly understood, are consistent with the behavioural record.

Finally, however, there are formidable difficulties about the record itself. Direct evidence of sexual activity in the past comes in just two guises: personal description and demographic quantities. At all periods, and perhaps especially in the nineteenth century, the first kind of evidence is immensely rare. This makes it very insecure as a foundation for any conclusions about the sexuality of the society as a whole, for individuals can vary to an almost incredible extent in their sexual behaviour. The point is perfectly illustrated by the two main personal sexual histories to have survived from the English nineteenth century: the diaries of Arthur J. Munby, and *My Secret Life* by the unidentified 'Walter' (I take the latter to be factual: the improbability of this is not as great as the improbability of its being any kind of fiction or part-fiction). The two authors were of similar social standing, and there is a good deal of common ground between their experiences in respect of sexual milieu. But they represent extremes of sexual behaviour, each, probably, equally alien to the experience of the reader. Munby was a virgin, although he loved and lived with a woman. 'Walter' was a prodigiously active heterosexual, who had intercourse with many hundreds of women, and in his sexual prime habitually ejaculated several times a day.

This example of extreme variation is, incidentally, on the face of it awkward for the view that our sexual conduct is deeply influenced by our beliefs. I have already indicated—in citing the creed of *My Secret Life* as that of a heterodox sexual subculture—how the anthropologists' wisdom on this matter may be reconciled with the coexistence of Munby and Walter in the same society. But I do not wish to be glib on this point, or minimize the problems posed by the case of Walter. On some aspects of sexuality he accepted prevailing beliefs which had a distinct anti-sensual potential. He took it that male masturbation could have debilitating effects, perhaps including impotence; in adolescence, especially, the male physique could be overtaxed by sex. He believed that women risked ill health and even mental impairment from 'libidinous excesses'. He recognized some connection between sperm-production and the condition of the rest of the male system.

The evidence of *My Secret Life* as to the impact of these beliefs is not simple. Walter never refrains from giving his female partners orgasms, but he does note with satisfaction that one of the most sexually active courtesans of his acquaintance suffered no ill effects: 'all this did not give her an excess of sexual pleasure, with all her fucking, frigging, and gamahuching, she looked the very picture of health and strength'. His beliefs about male sexuality, which evidently bore more closely on his own behaviour, had some restraining influence. He consistently refrained from masturbation, and on one occasion apparently moderated his rate of intercourse because a doctor 'warned that unlimited indulgence would lead to impotence, and perhaps worse'. On the other hand he expresses no anxiety about over-production of sperm, and he recounts with some pride and amusement an episode of involuntary ejaculation very much in the mould of the anecdotes which sexual quacks and some practitioners used at this date to excite fears about 'spermatorrhoea'. Walter's ideas about sperm are unclear, however: he does imply that frequent ejaculation could make a man lose weight, but his use of the phraseology of 'blood's essence' about sperm may be no more than an unthinking hangover from obsolete haematic theories (such as I describe in Chapter 4).

It is worth stressing that Walter has a very explicit libertarian creed, conceived as antithetical to codes of sexual abstinence and restraint. He frequently offers this creed as the ideological context of his promiscuity, and the latter does seem in some measure to have been ideologically driven. He once describes himself watching the prostitutes on Oxford Street, 'looking at them, pleased and yet sorry as they often made me feel, when in unphilosophic mood'. The oddity of this remark, if I read it correctly, is that pity for the prostitutes is treated as an involuntary impulse, while a more deliberate ('philosophic') attitude would dictate that they be sexually desired.[3]

As I have mentioned, there is a dearth of personal sexual records from the period covered by this book. From a slightly later date there is the interesting archive of requests for sexual advice received by Marie Stopes, now in the Wellcome Institute. This material shows that some husbands in the 1920s and 1930s, if not actually arriving at a lowered estimate of physiological possibilities because of their cultural environment, were at least convinced that a man should and could refrain from maximum sexual arousal. The following remark expresses an attitude which, perhaps, would be encountered in a comparable Victorian archive, if such a thing had survived: 'You . . . suggest (what appears to me to be extraordinary) that in most cases an average would be 5 or 6 times a week . . . I would not doubt the

[3] *My Secret Life* 1966: 124, 130, 557, 665, 1229, 1273, 1381, 1476, 1537, 1555, 1621, 1735, 1852, 1979, 2017, 2301.

desire for union as frequently as this but I cannot help thinking that the desire must be suppressed if one wishes to maintain one's health.'[4]

In the demographic record the huge variations between a Walter and a Munby become invisible. And even if the averages which emerge correspond to the actual behaviour of many individuals the story they tell is coarse-grained. The demographic data are aggregates: of those marrying at various ages, of children born inside and outside marriage, and so on. Admittedly these totals can, even with the limitations of the nineteenth-century demographic record, be narrowed approximately to particular groups in the community in many cases. We can say roughly what coalminers were doing about birth control at the end of the period, for example. But we cannot usually observe the demographic activity of a known group and their descendants.

A brilliant exception to this rule has been achieved by the recent technique of family reconstitution; but the only communities for which family reconstitution seems possible are rural parishes. And *all* demographic analysis is coarse-grained for our purposes because it is obliged to treat as indivisible atoms of information events which are actually multiple in nature. Births and marriages are overdetermined and inexpressive human events, converging points for numerous processes which can only take effect in the stark alternatives of an entry, or no entry, in registers and census enumerations. They cannot be unpacked for their original balance of causes—which may or may not have been instructive about beliefs.

II

Getting Married and Conceiving Children

A good deal is known about the rate at which men and women married, the ages at which they married, and their tendency to produce children, inside and outside marriage, in the English nineteenth century. But our knowledge comes in great part from official investigations and compilations of the period, and so it improves with the increasing sophistication of these inquiries.[5] To balance the deficien-

---

[4] L. Hall 1991: 108.

[5] It is not until well into the century—or even until its last decades—that full and reliable facts are available on some questions. The main innovation after the founding of the decen-

cies in the contemporary official analysis we do have the remarkable extrapolations from selected parish registrations which have been performed by modern demographic historians. However, in the nature of the case, these calculations have generally been done on the period before 1837. In some respects we are more ignorant about the early Victorian years than about the Georgian era.

One of the great discoveries of the new work on parish registers has been that age of marriage declined, and rate of marriage increased, in eighteenth-century England (and thus has been settled the controversy, vigorously conducted over many years by historical demographers but marginal to the concerns of the present study, about the cause of the eighteenth-century rise of the English population).[6] To what extent were these tendencies continued, arrested, or reversed in the nineteenth century? On the face of it, rates of marriage start to decline, after more than a century of almost unbroken rise, around 1800. There have been various attempts to argue that the evidence is misleading—that there was a period of unusually poor recording of marriages at this period, for example, or that only remarriages experienced a reduction, due perhaps to improved life expectancy. But the newest and most thorough work on the question suggests that there was a true drop, even allowing for the age distribution of the population, in rates of first marriage—that is, of numbers of marriages per thousand individuals aged between 15 and 34—late in the eighteenth century (similarly, from around 1770 there is a progressively higher proportion of individuals never marrying).[7]

The scale of the event should not be exaggerated. By the 1830s, at its lowest point, the decline had reached the levels of the early eighteenth century (around 7.8 per thousand, while the generation with the highest proportion not marrying is born around 1815), and was still well above the unusually low levels of the 1660s. Moreover the whole chronological block of seventeenth, eighteenth, and nineteenth centuries represents an episode of relatively constant low

nial census in 1801 is the Registrar General's annual table recording civil registrations of births and marriages. Civil registration did not start until 1837; the information requested and its presentation were not standardized for several years; and under-registration, especially of births, was a problem that took a long time to be corrected. The census enumerators' complete data (which do not appear in the official publication) had actually shed light on matters which the annual registration figures could not illuminate, but their potential was not exploited until the very end of the period covered here.

[6] Though see D. R. Weir 1984 and Schofield 1985 for the continuation of this debate.

[7] W. A. Armstrong 1965; Wrigley and Schofield 1989: 260, 428–9, 528–9.

marriage rates compared with the periods which flank it. Rates were at around 12 per thousand in the mid-sixteenth century; in our own day they are also considerably higher.[8]

All estimates agree that from about 1840 the English marriage rate then rose again steeply, and within a decade was not far from its highest eighteenth-century levels. Thereafter there is probably a decline by the end of the century, but its shape has been a matter of some disagreement. On the whole it is analysts in the nineteenth century, looking at short runs of rather crudely treated figures, who make the strongest claims for a decline, starting in the late 1860s or early 1870s. But since 1906 there have been more sophisticated treatments of the data, using more subtle notions of nuptiality, which suggest either that the marriage rate continued to rise rather markedly until 1870, and then fell off steadily for the rest of the century, or that there was only a shallow, even inconsiderable, decline from a plateau in the 1850s and 1860s.[9] In the present context it is not necessary to choose among these slightly different interpretations of the figures (which depend on different ways of adjusting them to take account of the demography of the whole population). Any variation after 1850 is fairly slight, and there is no suggestion of a decline until the last decade of the period directly covered in this book (though the end-of-century pattern should not be ignored: it may be relevant to the formation of early twentieth-century perceptions of the Victorian). The salient aspect of the story of marriage rates is the historically rather high, and perhaps still rising, level in the twenty years from the mid-century on. This high level had been achieved by an unusually steep rise in the rate in the 1840s.

What of age of marriage? The eighteenth-century tendency to marry increasingly early can still be detected in the first two decades of the nineteenth,[10] but the picture for the next thirty years on this important question is disappointingly uncertain. Civil registration came into force in 1837, but ages of those marrying were not recorded, except accidentally, beyond the categories of 'minor' and 'full age'. Successive Registrar Generals' reports did what they could with the data, to contradictory effect.[11] Modern analysis of the subject has found strong

---

[8] Barker and Drake 1982: 208–11.

[9] Ogle 1890; Longstaff 1891: 14; Hooker 1897–8; Yule 1906; Wrigley and Schofield 1989: 438; Teitelbaum 1984: 102; Woods and Hinde 1985.

[10] Wrigley and Schofield 1989: 255, 262; Tranter 1985: 50–1.

[11] The very small number of accidentally recorded ages in the two years 1840–1 shows a mean age for first-time grooms of 24.45 years and for first-time brides of 24.30; these are

indirect evidence of a *rise* in age of marriage in the second quarter of the century. This was certainly the experience of a group of Oxfordshire villages, which we do know about, in these years.[12] On balance it appears that from about 1820 to 1850—a period in which rates of marriage were at first falling, and then rose sharply—the average age of marriage went up slightly, and this perhaps despite a tendency for increasing numbers of very young individuals to marry (a tendency which itself is not in evidence until the latter 1840s).

This movement ceased at the mid-century, and then for twenty years or so there was a general tendency, with both sexes, to marry younger. A calculation of mean age of first marriages county by county in 1861, using census rather than registration figures, has found that there was already a slight drop in almost all counties from the 1851 levels. The movement towards younger marriage did in turn halt, probably sooner for men than for women. But while the male age of marriage then remained rather constant into the 1880s, women actually started, around the early 1870s, again to be increasingly older when they married.[13]

These nation-wide totals are very crude: the numbers of individuals marrying, and their ages, must conceal much that is significant about the pattern of nuptiality in particular groups. As I mention in the next chapter, the highest stratum in English society—the gentry and the professional class—seems to have married later and later, right through the period. This possibility emerged from an inquiry of 1874, and as long ago as 1890 the pioneering suggestion was made that high female rates of marriage (and to a lesser extent lower ages for brides) occur in regions where there is a high level of female employment—thus exploding 'laments on the unhappy condition of women, who are represented as driven to matrimony because they

similar to the levels at the beginning of the century. Ten years later the means, in the same very unsatisfactory sample, for both men and women were slightly lower, but in 1867 the Registrar General calculated that both had risen by a small amount over the whole period since 1841. On the other hand, his successor in 1896, when he came to review these figures in his report for that year, doubted if they were significant, and preferred the explanation that 'the practice of stating the actual age had during the interval increased more among the older persons than it had among the younger'. His reason was the increase in the proportion of minors, both male and female, among those who married over these years, and he deduced indeed that average age of marriage had declined right through to 1873.

[12] Outhwaite 1973; Wrigley and Schofield 1989: 626; Kuchemann, Boyce, and Harrison 1967.

[13] Crafts 1978; Ogle 1890; Teitelbaum 1984: 98–100; Carrier 1956; Wrigley and Schofield 1989: 436–7; Hutchins 1905; Matras 1965; Glass 1938.

are unable by any other means to support themselves'. Since then many studies have clarified how marriage behaviour varied from region to region in England during the last century, in response to occupation, economic conditions and social environment. A range of factors have been emphasized, and there is a certain amount of straight disagreement among historians about the relative importance of some of them. Interestingly, the level of female employment seems to have survived as one of the most robust of these explanatory factors, especially when it is associated with a favourable sex ratio in the population. It was capable of eclipsing the influence of industrialization, powerful though the latter was as a stimulus to marriage.[14]

If economic and social circumstances can explain regional variations in nuptiality, perhaps *national* trends were also much influenced by such factors. This is another venerable hypothesis, explored on several occasions by demographers well before the end of the nineteenth century, and recently assisted by an authoritative linking of nineteenth-century patterns of nuptiality (and of fertility) to wage-levels in the period.[15] All explanations of this sort are obviously in competition with cultural explanations of changed sexual behaviour, in terms of attitudes and beliefs. And culturally and economically minded historians have been in dispute over another topic, which has a particularly close bearing on sexuality: fertility in the English nineteenth century.

Fertility and nuptiality can go hand-in-hand. I have mentioned that the expanding population of the eighteenth century is now generally accepted to be the result, chiefly, of more marriage and younger marriage. This means that there is no significant change in what is called age-specific marital fertility in the period: couples did not produce more children, age for age, than their ancestors—they simply married younger and in larger numbers. The same logic, in converse form, seems to apply in the early nineteenth century. Rates of marriage were falling, and ages of marriage rising; a decline both in the numbers of children from each marriage and in the fertility of the population as a whole is clearly apparent from 1820. The effect is short-lived however, and both indices are levelling out and climbing again steadily from the latter 1840s.[16] The process continues until the

---

[14] Ogle 1890; Anderson 1976; Levine 1977: 47; Crafts 1978; Friedlander 1983; Woods and Hinde 1985; Friedlander and Moshe 1986.   [15] Wrigley and Schofield 1989: 402–53.
[16] Krause 1958; W. A. Armstrong 1965; Wrigley and Schofield 1989: 229–35; Tranter 1985: 58–60; Yule 1906; Innes 1938: 5; Teitelbaum 1984: 76–9, 114–18.

1870s, when there occurs the single most celebrated and controversial episode in nineteenth-century demography. It is not disputed that English fertility (along with Scottish, Irish, and continental fertility at about the same time) went into an accelerating, never-to-be-reversed decline in the 1870s which is novel in character. Neither changes in the pattern of marriages, nor any of the other factors (such as lowered biological fecundity, improved neonatal survival, and changed age of puberty) which until recently were invoked to explain earlier shifts in national fertility, can account for this decline.

It is a decline in marital fertility, though it seems to have had a precursor—very interesting in itself but not significant for the national totals—in a reduced rate of illegitimate fertility, which I will discuss shortly. It is true that married couples were slightly older on average towards the end of the nineteenth century, but they were having so many fewer children, and pacing their reproduction in such a way (in particular, they simply stopped having children after a certain point) that we know that they were also deliberately restricting their fertility, or practising 'family limitation'. As a national phenomenon, it is an unprecedented development. The controversy about it has to do with how it got under way, and what physical means were being used to limit numbers of births.

Even on a national scale the effects of family limitation may be detected, it is claimed, as early as 1861 if the right mathematical tools are used.[17] The movements are slight (perhaps a 5 per cent increase between wives born 1831–45 and those born 1841–55 in the number who were in some way deliberate controllers of their fertility) so it is possible that a fairly specific group is involved at this early stage, and that the increased resort to family limitation thereafter is to be understood as radiating from this point in the society. The 1911 census report included an analysis of fertility which permitted assessments of how far fertility had varied with class and occupation, at least as far back as 1861. When these assessments were performed they showed a definite correlation, from the start, between social rank and the degree of resort to birth control, with a widening of differences according to class as time went on, even though more and more groups were acquiring the habit of family limitation (and the link with class, occupationally defined, rather than by income, has since been confirmed).[18]

---

[17] Habakkuk 1971: 54–5; Matras 1965.
[18] Stevenson 1920; Innes 1938: 65–9; Haines 1989.

So, by a backward extrapolation, it seems that the core group, the original cell in the birth-control revolution, must be high up in the social hierarchy. There have been attempts to identify the mid-nineteenth-century birth-controllers more precisely, and other studies have incidentally shed light on who they might be. There is a suggestion of long standing that they were members of the middle classes, motivated both by higher material ambitions and an objectively more stringent economic situation to limit their numbers of dependants. In London (where birth control and class seem to be broadly correlated by 1861) there is evidence, though admittedly only from the crude registration figures, that family limitation was practised more in the middle-class district of Camberwell in the 1850s than in London generally.[19]

A more sophisticated analysis of several English districts has confirmed the general association between class and birth control, and added the interesting discovery that the middle-class pioneers, in Sheffield at least, were from the *bottom* of this group: shop-owners, hotel-keepers, and other non-manual but non-professional and non-managerial workers. While the handful of self-declared users of contraception tended to be of a superior middle-class stamp (and conversely, according to Annie Besant, there was some decrying of birth control from 'that lower portion of the shop-keeping class which wants to be thought "genteel"'), the *Saturday Review* was probably right in its intuition in 1866 that 'mothers of the lower middle-class' (in London in this instance) were in practice resorting to 'French precedents' more than suspected. In York also the middle classes, but above all the lower middle classes, were probably restricting their reproduction as early as the 1840s. At about this time Francis Place judged that birth control was used 'to a considerable extent among respectable people whose incomes are small', but was a rarity with those on 'large incomes' and with working-class families.[20]

These are not the only examples of complexity in the link between class and fertility control. It was inescapable even from the 1911 figures that there were certain surprising differences in marital fertility between various occupational groups among the working class. Miners were the least responsive to the possibilities of family limitation, and are indeed the one clear case where occupation has an over-

[19] Banks 1954: *passim*; Woods 1984; Branca 1975: 120–1.
[20] *National Reformer*, 29 (1877), 268; *Saturday Review*, 22 (1866), 481–2; Woods and Smith 1983; A. Armstrong 1974: 173–4; Miles 1988: 156.

riding influence on fertility patterns. Both miners and agricultural workers had higher fertility than unskilled workers, while textile-workers may have held their fertility to utterly anomalous levels: certainly below those of artisans and clerks and, on one interpretation, even below those of farmers and the lower ranks of businessmen. The West Riding was second only to London in the rate at which its marital fertility shrank in the national decline.[21]

In the heavier urban industries working-class families may have conformed to the miners' pattern of high fertility, but generally it seems that urban industrialization gave a considerable impulse to family limitation. In a small sample from Coventry and the surrounding countryside, that is none the less valuable because the families' occupations are known precisely from census enumerations, the wives of farm workers in the early 1870s have almost 9 per cent more children than industrial wives of the same age. Bigger differentials have been discovered separating the fertility rates of urban and rural working-class families in Nottingham and its neighbourhood twenty years earlier (an effect which was reinforced by social rank, so that the lowest fertility of all in the area is exhibited by upper-class families in the city). Even from an intermediate environment such as the industrialized village of Shepshed in Leicestershire there are indications of rather strict fertility control, from mid-century onwards, by the framework-weavers—in contrast to the practice of agricultural labourers, village artisans, and even shopkeepers in the neighbourhood.[22]

But when enquiries about nineteenth-century birth control are pushed this far back, and into communities as relatively unchanged as this, research starts to make contact, or so it seems, with an older tradition of family limitation. For Shepshed's agricultural neighbour, the village of Bottesford, while perhaps losing grip on its fertility by 1850, had shown signs of genuine and highly efficient family limitation practices before 1800. Indeed there is considerable evidence of such practices from all sorts of communities before the nineteenth century. The evidence does not call in question the novelty of the latter nineteenth-century fertility decline in its scale and speed, but it

---

[21] Innes 1938: 66; Yule 1920: 22–31; Haines 1977; Teitelbaum 1984: 140. See also Burr Litchfield 1978. See also Garrett 1990 for the proposal that the advantages of low fertility for Yorkshire textile-workers simply meant that individuals with *naturally* reduced fecundity stayed in employment.

[22] Haines 1979: 194–6; Galton 1873; R. Smith 1970; Levine 1977: 84–7.

does suggest, contrary to the original views on the subject, that the techniques being used so widely by late Victorian families to control their numbers, and the thinking behind their use, may not have been new.

These precursor birth-controlling communities are very diverse, but by the same token they make a very patchy appearance in the historical record.[23] Among them are the seventeenth-century Genevan bourgeoisie, the eighteenth-century French aristocracy, the upper classes of Philadelphia in the early nineteenth century, eighteenth-century American Quakers and more modern Amish, and several pre-industrial English communities in addition to the Bottesford case. The latter (parishes from Devon, Oxfordshire, and Lancashire are among them) have the appearance of a more coherent group, the still visible manifestations, perhaps, of a general pre-industrial culture of reproductive control. But, to judge by the non-English cases, they could equally be isolated from one another—communities which adopted birth-control practices independently—while the case of Bottesford after 1800 shows that these practices could come in some sense to be forgotten. It has been claimed that direct evidence of the old culture of reproductive control still survives in the written record,[24] and it is true that many allusions to abortion and contraceptive techniques can be recovered from a variety of sixteenth-, seventeenth-, and eighteenth-century sources. A problem with these is that many of the contraceptive recommendations (where they involve the menstrual cycle or positions for intercourse, for example) would simply not have worked.

Doubts have actually been voiced as to whether pre-industrial birth control is not a figment of historians' imaginations.[25] These sceptical studies have sometimes been vitiated by the assumption that authentic family limitation must be 'parity-specific', that is, designed to hold the number of offspring to a particular level. Earlier communities may have wished to control their reproduction in a different way: avoiding births for a time where this was desirable, but not intending any particular limit on total family size (in which case the historical evidence for birth control will have a different appearance). It seems best to accept that certain pre-industrial groups did deliberately restrict their fertility, but to be sceptical that they were drawing on a widely and continuously available wisdom about birth

---

[23] On this point, see Livi-Bacci 1986.   [24] McLaren 1984: ch. 3.
[25] Knodel 1977; C. Wilson 1984; Crafts and Ireland 1976.

control when they did so, even in pre-industrial England. The efficacious contraceptive measures available (unlike the inefficacious ones to be found in some of the literature) were, after all, the very obvious ones of abstinence and extra-vaginal ejaculation, and there is something rather absurd in the view that these must be learnt, or conversely could be forgotten—and that individuals were burdened with children they did not want because it never occurred to them that these methods would help their situation.

As I have mentioned, the fact of pre-industrial birth control may be thought to illuminate both the techniques and the motivations associated with the general English fertility decline of the late nineteenth century. The almost unanimous tendency, in recent studies, to forge links between the old and the new birth control has meant a thorough revision of the accepted account of what happened from about 1860 onwards to English fertility, and in particular of the accepted understanding of the contraceptive techniques involved.[26] Hitherto the issues of technique and motivation had been regarded as one and the same. On this view, English fertility declined simply because of the introduction of reliable barrier methods of contraception; there is no more to the story. These barrier methods—in which I include the douche along with the sponge, the pessary, and the condom—were not new, but they only became widely known with their deliberate publicizing by Charles Bradlaugh and Annie Besant, first in seeking prosecution for publishing the birth-control booklet *Fruits of Philosophy* in 1877 and then in their own written and spoken propaganda.

The mere fact of non-barrier techniques having been used in the past is no argument against this model of events (though some historians almost write as if it were).[27] The more solid objections are, first, that 1877 is too late, since the fertility decline certainly starts before this, in some quarters perhaps many years earlier. However, even the earliest starting-date for the decline (say, about 1860) is consistent with its being essentially a matter of new barrier methods, including the condom (which was manufactured in its modern form in large quantities from the mid-century),[28] so the objection can be met with a revision of the chronology. The second objection is that the barrier methods were too expensive for adoption by working-class families,

---

[26] See, as a notable recent statement, Woods 1987. Expert opinion is perhaps swinging back to the older view, however; see Boyer and Williamson 1989.

[27] e.g. R. V. Wells 1975.   [28] Woodruff 1958: 72.

an argument which usually takes the form of a comparison between the alleged price of a condom and working-class wages.

This is both a misrepresentation of the economic facts, and a simplification of the repertoire of available barrier contraception. Condoms cost about 10d. each before the era of mass-production, and were at that period regarded as a device for the gentlemanly libertine (though it was understood that they would be reused several times). But in the second half of the nineteenth century the price fell as low as ½d.: making every act of intercourse about twice as expensive for a Victorian worker as it is for his modern counterpart. By the early twentieth-century, at least, cost was not significant among the deterrents listed by a sample of working-class couples who had refrained from birth control.

It does appear that even the mass-produced condoms were, for some years at least, only sold from a few outlets. On the other hand the condom was the barrier method *least* favoured by those proselytizing for birth control, from Francis Place down to Annie Besant. All these writers (whose beliefs about birth control I discuss in the second volume of this study) emphasized devices that were cheaper and more available, either because they were home-made (as in the case of the sponge—reported to be still the dominant device in the 1870s), or because they were already in use for non-contraceptive purposes, as in the case of the douche and the solid pessary. Charles Knowlton's douching procedure, urged in *Fruits of Philosophy* in 1832, involved the adapting of the 'female syringe', which cost 1s. at apothecaries (to judge from the evidence of *My Secret Life* it was anyway commonplace for women to wash out their vaginas after intercourse, in the hope of preventing conception). Scores of different types of pessary were developed in the period, and their contraceptive potential was well-recognized and surely exploited. Doctors were in fact obliged to hint at it when they told their women patients to remove at night pessaries which had been inserted for non-contraceptive purposes.[29]

The problem for any model which denies that the fertility decline depended on barrier techniques is to say what *was* new after 1860, such that existing, non-barrier methods were abruptly and universally adopted to bring about parity-specific family limitation in a way

[29] P. Knight 1977; *My Secret Life* 1966: 605–6, 756; *Exquisite*, 3 (1843), 108–9, 117–18; G. Drysdale 1868: 136; Nichols 1873: 115; Chandrasekhar 1981: 138; Branca 1975: 133; Wood and Suitters 1970: 109–15; J. M. Sims 1866: 293–4; Blundell 1837: 47; Secombe 1990.

in which they had never been used before. Here the modern orthodoxy has been rather uncertain and divided, and has tended to
become entangled in simply verbal arguments about 'adjustment' and
'innovation'. Were English people responding, perhaps, to substan-
tially altered economic conditions? This would be in line with what
was probably the stimulus to birth control in pre-industrial communities, and the differing degrees of family limitation by different occupational groups (miners versus textile-workers for example), and by
groups with different patterns of employment (high and low numbers
of working children, for example), must point to economic motives.
Economic history is an accommodating thing, and it is not difficult to
find major economic change at the right period.[30]

But for what it is worth, economic factors do not seem to have
been decisive in any known modern example of a society undergoing
the 'fertility transition' to lower rates of conception.[31] Could any economic change have been so universally experienced in the English
nineteenth century as to bring about a universal change in reproductive practices? There remains a strong impression (although a simple
model of downward percolation in the social hierarchy is wrong) of
something learnt or realized by group after group in the 1860s and
1870s. It is true that the classic birth-control propaganda did give
some attention to coitus interruptus as a method, and in Robert Dale
Owen's *Moral Physiology*, in particular, the practice is represented as
both sensible and pleasurable. One miner recalled how he had read
the literature as a young husband and then opted for Owen's
approach.[32] I shall refer shortly to working-class families in the north
of England who appear to have resorted to coitus interruptus under
the influence of propaganda specifically recommending barrier
devices (and in this region even rates of abortion may have been
enhanced).

But the main lesson being apprehended by group after group was
surely the attractiveness of the condom, pessary, sponge, and douche.
It is worth stressing what would have been the positive attractions of
the new barrier methods if they were affordable. To put the matter
crudely, individuals seek pleasure in sex, and the new methods generally gave a better chance of more pleasure to both parties than
extra-vaginal ejaculation (there were admittedly some couples, even
into the twentieth century, who found their pleasure significantly

[30] See, most recently, Levine 1987 *passim*.   [31] Cleland and Wilson 1987.
[32] *National Reformer*, 29 (1877), 307.

reduced by the psychological effect of deploying barrier devices).[33] This is obvious to the point of banality (at least to the commercially successful manufacturers of pessaries, intra-uterine devices, and condoms in our day) but scarcely mentioned, if at all, by historians of the nineteenth-century fertility decline.

It is quite conceivable that a shift in attitudes eased the way for barrier methods of birth control here. In pre-industrial communities family limitation which reduced sexual satisfaction for the partners or eliminated it (in the case of abstinence) may have been perceived as an acceptable or at least less culpable violation of the principle that reproduction should not be interfered with. In fact a new moral evaluation of birth control, in general, seems to me to be the one message, other than the message of the barrier devices, which could have spread far and fast through England from about 1860. Charles Drysdale, the neo-Malthusian, had the impression in 1866 that 'a priori views of providential interference, and other fallacies' were still an obstacle to general family limitation. An observer of the fertility decline in urban Cheshire counted as one of its causes 'decay of religious sentiment and the decline of the idea that the prevention of conception is an immoral act'.[34]

Modern studies of the question have not much alluded to a possible weakening of taboos against birth control, perhaps because this raises problems about its practice in pre-industrial communities (moreover, as I have mentioned, women of all classes, from well before the mid-century, seem routinely to have washed their vaginas after intercourse unless conception was positively desired). Historians have spoken of a new perception of the rewards and advantages of small families, but this is virtually to argue in a circle (and implies an implausible lack of innovativeness in previous societies). It would be interesting also to explore the thought that non-parity-specific fertility restriction, the mere spacing of births, was more compatible with traditional religious and ethical notions than the parity-specific strategies that appeared in the late nineteenth century.

The new evaluation of contraception may have emanated to a significant extent from women, whose huge personal interest in the matter of childbirth and family size was being given something like due weight—even though there is one respect (particularly impres-

---

[33] L. Hall 1991: 94.   [34] G. Drysdale 1866: 30; Elderton 1914: 85.

sive to a modern reader perhaps) in which women were disadvan-
taged by the new power to control family size. The evidence is that
from the earliest years of the fertility decline, in the 1860s, birth control was parity-specific in a strong sense: couples adopted it once
some desired total of offspring had been reached, and not before.
Indeed—if still rather surprisingly—births in the first years of marriage, when this total was being reached, tended to be *more* frequent
for these couples than for couples in earlier decades.[35] Techniques
(not used systematically enough to count statistically as family limitation however) for holding births below their maximum for these years
must have been successfully adopted by the married before the fertility decline but then abandoned. Whatever these techniques were,
they will have tended to reduce the quantity and quality of early marital sexual activity: but if women of the late 1860s and thereafter had
better sex-lives they also gave birth more frequently.

To our minds this might imply that in the early phase of the fertility decline women had less control than men over the deployment of
contraception in their marriages, even though the new methods
would seem to give them a greater possibility of control. I doubt,
however, if wives were being obliged to adopt a faster programme of
childbearing than they would have wished. Couples married with the
intention of having children (divorce and childlessness were strongly
correlated, with causation probably flowing both ways).[36] It was hard
to tell what rate of procreation would yield the desired total of births
for a haphazardly, primitively birth-controlling couple: Charles
Ansell, writing in 1874 but evidently not taking modern contraception into account, has figures on the relation between the date of first
delivery and total family size to give partners 'while yet in the early
years of their wedded life, the means of forming an approximately
correct estimate as to the total number of children that they would be
likely to have.'[37] For wives strongly interested in being able to determine the latter quantity, birth control blessedly meant that slowing
down one's early rate of conception was no longer the only way to
reduce the risk of far more pregnancies than were desired or could
be faced.

There is one birth-control technique which I have not discussed,

[35] Habakkuk 1971: 55; Carrier 1956; Pearce 1973.
[36] Rowntree and Carrier 1957. For a case from the 1860s where three-year spacings of
births arranged by a husband were considered cruel to the wife see Hammerton 1992: 145.
[37] Ansell 1874: 61.

and which is relevant here. Abortion is a frequent topic in pre-nineteenth-century references to fertility control; one cannot doubt that it was resorted to, perhaps a great deal, but there is no way of checking claims that have been made to this effect. In the nineteenth century there are frequent allegations that abortion was routinely practised by the working class, and even by the upper class, though again no relevant evidence is ever likely to come forward (there is a possible allusion to abortion in a divorce suit of 1858, involving parties from the professional middle class). We know what incidence of miscarriage there was in some parts of the working class, and it has been suggested that as many as 7 per cent of working-class pregnancies were aborted.[38]

In the 1870s, at the time of the great controversy over *Fruits of Philosophy*, a good deal of evidence about current contraceptive practices was reported by the advocates of birth control, especially in the pages of the *National Reformer*. But this material is obviously extremely biased (Annie Besant particularly liked to draw attention to clergymen and their wives who endorsed contraception). The nearest thing we have to a balanced account of birth-control behaviour during the onset of the fertility decline is a rather later survey of practices (chiefly working-class) in the North of England, conducted by the eugenicist Ethel Elderton. She concentrated on the working class because she had a eugenicist fear that the best elements in the nation were restricting their reproduction more than the inferior elements; her study is disfigured by a closing diatribe about the genetic calamity facing the British Empire unless birth control is thwarted by a movement with 'religious' fervour and an inspiring 'leader' (no doubt Karl Pearson, whose Eugenics Laboratory commissioned the survey). But these shrill pages are in abrupt contrast to the study itself, which is balanced and numerate. Elderton puts the fertility statistics on each area beside qualitative accounts which she has elicited from local 'correspondents'. Since the study dates from 1914 none of these personal impressions goes back before the mid-1870s, and they are just impressions, but they are instructive for all that.

The statistics show a large variation in the timing of the fertility decline in different regions in the North (Dewsbury in the West Riding had falling rates in the mid-1860s, but in nearby Skipton not even the middle classes were using birth control detectably until the

[38] McLaren 1984: ch. 4; Greaves 1862–3; McLaren 1977; Sauer 1978; Granville 1860; *The Times*, 15 June 1858, p. 11.

1890s); this is reflected in the observations of the correspondents about the selling and advertising of contraceptives (in most areas both activities are conspicuous from the latter 1870s, but in Cockermouth the working class did not appear to be buying condoms until much later, and newspapers in Middlesborough had always carried exceptionally few contraceptive advertisements). Some correspondents believed that the middle classes in their region had pioneered the local use of contraception (the rural middle class near Stockton, for example, well before the Bradlaugh–Besant trial) and that this had influenced working-class practice (as in Bacup). But one striking lesson reinforced by correspondent after correspondent is the importance of active propaganda, both ideological and commercial. One or both of the Bradlaugh–Besant team had visited many of the areas after the trial of 1877, lecturing on birth control, with an effect which could still be remembered.

They were followed by other lecturers and pamphleteers, but the great mass of contraceptive propaganda was apparently commercial. The range of marketing techniques was wide and the advertising in a single area could be intensive: literature in chemists' shops, announcements in urinals, lectures by travelling salesmen, fly posters, advertisements in papers, and (with interesting frequency) circulars sent to couples who had announced a birth in the press. The energetic commercial thrust given to birth control after 1877 has perhaps been underestimated: one historian, however, has pointed out that from this date it is the manufactured devices which dictate the form of the non-commercial propaganda, however disinterested.[39] The impact of such advertising as reported in the survey does give some support, in an unexpected fashion, to the recent notion that families employed traditional means of restricting fertility on a new scale once the idea of family limitation had made its impact (which is ironical, in this case, because the idea was imparted by publicity for the new techniques). In Nantwich it was believed that fifteen years of propaganda had encouraged resort to coitus interruptus, while in Gorton both this technique and the condom had allegedly become popular.

But in the Blackburn and Burnley areas there was an avidity for the most up-to-date ways of implementing a principle long 'taken as accepted'. One York wife would have no truck with abstaining: 'Self-

---

[39] Peel 1964.

restraint? . . . Not much! If my husband started on self-restraint, I should jolly well know there was another woman in the case'. In Birkenhead 'douche tins can be seen unscreened in many bedrooms'. It is interesting that Elderton's correspondents make hardly any allusion to the cost of birth-control devices as a deterrent to their use by working-class families, and then only in reference to the very poorest cases. Abortion makes a conspicuous appearance in the survey; in several areas abortifacients are reported to be widely promoted and responsible for considerable mortality. There is an implication, in fact, that an increased market for these substances may also have come in on the back of the campaign for contraceptive devices.

III

Illegitimacy and Pre-Marital Sex

The view I have taken here, unfashionably, is that awareness of new barrier methods of contraception was an extremely important part of the explanation of the late nineteenth-century fertility decline. There seems to be no good ground for denying that these methods had *some* importance in this episode (and not just among higher social groups), and once this is conceded it would be perverse, I believe, not to grant that they had attractions which would have recommended them very widely. One of the most persuasive indications that the English fertility decline was very strongly stimulated by new barrier methods of contraception is the pattern of illegitimate fertility in the immediately preceding period—just one intriguing feature of a demographic topic particularly relevant to sexual morality which, though attended by difficulties of evidence, has produced both unexpected results and some radical controversy.

By 1861, before a decline is clearly detectable in the national fertility levels as a whole, English illegitimate fertility is already conspicuously reduced. Its fall thereafter was sharp and (with the proviso that regional rankings maintained themselves to a remarkable extent) universal. When the figures have been looked at carefully it seems that the beginnings of the decline lie in the 1850s; the illegitimacy levels are already dropping in almost a quarter of English counties in this decade.[40]

[40] Glass 1938; Laslett, Oosterveen, and Smith 1980: 17–18; Teitelbaum 1984: 151; Shorter, Knodel, and van der Walle 1971. See also Hooker 1897–8.

The phenomenon closely resembles the national fertility decline, but with a ten years' difference in its timing, and it is generally agreed that the same mechanisms must be at work in both, whatever they might be. It is even less plausible that new material needs, objective or subjective, were the trigger for this first phase of fertility decline: in so far as couples having intercourse when they were not married had motives for preventing conception these motives would only have been, at the most, indirectly economic. And the need to control fertility was surely pressing for these partners, even if their intercourse was often or even usually part of courtship. Any contraceptive technique was attractive if it was also congenial. The barrier methods, more than traditional methods, passed this test. We know of one working-class Londoner who regarded the extra-vaginal ejaculation he had been forced to practise with his girlfriend as a deprivation of pleasure: 'I cannot believe that you have been burdened by me for I was never allowed to enjoy you sufficiently for that'. Recent analysis of the fertility decline has, very sensibly, fed the illegitimacy data into computer models as one index of the spread of barrier techniques.[41]

This 'prediction' of the national fertility decline by the illegitimacy figures is a novelty, for changes in illegitimacy levels hitherto tend to be in step with changes in general fertility, as well as with changes in rate and age of marriage, and in pre-nuptial pregnancy (high illegitimacy going with high rates of marriage and pre-nuptial pregnancy, and with lower age of marriage). I have mentioned that there is convincing evidence for a drop in English marriage rates, followed about ten years later by a rise in age of marriage, at the beginning of the century—each episode lasting for about thirty years. Something also happens at this time to bastardy levels, though it is less clearcut and less extreme. Peter Laslett, who has looked at the question more closely than anyone else, wrote in 1977 of a 'generally downward tendency . . . during the years from the 1800s to 1831', with a 'dip . . . in the 1810s', but three years later did not detect more than 'a little slump between 1825 and 1835'. In this pre-registration period a general picture can only be assembled by combining figures from a suitable range of parish registers, and there are large local variations which make this an insecure process.[42]

[41] Barret-Ducrocq 1991: 128; Boyer and Williamson 1989.

[42] Laslett 1977: 114; Laslett, Oosterveen, and Smith 1980: 17, 96–8; Levine 1977: ch. 9; 'Statistics of Old and New Malton', *JSSL* 8 (1845), 66–8.

The downward movement in the bastardy figures in the early part of the nineteenth century is inconsiderable in one important sense: levels are definitely high and rising by the late 1830s, and by the beginning of the next decade they have gone up nationally in a really dramatic leap of between 50 and 100 per cent (depending on how low the earlier slump is judged to have taken them). Eighteenth-century illegitimacy rates had been on a steady upward trajectory, along with rising marriage rates and lower age of marriage, but whereas the last two indices do not quite recover to their highest eighteenth-century levels after their early nineteenth-century falls, the illegitimacy figures not only recover, but continue to rise through most of the 1850s.

In other words, the secular picture is very much of two hundred years of rising illegitimacy in England, starting in the middle of the seventeenth century and only disturbed once, slightly, in the early nineteenth. To put the matter into quantities, about one birth in a hundred was illegitimate in 1650 and about seven in a hundred in 1845 (a level which was reached again in 1960). The illegitimacy *rate* for 1845 (the number of illegitimate births in relation to the number of unmarried women of childbearing age, and generally a more instructive index) was about eighteen births to every thousand possible mothers.

It is as a fundamentally expansive tendency that illegitimacy in the first half of the nineteenth century matches the trend in pre-nuptial pregnancy.[43] Information about the latter, which perhaps brings us closer to the personal sexuality of men and women in the past than any other demographic measure, can be gained by the simple but resourceful operation of comparing dates of marriage to dates of baptism of first child. The technique requires that named individuals can be traced through the two ceremonies, and most studies have dealt with fairly small communities; there is also obviously a problem about postponed baptisms.

The history of pre-nuptial pregnancy is nevertheless a clear and striking one of high and ever higher levels. Eighteenth-century rates were conservatively around 30 per cent of all marriages. In villages and small towns in Cambridgeshire, Leicestershire, Hampshire, Kent, and Devon around 40 per cent of brides in the first half of the nineteenth century were pregnant; in some areas the rate pushed up

---

[43] Shorter, Knodel, and van der Walle 1971.

past the half-way point as the century advanced. The evidence is too scanty to speak of a downturn interrupting this upward movement, such as has already been illustrated for the marriage and illegitimacy statistics, but for what it is worth there were reductions in the early decades of the century in half the parishes in a sample of sixteen.[44]

There is evidence that fertility control had its effect on pre-nuptial conception in something of the way it operated on married and illegitimate conception; the retailing class in the expanding railway town of Ashford, Kent, seems to have reduced its levels of such events by 1860. Rather strikingly, however, it is known for at least two areas (Medmenham and Colyton) that pre-nuptial conceptions remained at a high level right through the 1870s, or at least a decade after national illegitimacy levels were falling under the impact of birth control.[45] This hints, but no more, at the intriguing possibility that, in the fertility decline, pre-nuptial conception lost its linkage with illegitimacy, rather as the latter moved independently of marital fertility.

And what, in fact, is the nature of nineteenth-century illegitimacy? How are we to understand its surprising relationship to other kinds of sexual behaviour, and its variations socially and in time? Until the 1860s there is evidently a close affinity between the behaviour which led to marriage and that which led to non-marital conceptions and births; they seem to be two aspects of the same thing, always varying together and in the same direction. Given the fact that between a third and a half of all brides were pregnant (at least in many parts of England) it seems right to think of the common ground as courtship, or relations between the sexes—readily including full intercourse—which were expected to lead to marriage, or at least of which marriage was understood to be a possible outcome.

It is also necessary to assume that courtship in this sense might be engaged in to a varying extent by different groups at different times, that any variation would include the amount of full intercourse taking place between courting couples, and that when there was a reduction of this courtship intercourse individuals did not then have an equivalent amount of intercourse with partners whom they never intended to marry. On this view, an illegitimate birth was usually the result of a disruption of marriage intentions, when a courtship involving intercourse and pregnancy issued in an unmarried mother rather than in a

---

[44] Hair 1966; 1970; Mills 1980: *passim*; Levine 1977: ch. 9; Pearce 1973; Robin 1986; Laslett, Oosterveen, and Smith 1980: 23; Reay 1990.

[45] Pearce 1973; Hair 1970; Robin 1986.

pregnant bride. In a period of social change such as the English nineteenth century it is not hard to think of mechanisms which could
have thwarted the expected outcome of a couple's courtship.

It will be seen that this model can explain any pattern of variation
that might appear in the marriage and illegitimacy figures. If both
figures are equally high or low the level of 'courtship intensity' can
be invoked. If they move in opposite directions the notion of 'marriage frustrated' can be tuned to an appropriate level.[46] A theory is
not necessarily a bad one if there is no set of facts it cannot fit, but
this does mean that it cannot be disproved. Actually, the courtship
theory of illegitimacy is not in this unfortunate condition. There is
some anecdotal evidence from London and from rural Kent that
working-class illegitimate babies were usually conceived in intercourse that had been accompanied by an expectation of marriage.[47]
And there is a third set of figures, those for pre-nuptial pregnancy,
which have to be in step with the illegitimacy levels, so that certain
combinations of the three would clearly make the courtship theory
untenable. If a community exhibited a high level of illegitimacy and a
high level of marriage, but little pre-nuptial pregnancy, it would be
hard to argue that the numbers of illegitimate births and marriages
reflected a high intensity of courtship. Difficult cases of this sort do
not seem to have turned up. And there is apparently a good chronological fit, as far as the evidence goes, between the national patterns
for all these indices, at least until the new conditions of the fertility
decline came into play.

There is important potential evidence about the nature of illegitimacy in the form of the specific ages of those who conceived illegitimate children and those who married (and in particular of those
brides who were pregnant). While the national illegitimacy figures
seem to have moved in step with changing age of marriage as the
courtship theory would require—with a drop in illegitimacy levels in
the early nineteenth century when married couples were a little
older—it would be a difficulty for the theory, as its supporters recognize,[48] if unmarried mothers were found to be consistently younger
or older than pregnant brides. They would start to look like a special
group, with atypical sexual behaviour.

Pregnant brides seem to have been as old, on average, as other

    [46] Laslett 1981; Levine 1977: ch. 9.
    [47] Barret-Ducrocq 1991: 86–7, 98, 177; Reay 1990.
    [48] Laslett, Oosterveen, and Smith 1980: 55–6.

brides; unmarried mothers did not differ greatly from the whole group and in some areas their ages may have converged in the nineteenth century. But the gap, if narrow, was consistently in one direction: unmarried mothers were younger than brides by perhaps something rather under a year on average, to which may presumably be added at least a few months for the date of first intercourse. The difference between the ages of the mothers of first children, legitimate and illegitimate, is over a year in one sample. And such aggregates and averages, although they emerge as roughly consistent with the courtship theory of illegitimacy, can conceal bigger gaps, suggesting that there were other aspects to illegitimacy which could become important in particular communities. The sample mentioned above contains the much-studied small Devon town of Colyton and here, after the middle of the nineteenth century at least, there is a substantial interval, of about two and a quarter years on average, between the age at which unmarried mothers baptized their children and the age at which women were first married.[49] So there is some indication that girls who had an illegitimate child often started having intercourse considerably younger than those whose first child was legitimate (even if, as was often the case, it was conceived outside marriage). This suggests that illegitimacy cannot always be thought of as the result of a disrupted courtship (though it might be argued that the younger the courting couple the more likely their plans were to fail, on some ground).

Age is only one of several respects in which unmarried and married mothers may be compared, with a view to testing the courtship theory of illegitimacy. It is possible to look for distinguishing characteristics of unmarried mothers as a group which more directly imply that they did not have intercourse with the intention or expectation that marriage would follow pregnancy. For example, what of mothers with several illegitimate children? The more of these there are in a community, the less important disrupted courtship would seem to be. And if unmarried mothers are found to be clustered in particular families, or particular neighbourhoods, their pregnancies also would seem that much less likely to have come about with marriage as a prospect or consequence. It does seem in fact that multiple illegitimacies not only contributed importantly to the rise and fall in the national figures, but could be high in a community with otherwise

[49] Hair 1970; Levine 1977: 134, 142; Laslett, Oosterveen, and Smith 1980: 107; Robin 1987.

low levels of bastardy: Colyton is such a community in the period 1850–80, and yet 30 per cent of its unmarried mothers had more than one illegitimate child. There is also definite evidence in Colyton that a woman's likelihood of having an illegitimate child was greater if her sister had one (whereas pre-nuptial pregnancy did not run in families), and that households with bastards clustered together in neighbourhoods. In other parishes a significant recurrence of particular family names in connection with bastardy has been detected. But it would seem that in a couple of Kent parishes the contribution made to the illegitimacy figures by a morally distinctive group within the community, if such a thing existed at all, was small.[50]

Finally, there are certain occupational and class differences between unmarried mothers and pregnant brides. But it would be unwise to think of these as evidence against the courtship theory. We know that illegitimacy is quite strongly associated with low social rank, for example, both in the country and in the town—so much so that pauper illegitimacy is as high in London as it is anywhere, although London has very low illegitimacy levels in general. But it is easy to see that 'frustrated marriage' might have been a particular risk for the most economically vulnerable groups in the population. A similar qualification must be entered concerning domestic servants, a group with a long-standing reputation for bearing bastards. About two-thirds of unmarried mothers applying to the London Foundling Hospital were servants, and the prostitute rescue organizations often reported that a high number of their clients had been servants, sometimes as many as three-quarters. But both these figures may just reflect the pressure there was on servants to be sexually respectable, so that the outcome of extra-marital intercourse or conception was more likely in their case to be dismissal or adoption of a child (and it may be significant that the orphanage was resorted to by superior servants in disproportionately large numbers). New findings in Scotland (admittedly a country with a pattern of illegitimacy very different to England's) show that urban domestic servants had low rates of illegitimacy, in strong contrast to their rural colleagues.[51]

Nineteenth-century illegitimacy is evidently a complicated phenomenon, with some aspects that are very poorly understood.

[50] Laslett, Oosterveen, and Smith 1980: 87–8, 113–20, 133–40, 234, 237; Robin 1986, 1987; Levine 1977: 143; Reay 1990. Cf. Gittins 1983, 1986.

[51] Robin 1987; Laslett, Oosterveen, and Smith 1980: 112–13, 133; Lumley 1862; Gillis 1983; 'The Greatest Social Evil', *Taits*, 24 (1857), 747–52; Hollingsworth 1981.

Perhaps the most intriguing is the powerful influence which local tradition seems to have had on bastardy levels. Regions varied considerably, one from another, and there was a strong tendency for these relative levels to persist across decades (and even through the fertility decline, when new differentials in marital fertility were tending to emerge). Of the eight counties with the highest rates in 1842, five were still in this group sixty years later: Cumberland, Norfolk, Shropshire, Nottinghamshire, and the North Riding. This is a fairly rural group of counties, and one tendency in the evidence does seem to be that illegitimacy is lower in urban areas. This can be detected locally: often even a market town will have lower rates than its rural surroundings, and in London—the outstanding example of low urban illegitimacy, with the lowest levels in the nation around mid-century—all areas, rich and poor alike, obey the law of low metropolitan bastardy.

But the relation between the town and illegitimacy is by no means clearcut, and has been denied by some commentators. There are paradoxes about the towns, which cannot even be resolved when their economic character as well as their scale and density is taken into account. Bristol, Birmingham, Liverpool, Portsmouth, and Sheffield have low rates; Nottingham, Preston, and Bolton rates more than twice as high—though none of them as high as Norwich. Both Norwich and Nottingham are within the counties with continuously high illegitimacy mentioned above, and they seem to indicate the curious power of regionalism, and its tendency to persist in time, in the pattern of nineteenth-century illegitimacy. Nottingham had less illegitimacy than its hinterland, but a higher level than most comparable cities because it was in a high area—and why illegitimacy figures were high there we do not know. Of the fifteen highest districts in 1860 more than half are from Norfolk or Nottinghamshire. It is tempting to regard London's very striking figures as an extreme instance of the impact of urbanization on illegitimacy, but the pattern elsewhere suggests that other causes, to do with regional traditions, may be at work.[52]

Illegitimacy is, however, a fairly small component of English fertility as a whole in the nineteenth century—on average around 7 per cent of all births at the mid-century. It is also, whatever the limitations of the courtship theory, obviously bound up with pre-marital

[52] Laslett, Oosterveen, and Smith 1980: 29–32, 62–5; Teitelbaum 1984: 144–9; Hollingsworth 1981; Annual Report of the Registrar General 1879; Lumley 1862.

behaviour to a great extent. In other words, the very much more important phenomenon, and not just numerically, is pre-nuptial conception. Moreover, its scale is a recent discovery, and constitutes a very novel element in the study of nineteenth-century sexuality: many secrets have been said to lie on the dark side of this topic, but the idea that two-fifths of all nineteenth-century brides were pregnant has not been among them.

It must be stressed, in fact, that this figure is not certain. It derives entirely from communities that are no larger than market towns; we have absolutely no idea what the pre-nuptial pregnancy levels were in London, Leeds, or even Lincoln, and they might be intriguingly different (and there is some impressionistic evidence that urban working-class couples managed to refrain from sex more than their rural counterparts). For what it is worth, however, there is no sign that semi-industrial Shepshed experienced a less steep rise in bridal pregnancy rates than more rural communities.[53]

Only a little can be said about the social characteristics of the pregnant brides other than that the ones we know of are, perforce, more or less rural. Not surprisingly, brides from higher social groups were less likely to be pregnant. This may be the case with shopkeeping families in Ashford, but only applies to the really élite 8 per cent of the Colyton population: below this élite the habit of pre-nuptial conception is common and general, so that farmers' daughters (like their peers in Kent) are as much involved as those of labourers (in contrast to the pattern for illegitimacy, as mentioned above).[54] On balance, to judge by the restricted evidence, pre-nuptial pregnancy and therefore pre-nuptial intercourse were indeed widespread phenomena, vertically and horizontally, in nineteenth-century England.

IV

Illicit Unions

> The Strand was once her favourite beat,
> But now she thinks it is not meet
> She should display her beauty there,
> So to Regent Street she must repair.
> Now in her silks she looks so nice,
> And if you wish to know her price,

[53] Burnett 1982: 256; Levine 1977: 139.   [54] Pearce 1973; Robin 1986; Reay 1990.

She'll tell you, if you do her greet,
'A guinea, sir,' in Regent Street.[55]

Reflected in all these data on English nineteenth-century fertility and nuptiality, but in a tantalizingly cryptic way, must be the formalized non-marital intercourse represented by prostitution, courtesanship, and concubinage. These phenomena—and especially street prostitution—are among the most notorious topics in the sexual culture of the period, and their real dimensions and character are very obscure. Demography, indeed, says nothing definite on this question. It is possible that the tendency towards lower urban illegitimacy reflects the fact of prostitution, which was certainly commoner in towns than in the country. On the other hand, what seems to be a kind of rural prostitution is detectable in the multiple illegitimacies recorded for some women in Colyton. And the high illegitimacy rates of urban East Anglia have an anecdotal link with high prostitute numbers in these communities.[56] The mechanisms of infertility among prostitutes in the period, and how they may have affected various types of prostitute, need to be much better understood than they are ever likely to be before the fertility figures can yield anything.

A potentially worthwhile exercise would be to compare illegitimacy rates with rates of conviction for prostitution in a range of towns, as given by the judicial statistics. The latter vary by a factor of more than five if, say, ports are compared with the woollen towns, and it would be significant if the illegitimacy figures varied in step.[57] There have been isolated attempts by modern researchers to draw conclusions from the legal record of prostitutes in the courts in particular localities. This is an effort to perform more thoroughly and objectively an exercise, or type of exercise, which was also attempted quite frequently by nineteenth-century investigators. Indeed, the historian is thrown back almost entirely on contemporary description and analysis where prostitution is concerned.

Writing about prostitution, and in particular writing that is expressly about prostitution, is not as abundant in the nineteenth century as might be supposed. It has been pointed out that many more books on the subject were published between 1838 and 1859 than between 1939 and 1959,[58] but the former was an altogether

[55] 'The Cockchafer', *Rambler's Flash Songster* ?1865: 13–15.
[56] Razzell and Wainwright 1973: 56–7.   [57] *JSSL* 30 (1867), 391.
[58] H. R. E. Ware 1969: 10.

exceptional period. Prostitution does not seem to have been a topic of constantly burning interest; writers gave it their attention in spasms, when it became topical for some reason or other, and much of the time they were not sufficiently curious about it, even when they did put pen to paper, to do more than rehash the claims of years and even decades earlier. Only a handful of commentators, at least until the agitation over the Contagious Diseases Acts of the 1870s, can be said to have specialized in the subject of prostitution.

If the weight of the material is not a problem its diversity certainly is. There are huge discrepancies in the contemporary literature over the quantity and quality of prostitution. Sometimes apparently conflicting evidence can be harmonized. In estimating numbers, for example, it is obviously important to know what was the basis for a particular contemporary calculation: there was a span here from local police figures all the way up to total illegitimacy rates (any woman who had an illegitimate child, in this instance, being counted as a prostitute). And in seeking to judge the character of prostitution—the demeanour, attitudes, and habits of prostitutes—it is important to remember that generalizations are fallible even when quite modest in their scope. Sheer individual variety among prostitutes must not be underestimated, though it is rarely allowed for in the contemporary accounts. Unusually, a French visitor of the early 1860s describes how the prostitutes outside a single pub near the Strand differed in manner, some being supplicating, others audacious.[59] One often feels that commentators who generalized about the blatancy, or refinement, or tawdriness, or demureness of prostitutes were greatly simplifying the reality.

Not only in London, but wherever prostitution is reported at all richly, the picture is complex. It is hard to form a clear idea of the character of prostitution in Liverpool, for instance, from the surviving accounts. Frederick Olmsted, an American agriculturalist who toured England in 1850, was struck by the demeanour of the women on the quay as he landed:

I was surprised at the quietness and decency of these 'sailors' wives', as they called themselves; they were plainly and generally neatly dressed, and talked quietly and in kind tones to each other, and I heard no profanity and ribaldry at all . . . they stood, companioned together with each other, but friendless, some with not even hats to protect them from the rain, others, with their

[59] Rémusat 1862: 25.

gowns drawn up over their head and others, two together, under a scanty shawl . . . We could not but think the cheerful words with which the sailors recognized and greeted them . . . were as much dictated by pity and sympathy as by any worse impulses.[60]

This is difficult to reconcile with various accounts (such as that filed by the *Morning Chronicle*'s 'Labour and the Poor' correspondent) in which the prostitutes of dockland Liverpool are depicted as extremely blatant or predatory or both. It is outnumbered by the latter, but its specificity carries some conviction and it is not without support. As early as 1815 another disembarking American had felt 'welcomed . . . most cheerfully' by the prostitutes and yet another, a year later, noted that they were at least not insolent; one native commentator at the mid-century believed that prostitution in Liverpool was discreet by comparison with the 1780s and 1790s.[61]

Among the writers on the blatancy side there was disagreement too. What for the local journalist Hugh Shimmin was 'unbridled lewdness' in the demeanour of the prostitutes produced in Jean Larocque, a French visitor, a rapturous impression of 'les plus ravissantes créatures du monde', of images by Praxiteles or Phidias equipped with flashing blue eyes, clouds of blonde hair, and 'sourires païens derobés à Venus'.[62] Differences of taste and moral standards are obviously strongly at work, but the two accounts are separated by almost twenty-five years, and there may also be an objective difference, a change over time, registered here. By 1877 the prostitutes of Liverpool, though evidently varying in many respects, are described as being uniformly elegant in dress.[63]

These Liverpool descriptions are also at odds, or at least discordant, on the important matter of the professionalism of the women they depict. Olmsted, indeed, is almost at odds with himself over this, since he raises the possibility in the expression 'sailors' wives' that these girls are in a relationship of partial concubinage with their clients, though he represents them as soliciting casually.[64] For Shimmin any woman who consorts with a sailor publicly seems to be a 'prostitute', while Larocque is convinced that the enchanting

---

[60] Olmsted 1967: 31–2.

[61] Ballard 1913; Razzell and Wainwright 1973: 272–4; J. E. White 1816: i. 19; Brooke 1853: 300.

[62] Shimmin 1856: 4; Larocque 1882: 321–6. [63] *Liverpool Critic*, 27 Jan. 1877, p. 59.

[64] Dickens, in his generally valuable account of the Liverpool night-resorts awaiting the average sailor, in Chapter 5 of *The Uncommercial Traveller* (1861), writes of 'a man crimp and a woman crimp, who always introduced themselves as united in holy matrimony'.

women he meets are such because they are only prostitutes temporarily, for a few years of their youth, while they collect money for their trousseaus, and that in this period they remain 'femmes, êtres humains, membres de la société et de la famille, decentes sauf un point'.

Evidently, the nature of the career of a girl perceived to be a 'prostitute', and its outcome, is the topic on which commentators are most likely to be in the dark, and where mere speculation can most readily abound. The possibility must be borne in mind that various quasi-prostitutional careers were followed by nineteenth-century girls, and even that certain kinds of uninhibited public liaison between the sexes did not denote sexual intercourse at all. There may seem to be an element of impertinence in suggesting that writers of the day, trained in all the relevant cultural cues, could be detected as mistaken in their sense of who were prostitutes by a twentieth-century reader, but the confidence with which the label 'prostitute' is used by some observers does sound excessive, especially when it is not echoed by other observers of the same social scene, and in the light of the many reports of the increasing decorousness and refinement noticeable among prostitutes. Occasionally one writer will have fun at the expense of another for allegedly failing to realize that a particular group of women are prostitutes.

These are preliminary remarks, to suggest that the inconsistencies in the contemporary literature of prostitution, though surely due in part to fantasy and prejudice, may also reflect the complexities of the subject, which are multiplied if adjacent phenomena such as concubinage and merely 'fast' living are brought into view. Discrepancies over numbers, it has been suggested, often flow from differences over sources and definitions (though a writer's choice in these matters may well be the result of his or her preconceptions). Roughly speaking, there are two widely separated levels at which prostitute numbers are pitched, differing by a factor of ten. The low level is fairly consistently associated with police and court data, plus in a few instances counts of brothels and their occupants performed by lay observers. The high level is based on a variety of other evidence or, very often, on no cited evidence at all.

This generalization must immediately be qualified, however, for the first published calculation of prostitute numbers (which may have been circulating informally for some while)[65] was made in respect of

[65] Wendeborn 1791: i. 288.

London by the magistrate and penal theorist Patrick Colquhuon in the last years of the eighteenth century, in his *Treatise on the Police of the Metropolis*. It not only excited great interest at the time for its novelty but was the ancestor of most later high estimates. Colquhuon claimed that there were 50,000 prostitutes in London. The figure carried the authority of a magistrate, but Colquhuon did not in fact purport to be using official evidence, and is frank in calling his totals 'estimated' and 'conjectured'. He also employed a broad definition of prostitution which included courtesans, part-time prostitutes, and working-class concubines. These categories, which by their nature could never have been calculated from legal sources anyway, make up over half of Colquhuon's total: common prostitutes, in the sense of working-class girls living wholly by prostitution, are put at 20,000.[66] This is still much higher than the kind of low figure offered for London by various writers in the next century, but it narrows the gap significantly: writers who favoured a high figure tended to ignore the fact that Colquhuon's 50,000 included large numbers of women who could only be called prostitutes in a very imprecise sense.

Later editions of the *Treatise* continue to offer the 50,000 figure but, whether under Colquhuon's influence or not (and I cannot trace another source), new high estimates are current of 70,000 in 1802 and of 80,000 in 1817. The latter installs itself as the orthodox bullish London estimate for many decades thereafter, being especially cited in the 1830s, when it seems also to have been receiving the private endorsement of the secretary of one of London's major prostitute rescue societies, James Beard Talbot. Even higher estimates, almost certainly sheer moralistic fantasies, are not wanting; in the writings of chauvinistic French observers in the 1860s they range up to a grotesque 220,000.[67] Many intermediate figures between these and the main body of low estimates could be cited (guesses in the region of Colquhuon's original figure are still being offered in the late 1850s and early 1860s), but by far the most important rival calculation of the number of prostitutes in London is the police total, which fluctuates between 5,500 and 9,500—thus being bizarrely close to an exact tenth of the most favoured high estimate.

What is one to make of the contemporary calculations of prostitution levels in London, and elsewhere? An important initial point is

[66] Colquhuon 1800: 340.
[67] Goede 1807: i. 118; *De Londres* 1817: 21; M. Ryan 1839: 168; PP 1839, xix. 16; Larcher 1860: 236; Mirecourt 1862: 90.

that the extreme ambiguity of the London figures is not repeated in relation to other centres. While the more anxious commentators were certainly prepared to deliver high national estimates, of up to half a million, for all the prostitutes in England[68] (in contrast to police totals of around 30,000), it is only very rarely, if at all, that calculations grossly in excess of the local police figures are proposed for large cities such as Liverpool and Manchester. Talbot, from afar, gave guesses for such centres very much closer to the official figures than he proposed for London, while workers on the ground, like William Bevan and F. W. Lowndes in Liverpool and William Logan in Leeds, Manchester, and elsewhere, either accept the police data or come out at around twice the official levels after doing personal research (in Logan's case, pioneering research) into local prostitution.[69] This says much for the psychological impact of London, and for the power of this uniquely large and unknowable city to stimulate, and draw towards itself, fearful imaginings about its moral life.

A second fundamental observation is that on scarcely anyone's showing do prostitution levels rise in nineteenth-century England; in real terms, indeed, there is almost unanimity that they fall. Even if the numbers of prostitutes in London had risen in the 1860s to the absurdly alleged 220,000 (over 7 per cent of the whole population of the city) this would be about the same proportion as Colquhuon's 50,000 in the 1790s, and the fashionable 80,000 in 1810. The police figures in London and every other city remain very flat, which in this country of rapid urban expansion means, for what it is worth, a decline in actual proportions.

When William Logan returned to the subject of prostitution in *The Great Social Evil* (1871) almost thirty years after his *Exposure . . . of Female Prostitution* (1843) he put a brave face on the fact that his totals had not changed (they are 'equally applicable to the vile system at the present day'), but this cannot disguise the point that if, say, his earlier estimate for Leeds of 700 prostitutes holds into the 1870s the ratio of prostitutes to the population had fallen by over half, from a little under 0.6 per cent to a little under 0.3 per cent. Lowndes, claiming an increase in Liverpool prostitution since the mid-century, prudently found that 'whether this be in proportion to the increase of population . . . we need not here stop to inquire'. Occasionally there

[68] e.g. 'Le Plus Bas' 1859: 18; 1865: 34; *London Review*, 6 (1863), 402; *British Controversialist*, NS 1 (1859), 107.

[69] Talbot 1844: 22; Bevan 1843: 10–11; Lowndes 1876: 5–9; 1886: 7; Logan 1843: 9–11.

may occur a temporary rise in the police figures (in Liverpool in the early 1840s and mid-1860s, for example), but over a long enough period absolute declines are almost universal—being clearly apparent in London and Manchester, for instance, over the 1840s and 1850s, and more or less marked in major towns not covered by the Contagious Diseases Acts in the 1860s and 1870s.[70]

Police figures on prostitution are more instructive than might be thought. Since they reflect police wisdom rather than the judgements of a court, they are to some extent exempt from the arbitrariness that makes most crime statistics uninformative. And they are not just a matter of heads counted by a bobby on his beat. Most of the local police forces who provided figures seem to have taken pains to calculate the various kinds of clandestine prostitution in their areas, and in London at least this included 'well-dressed living in private lodgings'. Lay observers with a similar practical experience did not disagree wildly with their totals, as we have seen. But there is an element of spurious tidiness in these police tables with their aggregated categories of 'well-dressed' or 'low', and brothel-dwelling or street-walking prostitutes. One brothel at least made its staff restrict their street soliciting to daytime, to avoid clashes with a militant local police force.[71] A notorious court case of 1854, in which a French prostitute, Margaret Reginbol, sued a brothel-keeper for property and wages allegedly detained by him, confirms that the distinction between brothel-dwelling and street-walking is artificial: Margaret moved freely from one mode of operation to the other.[72] When she walked the pavements of the Haymarket, the hub of London's prostitution, she was practically on the doorstep of her brothel-base in Waterloo Place, and would presumably have been counted by the police, perhaps twice, as a prostitute in the neighbourhood.

William Acton claimed that the figures for street-walkers in this whole area in 1857 should be more than doubled, to allow for prostitutes who came in from poorer areas. Did these women get enumerated in Southwark, or Bethnal Green, or wherever else they took their clients? The women who made the short trip from the Covent Garden area to the more westerly streets, as recorded by Bracebridge Hemyng for Mayhew, must have stood a very good chance of being officially counted in the former district, for they were simply

---

[70] Logan 1871: 76; Lowndes 1876: 5, 1886: 51; Bevan 1843: 10–11; Aspland 1868: 6–7; Knox 1857: 218–20; W. Acton 1968: 33, 38; Nevins 1876.
[71] PP 1817, vii. 457.   [72] *The Times*, 21 June 1854, p. 11.

migrating from a venerable brothel zone as the main centre of
London operations shifted. But one commentator stressed the new
phenomenon of apparently decorous outlying streets, 'presenting
nothing offensive by day or by night', full of brothels where clients
were brought after they had been picked up on the West End streets,
and Charles Booth found much the same in respectable Mile End. It
seems likely that some of these establishments could have been
unobtrusive to the point of escaping detection altogether. There is
also evidence that women simply took their clients to rented rooms
in the 'night houses' or where proprietors were indifferent as to
whether their guests were bona fide couples; indeed, in view of the
importance of cheap hotels in today's London prostitution, it would
be surprising if this were not quite a regular nineteenth-century
practice.[73]

This is all to suggest the limitations of the official figures as a guide
to the real extent of nineteenth-century prostitution in London and
elsewhere. The net result is to indicate that the police totals err on
the low side; they do not claim to comprise more than the prostitutes
known to the constabularies. But as a calculation of the numbers of
women who made a poor or modest living from sex with casually
acquired clients they are probably not far from the truth, and surely
nearer the truth than figures such as 80,000 for London's prostitutes.
It is true that the more thoughtful advocates of these high estimates,
from Colquhuon, to Acton, and John Chapman, argued that the numbers of detectable prostitutes must be supplemented with various
categories of quasi-prostitution, and it is surely the more part-time,
refined, and not directly mercenary forms of prostitution that are
most likely to have escaped enumeration by the police. Many of
these activities fell quite outside the scope of police interest.
According to Hemyng, 'the metropolitan police do not concern themselves with the higher classes of prostitutes'.[74]

However, the uniquely high estimates so often attached to prostitution in London, as opposed to other centres, cannot gain more than
rather slight support from this line of argument. There is no reason to
think that part-time prostitution or temporary concubinage among
working-class girls, for example, would be more the rule in London
than elsewhere. Refined prostitution, or courtesanship, was probably

---

[73] W. Acton 1857b: 17; Mayhew 1861–2: iv. 75–6, 249; J. E. Davis 1854: 226, 229;
C. Booth 1887; 'Le Plus Bas' 1865: 27; Fiske 1869: 175; *My Secret Life* 1966: 1337, 2113.

[74] Mayhew 1861–2: iv. 215.

more common in London, but not to an extent which would have had a big effect on numbers. There was a perception at the time that most prostitutes in provincial centres such as Leeds were 'of a very low class', but it is certain that some of these cities had their share of elegant prostitution. The audiences at Midnight Movement meetings in Liverpool were perhaps not as disconcertingly decorous as those in London, but many crinolines could be notices, and it was claimed that many of the city's prostitutes rented rooms in brothels for business purposes while passing as respectable women in their own lodgings.[75]

Manchester was recognized as superior in the tone of its prostitution (though at the expense of the tone of that in neighbouring Rochdale, it seems), and in 1865 a successful Manchester brothel-keeper, Polly Evans, published a memoir which gives glimpses of a luxurious club-like establishment patronized by some very wealthy swells. The reality in this brothel may have been rather nearer to conveyor-belt bought sex than the memoir admits (and it is apparent from the text that the police were well acquainted with its operations), but Polly at least has fairly non-prostitutional relationships with various lovers which seem to be authentic in spirit, since she was a known long-term companion of Manchester MP and mayor Sir John Potter.[76]

Discounting the morbid exaggerations provoked by London, what is the scale of quasi-prostitutional activity in England either ignored or not detected by official inquiry? There is a fairly impressive weight of allusion to working-class girls (nursemaids, seamstresses, and shopgirls in London, servants looking after London townhouses in the summer, girls of all types in the East Anglian centres of Norwich and Ipswich, wives in Preston, and so forth) supplementing their earnings by occasional prostitution, but estimates of numbers vary a lot, not surprisingly, with this element being judged to contribute perhaps about 6 per cent of the prostitution of Leeds, but well over half that of Norwich.[77] When a particular group is said by one observer to consist of prostitutes, but this is not detected by another, one may suspect that the explanation is occasional prostitution.

---

[75] Wade 1859: 385; *Magdalen's Friend*, 2 (1862), 22; Lowndes 1886: 12–15.

[76] Faucher 1844: 41; Logan 1843: 10; Evans 1865 *passim*; Marx and Engels 1930: ii/3. 181–2.

[77] Mayhew 1980: i. 234; Hale 1812: 12–13; Talbot 1844: 12; Davey 1983: 33; Clyde 1850: 57; Beggs 1849: 109; Mayhew 1861–2: iv. 217, 234; Logan 1843: 23; Remo 1888: 217.

Shepherd Taylor was a medical student in London in the early 1860s and his diary for these years has many references to his flirting with casually encountered working-class girls, among them a milliner near Tottenham Court Road, but none of this seems to lead to intercourse, on whatever footing. John Blackmore, the celebrated magdalenist, would have identified the milliner as a prostitute, to judge from his description of the 'mostly young and beautiful' girls on Tottenham Court Road that he saw being picked up by young men and taken off to dance-halls.[78]

Blackmore may in fact have misjudged these girls altogether, and mistaken uninhibited manners between the sexes in the working class for prostitutional behaviour: such blurrings of the outward distinction between prostitutes and others will be discussed shortly. But even if he is right the transaction between the girl and her client here is evidently not raw prostitution: they start, at least, by going off to a dance-hall. It is quite common for 'prostitutes' to be noticed, with partners, at places of public entertainment, such as the music saloons of pubs. Even if these girls met their companions casually at these sites it is surely significant that they danced and drank with them. Such associations could lead, one imagines, to sex that was not strictly prostitutional at all, but rather what Hemyng calls 'the illicit intercourse of the not yet completely depraved portion . . . who only prostitute themselves occasionally to men they are well acquainted with, for whom they may have some sort of a partiality—women who do not lower themselves . . . for money, but for their own gratification': in other words, affectionate casual sex.[79]

In the case of sailors' prostitutes particularly, it seems, the women seen in pubs and elsewhere might be enjoying affectionate, orderly, and fairly durable relationships with their companions: 'an illegitimate sort of faithfulness', in one observer's words. If Hemyng's reported conversation with a London dockland prostitute is anything to go by, the 'sailors' wives' of Liverpool may have deserved their label, and acted as the concubines of a dozen or so sailors who each lived with them for a month at a time and regarded themselves as their husbands. Even the promiscuous prostitution of these areas may have had a less automatic character than elsewhere: Hemyng, again, thought that the prostitutes in a pub dancing-room 'appeared too business-like' to have 'come there for pleasure exactly', but 'did

[78] S. T. Taylor 1927: 82; Blackmore 1854: i. 4.   [79] Mayhew 1861–2: iv. 249–50.

seem as if they would like, and intended, to unite the two, business and pleasure'. For another commentator these women were 'business-like' precisely in the sense that their behaviour was rather wifely; they picked up their clients in such a 'matter-of-fact' and commanding way that the 'suddenly affectionate couples' looked like 'husbands and wives walking out of church'. Unlike elsewhere, these East End prostitutes could be seen with knitting in their hands, or carrying their babies, even as they solicited on the streets.[80]

How commonly did prostitutes marry clients, or any man? Here the uncertainty affecting this whole field is compounded by the polemical guesswork of two rival schools of thought on the issue: of the magdalenists, who saw the trajectory of the prostitute's career as steeply descending into social dereliction and chronic illness or death, and of William Acton and his disciples, who agreed that her career could be short, but claimed that it generally terminated in marriage and respectability. The two views each have their fairly evident emotional and psychological roots, but if one had to adjudicate between them on the strength of what empirical foundation, in addition, they possess one might favour Acton's account (always bearing in mind that both could have some truth to them).

While there is a distinct element of panic in Acton's picture of middle-class wifedom being secretly contaminated by a large and enlarging fraction of ex-prostitutes, and a sense in which his is just a more sophisticated version of older scare stories about predatory harlots bamboozling respectable men into marriage,[81] it is plausible that many prostitutes should have sooner or later sought to settle down as respectable wives (while the sequence of events envisaged by the magdalenists when they saw a drunken or degraded prostitute is not the only plausible one: prostitution may be the consequence, not the cause, of alcoholism or extreme dereliction).

Such an outcome seems most probable in the instance of working-class or lower-middle-class prostitutes marrying at their own social level, and when this is described, whether in a spirit of man-about-town knowledgeability or as the boasted achievement of a social missionary, it deserves taking seriously. In such cases, however, respectability may have been difficult to maintain or never even have been attempted, since among low London prostitutes quite a high

[80] *My Secret Life* 1966: 1241–3; H. Jones 1875: 219; Mayhew 1861–2: iv. 229–30; R. Rowe 1880: 13; E. W. Thomas 1879: 36–7. See also PP 1866, xvi. 44.
[81] e.g. *London Guide* 1818: 135–7.

proportion seem to have been married.[82] At the opposite extreme of
the English social hierarchy, among the gentry, marriage to a prostitute was certainly a great rarity (as will be mentioned in the next
chapter), and its prevalence among the middle classes is an unknown
quantity. It is natural to think that there would have been great
obstacles of attitude at this level, but Acton's account has the merit
that it involves a claim about a recent and continuing shift in middle-
class ideas on these matters: 'The ball is rolling, the Rubicon has
been crossed by many who have not drowned in the attempt, nor
found a state of things on the other side more distasteful than compulsory celibacy'.[83] We shall never know if middle-class men were
marrying ex-prostitutes in increasing numbers from the 1850s, but if
they were it was surely with their eyes open, for the most part, and
thus in a climate of increasingly lenient attitudes to a woman's sexual
history.

Acton also thinks his rolling ball of attitudes has contributed to a
quite separate development in middle-class sexual behaviour, the
growth of concubinage (because this career is regarded as distinct
from the career of prostitution it really has no place in Acton's famous
1857 study, which is supposed to be addressing itself to the spread of
venereal disease—and Acton admits that concubines are not agents
of infection—but he is too intrigued by all tokens of hidden illicit sexuality in his society to refrain from discussing concubinage). Such
concubinage is an especially significant possibility, because within it
would presumably be included the majority of whatever practical
attempts were made to implement free-love doctrines, such as
George Drysdale started to advocate in the 1850s. (There was also a
great deal of comment in the period on concubinage among the
working class, but this is interesting as a possible element in the code
of particular groups, and I therefore discuss it in the next chapter.)

Unfortunately it is impossible to assess the phenomenon, other
than to say that the familiar claims about the upper and upper middle
classes keeping mistresses, though not dying out, start to be supplemented after the mid-century by allusions to clandestine households
involving unmarried couples, from the *petit bourgeois* upwards.
Acton writes of the apparently unattached men, in various walks, for
whom the 'real bower of rest is in some unpretending retreat, perhaps a suburban cottage, or perhaps a London lodging', where there

[82] Hanger 1801: i. 186; Vanderkiste 1852: 288; Merrick 1891: 32, 43.
[83] W. Acton 1857b: 65.

is a 'little educated' but superficially refined girl. The vignette acquires lineaments of greater domesticity, and greater companionship, in Taine's remarks on how an English bachelor, once you have got to know him well, may take you home to 'a young person busy with her household, modest and well-behaved'.[84]

These do sound like accounts of concubinage arrangements in the strong sense: of relationships centred on a joint home which are understood to replace and therefore exclude marriage elsewhere. So analogous to marriage had these become by the 1880s that it was apparently feasible to imagine a couple who had agreed to live together deciding 'at the last moment' to marry instead. But it is often not possible to tell if a particular partnership described in the literature is on this footing, or a looser one. Certainly there could be very domestic, companionable and sustained partnerships which differed from full concubinage mainly in the fact that eventual marriage elsewhere was accepted for the man (and probably also in the exclusion of parenthood from the household plans). Bracebridge Hemyng says it is surprisingly common to find that a gentleman bachelor who 'exhibits an invincible distaste to marriage' is privately 'already to all intents and purposes united to one who possesses charms, talent, and accomplishments', but he also envisages these qualities exerting an influence only 'as long as . . .[they] continue to exist'.[85]

It is relationships of this sort which seem to be in the minds of the various contributors to the famous 'Belgravian Lament' correspondence in *The Times* of 1861 who describe the refined domestic establishments which are allegedly proving too attractive an alternative to marriage. Such liaisons have a long history in the century, to judge from the advice of the early sexologist Henry Kitchener: 'an election must be made; and the parties who form the connexion must feel such an attachment to each other as shall prevent any desire of change' (this 'delicacy of friendship' is none the less regarded as a kind of rehearsal for marriage on the part of the man).[86]

In such non-matrimonial concubinage (as opposed to paramatrimonial concubinage) the woman's career has important affinities with prostitution or courtesanship; indeed there seems to have been in practice a constant overlap with these more mercenary

[84] 'How to get Married', *Belgravia*, 6 (1868), 531–7; Tristan 1980: 197; *British Controversialist*, NS 1 (1859), 44; Faucher 1845: i. 77; Acton 1857: 66; Taine 1957: 98.
[85] *The Ethics of Love* 1881: 23; Mayhew 1861–2: iv. 215–16.
[86] *The Times*, 28 June 1861, p. 11; 12 June 1861, p. 12; Kitchener 1812: ii. 2, 13.

and casual kinds of liaison. Francis Newman believed that many of the 'vast diversity' of self-reliant prostitutes—women living in their own lodgings and being discreetly visited by a small number of clients—became an individual man's exclusive mistress from time to time,[87] and this may have been in some sense the goal of more refined prostitutes, to judge by the emphasis which is put on such phases of the heroines' lives in the intriguing 'Anonyma' series of novels of the mid-1860s.

For all their feeling of verisimilitude, however, these novels are fictions, or at least factions, and the attention given to episodes of affectionate domesticity in a villa in Brompton or St John's Wood (while intervening periods of promiscuous prostitution are skated over) is in keeping with their general refusal to be moralistic or prurient about courtesanship. The publisher of the Anonyma series, George Vickers, brought out the *Memoirs* of Manchester's Polly Evans, and a certain romantizing of her life is apparent in this volume also. But there is presumably some general foundation in fact for Polly's seven years long liaison with the aristocrat 'Percy Graham', which is depicted as exclusive of all other relationships except his marriage ('unluckily, being a married man, I have certain duties to perform, and a position in society to maintain'); once it is over Polly returns to her earlier pattern of activity: 'I resumed the mode of life I had been leading previous to his acquaintance, and got on better than ever, for all my old friends who had held aloof while he remained with me, now returned to me, and courted, flattered, and petted me more than ever.' Perhaps more accurate as autobiography is the much earlier account of his life by the transported thief James Hardy Vaux. Twice, it seems, Vaux set up house and dwelt affectionately and connubially with prostitutes who were keen to give up the life: once with a high-class St James's girl, and once with a girl of respectable working-class origins and 'innate modesty', whom he eventually married.[88]

Polly Evans depicts herself as 'courted' by her clients when she resumed prostitution, but one may doubt if even the high grades of prostitute had much autonomy. Towards the end of the century there are signs that a new category of sexually transgressive woman was emerging, cultured women who lived on their own but took lovers when moved by a genuine and reciprocated liking: one French

[87] Newman 1889.   [88] Evans 1865: 116, 151; Vaux 1819: i. 71–81, ii. 26–31.

observer believed them to be a distinctive element in London's *demi-monde*, while Grant Allen claimed that 'Free Temporary Unions' were a 'growing actuality' in 1890. There seems also to have been emerging a commercially motivated class of transgressive women, in all other respects utterly unlike traditional prostitutes, whom they despised—women living undetected in households with the 'strictest views', whose families supposed them to be perfectly respectable.[89] But in earlier decades, with the proviso that the stars like 'Skittles' (Catherine Waters) could reserve themselves for the wealthiest clients, the limited personal autonomy of the refined prostitute is probably well indicated by an anecdote in the letters of an American visitor right at the start of the century. He recounts how a friend, to demonstrate 'how far a little genteel impudence would carry him', knocks at the doors of a series of respectable houses in a street north of Oxford Street, asking for a 'Miss Grey'. He strikes lucky at the third house and, having been shown up as a 'particular friend' of the lodger, convinces her that he is one of her many clients whom she has forgotten—whereupon this young girl, whose 'conversation is so sensible, that it . . . dignifies immodesty' apologizes for not having told him of her change of address and takes him on as one of her lovers.[90]

The numerical extent of this superior prostitution-cum-courtesan-ship should be a more definite quantity than that of the varieties of quasi-prostitution discussed earlier, though the best estimates are speculative. This is learnt painfully by Samuel Butler's Ernest Pontifex, in chapter 60 of *The Way of All Flesh*. Once he has made the surprising discovery that his apparently respectable co-tenant in an East End lodging-house, Miss Snow, is actually a prostitute who receives visits from gentlemen, Ernest comes to the reasonable con-clusion that the outwardly indistinguishable Miss Maitland is a pros-titute too. She turns out to be truly respectable, and is shocked by his advances. Even worldly-wise inquirers must have been unsure of their ground: 'who would dare to question gentlemens' business, who call ostensibly and frequently to spend an hour with cousin Miss A., or aunt Mrs M., whose greatest pleasure consists in receiving friendly visits from attached relatives?'[91] However Colquhuon and later police estimates (for the police did have opinions on the phe-nomenon) are more in agreement here than usual: Colquhuon

---

[89] Remo 1888: 44–5; G. Allen 1890; Nevill and Jerningham 1908: 134–5.
[90] Austin 1804: 57–9, 123–8. [91] 'Le Plus Bas' 1865: 28.

guessed 2,000 as the number of well-educated prostitutes in London at the turn of the century, and some police opinion in the late 1860s apparently put the figure at 7,000.[92] This would imply a more or less constant proportion of superior prostitutes in the city's population, in contrast to a shrinking proportion of women engaged in ordinary street prostitution.

This harmonizes with the broad tenor of the evidence about the demeanour of those prostitutes who did remain visible on the streets, which is to the effect that the outward face of this prostitution became much more refined as the century advanced. If this was the truth on the street it seems plausible to suppose that much prostitution was taking the next step towards gentility, and leaving the street altogether. But the evidence about this is not without complications, and needs to be reviewed. And the whole question of changes in the demeanour of prostitution is important quite apart from its numerical implications. It may say something about values and about the social standing of prostitutes' clients. An increasing refinement in the outward character of prostitution brings the prostitute closer in her demeanour to bourgeois and respectable sections of the population: how significant was this convergence?

Prostitution as a street spectacle is liable to be strongly influenced by merely local and temporary factors, such as the activity of police and magistrates, and changes in the physical environment (it has already been suggested that Francis Place was observing an effect of the creation of Trafalgar Square when he recorded the decrease of brothels at Charing Cross). The law, with no powers directly to prevent soliciting or prostitution, was always bound to be in a complex, give-and-take relationship with the women on the streets. The police probably acted increasingly to inhibit the blatancy and aggressiveness of prostitutes, though it could still be found necessary in 1848 to walk all the way from Pall Mall to Bow Street in search of a policeman to scare off a prostitute clinging to one's arm.[93] Much more direct powers were available against the ancillary institutions of prostitution through the magistrates as granters of licences for drinking and music, and by virtue of legislation such as the Early Closing Act of 1872. But action through these channels did not have a straightforward effect. In the early 1870s the police and magistrates famously cleaned up the West End, the magistrates acting against the big

---

[92] Kirwan 1963: 183.　　[93] *The Times*, 20 Dec. 1848, p. 2.

dancing establishments and the police hitting the after-hours 'night-houses'. Though this seems in due course to have reduced casual prostitution in the area it is well attested that there was a temporary big increase in the numbers of women soliciting on the street, as old haunts were closed to them.[94]

Changes in the geography of prostitution were unpredictable. Individual streets could wax and wane and then wax again as sites of prostitution for no clear reason and this may explain some of the conflicts in the evidence.[95] It does seem, incidentally, as if Place's claims about improvements in the quantity and quality, or at least relative quality, of prostitution in the Strand were premature. Actually, as we have seen, Place was perhaps not himself clear on the question of prostitute numbers and the Strand may have had its share of temporary rises and falls: one such recent rise was complained of in 1828. But in terms of longer tendencies the whole area remained a centre of conspicuous prostitution, and probably the most important in London, into the 1820s—with the Strand especially prominent and often the first to be referred to by commentators, but with streets to the east such as Holborn and Fleet Street also significant.[96] From about this time the Leicester Square–Regent Street axis appears as a real rival, and soon afterwards some parts of the Strand neighbour-hood, such as Covent Garden, were certainly depleted of prostitutes by the westerly migration. But the Strand itself contributed significantly to London's prostitution for decades after. It is some-times omitted from surveys of the phenomenon, while the Haymarket never is, or it is ranked below the latter site, but there are plenty of references to its conspicuous street prostitution, and there were still brothels at Charing Cross towards the mid-century. It was always sufficiently close to the core of things at the Haymarket to be high on a gradient of prostitute density (with 'files' but not 'cohorts' of women) that is reported as rising from the City westwards; indeed, it was an outlying part of the central zone of London's prostitution.[97]

[94] Storch 1977; Williams 1890: i. 263; D. Shaw 1908: 57.

[95] 'Man about Town' 1857: 4.

[96] Barret-Ducrocq 1991: 54; *My Secret Life* 1966: 430, 436–9; *The Times*, 11 Sept. 1828 n.p.; *Anti-Jacobin*, 13 (1802), 185; Andrewes 1810: 10; Defauconpret 1817: i. 97; Desquiron de Saint-Agnan 1817: ii. 183; Wade 1859: 384.

[97] A. Spencer 1913–25: i. 71; Nicholson 1965: 41; Mayhew 1861–2: iv. 240; *London Guide* 1818: 122; *The Times*, 4 Jan. 1858, p. 4; 8 Jan. 1858, p. 6; *British Controversialist*, NS 1 (1859), 39; Vintras 1867: 40; *Magdalen's Friend*, 1 (1860), 118; Wardlaw 1842: 83; Texier 1851: 14; *House of Lords Sessional Papers*, 1883 ix (109), i. 64. Malot 1862: 230; Laver 1966: 91.

There is also plenty of evidence that the tone of prostitution here was correspondingly lower and the street beyond the pale for the smarter West End women. This does not impugn Place's basic perception of an improvement, since the Strand participated in the general dramatic change in prostitute demeanour. In due course this led to the disappearance of low brothel-based girls from the Strand (the very lowest prostitutes of all turned to St James's Park, conveniently adjacent to the Haymarket). But even in the 1860s some of the Strand prostitutes made a contrast in their squalor with the prosperous and cheerful passers-by, and their shamelessness seems to have been sufficient to embarrass respectable girls into the 1880s.[98]

The change in the public character of English prostitution in the nineteenth century is too widely commented on to be doubted, and apparently occurs in all centres, though there is much more record of it in London than elsewhere. As a nationally noticeable phenomenon it seems to go back to the late 1820s but in London it is claimed from rather earlier, and thereafter is regularly attested.[99] These are chiefly records of decreasing blatancy: of less thronging of prostitutes, and less insistence and eroticism in their soliciting. Improvement in physical appearance, though it converges with this development, may have a separate and prior origin: at all events, there are descriptions from somewhat earlier of strikingly smart and well-groomed London prostitutes who none the less are foul-mouthed and 'forward and lascivious', capable of an approach, at night, 'addressed to your grosser animal faculties and functions'.[100] Place's impressions, it will be remembered, are predominantly of prostitutes becoming cleaner and better-dressed around the turn of the century.

None of the writers who note the accompanying but perhaps slightly later change in the degree of prostitute blatancy achieves Place's level of vivid detail however; most offer fairly general retrospective accounts of this shift, and for a fuller picture it is necessary also to piece together the descriptive comment of the time on what it was like to walk around London or Manchester at night. Even then it is not always easy to put flesh on this broad sense that prostitution was changing in its character. When a writer says that there are

[98] J. E. Ritchie 1857: 37–40, 1859: 189; Remo 1888: 214; Blouet 1884: 53; Smeeton 1828: 41; Mayhew 1861–2: iv. 247; *Meliora*, 1 (1858), 73; Budgett 1865: 24; Merrick 1891: 55.

[99] Knox 1857: 2; Wade 1859: 384; Faucher 1845: i. 85; B. Scott 1884: 4; Perthes 1868: 57; J. E. Davis 1854: 239; 'Moral and Physical Evils of Large Towns', *Foreign Quarterly Review*, 38 (1837), 338–57; Hansard 1844: 14; Mayhew 1861–2: iv. 226; Schlesinger 1853: 285–6.

[100] Hutton 1785: 73–9; *London Guide* 1818: 122–8; J. E. White 1816: ii. 25.

'swarms' of prostitutes, or that they have a 'shameless' air, what does this mean? What does a man mean by 'molested'?

Prostitution was a phenomenon which everyone was inclined to feel they must make a judgment about, even when they had little to go on. In a moment of unconscious candour a German visitor to London in 1819 recorded the difficulty he had, as one primed by Colquhoun's statistics, in seeing what he should see: 'one can scarcely believe that . . . a countless number of the most despicable human beings, a depraved class of people, are to be met with', he wrote, when 'we see ourselves surrounded with such a number of people, in whose countenance and deportment, health, ease, spiritual cultivation, honesty . . . nobility of mind . . . are so visibly imprinted'.[101] No doubt many observers persevered despite the irritating refusal of direct experience to conform to alarmed preconceptions, statistical or otherwise. Conversely, such a record, coming from a fairly early date, is a warning that when later commentators read the opposite lesson into the public appearance of London—that it is orderly, respectable, and moral—they may simply be noticing the neutral reality of the city's life.

It is surprisingly hard to derive answers from the contemporary literature on some matters which should be uncontroversial. Did London prostitutes solicit from windows and doors, for example? According to some authorities in the second decade of the century, soliciting from windows, by day at least, was not practised or had been stamped out (it is specifically described in Newman Street near the turn of the century). But there is plenty of evidence from this date and subsequently that prostitutes solicited routinely from windows and doorways in slum areas in the East End, south of the river, and Westminster. And even in the smarter areas a genteel-looking lady at a window might have continued to be a signal for the initiated; such ambiguities in the appearance of prostitution seem already to have been current in the first years of the century, and Charles Babbage, much later, writes of how women will solicit in this way as long as they have 'the excuse of a street musician' to justify their coming to an open window.[102]

What does seem certain is a broad shift towards more subtle and

---

[101] Niemeyer 1823: 73.

[102] *My Secret Life* 1966: 120; Nougaret 1816: i. 326; *London Guide* 1818: 124; Austin 1804: 57; *Scourge*, 4 (1812), 79; Badcock 1828: 64; Bartlett 1852: 120; Mayhew 1861–2: iv. 263, 332; Malcolm 1810: i. 333; Babbage 1864: 5.

ambiguous means of soliciting, especially as certain smart West End streets became such active centres. Opening ploys such as asking the time or requesting a gentleman's arm across the street were venerable but became more the rule, and by the 1850s much was transacted by 'mute but intelligible signs . . . a look, wink, or a smile' and even in the Haymarket at night one needed one's 'eyes open' to identify all the prostitutes. Some writers go so far as to claim that the women always expected the client to make the first approach, but this can only have applied to a limited group.[103]

In the first twenty years of the century, prostitution in English cities might be found not 'insolent', but the 'salutations' involved were 'unmistakeable' even if 'easily repulsed'. There are continuing complaints up until about 1830 of fairly aggressive soliciting in London and other big cities: of pertinacious individual women and obstructive crowds of prostitutes—especially outside the theatres—on the London pavements, of urgent, repeated, even violent accostings in Manchester and Liverpool, and of groups competing in flagrancy in Birmingham. A flaunting indecency is often noted in London prostitutes, and in those of Portsmouth as late as 1836.[104] It would be wrong to suggest that such complaints then die out from the literature entirely; as I have already stressed, prostitution was never a monolithic phenomenon. But these complaints must be judged against a background of recalibration of what counted as an unacceptable level of accosting, or even of accosting at all. The *Times* leader of 8 January 1858, which complains that a man cannot traverse the Haymarket 'without molestation', may be thought to be paying an inadvertent compliment to a changed aspect of things. William Acton, in the 1870 edition of his *Prostitution*, comments on the 'marked improvement' of the streets since the first edition of 1857: 'of pertinacious solicitation there appears to be little or none'. But in that first edition he had already emphasized the restraint of London's prostitutes: how their soliciting is 'of the most trifling and transient description', and how the Haymarket never contains sights that would offend even 'the most fastidious'.[105]

[103] Defauconpret 1817: i. 98; Mayhew 1861–2, iv. 258; *London Guide* 1818: 125; Wade 1859: 384; 'The Greatest Social Evil' *Tait's*, 24 (1857), 747–52; W. Acton 1857a: 113; Hansard 1844: 14.

[104] J. E. White 1816: i. 19, ii. 25; Griscom 1823: i. 136; Nougaret 1816: i. 326; *De Londres* 1817: 21; Ducos 1834: ii. 73, iv. 107–8, 204–5; Z. Allen 1832: i. 148; Paulding 1822: 12; Haussez 1833: i. 13; Geiger 1932: 249; Slidell 1836: i. 73.

[105] W. Acton 1968: 167; 1857: 107, 117.

And though the old talk of entangling swarms of London prostitutes may still be encountered in the 1840s and 1850s, especially
from the more hostile foreign visitors, there are some actual counts of
peak street-prostitute density in its West End heartland to serve as a
corrective: of something under two hundred women along the
Haymarket–Regent Street axis (with about half of these in the
Haymarket) in 1857, and of about five hundred women in the whole
Haymarket zone in 1883. The two figures can be somewhat reconciled if the two hundred women said to be in the Haymarket pubs
and restaurants in 1857 are added in to the first of these estimates.
When a Midnight Meeting in the area drew about two hundred prostitutes the numbers on the street were said to be visibly depleted.
Several hundred women selling their bodies in a small area of streets
is certainly a large number, but does not constitute a massed throng.
And under these conditions encounters with prostitutes would be
extremely frequent, but not in the nature of running a gauntlet: an
American visitor in the 1860s was accosted seventeen times as he
walked the half-mile from the Haymarket to his hotel in the Strand,
or on average once every fifty yards.[106]

There is nothing in this nineteenth-century transformation of the
face of prostitution that cannot in principle be explained as a
response to pressure from new laws and new legal agencies. Being
less aggressive, less lewd, and not forming gangs on the pavement,
are sensible strategies if the police are seeking an opportunity to use
their rather restricted powers to interfere with your operations. And
it is no accident that much of the old blatant behaviour seems to dis-
appear at the time of the creation of police forces. But it is possible
that enforced change coincided with some degree of spontaneous
change in the character of England's prostitutes. After all, police
pressure does not oblige a prostitute to be dressed and groomed to
the height of the best fashions, and there is general agreement that
the élite of London's street-prostitutes met just these standards; they
were 'studiously fashionable', and Nash's Quadrant at the bottom of
Regent Street looked like a 'ballroom' rather than a street full of
prostitutes. Admittedly, as we have seen, a new smartness in
prostitutes was detectable early in the century, independently of any
other change in their demeanour, and in this there were probably

---

[106] Vintras 1867: 40; Michiels 1844: 39; Verne 1989: 218; W. Acton 1857a: 17; *House of
Lords Sessional Papers*, 1883, ix. 109; i. 64; *Magdalen's Friend*, 1 (1860), 58; Budgett 1865:
25. See also Raumer 1836: ii. 24.

mechanisms at work that continued to have an effect: a new gentility in the clients' values, for instance, and (especially for London's prostitutes) an increased prosperity.[107]

The organizers of the Midnight Meetings in London and elsewhere, with their magdalenist commitment to repentance and rescue, were keen to find a decency—whether of upbringing or of womanly nature—which would be an inner correlate for the very refined and orderly appearance of the women who attended these events. They undoubtedly neglected the other motives which might have made these women, along with their unrepentant colleagues, dress and comport themselves as they did. By contrast, A. J. Munby has a most expressive vignette of a girl, Sarah Tanner, he had first known as 'a maid of all work to a tradesman in Oxford Street':

I met her in Regent St. arrayed in gorgeous apparel. How is this? said I. Why, she had got tired of service, wanted to see life and be independent; and so she had become a prostitute, of her own accord and without being seduced. She saw no harm in it: enjoyed it very much, thought it might raise her and perhaps be profitable. She had taken it up as a profession, and that with much energy: she had read books, and was taking lessons in writing and other accomplishments, in order to fit herself to be a companion of gentlemen. And her manners were improved—she was no longer vulgar: her dress was handsome and good.[108]

Though thoroughly damaging to the magdalenist version of the prostitute (which I discuss more fully in the second volume of this study) this is not a description of a woman likely to form a companionate relationship with a socially elevated client. The heroines of the Anonyma novels are all likewise more-or-less hoydenish spirits, with a skin-deep refinement, after the fashion of the real-life 'Skittles' or Catherine Waters (to judge by the descriptions of her that survive), whether or not they share her lower-class origins.[109] None of them starts to aspire to the condition of the cultivated *demi-mondaine* heading her own off-limits *salon* (though such a world is glimpsed, briefly, in one of the novels, *The Soiled Dove*). They often have affectionate relationships of temporary concubinage with their men, but domestic life is a matter of horse-play and good times. Such a picture

[107] H. Jones 1875: 220; 'A German in London', *Bentley's Miscellany*, 52 (1862), 412–20; Schlesinger 1853: 285.

[108] Hudson 1974: 40.

[109] 'Anonyma' herself does not seem to have been Catherine Waters, as is often alleged; her real identity is given in J. O. Field 1926: 259–60.

of the mistress-cum-courtesan of the day is endorsed by Bracebridge Hemyng: 'if they appear accomplished you may rely that it is entirely superficial' (it must not be overlooked, however, that Hemyng may be the author of the Anonyma novels, or of some of them). W. R. Greg believed that there had been a levelling of the *monde* and the *demi-monde*, but partly because 'the *monde* has been deteriorating' (and it is true that the men in the Anonyma series resemble the most Neanderthal of today's Hooray Henrys). Others judged that the prostitute had lost her old equality with 'artists, poets, and philosophers', and that mistresses were 'rarely' from the 'educated classes'.[110] Laura Bell seems to have been the only *demi-mondaine* of the period who compelled admiration for her intellectual capacities.

From the early decades of the century, however, there are striking descriptions of a type of prostitute who is distinguished from her peers, including the most genteel of these, by her air of thoroughgoing demureness and even prudery. It is hard to know what to make of these records, or of the fact that they do not seem to crop up at a later date. Sometimes the authors of these descriptions are cynically confident as to what is involved, namely, a sexual specialism much like any other:

There are hundreds who . . . may be seen out walking with a letter or a basket in their hands, as if out on some business; these women will pretend to anyone who falls into their company, that they are married, or kept, and thereby enhance the value of their favours. They will dress in the style of a neat servant-maid, with perhaps a key of the front door, or a plate in their hand, as if just stepping out upon an errand . . . she pretends to modesty at first . . . but, if her admirer knows a little too much to take that in, she changes her tone to an expected meeting, or an appointment with a gentleman of consequence (a married man); but the time of meeting being passed she thinks of walking homewards. Very many . . . have pretty faces, and appear as if just escaped the trammels of a parent's care, or the drudgery of a manufactory, and thus it is they arouse the lecherous *gusto* of their paramours.

Other commentators, however, report a similar or overlapping phenomenon in very different terms: for them the 'reserve . . . decency . . . prudery' and 'coyness' of certain prostitutes as 'they pace the

---

[110] Mayhew 1861-2: iv. 216; Greg 1862; 'The Relations of the Sexes', *Westminster Review* 55 (1879), 312-18; G. Drysdale 1868: 377; *Fifty Years of London Society* 1920: 126. On the rowdy partners of the *demi-mondaines* see also Bailey 1986.

streets in silence' are puzzling and comparable to the prudery so marked in respectable English womankind.[111]

It would be a very wild speculation to suggest that what lies behind the second, more kindly group of comments is a strain of prostitution ancestral to the new decorum of prostitution in the Victorian years, showing that the latter was not just a protective guise adopted in new legal circumstances. But it seems a fairly safe guess that what lies behind the first group is not true prostitution at all. These passages are from so-called 'guides' to London of a complacently rakish cast and they are evidently 90 per cent prurient masculine fantasy. The girls they purport to describe need not be other than they appear to be (after all, betrayingly, the premiss of the passages is that there is a 'lecherous gusto' in seducing authentic housewives, servant girls and ex-factory hands), or they could be part-time prostitutes such as were discussed above. Another, rather later passage describes how the prostitutes returning in the early hours to a common lodging-house in St Giles include two 'genteel' girls with 'three ways of making a living . . . selling flowers . . . begging as servants out of place . . . and . . . to use their own phrase, "seeing gentlemen"'; they are disdainful of the other women, having 'the most singular audacity to style themselves modest girls'.[112]

Whatever the reality behind the ambiguities of such material it usefully introduces an important phenomenon: the blurring of the boundaries between the sexually transgressive and the sexually respectable which accompanies the growth of prostitutional decorum in the nineteenth century. When, as the *Saturday Review* complained, it was difficult 'to make out the true character of a vessel from the colours under which she sails', and solicitation was increasingly a matter of men addressing women who had offered some fairly inconspicuous gesture or expression, the possibilities of error were considerable. Respectable girls who knew the ropes would keep up an air of studied unawareness of the men winking at them and generally importuning them, as they shopped in the Burlington Arcade. But a woman who was not familiar with West End ways might find the 'glance after glance *poked* under my bonnet' very irksome. 'Staring' was the usual term for this activity.[113]

---

[111] Ferri di San Costante 1804: i. 215; J. E. White 1816: i. 23, 25; Gourbillon 1817: ii. 357; 'Two Citizens of the World' 1828: 107.   [112] *Sinks of London* 1848: 90.
[113] 'The Rape of the Glances', *Saturday Review*, 13 (1862), 124–5; Ducos 1834: i. 152; H. Wood 1843; Shonfield 1987: 51; Hillocks 1865: 249–50; Walkowitz 1992: 50–2.

'Paterfamilias' (who may, in reality, have been the gadfly journalist Matthew Jacob Higgins) complained in *The Times* in 1862 that his daughters kept being pestered on the West End streets. The really interesting possibility, which emerges in the subsequent correspondence, is that there was a true overlap between prostitutes and respectable girls in the sense that the latter were not averse to being picked up in an honourable way and having 'little harmless and interesting adventures', and that it was slight signals of encouragement in this spirit which were being misread by some men. Those girls who received unwished-for attentions may in fact have been mistaken for women bent on this kind of 'adventure' rather than prostitutes. Otherwise it is hard to understand why, as is alleged, the problem should have been worse by day than by night, with a 'reasonably good-looking' girl being unable to walk a block without 'half-a-dozen' approaches (the morning was safe, because gentlemen were not abroad, for any purpose).[114] But this belongs with the topic of middle-class 'fast' behaviour, especially in the 1860s, and will be dealt with in the next chapter.

It was not only in the West End streets at daytime that these uncertainties could occur. The rising tone of prostitution made it advisable for better-off, respectable women to travel third class on the trains—when they could have afforded first or second—to avoid being accosted.[115] In so far as prostitutes resorted, perhaps increasingly, to certain off-street sites where respectable recreation was also being enjoyed the moral colouration of these places became indeterminate, and the sites themselves a kind of liminal zone. A tolerant observer in the mid-1860s, William Brighty Rands, assesses this phenomenon very interestingly. 'Social boundary lines are not so sharply drawn . . . as they used to be' because of a rising tide of sexual laxity ('the old *cordons sanitaires* have snapped under the pressure of multitudes'), but this mingling of 'the half-anchored, the drifting, and the drifted' with the morally uncontaminated is salutary: there is no threat to general standards, thanks to the huge improvement in morality over the last century or half-century.[116] The spirit of this— with its awareness of a vigorous culture of sexual transgression, but confidence about a larger moral consensus—seems to me characteristic of the 1860s.

[114] *The Times*, 7 Jan. 1862, p. 7; 18 Jan. 1862, p. 10; and intervening correspondence; L. Richardson 1886: 107–8; Shonfield 1987: 44.
[115] Hillocks 1865: 251.   [116] Rands 1866: 267–8.

Cremorne Gardens was well known for bringing together 'strange mixtures of the decent and the dissolute', so that 'the goats and sheep mingle'; William Acton was confident in being able to identify the several hundred girls who were goats, but in so far as this is in the context of recording the well-attested decorousness of the goings-on ('the intercourse of the sexes could hardly have been more reserved') the modern reader is bound to doubt if his scoring rate was perfect.[117]

Acton's confidence is representative of the spirit of almost all Victorian commentary on the public aspect of prostitution, and it may be that the sense which has transmitted itself into the twentieth century of a rigid distinction between prostitutes and respectable women in the period, with no half-world that it not the *demi-monde*, is in some measure an artefact of the unwarranted certainty with which these writers pigeon-hole their female contemporaries. There was definitely such an effect at work in the comment on music-hall audiences (on the whole a topic which lies outside the chronology of this study). Modern inquiry has shown most tellingly how these audiences routinely included considerable numbers of respectable, single, unaccompanied women, though the contemporary descriptions hardly ever acknowledge their presence.[118]

The ordinary theatres in London and large provincial towns were for several decades important centres of prostitution. In the early part of the century the contrast in demeanour between the prostitutes and the respectable theatre-goers was probably considerable but it later became a matter of frequent comment that the former, in London especially, were deceivingly well turned out (and many visitors seem indeed to have been deceived, as they describe the elegance of the audiences without any recognition of a prostitute fraction). Interestingly, for some commentators the homogeneity of the women's looks was due more to an approximation of the respectable to the non-respectable than to the opposite movement. Full evening-dress, with the extreme *décolletage* that was often censured by foreign observers and even by servants, was the rule at the major theatres; to the eyes of one of these visitors, it left upper-class women in the audiences virtually naked except for their jewels

---

[117] W. E. Adams 1903: ii. 310; Forney 1867: 58; W. Acton 1857*b*: 104; J. E. Ritchie 1857: 187–91; PP 1866, xvi. 133–4; Nevill 1912: 135–8. On Vauxhall Gardens Montulé 1825: i. 260–1 has interesting details.

[118] Nead 1988: 179–81; Walkowitz 1992: 129–31; Hoher 1986.

and hair, and indistinguishable from the girls on the pavement out-side.[119]

There is a further sense in which moral boundaries were probably blurred in the theatres. While the foyers, lobbies, and bars may have been frequented by prostitutes to solicit business, the latter surely entered the auditoriums in part for the same reason as everyone else: to see plays and operas (this is certainly how the matter is understood in Polly Evans's memoir and in the Anonyma novels). The evidence is that their dealings with men inside the theatre proper were by way of hobnobbing with admirers and escorts rather than soliciting.[120] In general, like their working-class counterparts discussed earlier, these superior prostitutes in the West End and elsewhere were not plying their trade during every moment that they spent in the sites of prosti-tution. It must always be remembered that prostitutes and their haunts were to an important extent just part of the broad pleasure-seeking culture of any town (which at one extreme included young men, like the medical student Shepherd Taylor, who could afford or were inclined only to stroll and watch).

Sex for money was a less significant bond in this culture than a general idea of hedonistic good times, which might include sex on various footings. The formulation which *The Times* used, with an air of astonishment, about the Haymarket household in which the famous Lani murder took place in 1857 could be applied to this wider grouping: 'a community which is existing in the most self-com-placent manner on the wages of infamy, and in which each individual has the air of considering that he or she is doing nothing in the world to be ashamed of'. A way of avoiding such painful recognitions—and another pigeon-holing strategy—was to represent those individuals in the West End night spots who were not buying or selling sex as *ingénus*, innocents lured unawares into these attractive haunts who were likely to be shocked and disgusted by what they then wit-nessed.[121]

As the century advances, another cultural model, which has been stimulatingly proposed by the historian Peter Bailey and labelled by him 'parasexuality', may come increasingly to be the explanation of these and other comparably ambiguous phenomena. Parasexuality is

[119] Gourbillon 1817: i. 200; Weyden 1854: 128; Slidell 1836: 267; Wikoff 1880: 188; Pichot 1825: i. 218; Tayler 1962: 36; Texier 1851: 14.

[120] Defauconpret 1817: i. 99; Weyden 1854: 128.

[121] *The Times*, 10 Apr. 1858, p. 8; J. E. Ritchie 1859: 84, 106.

eroticism of demeanour only, not of actual relations. Bailey sees its growth in this period as both commercially driven, an aspect of the marketing of commodities, recreations, and so forth (he identifies the friendly barmaid as the first parasexual type), and as a creation of the ordinary public 'in a self-conscious and mutual . . . working out of new modes of relationship between men and women'. In this latter form 'parasexuality' is also a very promising notion for the under-standing of certain ambiguities of sexual behaviour which I mention in the next chapter: such as the 'fastness' craze of the 1860s, and the behaviour of young working-class people consorting in places of pub-lic entertainment.[122]

Due to the efforts of Macready and others prostitution was forced out of the theatres after the mid-century, and in London at least the dance-halls or 'casinos' became in turn important off-street resorts of prostitutes. Some of these establishments, like Mott's, the Argyll Rooms, and the Holborn, were in the network of places favoured by the polymorphously hedonistic culture just described: Mott's, it was said, was frequented by dancing-girls and by 'actresses of note, who, if not Magdalens, sympathized with them', and most or at least some of the men at the Argyll and the Holborn may have been there to meet friends, dance and take in the spectacle.[123] But the casinos seem to have been very various in character. Some may have special-ized in prostitution and served as a kind of indoor version of the streets, the business being conducted with considerable blatancy. Others were handsome, orderly establishments patronized in part by middle-class married couples and completely genteel customers who would have appreciated the warning, as given by a guidebook, that the visitors were 'unselect' (and where unselectness in the sense of any kind of soliciting was punished by the management with expul-sion). Yet others seem to have been resorted to entirely by lower-middle-class girls associating with young men without restraint but not as prostitutes. Overall, the casinos were not nearly as bad on the face of it as their enemies would have liked; the latter had to deploy a reverse logic which is often to be found in the moralistic comment on recreations of the day: 'for a dancing hall there is so much of apparent

[122] Bailey 1990.
[123] A. Smith 1856: 64; D. Shaw 1908: 2; Fiske 1869: 174; W. Acton 1857*b*: 51; C. Scott 1897: 45; 'The Holborn Casino', *Paul Pry*, 18 (17 Feb. 1857), 1–2; Rendle 1919: 266; Holden 1950: ch. 4 and *passim*.

propriety . . . that a young man . . . is as safe as on the edge of a heaving volcano'.[124]

The cues distinguishing the respectable from the disreputable may have been extremely slight (it was said that you could only identify the prostitutes at the Argyll Rooms by the fact that they left in cabs), but it is always wise to doubt claims that the girls to be seen either in the casinos or in the more working-class dance-halls were largely or exclusively prostitutes because the drive in the literature to assimilate the innocent female dancer to the depraved is so palpable. A girl who is not 'disreputable' must at least be 'doubtful', one who is 'innocent-*looking*' cannot be what she seems, and, as a last resort, one who is innocent now may as well not be, since she 'in twelve months time will have lost her maiden shame'. The process can be seen at work between the two editions of Acton's *Prostitution*: in 1857 'a third at least' of the girls at the Holborn are prostitutes, but in 1870 they are 'of course all prostitutes'. The doubt a visitor might feel about this, faced with the way in which 'all the outward proprieties of demeanour and gesture are strictly observed', is magisterially dismissed but, given Acton's inconsistency, one could decline to be impressed, and question whether even his lower, earlier estimate means very much.[125]

Sexual codes as they relate to social class will mainly be dealt with in the next chapter, but it is appropriate to ask whether the changing levels of refinement of prostitution in the nineteenth century shed any light on the difficult and very important question of who were the clients of prostitutes. After all there do seem to have been sizeable changes in the make-up of London's prostitute numbers, for example, with street-prostitution dwindling but the superior clandestine varieties staying at a fairly constant ratio to the population. Much of the preceding discussion has been about the prostitution of London's West End, because this is the most richly documented kind of prostitution in nineteenth-century England, and one of the strongest popular stereotypes of Victorian sexual culture is of middle-class men, perhaps married, resorting to West End prostitutes. It is certainly plausible that the girls in the Haymarket or the Argyll

---

[124] Wade 1859: 385; Prémaray 1851: 101; Hibbert 1916: 123; PP 1854, xiv. 91; 1866, xvi. 35, 45; *London Life* 1851: 51; J. E. Ritchie 1859: 85; Burnand 1904: i. 247; A. Smith 1849: 14–15; Hudson 1974: 22, 155–6; C. Scott 1897: 45; Corderoy 1880.

[125] Judge 1874: 27–9; *The Times*, 3 June 1857, p. 9; R. Rowe 1880: 16; J. E. Ritchie 1859: 184; W. Acton 1857*b*: 102, 1870: 52.

Rooms sold themselves mainly to middle- to upper-class clients (their fee was between £1 and £3, perhaps with entertainment expenses on top).[126]

There were of course larger number of prostitutes in the less smart areas of London, as well as thousands spread through England's other cities, cities in which there was often a much more sizeable working-class sector than in London. On the other hand, in London's only female prison, the Millbank Penitentiary, in the 1880s there do not seem to have been significantly greater numbers of prostitutes from the East End than from the West, and just on arithmetical grounds one would expect the biggest proportion of prostitutes' clients to be working-class men. Was there any departure from proportionality? Are there any signs that, man for man, the bourgeoisie were more likely, or became more likely, to resort to prostitutes than the workers, or vice versa? To judge from the judicial statistics, the numbers of prostitutes in different towns varied considerably and in a way that is related to the permanent social composition of these communities, even if much can also be attributed to transient elements in the population: resort towns and agricultural centres are high on the list (but commercial ports are highest of all), while the mill and factory towns are at the bottom.[127]

It was estimated in 1860, though it is not clear on what grounds, that for every middle-class client of a prostitute there were a hundred working-class clients, but such views of the level of working-class resort to prostitutes tend to be linked to the inaccurate 'high' tradition of supposed prostitute numbers. To nineteenth-century writers and readers the dizzying scale of these figures may often have spoken, silently, of their supposed explanation, namely, proletarian depravity. Magdalenists (for whom many prostitutes were decent girls seduced by heartless upper-class men) tended to believe that both the working-class and bourgeois fraction of the client population was shrinking.[128] But the commonest perception—and it is ubiquitous—was that both prostitution and concubinage were being increasingly sustained by young middle-class men reluctant to incur the costs of marriage in a newly plutocratic society.

It is impossible to adjudicate between these different perceptions

---

[126] W. Acton 1870: 52; *The Times*, 21 June 1854, p. 11.

[127] Merrick 1891: 22; *JSSL* 30 (1867), 391.

[128] 'Midnight Meetings' *Leader* (28 Apr. 1860), 397–8; Grant 1837: i. 294; *Female's Friend* (Apr. 1846), 79.

with any confidence. It seems that the concentration of brothels and prostitutes in working-class areas such as Manchester's Deansgate was greater the 'lower' the nature of the neighbourhood, but there is obviously a danger of circularity in such judgements, and in London and York brothels in the poor areas were certainly patronized by middle-class clients. Contributing to the appearance of superiority in these establishments may have been a change in the character of the old 'disorderly house' type of working-class brothel; new ideas of gentility and refinement had their impact on working-class prostitution as they did on the higher varieties, despite the residual influence here of old traditions of gaudiness.[129]

Modern surveys of the evidence have concluded that working-class resort to prostitution was always at least up to the proportion of workers in the population at large (in other words, was numerically the overwhelming source of prostitute business), but the author of the most searching of these studies admits that her evidence—of which a significant component is criminal proceedings—tends to emphasize the lower groups of prostitutes. Certainly those girls who ended up in prison may have been very unrepresentative of the generality of prostitutes: judging from surveys by prison chaplains in the 1880s between a third and a quarter of such inmates were completely illiterate. The safest conclusion is probably that men at all social levels used prostitutes to much the same extent, and continued to do so, and that in assessing the sexual codes of the different classes in nineteenth-century England it may be assumed that prostitution was a familiar part of all of them—perhaps even to the point, as one commentator believed, where 'there are few men who, in some period of their lives, have not dealt in mercenary sex'.[130]

---

[129] Oats 1864–5; C. Booth 1887; PP 1817, vii. 465; Finnegan 1979: 119; H. Jones 1875: 220, 239; *British Controversialist*, NS 1 (1859), 105.

[130] Walkowitz 1980: 17; Finnegan 1979: 17–18; *House of Lords Sessional Papers*, 1883, ix (109), ii. 52; Merrick 1891: 50; Wade 1859: 371.

Chapter Three

CODES AND CLASSES

I

Class Structure

THE cliché that links social rank and resort to prostitutes in the English nineteenth century is not secure, but it is very plausible that rank and sexual codes did go hand in hand. One such correlation, in a perhaps unexpectedly complicated form, emerged in the last chapter: linking class and the early adoption of birth control. A good deal of the contemporary comment on sexual culture can, in fact, only illuminate the behaviour and attitudes of certain social groups, because this is all it claims to illuminate. In particular, there is an enormous volume of comment on working-class sexuality in the period. Francis Place's writings are a highly distinguished founding example of the phenomenon.

Place does not offer an opinion about resemblances between the growing respectability he claimed to observe in his own social environment and changes in sexual codes higher up the social scale. He may have believed that the working classes in late eighteenth-century England pioneered the 'Victorian': he clearly thought that they adopted such a code autonomously. The radical Sir Richard Phillips, a contemporary of Place's, claimed it was the moral opinion of the 'populace' which checked the sexual licence of the English élite. We know of one aristocratic employer who wanted to condone a servant's sexual misconduct, but was prevented by 'the unpleasant-ness it would have caused with the other servants'.[1] By contrast, the

---

[1] Phillips 1817: 140; Barret-Ducrocq 1991: 174.

commonly accepted model of nineteenth-century anti-sensualism holds it to be an invention of the middle class, or of some section of the middle class. The two versions of events obviously imply very different processes, mainly because of the relative scale of the groups involved. We either have a mass movement, or hegemony exerted by a small sector. But what do these quantitative expressions, 'mass' and 'small', mean exactly? Most of us have a vague sense, probably, that the nineteenth-century working class amounted to a vast fraction of England's population, and that other groups, even all other groups, amounted to a tiny one. This intuition makes the contrast between the two versions of Victorianization very stark. How justifiable is it? Answers to this question are not as clearcut as might be thought.

The population of England and Wales was somewhere just in excess of eight million in 1790, had grown by at least a million by 1800, and was then boosted by a vigorous rate of growth to a remarkable twenty-five million by 1880. In 1800 about a ninth of the population lived in London, and as many again in the forty-eight next largest towns (towns of over 10,000 inhabitants, it should be said, and therefore sometimes scarcely urban by later standards). The picture over the next three decades is, of course, of expanding urban populations and shrinking rural. The effect was universal, but the already heavily urbanized areas, such as Lancashire, mushroomed at about twice the rate of even the newly urbanizing, such as the West Riding. The interesting exception to this rule is London, where the rate was close to the average for the whole country.[2]

In the Victorian period proper the pattern changed somewhat. The more established and largest industrial centres experienced some slowing down of their growth. After 1850 South Wales and the East Midlands show a spectacular rise in the number of towns exceeding 100,000 in population, for example, while such conglomerations do not increase very markedly in Lancashire, the West Riding, or Durham. But it was still increasingly likely for any individual that he or she would live in a town or city. Industrial urbanization was still an overwhelming demographic force, driving the fledgling urbanized areas of 1850, and especially the urban-industrial areas, to the nation's fastest rates of growth in the next half of the century. There was an increasing division in character between rural and urban England: areas were becoming more markedly one or the other.

[2] W. A. Armstrong 1965; Deane and Cole 1967: 103.

Eight million people out of twenty-six million lived in the country in 1880; in 1800 there had already been six million—but out of a total English population of only nine million. London, which had anticipated the pattern of rather slower growth by the very largest cities, continued its fairly modest rate of expansion. Given London's scale, this was not modest in its demographic effects if you were a Londoner, as the capital grew from around a million in 1800 to almost four million in 1880, or even if you lived elsewhere, as London accommodated a growing proportion of the country's inhabitants (about a ninth in 1800 and more than a seventh in 1880).[3]

This huge, continuous shift meant that patterns of employment were also transformed. In 1801 about half the working population was doing agricultural work and half manufacturing or commercial. In 1811, when the census information is expressed in terms of *families* associated with various occupations, a rough picture of the whole society emerges: 36 per cent involved in agriculture, 45 per cent in manufacture and commerce, 19 per cent elsewhere. Modern historians, working backwards from later census data, have proposed a more detailed picture for the pre-Victorian years. They have suggested that the manufacturing-commercial sector broke down into a ratio of about 24 (manufacturing) to 11 (commercial) in 1789, and that this shifted to 41 to 12 by 1831.[4] By the middle of the century more than half the population depended on manufacture and trade for a livelihood, and manufacture in a narrow sense (excluding mining and building) supported about 30 per cent. The latter proportion, interestingly, then remained fairly constant for the rest of the century— the continuing shrinkage of the agricultural part of the population now being achieved more by a shift to occupations such as building and transport.[5]

Patterns of occupation and settlement are themselves relevant to sexuality, especially in view of certain impressions of the day (concerning, for instance, the morals of factories versus farms, and of domestic servants), but their main interest here is what they indicate about nineteenth-century class structure. Rather frustratingly, the direction taken by enquiries into occupation in the nineteenth-century census makes this, the obvious instrument, progressively more cryptic about class. There is an important supplement, therefore, in

[3] Law 1967; Friedlander 1970. [4] W. A. Armstrong 1965; Banks 1978.
[5] C. Booth 1886.

information about *income* in the period, which is furnished by some contemporary inquiry and by tax receipts.

I give more detail on various studies of nineteenth-century class, based on these sources, in an appendix to this volume. To abbreviate these findings drastically, it may be said that right through the century the upper and middle classes composed something over 20 per cent of England's population, and what modern sociologists call Class III groups—craftsmen, clerks, and so forth with their families— much the same proportion. Working-class groups of all kinds amounted to around 56 per cent, but there was certainly a very lowly fraction in Class III, and it may be more correct to think of England's working class as approaching two-thirds of the population. London differed chiefly in having a smaller working-class component than the rest of the country. The main shift in time, unexpectedly, was in the direction of greater polarization: the semi-skilled fraction of the working class shrank, with an expansion of groups both above and below them but especially of the latter, the unskilled workforce. This change may have been especially marked in London.

So the picture is Janus-faced: of a society in which *both* gentility and lumpen proletarianism were large components, which became larger. It allows the possibility that Francis Place's phenomenon of working-class respectability was, at its upper end and as represented by Place himself, just a matter of rising status. And the growth of a very different sector, the true, unskilled, labouring poor, also at the expense of higher ranks in the working class, might suggest that Place's concept of an autonomously respectabilizing proletariat is implausible. Conversely, élite and bourgeois groups were not only privileged and powerful in the nineteenth century, they were quite numerous: well-placed, perhaps, to bring the working class morally to heel.

But these are just slight likelihoods, based on crude aggregates. There are many other important considerations: the relative timing of respectabilizing processes among different groups, the solidarity of moralistic codes in the quarter of England's population that was middle-class or higher, the degree of authentic penetration of respectable values at the working-class level, the contribution of occupation and settlement as influences on moral codes. Verdicts on these matters could (and, I believe, do) run counter to the implications of the class totals. This inquiry will involve stitching together contemporary impressions and definitions, with a due sense of the ignorance and bias that often underlies them, but with a responsiveness to the social realities they can nevertheless attest.

II

Élite and Bourgeois Sexuality

The nineteenth-century English aristocracy as such is a well-defined and well-recorded class but also an extremely small one, whose sexual manners and morals may reasonably be expected to have had a lot in common with those of the larger and more poorly defined élite which is 'society' or the 'gentry' (if the latter term is not understood to denote only a rural or even land-owning group). The sexual code of the highest professional class may also have had much in common with that of these socially superior grades. But in the contemporary anecdotal evidence it is often hard to know where lines are drawn (if the conduct of 'gentlemen', for example, is being reported), and how tight the social blinkers are in a particular case: whether a complaint about wifely infidelity is directed at titled adulteresses or easy-going wives of doctors and businessmen, or just who is meant to fall foul of an accusation of prudery in demeanour and language. Sometimes a particular behaviour is identified as aristocratic, but it does not appear that commentators made a distinction, in general, between the peerage and the larger élite. The latter is also the group which is most likely to be described without being identified for what it is; it tends to be treated as if it were coextensive with the nation, as if it were both 'society' and society (foreign visitors are especially prone to write in this spirit).

A nostalgic memoirist of the swinging London of the 1860s, writing in 1908, retained the impression that many of the aristocratic companions he had roistered with had married courtesans and high-class prostitutes. The demographic evidence is against him. The English peerage proper, at least, were marrying 'out' more and more in the nineteenth century but the increase is attributable mainly to marriages with foreigners; and the English commoners taken as wives by English peers were still predominantly from the squirearchy (not prostitutes, and seldom even actresses, but not the daughters of ironmasters either).[6] In other words, the wider grouping

---

[6] D. Shaw 1908: *passim*; D. Thomas 1972; Horn 1991:73.

of upper-class society generally was maintaining its old demographic outlines.

The peerage conformed to national patterns by adopting birth control in the 1860s and by marrying in increasing numbers, but the whole of the English élite, understood here to include the professional classes, had been unusual in marrying progressively later than the rest of the population since the beginning of the century—so that for them the tendency of the first decades of the century seems never to have been reversed as it was for the rest of the population. It would not be surprising if actual celibacy rates were also sometimes higher in such circles, and the figures concerning unmarried women aged 35–45, in different social bands in London, seem to confirm that this was the case.[7]

If the idea that courtesans entered the ranks of the aristocracy in any numbers is wrong, some aristocrats did have affectionate and sustained relationships with prostitutes. One marquis was so close to the notorious Skittles for so long that rumour made him her clandestine husband. Brothels catering for the aristocracy were alleged to be on an almost domestic scale, with usually no more than three women, each primarily the companion of one client.[8] To consort with Skittles so devotedly, or to maintain a private brothel with a couple of friends, was libertine behaviour in an aristocrat at this or any other period, but it was perhaps tinged with a more decorous and controlled idea of sexual licence than the libertinism of a century earlier, and in general it is clear that the face of upper-class sexual recreation became much more refined, especially from the early 1830s.

The evening behaviour of young gentlemen in London is first recorded as 'wonderfully improved' from about this time (with the West End clubs cited as an important new recreation, as they would be often). The survival of a scattering of conspicuously debauched gentry is attested into the early 1840s, but from an early date there is some agreement that the ranks of the old libertine aristocracy are on the defensive and thinning. There are allusions to the 'barefaced profligacy' still 'flaunted in defiance of a better sense of feeling' in the first quarter of the century, but the American Episcopalian minister Nathaniel Wheaton thought that a few noblemen were giving a misleading impression of their class, and one satirical commentator who wrote accounts of London in 1800 and again in 1820 was struck,

[7] Hollingsworth 1957, 1964; Ansell 1874: 44; Hammerton 1979: 30.
[8] D. Shaw 1908: 169; *Town* (1837), 13.

among the tokens of general moral improvement in the interval, especially by the dwindling numbers of 'worthless and . . . profligate individuals among our nobility'. By 1855 the really debauched peerage
was said to be 'fortunately extinct', and from the mid-century on, even
when you did turn out from your club, slumming it in low dives—as
'members of both Houses, the pick of the Universities, and the bucks
of the Row' had recently been wont to do—was no longer the fashion.[9]

Not unexpectedly, there are large differences of opinion as to the
authenticity of these appearances. While Wheaton and others
believed that the prevailing improvement in upper-class demeanour
betokened a real reduction in licentiousness, or at least a determined
commitment to respectability, other commentators saw it as the
worst kind of sneaking hypocrisy. The previous chapter has argued
that there was no real increase in the numbers of prostitutes in
England, but also that the most genteel categories of prostitute were
probably an exception to this rule—while there is no reason to think
that courtesans at this period were on anything like a matrimonial
footing with their lovers, however domestic and orderly the appearance. A shift towards some degree of concubinage may have been
associated with less sexual transgression on the part of upper-class
girls and wives. *Frasers Magazine* claimed in the 1840s that 'the days
of Lovelaces and Lotharios are past . . . gentlemen are less accomplished, or ladies more prudent: the seducer now reserves his skill
for the humbler sphere'. A Marylebone footman, writing in his diary
in 1837, knew which sex was to blame: the elaborate wiles of young
ladies at parties (dropping their handkerchiefs or gloves, and so forth)
did not usually ensnare the gentlemen, who 'generally place their
affections on some poor but pretty girl and takes her into keeping
and when tired of her, turns her off and gets another'.[10]

It was still believed elsewhere that seducing married and unmarried women was 'almost the only business of their life' of 'hundreds'
of aristocratic youth. But a powerful taboo on the first category of victim is reported as being in place later in the century, and the extent
of sexual transgression by upper-class women once they were
married is a topic fraught with contradictions.[11] One must beware of

[9] Symons 1860: 52; J. Richardson 1855: ii. 127, 226; H. Wood 1843: 90; Wheaton 1830:
201; Corry 1820: 34–5; Doré and Jerrold 1872: 168.

[10] Channing 1874: 210–11; Tolly 1843: ii. 192–205; Weyden 1854: 128; J. Mitchell 1842;
Tayler 1962: 56–7. See also *Old Bachelors* 1877: 4–12, Morley 1862.

[11] Grant 1837: i. 230; Warwick 1929: 171.

supposing that in this area a single group, even a small close-knit group such as the titled gentry, would necessarily possess a code that was shared or even known by all its members (and not just because of the anomalous standards of a few Evangelically minded individuals). When the House of Lords debated in 1800 a Bill designed to deter adultery by prohibiting the marriage of adulterous parties in a divorce suit it was clear that there were perfectly genuine disagreements among English peers as to the extent of marital transgression in their own class. The aristocracy were not internally transparent in their sexual code, so to speak, so even the direct testimony of an aristocrat is not to be trusted implicitly. A good illustration of the principle is Lady Morgan, who declared with insider-like confidence that the Parisian upper classes were 'to the full as indulgent, as those of London' when it came to adultery, although she herself was a complete newcomer to the peerage. To the extent that the typical aristocratic sexual 'freemasonry' would include in its code a rigorous secrecy about all activities, it may easily be imagined that even social equals, if uninitiated, were fooled: 'never by a word or movement of an eyelid' did one durable pair of lovers from this tier 'give themselves away'.[12] But the axiom of internal opacity should be borne in mind in judging insider comment on all nineteenth-century social groups.

One student of aristocratic morals in the 1830s tried to put things on a more objective footing by systematically annotating a *Burke's Peerage* with information on adulteries, and the result showed, it is said, 'nearly universal immorality' and 'a regular transfer of husband and wife'.[13] There was of course a vigorous tradition of satirical attack on aristocratic vice—particularly in the form of anti-court satire in the pre-Victorian period—and this story belongs somewhere in that tradition, but should not necessary be taken lightly. The less there is of axe-grinding in the tone of contemporary claims about a prevalence of aristocratic adultery the more confidence they inspire. It is at least plausible that for many wives in this group 'chastity is not considered the most important of the cardinal virtues' and 'alliances . . . are . . . contracted with persons of agreeable physical endowments', especially when the assent to such a code is linked to the natural erosion of false modesty through the experiences of marriage and motherhood: 'as life advances, the duties of a wife render the

[12] Morgan 1817: i. 309; Warwick 1929: 176–7.   [13] *VPNL* 12 (1971), 7.

indulgence of such tastes more difficult: those of a mother render them more so. The mature woman often concludes, by considering the tastes and delicacies of the young one, as so many fantasies and affectations.'[14]

One anecdote, at least, carries an irresistible conviction of an extremely well-entrenched and conscious ethic of adulterous sex within one coterie of the aristocracy, well into the century. In her memoirs, the Countess of Cardigan and Lancastre described an extra-marital ménage of the 1850s known as the Parrot Club which was set up by two ladies and a commoner with their three lovers; all went well in the house in Seymour Street until Lady K. began to diversify and 'commenced to change her lovers with such rapidity that the other two members were obliged to ask her to resign', and the commoner's lover, a Captain Vivian, discovered that she had seduced his surviving fellow member, Lord Strathmore.[15] This certainly bespeaks a cool, deliberate, and more-or-less communal philosophy of free love in this circle, but not a notably licentious one. What these wives had established is a mirror of the small, semi-domestic brothels of the male aristocracy mentioned earlier; it was in intention a decorous, not to say respectable institution, with fidelity between the couples as one of its principles. Sustained extra-marital liaisons are the burden of many of the contemporary allegations about aristocratic adultery, and such patterns of behaviour would be consistent with maintaining a thoroughly decent matrimonial front. In 1833 it was allegedly a familiar fact that abductions had decreased, but it was controversial whether this reflected a real decrease in adulteries; either way an improvement in appearances had occurred. Hence also arose such 'hypocrisies' as that related of a peeress in 1819, who strongly commiserated a friend whose ten-year affair (starting at the time of her marriage) with 'the Colonel' had been exposed, but who would not employ a servant who had been seduced because 'I cannot encourage vice'.[16]

Such discontinuities, or apparent discontinuities, between manners and morals may explain some of the contradictions in the descriptive comment of the day. For there is an awkward body of evidence, which has to be reconciled with the image of a much-glossed *Burke's Peerage*, to suggest that there was substantial upper-class

[14] W. B. Adams 1832: 49; Walker 1840: 177.
[15] Cardigan and Lancastre 1909: 143–4.
[16] Haussez 1833: i. 53; MacDonogh 1819–20: i. 119. See also Crapelet 1817: 255.

marital fidelity. This is mainly in the form of opinions recorded by
foreign visitors on the strength of what they saw of the social behaviour of husbands and wives, and as such suffers the additional disad-
vantage that it may be influenced by inappropriate comparisons with
foreign manners. But the conviction, as expressed by a German traveller in 1802, of the 'unblemished virtue in the women, and an honourable fidelity in the men' is quite widely shared, and sometimes
uttered with great confidence.[17] It is also true that such claims are to
be found as early as the 1780s, and it may well be that a fairly persistent difference between English and continental standards, or at least
demeanour, is being recorded, which has nothing to do with
Victorian or proto-Victorian culture. Moreover, the topic of sexual
morals in marriage tends to drop out of foreign comment from
around 1810 (probably because of changed literary tastes), and the
scattered later observations are bewilderingly contradictory: in contrast to the confidence of certain French observers around the mid-
century that adultery was rare in aristocratic circles, and 'gallantry' a
scarcely intelligible notion, there are declarations, though perhaps
rather sensationalist, that it was rife, if improving.[18]

If a verdict on this difficult subject can be ventured, it must be that
in some upper-class circles there was a very lenient code on adultery,
especially when this involved sustained liaisons that did not violate
the appearance of strict marital decorum. In other circles in the same
élite, however, such practices would have caused surprise and disapproval. The standards of the rural gentry were probably different
from those of their town-based equivalents, but the fissure between
pro- and anti-transgressive thinking, as such, did not necessarily run
down this divide. Town versus country was a major source of moral
heterogeneity according to a very interesting account of London
morals written in 1829. The author is completely in accord with
Francis Place on the huge change which has occurred in the moral
face of the capital, but believes that it is entirely superficial: under
the surface 'there are fewer conscientious scruples entertained
respecting sexual intercourse than at any former period'. This 'laxity
of manners among the females of London' would be 'quite startling in
a provincial town'. Even on this account, however, country morals
are not particularly high: because provincial society is less concerned

---

[17] Goede 1807: i. 120; Simond 1817: i. 45; Meister 1799: 283–4; Ségur 1803: iii. 164.
[18] Archenholz 1797: 327; Wendeborn 1791: i. 441; Taine 1957: 80; Tolly 1843: ii. 12;
Anichini 1836: 18; Larcher 1860: ii. 40; Delfau 1971: 390.

with mere appearances, 'faux pas and kept mistresses are considered in the country among the phenomena of nature'.[19]

This particular author sometimes has in his sights distinctly bourgeois groups but, as I have mentioned, there are great uncertainties in the literature concerning approximately upper-class sexuality as to the social range over which élite codes are thought to extend. For example, when 'rinkomania', dancing on roller-skates, became the rage in the late 1870s it was interpreted by one observer as a 'revolt of the sons and daughters of the middle class against their exclusion from modes of social enjoyment that to their contemporaries slightly above them in the social scale had long been allowed', because at the rinks young people could meet and dance without being formally introduced, as was already the case at subscription dances. And while the roller-skating bourgeoisie were making up lost ground their superiors were allegedly setting an even hotter pace: 'meanwhile, the gentlemen and ladies who called themselves society . . . were indulging more enterprising tastes still . . . The rage for "making up a party" for everything came in; superstitious veneration for the ceremonial etiquette of a past day went out'.[20] There is certainly evidence here of bridges being thrown across a division in moral codes, and of a more emancipated élite having a defrosting effect on middle-class moralism, but who composed this élite? The social calibration in this account is complicated, because the fast set described evidently thought of itself as upper-class, but the author wants to suggest that their claim was bogus. Almost certainly these were not the lineal descendants of fiercely dissipated Regency bucks, nor of coolly adulterous Mayfair wives, nor even of the pub-crawling MPs and Oxbridge men, who had died out in the mid-century.

It is probable that a fairly sharp distinction should be made, in fact, between a narrow élite and the next rung of the bourgeoisie (with the highest professional grades perhaps belonging to, or aspiring to belong to, the élite: the wealthy West End surgeon's daughter Jeannette Marshall would only go 'rinking' if accompanied by a gentleman). James Fenimore Cooper received the impression in the 1830s that English girls of the 'higher classes' were under a 'good deal of restraint' before marriage, but 'a caste or two lower' and the 'exuberant mode' is 'not uncommon' or 'actually . . . the *mode*'.[21]

[19] Wade 1829: 150–1.
[20] Escott 1897: 195–7; see also Fayet 1846: i. 218, 'The Man in the Club-Window' 1859: 271.
[21] Shonfield 1987: 73; J. F. Cooper 1837: ii. 194.

There is good evidence for a distinctive collocation, at the level of English society 'a caste or two' below the top, of a strict code for wives and a relaxed code for unmarried girls. One claim about English marriages made with astonishing frequency and persistence by foreign observers is that English wives, by comparison with their continental peers, lost freedom when they married. They had more before marriage, and less afterwards.[22] It was generally agreed that the foundation of most English marriages was more in affection and less in convenience than abroad, and some commentators judged that marriages remained companionable and affectionate,[23] but there was also a consensus that wives were much subordinated: according to some without coldness in the relationship but, according to others, to an extent that made the wife a stranger and slave or, in a more optimistic impression, an individual left free to educate herself. The French feminist Flora Tristan, who recorded the bleakest of these views of a Victorian wife's life (and who is also fairly clearly embracing bourgeois experience), thought that the husband's tyranny included rampant infidelity.[24]

The remarkable reiteration, to the point of cliché, of this sense that nineteenth-century English women from the higher ranks lost freedom by marriage more thoroughly than in other countries, does suggest that some observers were simply persuaded they had discovered something they expected to discover. But it is a cliché endorsed occasionally by native commentators, including one whose three-year residence in France also left her with the impression that it was French marriages which were the more companionable.[25] And the interesting first half of the cliché, the claim about *pre*-marital freedom for young English women, is supported by a great deal of further comment. Time and again foreign observers were struck by the uninhibited demeanour of unmarried girls—an effect which they interpreted, sexually, as denoting frigidity, or licentiousness, or something in between. There can scarcely be found a comment on young women's demeanour which is not to this effect, and while the

[22] Wey 1856: 169; Blouet 1884: 17; Lecomte 1859: 256; Hennequin 1836: 137; Larcher 1860: ii. 30.

[23] Nougaret 1816: i. 318; Blanc 1867: ii. 89; Trabaud 1853: 191; Wall and Hirsch 1878: 74; Stael-Holstein 1825: 86.

[24] Haussez 1833: i. 48; Simond 1817: i. 36; Tolly 1843: ii. 32; Tristan 1980: 195; Larcher 1860: ii. 36; Defauconpret 1817: ii. 94.

[25] *London Journal*, 20 (1854), 91; *The Key*, 3 (1864), 377; 'Old Maids', *Dublin University Magazine*, 86 (1860), 702–17; Strutt 1857: 138.

occasional dissenting observations do indicate that there was an element of cultural bias involved (with German witnesses sometimes diverging from the consensus, which is mainly French and American in origin)[26] the accumulating picture is impressive. It was not just a matter of how these English girls reacted to foreign interlocutors, but also of their observed behaviour with their English male coevals; and here the impression can be fleshed out with native evidence about the freedom of young people to associate unsupervised, and the conventions which obtained for courting or betrothed couples.

Visitors commented as readily on the easy-going affability of English girls in 1791 or 1809 as they did in the 1860s.[27] To some the content of this easy intercourse seemed entirely high-brow and earnest (even disturbingly so, given the exposed white shoulders of the young women), or the effect was 'remarkably natural' but also 'negatively natural', and possessed of a 'determined innocence'. Many gained an impression that was less null and asexual, even coquettish, but still fundamentally ingenuous. But the unflustered attitude of girls (here again probably middle-class) towards men meant that they responded all too calmly to 'propositions indiscrètes' in the street. Girls were flirtatious in effect if not in intention, and struck some—in fact many—commentators as frankly indecent in their conversation, or sexually shameless and predatory.[28]

The context of this was a greater freedom of movement and association granted to English girls than to their equivalents in other countries. This struck French visitors particularly, it seems, at all periods, but also appeared noteworthy to occasional English commentators.[29] It is well-attested that upper-middle-class girls in London could go shopping and pay visits, for example, without any attendant—and perhaps, as has been suggested in the previous chapter, with enough responsiveness to male passers-by to provoke approaches from them. This freedom ran to a much less restricted and supervised contact between individuals than might be expected, both directly—on social

[26] *Letters from Albion* 1814: i. 91; Niemeyer 1823: 22; Wall and Hirsch 1878: 184.

[27] Geiger 1932: 248; Meister 1799: 55; Taine 1957: 69; J. E. White 1816: i. 41; Austin 1804: 118; Avot 1821: 216.

[28] Andersen 1809: i. 126; Texier 1851: 110; Nadal 1875: 22; J. F. Cooper 1837: ii. 194; Angiolini 1790: i. 91; Fontréal 1875: 61–2, 64; Gourbillon 1817: iii. 349; Nougaret 1816: i. 128; Blouet 1884: 3; Wendeborn 1791: i. 290; Fayet 1846: ii. 840; Larocque 1882: 326; Narjoux 1886: 38; Custine 1830: ii. 474; Prémaray 1851: 87; Pillet 1818: 168–70.

[29] Taine 1957: 71; Lecomte 1859: i. 256; Simond 1817: 36, 46; Fayet 1846: ii. 831; Haussez 1833: i. 85; Ducos 1834: i. 152; Prémaray 1851: 87; Mirecourt 1862: 283; 'Father North' 1844: 72. Also Slidell 1836: ii. 171, Lewald 1851: i. 320, ii. 126.

occasions, domestic visits, and chance outdoor meetings—and indirectly via correspondence (which was not considered a field for
supervision for either betrothed or unbetrothed couples).[30] It is often
implied or expressly said in contemporary accounts of socializing by
the sexes that supervision is perfunctorily performed and readily,
even systematically, avoidable—and there was always the possibility
of footsy-footsy under the table. The chaperonage principle seems to
have been very much an aspect of élite protocol, and no doubt
regarded as a mark of status. This did not prevent its decay over the
century.[31]

A formal betrothal did not have to be ratified before a couple could
detach themselves from the ruck of young things and have an exclusive intimacy; like many of their social inferiors these upper ranks
had a relationship of courtship which might or might not lead to a
privately communicated proposal of marriage. The intimacies
allowed would in France have only been permitted after a firm
betrothal.[32] Above all, however, the relations of betrothed couples
were notably free and close at this level of English society. The sense
that, compared with England, 'there is no other country where two
young people are allowed to know one another well before they
marry' was an impression endorsed often, and in the fullest sense. A
modern historian, weighing the evidence of several groups of family
papers, has concluded that 'extensive physical intimacy was a
respectable and acceptable part of Victorian engagement'.[33] Such
contacts were occasionally, but not normally, visible in public.
However there was little doubt in the minds of commentators that
the more private kinds of contact permitted might lead to sexual
arousal and consummation; the only dispute was over whether this
occurred. An observer at the beginning of the century thought that
betrothed couples remained extraordinarily shy and constrained
despite all the freedoms granted them (this writer is one of the very
few who finds unmarried upper and upper-middle-class English girls

[30] Morgan 1817: i. 315; Haussez 1833: i. 85; *Cassells*, NS 6 (1860), 197; *The Science of Love*
1792: *passim*.

[31] 'Chaperones', *Saturday Review*, 13 (1862), 737–8; 'Match-making Mammas', ibid., 12
(1861), 374–5; Tolly 1843: ii. 32; Shonfield 1987: 42; A. Smith 1856: 91–3, 101; Blanchard
1874; 'Courtship and Marriage', *London Magazine*, NS 4 (1826), 37–44; Curtin 1987:
243–6; Horn 1991: 54.

[32] Taine 1957: 78–9; Fayet 1846: ii. 838.

[33] 'Old Maids', *Dublin University Magazine*, 56 (1860), 702–17; Pontès 1865: 328;
Hennequin 1836: 137; Tolly 1843: ii. 35; Peterson 1989: 75–6.

inhibited in demeanour), but for others 'the familiarities of courtship . . . call the passions into expressive life' in a woman, and could lead to pregnancy.[34]

The evidence almost exclusively points in one direction, but with important divergences: it is united on the freedom and intimacy of young men and women, but divided on sexual meanings and consequences (and here the idea that girls were 'more prudent' in 1842 should be recalled). Can the evidence be harmonized? Much hinges on what one imagines was transacted by the average young girl given that 'dans les receptions et dans les bals, pendant des nuits entières, elle peut . . . aller s'asseoir, les épaules nues et les seins à demi découverts, dans le coin obscur d'une serre . . . en tête-à-tête avec un jeune homme'.[35] Though in its original context this image is meant to suggest the moral tarnishing of English girls it gives the sense of sexually charged, rhapsodic conversation rather than of clandestine physical licence, and such may have been the spirit of much of this young intercourse. In the fashionable world of 1827, it was judged, 'the channels of impure passion, if still broad and deep, are less exposed; the public mind, if not less sensual, is more imaginative'. It is interesting that upper-middle-class girls, at least early in the century, are often deemed 'romantic', by which is meant, quite narrowly, much influenced by modern prose romances.[36]

Another problem with the picture is that it may not be very instructive as to specifically nineteenth-century developments. As in the case of impressions of English marital probity, remarks about what is called, admittedly, a 'modern forwardness' can be traced back at least to the 1780s,[37] and several of the texts I have cited are virtually from this period. It would be hard to make out a case for unmistakable change in the frequency or character of reports of young women's behaviour over the successive decades of the nineteenth century—except in the case of one decade, the 1860s. I have generally refrained from using material from these years, because here the impression of girls' freedom and sexual adventurousness becomes so emphatic that the episode deserves isolating and considering on its own. It is however reasonable to suppose that the 1860s, if they were

---

[34] Wall and Hirsch 1878: 184; Baert 1800: iv. 186; Wade 1859: 373; Blouet 1884: 17; Larocque 1882: 326.

[35] Fontréal 1875: 64.

[36] Thomason 1827: 37; Angiolini 1790: i. 91; Tolly 1843: ii. 32; Avot 1821: 85.

[37] J. Bennett 1789: ii. 169.

being accurately reported, were the climax of some process of intensification of quite long-established tendencies towards free demeanour for young women, and free intercourse of the unmarried, in English upper-middle-class circles.[38]

The evidence for 1860s emancipation comes from an encouragingly wide range of texts, including complaints of a new decline in standards, reminiscences about the period that are nostalgic for the good times it offered, and non-polemical writings (among them some fiction) which incidentally depict emancipated habits. These pieces of evidence would not be very convincing in isolation but they become convincing in the mass. 'Fast'-ness is a key notion (it is primarily girls who are 'fast', but the term could be more widely applied). When a silverfork novelist of 1862 turns aside from her tale of an imaginary *very fast* young lady' to assure her readers that, unthinkably, real-life girls pride themselves on being fast ('Oh, that any British maiden should unblushingly, nay, and without the slightest feeling of shame, even glory in such a title! But so it is, in the year 1861'),[39] she may very naturally strike us as uttering moralistic fustian, but there are impressively many allusions, in an impressive variety of registers, to consciously, cheerfully 'fast' behaviour.

Specific practices indicated a girl's allegiance to the fashion: smoking, for example, or addressing young men by their Christian names.[40] Sexually to be fast was to be daringly uninhibited in talk ('to talk of the young men who "spoon" with them, and discuss with them the merits of "Skittles"'),[41] and daringly intimate with slightly or casually known members of the other sex. There are accounts of flirting carried to a remarkable extreme, to a kind of simulacrum of courtship ('half-engagement', 'playing at lovers').[42] The main issue about the phenomenon of 1860s 'fastness', in the present context, is indeed its relationship to courtship, in an era of flattening nuptial statistics (statistics which were probably even more depressed in the general social ambit of the practitioners of the fast way of life). Was fast behaviour an aspect of the avoidance of marriage, or was it a response by women to shrinking matrimonial prospects?

[38] There are signs that the top tier of English society escaped the influence of 1860s fastness rather fully: see *Fifty Years of London Society* 1920: 11–18 and St Helier 1909: 66–7.

[39] Grey 1862: iii. 304.

[40] *London Reader*, 1 (1863), 665; *Saturday Review*, 11 (1861), 629; 'Modern Manners', *Temple Bar*, 34 (1872), 453–62.   [41] Gronow 1863: 65.

[42] 'Flirts and Flirtation', *Temple Bar*, 26 (1869), 58–67; 'Marriage *versus* Celibacy', *Belgravia*, 6 (1868), 290–7.

There was an enhanced need, or enhanced confidence, or both, among unmarried men and women of the day, in the sense that the *Matrimonial News*, the first periodical to specialize in matrimonial advertisements (they had appeared for many years as part of the ordinary personal advertising of the press), started its long life in 1870. Fast behaviour was interpreted in some quarters as a kind of advertising for marriage, a means of making a more satisfactory choice of husband, and becoming more conspicuous as a potential bride in the 'steeplechase after husbands'. But just as the probity of the literal advertising was doubted ('do all these notices point to something which is not exactly marriage?'), so the behaviour—predictably, but nevertheless with an interesting definiteness—was compared to, and even attributed to, the example of prostitution and courtesanship. The new 'skating over thin ice' indicated that 'the Haymarket gives the law of tone, dress, manner to Rotten-row', and that modern girls wanted to be 'mistaken for a "femme-du-demi-monde", to be insulted when they walk out with their petticoats girt up to their knees . . . and . . . with that indescribably jaunty, "devil-may-care" look'. One account specifies the influence of the Anonyma novels, an interesting group of 1860s publications which do seem to be accurate about prostitution and which were certainly popular in high circles.[43]

In practice even the most rancorous commentators only claimed that this *demi-mondaine* appearance was a precursor of literal unchastity, outside marriage or within it. W. R. Greg seems confident that it was an inevitable extension of the process of matrimonial self-publicizing in an environment in which the courtesan or mistress was a competitor: 'they must imitate that rival circle . . . in its charms . . . its ease and simplicity . . . in the cheerfulness and kindliness of demeanour'.[44] But there does survive one interesting vignette—in the form of a fictional but naturalistic sketch—of an 1860s girl from a 'carriage-people family' who seems to be precisely in a limbo between sexually transgressive behaviour (she lets herself be freely picked up and taken about by men in a manner her parents would never approve) and respectability (she does not appear to have intercourse with the author or with her other casual acquaintances): 'I have . . . tried to ascertain what was the final aim of her gallant

---

[43] 'Love's Fits and Fevers', *Temple Bar*, 26 (1869), 213–23; Gronow 1863: 64–5; 'How to get Married', *Belgravia*, 6 (1868), 531–7; 'Marriage Settlements', *Saturday Review*, 11 (1861), 336–7; Linton 1868; McCarthy 1864; J. E. Ritchie 1859: 82–3.
[44] *Medical Press and Circular*, 1869(2), 92; Greg 1862.

escapades . . . The answers can be reduced to a few words: "Life is dull; I am bored and want some change . . . [my parents] neither know nor care much about what I am doing."[45]

And the phenomenon of fastness was not perceived to be restricted necessarily to the behaviour of unmarried girls; in 'refined society', it was said, 'no one in these days minds being considered *fast*'. There had been a general falling-off in standards back to late eighteenth-century levels, after a recent 'moral oasis . . . which extended at least over the surface of society'. George Sims, a celebrated exposer of slum conditions in the 1880s, thought that 'the serious early and mid-Victorians would have been aghast' at the London night-life of the 'late sixties and well on into the seventies'. Sims, born in 1847, was actually too young to have had much relevant personal experience of the 1860s, and he is writing at a date when anti-Victorianism is already installed; more suggestive is his belief that *later* generations will be taken aback (there was 'a gayer London by night than the twentieth century has ever known'). A writer who had directly experienced and enjoyed 1860s London looked back on the period as the heyday of a vanished boisterousness and freedom, a contrast not to earlier decades (it was 'the tail end of the days of the Regency') but, again, to stifling later ones. Such tributes to the spirit of the 1860s are not negligible.[46]

The free behaviour of young unmarried women in higher circles seems to be echoed right through the English middle class, though ideas were certainly stricter in the heart of this group. The small social band in Colyton's population who had a low rate of pre-nuptial pregnancy (cited in Chapter 2) was mainly composed of a bourgeoisie with teachers, vets, commercial men, and so forth as heads of family. Unless there was some such group, contrasting in its ideas and conventions with the stratum above, the description of the spread of 'rinkomania' quoted above makes no sense. If it is accurate, it is a record of much freer standards prevailing in upper-middle-class families making their impact at the end of the 1870s on the world of the 'parlour' (as this writer labels it).

Quite how substantial this hard centre of the bourgeoisie was is

---

[45] Thieblin 1870: 38.

[46] 'Manners and Morals, as Affected by Civilisation', *Frasers*, 64 (1861), 307–16; Gronow 1863: 324; G. R. Sims 1917: 2, 97–8; D. Shaw 1908: 2. In the early decades of this century the popular historian Ralph Nevill made something of a specialism of nostalgia for a lost gaiety in the period 1860–80.

impossible to assess. It could have extended over the boundary between classes III and IV in the conventional modern scheme, but it is likely that parental supervision and restraint of young people ceased almost completely at the bottom end of the nineteenth-century English middle class. No doubt this was a very different phenomenon, culturally, from the freedom enjoyed by young ladies on their shopping expeditions in Mayfair, but it should not be thought that the effect was a ruffianly orgy of apprentices and their girl-friends. 'When Miss Jemima Higgs has "her young man" . . . he may go to the house and take her out whenever he pleases, and no one dreams of interfering'—though what the couple did when they went out made a strong impression on some foreign observers because it was perforce in public. The girls let themselves be kissed on their lips by their sweethearts in broad daylight and cuddled closely on benches (kisses were essential for the happiness of married and unmarried women alike, raved the *Halfpenny Journal*); the couple strolled about on holidays pressed closely together, holding hands, girl's head on boy's shoulder; they wandered in the evenings—'clerks, shopmen, and shopgirls, very well dressed, and for the most part very respectable'—arms around waists and necks.[47]

These pieces of evidence, cited because they seem to be specifically descriptive of lower-middle-class 'sweethearting', are all late however. They are even arguably a record of the recent influence of sexual conduct in higher social ranks: shopworkers aping the freedoms of the ballroom? or, more plausibly, shopworkers aping the decorums of the ballroom? We are at the difficult boundary or non-boundary between this group and the skilled working class, exactly Francis Place's territory, and more light will be shed on the lower middle class in courtship, and other phases of their sexuality, in connection with the working class.

In general a distinctive *bourgeois* moral culture is hard to identify from the literature, though it is certainly a plausible assumption that such a thing existed. The marital sexuality of this group must remain even more of an enigma than that of the élite above them: almost the only thing that can be said with confidence is that many of them were among the first to use birth control. The extreme rarity of divorce before 1858 means that we have no indications about adultery. Once statutory divorce was introduced the number of suits steadily

[47] Blanchard 1874; Fontréal 1875: 65; Valles 1884: 185; *Halfpenny Journal*, 4 (1864–5), 151; Blouet 1884: 5.

increased, but was always small. It was claimed in 1859 that the middle class in the broadest sense was adulterous: 'the schoolmaster runs away with the wife of his apothecary; the brewer does the fashionable with the attorney's wife; the baker intrigues with the green-grocer's hitherto worthy helpmate'. Is there anything to this other than witty slander? Even harder to assess is a maverick commentator of the 1830s who believed, and was happy to believe, that 'there are, perhaps, few men, and fewer women than is commonly imagined, who have not indulged irregular passions' (he appears to have the middle class in mind). He is happy with the situation because these liaisons are short-term, controlled, and often condoned affairs undertaken with social equals for the sake of sexual variety. They are only reprehensible if they involve 'low and degrading or improper association, indecent exposure of sensual indulgence, and great waste of either time or fortune'.[48]

These are certainly rules of the game that sound likely for a discreetly wife-swapping bourgeoisie; how widely were they played under? The kind of matrimonial partnership implied here does not harmonize with the picture of unequal marriages and subordinated wives so reiterated by foreign observers, and which Flora Tristan, for example, seems to have thought accurate for most of the bourgeoisie, with universal infidelity by husbands its result. Here enters the modern commonplace that Victorian prostitutes were much resorted to by middle-class husbands; but what evidence there is does not support this conjecture, nor the cliché of master–maid liaisons which Tristan favoured.

There was of course also available a burger stereotype, and when this is at work the assumption is that middle-class wives, particularly, are the chastest in the nation. But one may be struck by how relatively powerless this stereotype seems to be in the period. The *Scourge*, an important and still very readable satirical vehicle for mercantile middle-class views in the second decade of the century, shows an interesting instability on this: sometimes virtue is centred in 'the middle classes of society; the wives and daughters of professional men; the families of individuals of respectable connections; and the fair inhabitants of our provinces'. But for the *Scourge* in another mood 'the family parlour of the middle classes' where 'morality holds her court' is being destroyed. The burger stereotype is modulated by one

---

[48] 'Man in the Club-Window' 1859: 371; Walker 1840: 181–2.

commentator (admittedly a devout Calvinist) so that the moral pre-eminence of the bourgeoisie is only relative: 'immeasurably fewer' adulteries occur among them than among the aristocracy, but immorality still 'prevails to a considerable extent'. The more usual comparative framework within which middle-class behaviour was set was probably that of its own past, where Francis Place set it, with a great improvement noted after about 1800, again like Place. Often, perhaps generally, this is seen as part of an escalator-like movement, with the middle-class family simply riding upwards morally, together with all higher ranks (and occasionally some lower).[49]

Such reports tell us that middle-class family life was getting more decorous (for example, that around 1780 the wives of respectable tradesmen had sung songs to their guests which by the 1830s could not be among the wares of a decent bookseller), but they do not say anything directly about marital sexuality. Rather more can be gleaned about male pre-marital behaviour. In terms of London night-life there is good evidence that the specifically middle-class bachelor stepped on the escalator of restraint before his upper-class colleague. William Acton, whose brilliant and strangely toned accounts of London night-life in *Prostitution* are the most valuable things he wrote, and exceptional in the period, is very precise about this. As a qualified doctor returning from his studies in Paris in 1840 he found himself among 'compeers of the middle-classes', 'gents', 'snobs' who, while not behaving with the 'disorder' of their fathers, still surprised him by their 'promiscuous viciousness and constant craving after fresh artificial excitements'. By 1857, the time at which he writes, 'your snob *pur sang*' has left the West End and is 'girding up his loins for the race of life, is "coaching" himself in his Crosby Halls and in the public libraries, chess clubs, debating societies' (Shepherd Taylor, whose diary is quoted in the previous chapter, was a medical student of exactly this generation). According to Acton, the 'gently born and bred . . . now rule at Cremorne and in the Haymarket'; on the other hand he would have agreed that the 'gent' (who was 'in his glory about the year 1847') was by 1860 'nowhere to be seen'.[50]

This may seem rather inconsistent with the degree of reform of

[49] W. B. Adams 1832: 49; *Scourge*, 5 (1813), 204; 2 (1811), 23; Grant 1837: i. 274; Corry 1820: 35; G. R. Porter 1836: 239–40; C. Knight 1864: i. 221; Tolly 1843: ii. 181–2; Angelo 1828: i. 284; Sargant 1857: 384.

[50] W. Acton 1857b: 166; 'The Morals of the Decade', *Temple Bar*, 4 (1862), 288–94. For medical students see also J. E. Ritchie 1857: 109–10.

(authentically) gentlemanly night-life by mid-century claimed by the observers I cited at the beginning of this section, but all these chronological markers are just breaks in a continuum made according to taste. The important point is the relatively early buttoning-up of groups like medical students. Others dated even this change somewhat further back, like a writer of 1844: 'we find an obvious difference of characteristic between the bachelor of (say) some ten years ago, and today. Science and Utilitarianism have marvellously modified the objects of his ambition'; then it was all-night roistering, now the Regent Street Polytechnic and the hope of meeting a girl in a lecture. A late 1850s guide to *London by Night* is not tongue-in-cheek (as any book with such a title thirty years earlier surely would have been) when it announces that 'to indulge moderately in the gaieties of life forms, in some measure, a CORRECT portion of the education of the man of the world'. This is just a rather timid assertion of a young man's right to have a good time, on behalf of a readership who genuinely would not have welcomed too rakish a programme of entertainments (and the listings include the Polytechnic as well as the Holborn Casino, the Soane Museum as well as the Coal Hole).[51]

One of the most familiar features of the Victorian stereotype is prudery. To the extent that prudery was a real phenomenon it was probably (as, indeed, the stereotype would have it) most notably an aspect of the behaviour of the social groups discussed so far, especially the middle-class groups. But the evidence about it is also too problematical simply to be put alongside relatively solid evidence about other aspects of sexual behaviour, and must be dealt with on its own. The worst problems concern the quality of the available information and not, or not to the extent that is sometimes alleged, its possible significance. That is to say, I can see no reason for declining to treat some kinds of linguistic euphemism, for example, or the tabooing of sexual topics in conversation, as good evidence about sexual beliefs and even practices. It is plausible that a married woman who exhibited this behaviour in public would be reticent about sex to some degree in private, with her husband, and plausible in turn that this reticence would have some inhibiting effect on the character of her sexual relations with him. In fact one reason for concluding that prudery was not as widespread in the Victorian middle class as we may suppose is the onset of contraception, examined in the previous

---

[51] 'Father North' 1844: 12; *London by Night* ?1857: p. v.

chapter. The barrier methods resorted to would generally have required candid reference to organs and actions as between husband and wife. Peter Gay has argued that even withdrawal by the husband would have been agreed upon by both partners in advance.[52]

It is true, as is often pointed out, that to avoid or repress a sexual implication is to show that you are conscious of it (and some euphemisms—such as 'unmentionables' for trousers—seem almost to be jocular about the matter), but such a consciousness, even if it were significant, was supposedly evinced in a group of alleged usages—those, such as 'bosom' for 'breast' of chicken, where a secondary or unapparent meaning is censored—of generally rather doubtful authenticity. Speaking of 'prostitutes' rather than 'whores', or declining to mention these individuals at all, does not show a betraying alertness to sexual meanings.

People can, of course, be hypocrites, and it is not only twentieth-century popular opinion which has been quick to resort to this thought in passing judgement on the Victorians; the contemporary literature is rich in allegations that the famous 'English prudery' was all 'cant'. But it is important in assessing these accusations, when they make a show of offering some kind of evidence, to ask whether the inconsistencies that are being pointed out (the wearing of low-cut dresses by verbally prim ladies, for instance) can only be explained as dishonesties. Codes about what can be uttered or mentioned or countenanced socially may be genuinely more severe than codes about physical exposure in some contexts—such as sea-bathing, male urination, and women's evening-dress. And while sexual prudishness obviously has an affinity, in its effects, with notions of etiquette and refined or polite behaviour, the development of the latter, which has been traced over many centuries of European history by Norbert Elias, seems to be independent of sexual codes. In the modern West we have conventions about recreational nudity and about privacy for washing and evacuation which may appear completely out of step with one another: nudists do not use multiple or mixed sex latrines. Here, in fact, lies a better possibility of driving a wedge between the behaviour of a bourgeois wife in the drawing-room and her behaviour in the bedroom. Is it really, or at least only, a *sexual* prudishness which makes trousers 'unmentionables' and, even, makes it incorrect to allude to a woman's pregnancy?

[52] Gay 1984: 275.

If the evidence about prudery were definite and detailed, in other words, it might be possible to make quite confident speculations about aspects of middle-class sexual behaviour. The trouble is that the evidence is so poor. On one hand there is a linguistic record in the form of the history of certain coinages, the character of middle-class conversation as recorded in fiction, and the lexis and semantics of the texts which the middle classes liked to read—of their newspapers and magazines for example. This is directly available for us to judge today and it obviously has a story to tell. The host of prudish innovations in English vocabulary collected by Peter Fryer in *Mrs Grundy* (1963) is impressive. And no reader adjusted to late twentieth-century standards of use and mention can escape the sense of strict exclusion of certain kinds of material wherever he or she may turn in the domain of respectable middle-class reading in the nineteenth century: the point is so familiar that it would be platitudinous to dwell on it.

This surviving linguistic record is none the less fairly inscrutable. It points to an early date for the upsurge of English euphemism, as most of Fryer's examples come from the late eighteenth century, but who was using the new shamefaced vocabulary, and in what contexts? One of the most commonly cited anecdotes concerning changed linguistic standards—Scott's story of his elderly female relation who is startled to remind herself of the vocabulary that was used in the reading of her girlhood (in this case, the novels of Aphra Behn)—dates from about the turn of the century.[53] It may indicate both the social level from which a new prudery first radiated, and the area in which it first made an impact, namely, leisure reading. The celebrated operations of the Bowdler family on Shakespeare (though there are some precedents for these as far back as the 1740s) date from 1807.

It would however be wrong to think of the new tone of the written word just as a matter of militant middle-class Evangelicalism forcing itself on society. John Keats's publishers, Taylor and Hessey, wanted him to fudge the fact that Porphyro and Madeleine, in 'The Eve of St Agnes', have sexual intercourse, and a few years later a man who also wrote for them sometimes, William Hazlitt, was cleaning up his letters to his friend Patmore for publication in *Liber Amoris*. The latter, Hazlitt's account of his futile infatuation with his London landlady's

[53] Lockhart 1837: v. 136–7.

daughter, Sarah Walker, seemed embarrassingly candid to some contemporaries, and still has a power to disturb by its raw self-exposure.
A good deal in the way of direct sexual allusion is omitted in the published version, however. While some of these omissions may have
been motivated by embarrassment—as when Hazlitt deletes certain
anxious-sounding references to the size of the penises of potential
rivals for Sarah's favours—he also leaves out boastful remarks about
how he will 'make her the best bedfellow in the world' and how
'she'll have enough of my conversation and of something else before
she has done with me'. Although there is a general tendency in *Liber
Amoris* to make the whole experience, on the author's side, rather
more high-minded than it had been in practice, there is no shunning
the possibility—far from it, indeed—that Sarah Walker may have
been a cold-hearted flirt.

The main difference between the original accounts and the published version is that, for example, Sarah's sitting on Hazlitt's lap and
'fondling' of him 'sometimes for half a day together' is specified, in
the former, to be 'rubbing against me, hard at it for an hour together'
while 'I poked her up'. In another omission, what the published text
calls darkly 'exposures from the conversations below-stairs' is spelt
out as an overheard exchange, traumatic for Hazlitt, about the 'seven
inches' of another lodger. This ribald conversation, if it really took
place, is instructive in itself. It involved Sarah's mother (whose husband was a tailor) and her staff in the lodging-house. Sarah is present
but Hazlitt does not have her joining in, and while he often broods
on how 'she wanted only a codpiece' and 'runs mad for size' he also
consistently described her as refined and even puritanical in her
demeanour. The briefly glimpsed Walker household in Southampton
Buildings, Chancery Lane, thus makes an intriguing adjunct to
Francis Place's picture of life in the same setting, at the same
period.[54]

The second kind of evidence about prudery is indirect, in the form
of contemporary depictions of prudish speech and behaviour. Since
these are always more or less disparaging in their approach, and frequently contaminated by the chauvinism of foreign observers, it is
hard to draw conclusions from them about real practices. They too
point to an early date for a vigorous prudery in some quarters: Mrs
Grundy, after all, the byword for censoriousness right through the

---

[54] Sikes 1979: 265, 270–1, 286–7; Hazlitt 1985: 80–1.

nineteenth century, makes her appearance (or more strictly non-appearance) in a play of 1792. In 1835 Byron seems to have thought that 'cant and . . . squeamishness in point of language' were of at least several decades standing, and from the outset of the century there are suggestions of a very considerable percolation of some kinds of prudishness through the ranks of English society—down to servant level or lower, so that 'even the coal-porter and the butcher's-boy *perspire*'.[55]

But this particular example of prudishness is so hackneyed that one may well doubt if the writer ever heard a worker, of any sort, use the word 'perspire'. In general there is a suspiciously small repertoire of linguistic usages which is continually cited in the literature about English prudery. When these also crop up in English jibes about America the whole business starts to look like a hall of mirrors in which only fantasies are reflected. Chickens, with their legs and breasts, and furniture, with its legs, are the commonest elements in these symmetrical accusations. There was some confusion, apparently, in the minds of French commentators as to whether in the case of furniture the concealment was verbal (sometimes said to involve substituting 'feet' for 'legs', which seems odd) or physical, so that the English housewife inoffensively deploying a tablecloth could fall foul of these Gallic thought-police. Occasionally a French observer will break ranks and deny that a breast of chicken is called anything but a breast of chicken in English households. A French critic will sometimes be unable to find expressions permissible in his *own* language to refer to the spade that is no longer being called a spade in English, so that English doctors are twitted for speaking of 'brisements du vent' rather than 'flatuosités' and of 'emotions exterieures' rather than 'evacuations naturelles'.[56]

In the last resort it is really very uncertain that there was any significant difference in levels of linguistic prudery between France and England in the nineteenth century. However, both countries may well have been more notable for a prudishness of etiquette than Germany[57] and, despite the strong presence of stereotype in English satire on American manners, it does seem that prudishness had its firmest grip on society on the other side of the Atlantic. The best evidence for this is not so much the quality of some English descriptions

[55] 'A.D.' 1835; Gourbillon 1817: iii. 356; *A View of London* 1803–4: 121.
[56] Texier 1851: 39; Sarrazin 1816: i. 173; Gourbillon 1817: iii. 358.
[57] Fontane 1939: 61.

(though Frances Trollope's examples of American prudishness have an unhackneyed, authentic feel to them) but rather the readiness with which American writers accuse their own society of being prudish, or accept and even welcome accusations to this effect, plus—what is more interesting for our purposes—a general agreement among them that England is less so. This marks American opinion off from French, which liked to accuse Albion of combining stuffiness and coarseness.

Some Americans simply shared Mrs Trollope's sense that American girls exhibited prudery rather than probity, while others defended their society with the argument that what she saw as prudery was a justified moral indignation. Some even embraced the accusation in its raw form: 'I hope the charge will always remain a true one'.[58] Conversely, many Americans noticed (whether approvingly or disapprovingly) the relative lack of inhibition in English manners. Their remarks about the behaviour of girls in the upper and middle classes have already been cited. They also found the performances and the audiences in the theatres lubricious, the tone of conversation between strangers too lax. They noticed 'less sham' on illegitimacy and other sexual topics, more 'contempt for any fine-strained purity, any special squeamishness' at all levels, 'from peer to peasant'. They reported that English and French opinion concurred in attributing to reduced American virility the American distaste for discussion of mistresses, among élite cultivated men.[59] (Comments in the latter vein are particularly interesting, both because they are unexpected and because they presumably have a close bearing on sexual codes.)

As I mentioned in connection with popular perceptions of hypocrisy in sexual matters, some of the things which could have shocked a prudish American in England (or even gratified an unbuttoned one) may be less relevant to sexuality than appears. Men bathed naked in sight of women well on in the century, and were apparently still urinating in primitive conveniences close to the pavements of major streets in the 1850s. When contemporaries tried to relate such features of the society's etiquette to sexual standards there was no unanimity as to their meaning. On one account the fact

[58] Lester 1841: i. 323; Trollope 1949: 135–6; Child 1835: ii. 267; Bartlett 1852: 93; Silliman 1812: i. 266.
[59] Thorburn 1835: 35; Slidell 1836: i. 265–6; Ballard 1913: 31; Wheaton 1830: 193; R. G. White 1881: 88–9; J. F. Cooper 1837: ii. 197; Hawthorne 1863: ii. 127–8; Dana 1921: 162–3.

that respectable women remained where they could see men coming
naked out of the sea was Mrs Grundyish—since to move away would
be to betray a compromising awareness of the spectacle—but on
another view these women were indeed avid for the sight of male
nudity (even if they were likely to be disappointed by 'the action of
cold water').[60] The 'indifference' and 'unabashed' air with which men
turned aside, even when accompanied by women, to urinate within
public view could seem a disgusting anomaly, especially as 'we see
him unbutton a garment which our conventional decency forbids us
to name', and the scantiness of the tent-lavatories at Ascot—and the
lightheartedness with which the resulting exposure was treated—
were invoked as evidence that English prudery was superficial. But
later in the century the very absence of lavatories in streets and other
places of public resort was interpreted as a prudish evasion of physical realities.[61]

On the behaviour which relates more directly to sexual codes it is
very hard to come to a verdict. Different contexts undoubtedly called
forth different behaviours: men going out together in London's West
End or women at the theatre would be more receptive to dirty jokes
and loose talk than they were at home, but was the difference in standards a massive discontinuity, a towering precipice of Podsnappery?
Dickens's caricature of bourgeois *pudeur* recalls one thing which
probably always acted to mitigate extremes of prudishness, namely,
the readiness with which such behaviour was seen as absurd, especially when linked to religious narrowness or social pretension: the
pages of a popular and respectable family weekly such as *Cassells*,
around 1860, will be found to be full of humour about prudery.

But one might insist that there is no smoke without fire, and it is
significant that even a French observer who liked the repressive
demeanour of English middle-class wives judged that they took vigilance too far.[62] So were the American visitors who admired the lack
of 'fine-strained purity' in English etiquette just applying the wrong
measuring-rod? Their testimony would at least confirm that a really
ostentatious or extreme prudishness was not generally acceptable.
But another reality of middle-class culture seems also to have been a
genuine and deeply rooted commitment to a fineness or purity of

[60] Wey 1856: 302–3; S. M. Ellis 1925: 80–1. See also Gay 1984: 338; Lindridge 1850: 96;
Trudgill 1976: 6–7.
[61] Dolby 1830: 6; F. Cooper 1851: 18–19; Hamerton 1889: 310; Wey 1856: 304–5.
[62] Fayet 1846: ii. 849.

tone in respect of sexual matters, a commitment bound up, for example, with national pride. It was not necessarily a militant belief, and punctiliousness in this area may in fact have been unfashionable; indeed candour and intimacy in conversational etiquette between the sexes probably increased, while men's private talk became cleaner. Prudery, in other words, ran deep rather than shallow. It may have led in some cases to an actual exclusion of basic sexual knowledge from young people's awareness, but this was an extreme result which respectable opinion did not defend, and sometimes actively deplored.[63]

III

The Growth of Working-Class Respectability

There is usually no mistaking when the nineteenth-century working class is being reported in the contemporary literature. At this level, descriptions generally come clearly labelled as accounts of the working or 'labouring' population, or of some part of this population, such as the factory operatives, or the rural workers, or the metropolitan poor. These descriptions are almost always offered by outsiders conscious that they have something to report (or to claim to be reporting) which is unfamiliar to their readership, and very often with an axe to grind. The element of partisanship and prejudice makes much of this material utterly untrustworthy as information about working-class sexuality, and only significant as an expression of various assumptions about sex (and in this connection some of it will be cited later in this study).

The fact that most observers were visiting working-class neighbourhoods, homes, and institutions as outsiders must also bear on the accuracy of their findings, but not in a way it is easy to make allowances for, and the internal evidence of individual texts is bound to become important, intuitive though judgements about this have to be. Some, perhaps even most, nineteenth-century descriptions of the private aspects of working-class life disable themselves—or, in extreme cases, reveal themselves to be imaginary—by failing to allow for the observer and his or her impact. It is one of the many distinctions of Mayhew's work (even by comparison with his fellow

[63] Hamerton 1889: 229–32; A. West 1897; S. Lewis 1839: 72–4; O'Donnoghue 1836: p. iv.

correspondents on the *Morning Chronicle*) that he describes himself as having human relations with working-class people—not only in listening to their stories, but also in arguing with them and even buying them meals.

Urban missionaries sometimes describe the reaction of the poor to their tract-distributing and sermonizing visits, but it is astonishing how seldom secular observers tell us how the occupants of a lodging-house dormitory or a Liverpool cellar, or the audience at a penny gaff or a music saloon, responded to the fact that a middle-class individual (probably censorious and sober) was observing them. Sometimes these visits were made in the company of policemen, but it is only very rarely that the poor are seen to be affected by the law. A sense of fantasy is in fact strong in much of this material: things are witnessed which the alleged conditions—of noise and darkness for example—should render unobservable. Texts in which a hypothetical mode is explicit ('imagine, if you will, that you are climbing the filthy, flimsy staircase to one of these abominable nests') are perhaps just being honest about a principle which informs a great deal of this writing.[64] Authors commonly wrote anonymously or pseudonymously, and this assisted the creation of imaginary personalities for the observers. Robert Lamb wrote about working-class life in *Frasers* as 'R.L.' but also as 'A Manchester Man', and these are such different personae that when he comes to pull the essays together in one volume, under his own name, he appears bizarrely inconsistent in his knowledge of Lancashire life.

Francis Place was less of an outsider than most commentators in the field, and he claimed that working-class sexual morality had undergone a revolution around the turn of the century. It was, however, a more limited claim than might appear. Place himself seems to have thought that it did apply outside London, his main area of observation, but not to an important non-metropolitan group of workers, the factory hands. He declared that he would 'rather be hanged here in London, than be compelled to live in one of our large manufacturing towns', no doubt partly because of the moral conditions he perceived to obtain in these centres. He accepted one of the most preposterous of all claims made about factories and sex—Gaskell's theory that the heat in the workspace excited sexual drives

---

[64] For a possible case of a middle-class author fabricating a night, *à la* Orwell, in a Bath lodging-house see G. Davis 1990.

precociously—and (against the grain of his meliorist temperament) thought that the working class in Manchester had deteriorated.[65]

One eminent historian of the period has argued that Place's picture, though accurate, applies very specifically to London, and that industrialization and the economic aftermath of the Napoleonic wars brought about very different results for working-class life in the rest of the country. There is also the important point that Place's London was vanishing demographically in the nineteenth century: for the city's expansion was due to in-migration as well as natural growth and, while the effects were interestingly less marked in strictly working-class areas, even here only half the residents were London-born by the 1860s (while the groups at the working- and middle-class borderline who mainly interested Place were experiencing particularly high levels of non-London infiltration).[66]

It is nevertheless possible to make a case—in the spirit of Place, though not according to his letter—for increasing English working-class respectability in most areas from early in the nineteenth century, and in this new respectability a change in sexual standards seems often to be involved (but there are certainly difficulties about the association of the two things, which will be tackled in due course). As far as the factory population goes, this means flatly dissenting from Place's view. And it entails that the demographic upheavals of nineteenth-century London did not disrupt processes of moral change which Place had discerned around 1800. Place's emphasis on a fairly superior stratum of the working class can be retained, but it must also be said that the aspirations that were so characteristic of the London artisans described by Place seem to have been widely pervasive right through the English working class. Even among the irreducible bottom tier of humanity, as surveyed by Mayhew at the mid-century in *London Labour and the London Poor*, sexual codes varied in strictness.[67]

---

[65] Miles 1988: 170; Ratcliffe and Chaloner 1977: 47.

[66] George 1925: 1, 17; Wohl 1977: 21–2; Dyos and Wolff 1973: ii. 362, 373.

[67] Mayhew sets the size of this class at 50,000, or about one-fortieth of the city's population, which is inadequate to his title. It is something of a mystery why Mayhew's 'cyclopaedia' of this subject became such a very restricted survey of, in effect, London street-folk, since his research, as first undertaken for the *Morning Chronicle*, had originally been much broader in coverage (see Himmelfarb 1971). The dimensions of the complete body of poor Londoners which the *Morning Chronicle* would have dealt with can be suggested on the strength of figures mentioned earlier in this chapter: a group at least five times the size of Mayhew's eventual cohort was involved in unskilled labour, when it was employed at all.

How poor, in fact, was 'poor'? What should we be visualizing as
the material conditions of the nineteenth-century working class when
we seek to reconstruct sexual codes? Working-class standards of
living, how much they altered, and in which direction, are intensely
controversial subjects with historians, which it would be pointless to
try to form a judgement on here.[68] But working-class housing is a less
obscure topic, and one very relevant to sexual morality, if only
because of the great emphasis put on overcrowding and sexual
licence by nineteenth-century observers. Nationally the ratio of
people to houses remained fairly constant through the century, or
improved slightly, but working-class densities per house were obviously higher than for other classes (perhaps half as high again in
accommodation less than a quarter the size). A constant national ratio
together with enlarging accommodation for the middle and upper
classes entailed an increase in working-class crowding in some areas.
There were rising densities in Liverpool in the 1830s, but on the
other hand levels were constant in the equally working-class cities of
Leeds and Wolverhampton in the first part of the century, and in
Newcastle after the mid-century. Even the Liverpool figures are
below the national average. In the Newcastle region as a whole, as
with the Liverpool region, even the early decades of industrialisation
did not bring increasing densities.[69]

The case for deteriorating working-class housing is in fact more
promising when argued in relation to a smaller scale (but by the same
token in relation to smaller numbers of workers). The image of small
and often inconspicuous but extremely crowded and squalid areas of
housing—'slums' and 'rookeries'—is a cliché of the period so frequently to be encountered that it needs no illustrating, but what
degree of objective degradation of working-class life does it represent? A problem that besets this enquiry is that contemporary comment was itself extremely rookery-minded and commonly restricts
itself for perfectly honourable reasons to the worst cases. This is a
general feature of reports of working-class deprivation and suffering
in the period: it was naturally considered a sufficient cause for concern if *some* families of six were forced to inhabit subterranean rooms
ten foot square, if *some* children were beaten to keep them working
for twelve hours in a mill, and if *some* Londoners were dirty, ragged,

---

[68] See A. J. Taylor 1975: *passim*, and Blythell 1974.
[69] Wohl 1971; Palgrave 1869; Chadwick 1965: 5; Beames 1850: 20; Burnett 1978: 91–2;
Daunton 1983: 16; Ginswick 1983: i. 216; Fleischman 1985: 308–9; D. J. Rowe 1990.

and emaciated beyond belief. In the case of investigations into housing it was perfectly normal practice simply to disregard the handful of superior houses in a predominantly poor neighbourhood. But without intending an impiety to the atrocious experiences of many thousands of nineteenth-century men and women, or any belittling of the compassion of Mayhew, the indignation of Engels, and the social dedication of Chadwick, the historian must ask what the whole picture was like. I have reviewed the evidence in an appendix, because the facts are somewhat surprising; it is important to bear them in mind when one is envisaging working-class domestic life in nineteenth-century England.

It emerges that at least a third of English working-class housing was decent or more than decent, and at least a third poor or wretched. It would be wrong to play down the latter proportion, of course, especially if it is judged that a good share of the remaining third of homes was also of a poor standard. But this seems unlikely. Vague though the vocabulary of contemporary inquiry was ('respectable', 'comfortable', 'uncomfortable', 'decent', 'wretched', 'indifferent', etc.) one can generally be confident that any underlying bias was towards a negative rather than positive verdict on working-class housing. In the stables from which most of the surveys come, especially the London and Manchester Statistical Societies and Chadwick's 1842 sanitary report testimony, there was a strong inclination to find evidence for what had already been assumed as a fact, namely, the dire condition of workers' housing. In view of this, the one-third figure for bad accommodation is likely to be about a maximum; certainly it would be wrong to suppose that such intermediate classifications as 'neat' or 'middling' were self-consoling middle-class euphemisms for something much worse.

The high levels of 'comfortable' accommodation found in the surveys do partly reflect the admixture of economically superior families in almost every working-class neighbourhood, which was so thorough as usually to frustrate the search for the pure slum. For most of the century the working-class residential districts in English towns, particularly, remained very unsegregated economically, often housing the whole range of working-class groups from the least skilled labourers through to skilled artisans in a mix that sorted them on no more than a street-by-street scale. In fact one may doubt if there was a single street in any nineteenth-century English city which was a complete Tom All Alone's, a site of absolutely uniform and abject poverty.[70] But it is also clear that a spontaneous drive towards domestic respectability was widespread, which often brought it about that any potential for decency was fully exploited—and without which a more-than average prosperity or especially favourable physical amenities would not have produced the high observed standards of some working-class accommodation.

The relative contributions of economic and moral factors are admittedly never easy to assess. Even the slums of Merthyr Tydfil (which one commentator said exhibited 'misery, degradation, and suffering, I shall remember to the end of my life') contained pockets of respectability, but was this because of the presence of ironworker-families, who had a reputation for turning their small and poorly built cottages into 'the very type of cleanliness and order'? In Liverpool the sharp contrasts in respectability to be observed from street to street were matched by variations of over 100 per cent in average numbers per house, but one observer put economic factors second as an explanation of these abrupt differences between streets ('it is not so much the mere earnings, as the *spending*, of wages which causes the change'), and quotes a comment by a housewife which does indicate an ideological dimension to such effects: 'in this court we are all trying to keep ourselves decent, and there are no prostitutes amongst us'. On the other hand when the *Morning Chronicle*'s correspondent—refining the scale still further—noticed within one Liverpool court a house of 'great propriety', the key to its difference turned out to be that the occupant was a bespoke dressmaker rather than a slop-worker. The chequering of domestic respectability in Manchester was often noted: in the late 1850s, round the corner from 'black spots', there were housewives who kept the pavement outside their houses even cleaner than their kitchens, and 'dirty' and 'clean' families were observed to come in clusters. The more respectable workers could be actually unaware of the degraded conditions in which their neighbours lived. In Oldham the very poorest accommodation, the cellars, varied from abominable to 'beautifully clean'.[71]

One group certainly at the bottom of nineteenth-century society was the Irish poor: yet in London Mayhew found among these a

---

[70] Dennis 1984: 66–7, 214–15, 218–20; Green and Parton 1990; G. Davis 1990. Cf. Ward 1978.

[71] Ginswick 1983: i. 98–9, iii. 52, 87; Kenrick 1846; Dennis 1984: 60; Shimmin 1862: 116, 1864: 58; *Morning Chronicle*, 24 June 1850, p. 5; Rushton 1909: 231; Lamb 1866: i. 3; W. E. Adams 1903: ii. 385; Oats 1864–5; Rowley 1899: 8.

degree of 'household care and neatness', and 'comfort and cleanliness', both in their slum dwellings and their lodging-houses, which he called startling. Mayhew also noted how far down the ranks of the London costermongers ran the effort to make their homes respectable: all but the most destitute achieved some decency against the odds. Less sympathetic observers than Mayhew (who are responsible for the mass of the surviving comment) greatly underestimated the scale of respectable living that was achieved in the slums and rookeries they demonized.[72] In the country too, there were abrupt moral discontinuities which seemed inexplicable: one village would be all drinking, betting and cock-fighting, while two miles away 'in a neighbouring village, or hamlet . . . you may find the bulk of the inhabitants fond of reading, and conversant with the poets'. The scene here is the North Midlands in the 1820s. Even among agricultural workers in this part of England too poor and hard-worked to know anything of books an exceptionally high moral spirit could prevail.[73]

Sexual moralism was an important aspect of the ideal of domestic respectability. That antagonism to the moral taint of prostitution evinced in one small neighbourhood in Liverpool crops up elsewhere (while in provincial Lancashire, in the last third of the century, even an unmarried couple aroused the indignation of 'virtuously vicious' women in the same street). Prostitute funerals in London's East End were apparently liable to be hooted and stoned by 'the virtuous matrons of the neighbourhood'—who, according to Nathaniel Hawthorne's impression, were often a conspicuous if small admixture in slum areas. (By contrast, with no apparent economic rhyme or reason, one London East End court is reported as being on excellent terms with its two resident prostitutes.) William Swan, admittedly a Baptist, twice felt forced to move from lodgings in the Stratford area of London because of the immorality of landladies (in the second house there was 'a married man constantly visiting and the husband not ignorant of it').[74]

The drive to working-class sexual respectability, where it arose, showed a remarkable power to overcome the most important physical constraint in working-class life, namely, domestic crowding. Nineteenth-century middle-class opinion had a strongly environmen-

---

[72] Mayhew 1861–2: i. 47–8, 111; G. Davis 1990.
[73] Thomson 1847: 227; Snell 1936: 24.
[74] Allen Clarke ('Ben Adhem'), *Liverpool Weekly Post*, 26 May 1934, p. 2; Rogers 1913: 4; Hawthorne 1863: ii. 200–1; T. Wright 1868: 142; Swan 1970: 77.

talist bias, as I explain in Chapter 5, and was on the whole incredu-
lous that physical proximity could be other than morally depraving.
The belief that individuals who dressed, slept, washed, and excreted
very near each other were much more likely to have sexual intercourse seems to have been practically universal. Some otherwise sensible commentators, such as Joseph Kay, dwelt obsessively on the
idea of incestuous and freely copulating working-class people in very
crowded environments. The proof usually offered of the connection
between crowding and sexual licence was simply a kind of thought
experiment: high densities of unmarried individuals in beds or bedrooms were alleged, and the reader then invited to draw the supposedly inevitable conclusion about sexual outcomes.

Only occasionally was evidence produced that the worst had happened. Apart from the broad truth of multi-occupied beds and bedrooms the facts mustered by investigators keen to prove the
crowding/sexual licence hypothesis now tend to seem strangely feeble. One much cited testimony was that of Riddall Wood, giving evidence in Chadwick's sanitary report. He had visited slum housing in
a variety of centres—Manchester, Liverpool, Ashton-under-Lyne,
Hull, and Pendelton—and gives several anecdotes of crowding of the
sexes, but this was the mouse that emerged when he was asked to
summarize his findings on 'persons of different sexes sleeping
promiscuously': 'I think I am speaking within bounds when I say I
have amongst my memoranda above 100 cases, including, of course,
cases of persons of different sexes sleeping in the same room.' Yet
these 'memoranda', amounting to very little more than a reiteration
of the familiar truth of overcrowding, are endlessly quoted by subsequent commentators as a proof of the fact of general working-class
sexual depravity under these conditions.[75]

Riddall Wood does cite a pair of prostitutes who said they had
been corrupted by sharing accommodation with married couples. We
also have, however, the very words of a prostitute from the Home
Counties on this question, and her testimony is oddly half-hearted:

If it hadn't been that we were all forced to undress ourselves before one
another, and five of us to sleep in the same room, I do think—though perhaps that wasn't the only reason—that I should not have been leading this
life I now am. If there had been no one else sleeping in the same room, I
might perhaps have fallen into this way, but I don't think I should have gone
wrong so soon.

[75] Chadwick 1965: 192–3.

A modern historian has concluded from a survey of statements made by unmarried mothers applying to London's Foundling Hospital that 'they throw serious doubt on the idea that housing and working conditions at that time gave the popular classes a broad familiarity with sexual matters'. In the last decades of the century parental reticence on sex in front of children was so great that some working-class sons and daughters in London remained ignorant about basic information into adult life.[76] Examples were reported in the literature of illegitimate births to women who had been made pregnant by men in crowded accommodation, but the general statistics of illegitimacy showed no correlation with density in housing; this was carefully demonstrated in 1862. Marriage rates tended to peak in the autumn and early winter, and, for country districts at least, this may be linked to the high known rates of pre-nuptial pregnancy; in other words, according to a modern study, 'in the crowded housing conditions of the period, courtships involving intimacy would be more likely to occur in the summer than in the winter months'. Mothers' depositions concerning illegitimate births in rural Kent often cite sexual encounters at summer festivities.[77]

This puts the relation between crowding and sexual licence in a startlingly new light—indeed it completely reverses the nineteenth-century wisdom on the question. While it may not have been universally true that courtships were conducted more intensely outdoors (the persistence of 'bundling' in some districts will be discussed later), and while acceptable thresholds of exposure of bodies and bodily functions may have been lower in working-class than in middle-class homes, there is much anecdotal evidence of working-class households trying to mitigate the effects of proximity—so much so that one historian of slum housing has written of her continual surprise at 'the extent to which the poor strove . . . to conform to middle-class standards of morality'.[78] Nineteenth-century observers were so keen to discern depravity that the meaning of their own observations sometimes has to be read against the grain of the surrounding argument. A writer who took refuge early in the morning in a Northumberland cottage, to wait for a coach, gives a vivid and important picture of how decency could be maintained in crowded rural accommodation:

---

[76] *Morning Chronicle*, 28 Oct. 1850, p. 5; Barret-Ducrocq 1991: 112; E. Ross 1982.
[77] Lumley 1862; Mills 1980: 12–14; Reay 1990.   [78] Gauldie 1974: 22.

we were at once astounded, and we will confess it, in some degree amused, to behold one after another of the family creeping forth from some unseen places in the room; some were still asleep; some, a married couple, were having breakfast, and some dressing themselves, thus, the whole of this large family slept, and had their meals in the same room.

But in the same volume this writer fulminates about the 'over-mastering circumstances' which result in incest, and about how it is 'beyond all conception' that 'unutterable horrors' do not take place in crowded cottages, apparently unconscious that he has convincingly described (though as a merely surprising and amusing feature of working-class life) how circumstances were resisted and horrors avoided.[79]

The *Morning Chronicle*, often unfashionable on such topics, gave due weight to the 'praiseworthy effort . . . for the conservation of decency' sometimes to be seen in one-roomed rural houses, and there are many inadvertent glimpses in the literature of very meagre accommodation being exploited for the maximum decorousness: of housewives in Northumberland mining villages running across the street to the 'pantry' (an outdoor foodstore) to change their clothes if a stranger visited, for example, and of expedients even in the lowest multi-occupied rooms in London, such as 'the decency of an old curtain' round a married couple's bed, or a neat separation of personal items showing 'the idea of *meum* and *tuum* . . . some clinging still as to a home'. Parliamentary officialdom too, in its stilted way, acknowledged 'numerous instances . . . of beauty, modesty, and intelligence in girls enduring the intensest cubicular crowding'.

The tenor of the small number of nineteenth-century working-class autobiographies that touch on this subject is that restraints and separations were achieved, even if sexual knowledge was learnt early. In one of these there is an account of two sisters and two brothers, occupying one room in Spitalfields in the 1860s, which beautifully indicates how working-class people strove to maintain standards: 'the men dressed first and came out into the street, or under an archway, while the women rose and dressed'. At one stage in his young life as a colliery worker Thomas Burt had to share a bedroom with six relations; the family were Methodists, and 'we managed, with mutual cordiality and goodwill, to get along very harmoniously'. Laurence Housman has a telling anecdote of how the local poacher's daughter,

---

[79] Hood 1850: 162, 228–9. Gilly 1841: 19, quoted by Hood, is similarly self-defeating.

who shared a bedroom with her three brothers, 'divided from them only by a curtain', one night 'had to flee away in her night-clothes to the home of the man she was to marry'. This suggests both how decorum was fought for at even the lowest rung of rural life, and the degree of sexual self-discipline in rural courtship.[80]

Sharing of beds and bedrooms was the subject of regret and even remorse. Researchers could have difficulty in eliciting the facts because of 'shame' felt by working-class families. Suffolk housewives deplored their own crowded circumstances as 'not respectable or decent . . . hardly bearable'. A Cornish widow pressed on whether she would have enough privacy from the lodger she was to take in retorted 'oh, sir . . . you mustn't think us so bad as we seem; we're drove often to do what we don't like to do, or we wouldn't have a roof at all to cover us.'[81] Even when working-class families were 'drove to do what we don't like to do' in a stronger sense it is apparent, despite the hostility of the contemporary researchers, that they were still trying to achieve the maximum sexual decency consistent with economic constraints. Having a grown-up daughter sleeping with her parents might be a means of avoiding the greater evil of her sharing a room with a mature brother; cases are known of husbands from neighbouring houses in rural areas agreeing to share beds so that their grown-up daughters could have the privacy of a single room. (Investigators never seem to have asked whether families were achieving the greatest *possible* separation of the sexes in the accommodation available—just as it seldom occurred to them that individuals might sleep naked because their limited clothing had been washed for wearing in the morning.)[82]

It would be wrong to suggest that these attitudes and impulses were universal; all that is being claimed is that they had a significant currency even very low on the social scale in nineteenth-century England. There are also cases where they do not seem to have been influential—where all the bedrooms in a house were not occupied, for example, leading to more sharing of beds than was presumably necessary (but it is important to realize that this was also a bourgeois

[80] Razzell and Wainwright 1973: 32; Ginswick 1983: ii. 39; Mayhew 1861–2: i. 135; Gore 1851: p. x; H. J. Hunter 1865: 146; Burnett 1982: 44; Okey 1930: 147; Burt 1924: 91; Housman 1937: 74.

[81] *JSSL* 5 (1843), 212–21; *Morning Chronicle*, 5 Dec. 1849, p. 5; 14 Nov 1849, p. 5.

[82] *Morning Chronicle*, 17 Nov. 1849, p. 5; Chadwick 1965: 194; Mingay 1990; Fontane 1970: i. 127.

habit).[83] A considerable range of behaviours is also to be found among the occupants of one of the very lowest types of accommodation, and one which aroused much comment in sexual-moral terms: the common lodging-house. In these establishments, overlapping with if not exactly parallel to the workhouses, were housed much of the large migrating portion of the working class as well as tramps and more stationary but homeless streetfolk. Estimates of the numbers in them vary widely, from 1.5 per cent of the population of Leeds in 1851, through 0.4 per cent of the population of London a decade later (and much the same proportion of the national population) to as much as 10 per cent in the case of Liverpool, where numbers would admittedly have been swelled by crews of ships.[84]

Assessing sexual behaviour in the working class from the evidence of the lodging-houses is greatly complicated by the wide variation in standards set by the lodging-house keepers and administrations, such that houses in one and the same neighbourhood could differ strikingly in their moral tone. There was probably a tendency for the laxest houses to die out as the century advanced (lodging-house registration became compulsory in 1851), and provincial houses, especially in the North, were said to be variable but better on average than those in London. On the other hand London did have its intensely respectable establishments, sometimes religious, where single women were not admitted on any terms, while all over the country, and right through the period, there were houses where no separation of the sexes, 'married' or not, was enforced. In Norwich there was a house which came so close to being a brothel that the keeper would try to charge extra for couples having casual sex. Rare but definite cases do seem to occur where lodging-houses were used by prostitutes, or where there was an understanding that casual sex would be available. Matters are further complicated by the possibility that some of the new model lodging-houses were a front for organized vice.[85]

The most common practice seems to have been that only couples who declared themselves married would be allowed to share a bed, but no documentary evidence of marriage was required. They would

[83] *JSSL* 11 (1848), 193–249; H. J. Hunter 1865: 137; Schopenhauer 1818: ii. 126.

[84] Burnett 1978: 62; Mayhew 1861–2: i. 253, 408; Treble 1971.

[85] Mayhew 1861–2: i. 257, 259, 317, 408–9, 423; Ginswick 1983: i. 75; *Morning Chronicle*, 15 Dec. 1849, p. 5; 12 Jan. 1850, p. 5; Chadwick 1965: 411–21; *JSSL* 3 (1841), 14–24; Williams 1890: i. 166; Worsley 1849: 68; *Sinks of London* 1848: 18; Katscher 1881: 231; Narjoux 1886: 61.

be accommodated in a room with other 'married' couples, while single males and single females were each accommodated separately. There are extremely lurid stories about what happened when this system was operated laxly, including reports of partners being swapped nightly or even more frequently; these are probably much exaggerated, as are the stories of more respectable working-class individuals being shocked by what they witnessed (a motif which is repeated too often to be much more than a trope). But behind these stories there can probably be discerned a considerable variety of sexual standards in the occupants and even conflict over standards (and variety can presumably also be deduced from the fact that different lodging-houses found it worthwhile to offer their customers different degrees of respectability). There are stories of rare inmates saying their prayers and, interestingly, being jeered at for it. More generally, there are said to have been fierce quarrels between girls who boasted of their 'wickedness' and those who deplored this (and even in the very lax Norwich house the occasional 'nice' married woman would make a screen of clothes on a line across the bedposts). There may have been a good deal of this militant non-respectability in the looser establishments, with sexual decorums being joked about and attacked.[86]

Mayhew, who provides many of the most convincing glimpses of lodging-houses and their chequered sexual morality, is an important source of evidence for the variety of lower-working-class sexual attitudes more generally. The value of marriage and the extent to which it was substituted by firm common-law bonds seem to have been aspects of sexuality that varied notably, even within the same small groups. A rubbish-carter's wife deplored not only 'going together in that bad way' but even civil marriage, as immoral alternatives to church marriage, but she was criticizing some of her peers, families in the same trade who thought of this 'going together' as being 'ready married'. Interestingly, she reported that there was a 'goodish deal' of this sort of thing in the Paddington area but little in Clerkenwell and Pentonville. The tendency for such habits to crop up in 'corners of London' was likened to the moral seclusion of 'some forest district in England'.

It emerges in Mayhew's account of costermonger families that in Clerkenwell a greater proportion of the latter were properly married

[86] Mayhew 1861–2: i. 248, 252, 256–7, 409, 412–13; iii. 391–2.

(allegedly a fifth as opposed to a tenth elsewhere) because the fee for church marriage was waived in that parish at Advent and Easter (as it apparently was also in Manchester Cathedral—with mass ceremonies being performed at the latter season). Formal marriage was perhaps thought of by some groups as simply an unaffordable or excessively expensive means of ratifying strong common-law ties: Mayhew says that unmarried costermonger women were as 'rigidly faithful' to their partners as married, and more inclined to jealousy. In Mayhew's *Morning Chronicle* reports there are frequent references to affectionate and loyal couples claiming to be deterred from marriage by its cost. On the other hand, Mayhew's own collaborator, Bracebrydge Hemyng, doubted if the small fee would really be an obstacle, and a later but comparably knowledgeable London observer, James Greenwood, regarded such claims as mere pretexts, and advised middle-class philanthropists against providing the financial help which turned concubinage into unwelcome marriage. According to Greenwood, interestingly, the former was a looser bond, distinct in the working-class mind from marriage—which was a state so highly esteemed that when it was entered into with full commitment the marriage certificate was often hung up in the living-room 'as a choice print or picture might be' (though the allusion to a living-room and its furnishing implies that Greenwood is confounding economic distinctions in this discussion). Mayhew, indeed, has evidence suggesting that the coster common-law marriages were less permanent than real marriages, even if just as faithful, and reports that concubinage among chimney-sweepers was especially short-lived.[87]

Mayhew's inclination is always to cling to occupation or economic niche as the determinant of sexual standards, on however small a scale, but his material often seems to show that these were a matter of purely personal inclination or conviction. In successive descriptions of two female tramps he has one who entered unconcerned into a strong unformalized relationship with a man she met while haymaking ('I liked him, and would have gone through trouble for him . . . We never talked about marrying. I didn't care, for I didn't think about it'), and another who still regretted having been persuaded into concubinage when she knew that it was wrong. In a quite different environment, that of rural Suffolk in the 1840s, individual working-class girls were differentiated over a broad range of sexual

[87] Mayhew 1861–2: i. 20, 44–5, 475; ii. 294, 370; iv. 259; Rands 1866: 276; Greenwood 1981: 15–16; Fiske 1869: 170–1; Hawthorne 1863: ii, 235–7.

demeanours and attitudes, from austere refusal of all thoughts of sex, marital or non-marital, to the distinctly 'frolicsome'.[88]

It has been my general argument so far that economic standing in the nineteenth-century English working class was not correlated in a simple way with moral respectability (and certainly not via the crude environmentalist mechanisms imagined by commentators of the day). But status and respectability were connected in the aggregate, with a general tendency towards such a code as groups rise in status. There was still variety as we move up from Mayhew's streetfolk. Workplaces of the same type, in the same area, and at the same date could have divergent sexual codes. A father testified to the Sadler committee in 1832 that he dared not leave his daughters working in certain Halifax mills once they had reached puberty, while at others their virtue would be secure. A young hand in the Staffordshire potteries in the 1850s witnessed drunken sex-parties at the second workshop he joined, but found in the third a climate of complete restraint and orderliness. A wide variety of 'moral atmospheres' could be breathed by the young miner in Northumberland.

These contrasts are especially telling because each appears at a single date. A misleading or at least exaggerated appearance of diversity in moral culture at this level can be created by comparing evidence from, say, 1810 and 1860, or by isolating examples of heterogeneity in the sexual codes of particular communities which should probably be interpreted as signs of transition. A religiously moralistic young tailor in the second decade of the century met only one kindred spirit, in a London workshop of forty men, who would join him in resisting the general dissoluteness and obscenity (as they perceived it). An equally high-minded—but in this case free-thinking and radical—young silk-weaver in Coventry about twenty-years later also found only a small group of 'more thoughtful youths' who shared his hatred of the laxity (especially the hard drinking) of his fellow workers. By mid-century a new generation's code had prevailed with the brass-makers of Birmingham, so that old habits of depravity 'only linger among the elder race of workmen, and are fast disappearing among the younger men'.[89]

Such sequences of evidence do, however, need to be treated sensitively (even if one discounts the fact that there could be

---

[88] Mayhew 1861–2: iii. 403–4; Betham-Edwards 1898: 57.

[89] PP 1831–2, xv. 88–9; C. Shaw 1977: 50–1, 81; Burt 1924: 104; T. Carter 1845: 155–6; Gutteridge 1969: 98; Razzell and Wainwright 1973: 298.

heterogeneity within one kind of workplace) because several kinds of occupation are involved, at several places. What 'progress' there was in working-class morals occurred with different timings in different localities. Sometimes such variations could be attributed to sheer geographical isolation (the Lancashire village of Smallbridge was alleged to have remained unusually uncouth and disorderly until the mid-1830s for this reason), but a difference of occupation was usually enough to override the effects of a common place of settlement. The edge-tool workers in Sheffield were reported to be very dissipated as late as 1839, but a notable improvement in the morals of the silver-platers was traced back as far as the 1780s.[90]

Superior groups in the working class such as the Sheffield silver-platers were probably more homogeneous in their moral codes than, say, the Staffordshire pottery-workers. These 'labour aristocracies' have attracted much attention from historians recently; in so far as the attitudes of their members have been studied the emphasis has been on their political and social outlook, but it is clear from the contemporary evidence that upward ambitions and superior status in the working class tended to go with an often very marked strictness and orderliness in moral demeanour (I discuss the third side of this triangle—the radical-respectable nexus—in the second volume of this study). Nineteenth-century commentators recorded the phenomenon of élite workers, with their concomitant respectability, both as a general fact and in particular environments. Francis Place's intuition of a progressive stretching of moral differences with rank was shared by several observers with respect to the middle and top of the working class as a whole—where they saw a considerable moral and economic self-improvement (up to or even beyond middle-class standards) being achieved by a select few, and perhaps an overall rise in the 'conduct, mind, and tastes' of all workers, but a huge and widening gap still separating the bulk of the class from the bourgeoisie.[91]

Place was not alone in finding the journeyman artisans of London, or at least their upper tier, to be notably moral by the very first years of the century, and a foreign visitor of the period felt this to be true of their peers throughout the country.[92] Some decades later, while he was still surveying a relatively broad range of working-class groups

---

[90] Waugh 1855: 107; Holland 1839: 21; S. Roberts 1849: 37–40; C. M. Smith 1853: 256–7. See also Housman 1937: 72.

[91] Morrison 1854: 264–5; Slaney 1847: 17; J. D. Milne 1857: 157–9.

[92] Malcolm 1810: ii. 407–10; Goede 1807: ii. 112.

for his *Morning Chronicle* articles, Mayhew was often struck by the large moral differences between the 'honourable' and non-honourable tiers of a particular craft: between the craftsmen tailors and the slopworkers, for example, and between the cabinet-makers and the joiners. Even in the narrower arena of *London Labour and the London Poor*, however, there was room for such contrasts: within the fairly lowly trade of chimney-sweeping, for example. 'Men . . . converse with shopmen in Bond-street', said a contemporary of Mayhew's, 'and cannot understand how the lower orders can be ignorant'. At much the same time William Acton commented on 'the improved morals . . . during my time . . . of young men engaged in the lower departments of commerce and trade'.[93]

About a year after Mayhew started his researches the pioneering French sociologist Le Play was collecting English material for a compilation of detailed studies of individual working families in Europe, Russia, and Turkey. For some reason his four English portraits are all of relatively privileged workers and their households (two craftsmen cutlers, a carpenter, and a foundry-worker), and the note of orderliness, restraint, and delicacy (as well as comfort and cleanliness) is sounded throughout Le Play's very comprehensive descriptions. The small workshops of Manchester were admitted, in an otherwise bleak reminiscence of the moral condition of Manchester workers in the 1830s, to have been islands in a sea of uncouthness and unchastity. This was probably too harsh, in fact: at the same date the great James Nasmyth, recruiting for his engineering works in the city (rather less élite employment, because unskilled), had no difficulty in finding 'able' workmen who were also 'steady, respectable, and well-conducted'.[94] The workforce of the industrial North-West continued to have many ranks for decades after this. Some were very degraded, but a degree of high-mindedness was exhibited by much more than a minority in these areas: membership of the local 'institutional vehicles of respectability' (such as the Mechanics' Institutes, Working Men's Colleges, friendly and co-operative societies, and so forth) is known to have had a long if tapering 'occupational tail'.[95]

The case of the North-West serves to raise a different issue about

[93] Mayhew 1980: ii. 96, v. 144, 211; Mayhew 1861-2: ii. 367-8; W. J. E. Bennett 1846: 7; Acton 1857: 165.

[94] Le Play 1855: *passim*; Ludlow and Jones 1867: 17-19; Nasmyth 1883: 216; Sargant 1869-70: 13.

[95] Barlee 1863: 5; Kirk 1985: 189-90. See also Waugh 1855: 189-90.

economic standing and working-class moral culture in the nineteenth century: the influence of urbanization and new industry on morality. This is a frustrating subject because, although there is a very big contemporary literature on various aspects of it, the amount of worthwhile evidence is, by comparison, minute. Usually this comment is quite consciously partisan—in favour of rural morality and hostile to urban, for example, or defensive of sexual morals on the shopfloor of the factory—and tends to cluster around certain particular controversies, such as the sexual consequences of the employment of women underground in the mines, which only involve a small fraction of the nineteenth-century workforce. Some major groups are virtually ignored in these debates, and where they are concerned modern inquiry does not even have the poor starting-point of highly coloured data. The emphasis on town and country itself tends to exclude certain occupations from attention from the start: domestic servants, for example—a large and expanding section of the working class about which this study will perforce have little to say. Even within the urban population servants certainly outnumbered a group which was the subject of endless comment quite disproportionate to its scale, the workers in textile factories.[96]

On the few occasions when the evidence concerning one of these vexed issues of working-class occupation and sexual conduct was investigated dispassionately the result was usually a blank. The evidence collected by the Royal Commission of 1833, set up to improve on the Sadler committee's inquiry into children in factories of the previous year, is massive and contains copious allusions to sexual behaviour which remain to be reviewed by a modern historian. But when the Benthamite authors of the summary of the Commission's first report came to look coolly at everything that had been alleged about sex in the factories their conclusion was undramatic: 'though the statements and depositions of the different witnesses that have been examined are to a considerable degree conflicting, yet there is

[96] When the factory question started to achieve national prominence in the 1830s there were only about 200,000 workers in the cotton mills of the North-West, as opposed to about a million agricultural labourers. It is true that the latter group shrank steadily as the century advanced, but the factory-workers, even when supplemented by woollen textile operatives and foundrymen and engineers, were only part of a manufacturing sector which continued to include large numbers working in older ways—in small workshops and with hand-operated machinery—and which, moreover, did not increase as a proportion of the whole workforce (F. M. L. Thompson 1988: 23–43). On domestic servants and illegitimacy rates see W. Acton 1859.

no evidence to show that vice and immorality are more prevalent among these people . . . than among any other portion of the community in the same station'. In the three reports submitted by the Commission altogether fifty-three witnesses deposed about sex and only seven thought the factory-workers more depraved than their peers.

Thirty years later the children's employment commissioners were still drawing attention to the way allegations of immorality in manufacture were more than balanced by conflicting evidence. Mixed agricultural fieldwork was also a subject widely felt to have a sexual-moral aspect, but about which twenty-five years of parliamentary enquiry was only able to expose uncertainty and disagreement. Investigation of the mining industry threw up perhaps the most direct confirmation of fears of sexual depravity in particular working environments—in the shape of miners describing their own sexual activity underground—but it was recognized that mining communities varied greatly in their sexual codes, and a modern survey of the material before Parliament finds no good evidence of a tendency to sexual licence in English mines.[97] On the broad question of rural versus urban morality the official judgement, in the form of the Registrar General's analysis of illegitimacy levels in different districts, which I cited in the last chapter, was also agnostic (in the context of numerous strong expressions of opinion on one side or the other).

Actually this was to be too cautious about the illegitimacy figures, which *were* normally higher in country areas than in local towns. Evidence of a more permissive attitude to pre-marital sex in the country will be mentioned shortly. Despite the very jagged profile of rural morality, when like is compared to like the urban nineteenth-century working class does seem to have the moral edge. A unique piece of research covering Suffolk in the years 1848–53 found that sexual crimes were apparently much more frequent in rural areas: there were twenty-six proven offences including sodomy and bestiality, to which the towns contributed only four rapes. An unusually careful American observer at the mid-century was consistently struck by the contrast, in moral demeanour at least, between urban and rural populations in England—no less marked near London, where he scrutinized rural labourers at Godalming alongside London boys commuting out to a factory in the area. When the future suffragist

[97] PP 1833, xx. 32; 1863, xviii. pp. lxxvii–lxxviii; 1843, xii. 161–2, 233, 309–10; 1867–8, xvii. 17; 1842, xv. 32, 156–66; Wheeler 1836: 186; John 1980: 41.

Hannah Mitchell moved from a remote Derbyshire farm to the town of Glossop she was surprised and delighted to find that men were not the quasi-rapists of her experience hitherto, but friendly individuals who only sought limited sexual familiarities.[98]

On the matter of factory morality also, the verdict of the official investigators may have been too neutral. In factories proper the evidence is on the whole against extensive licence, even at an early period, between bosses or supervisors and female workers, or between workers; there is reason to think that pre-marital sexual activity by factory hands seldom involved partners from the same factory, contrary to the widespread belief that factory conditions aroused sexual desire by the proximity and exposure of members of the other sex.[99] No store can be set by the many conscious defences of the morality of factories, but sometimes their gist is unconsciously confirmed by opponents of the system: as when Peter Gaskell (perhaps the most egregious of all writers on this question, though still much quoted) in his eagerness to measure the factory worker by a ruralist, Wordsworthian standard finds it by no means to his credit that he 'shows a high order of intelligence', and has rejected traditional rural intercourse-in-courtship because of a new 'high tone of public decency'. Likewise when an untiring commentator on Preston conditions, the local prison chaplain John Clay, finds the depravity of the local workers to be proved by their licentious behaviour when they have money, as opposed to their decent behaviour when out of work, he strengthens the case of those sympathetic observers of the Lancashire workers who took their restrained, respectable demeanour in times of great hardship as marks of their essential temperament.[100]

The theoretical propagandists for the factory system had their practical counterparts, moralistically minded owners who set out to regulate the conduct of their workers, both on the floor and, in many factory towns, at home. The influence of such men was often adduced by observers as the explanation of the good demeanour at a particular works, but there is also evidence, not to be ignored, that moral respectability in the factory, like the outcroppings of respectability in working-class neighbourhoods, often arose spontaneously. We know

---

[98] Glyde 1856; Olmsted 1967: 302; G. Mitchell 1968: 82.

[99] Smelser 1959: 284; Ginswick 1983: i. 39.

[100] Gaskell 1833: 24, 30; Clay 1855b; Barlee 1863: 59; Waugh 1867: 69; W. C. Taylor 1842: 79.

that sexual interference by senior males in a factory, when it was attempted, was fiercely resented and resisted by some women workers. In Manchester mills the girls were said to carry ideas of moral correctness to the point of 'a species of saucy prudery' (an intriguing conception, which certainly does not sound like owner-imposed respectability), and to make life hard for any of their number who was guilty of 'frailty'. And in a Birmingham steelpen works (probably more a workshop than a factory) a moral-minded owner was allegedly abetted by moral-minded working girls, so that they would tip him off if he inadvertently gave a job to a loose member of their sex. An ex-factory-worker declared in 1853 that, in contrast to his experiences of thirty years earlier, 'if any man would give utterance to a profane, or lewd, or filthy expression, he would be instantly rebuked'.[101]

So one generation of factory-life, for this participant, yielded a moral revolution. But factory-workers composed a small and non-expansive fraction of the population for most of Victoria's reign, while the semi-skilled workforce as a whole shrank in scale. Moral respectability was on the increase among the expanding unskilled labour force, but in trying to put a date on the process as a whole, and striking a balance across a great variety of generally very subjective evidence, one should incline to favour slow rather than fast estimates in order to register the broadest reality of the change. While every favourable description of working-class morals could be balanced, at least in the first few decades of the century, by a negative account, there are probably more claims that the working class is improving morally than claims that it is deteriorating. A few accounts date a general increase in working-class respectability even earlier than Place, but the point at which there is some agreement that it becomes notable lies in or around the first two decades of the century. And though sweepingly hostile pictures of working-class morality can be encountered up to the mid-century I do not know of one after that date. About this time there appear the first authentically celebratory descriptions of the working class and their modes of private life (including praise for their moral standards)—as opposed to descriptions in the service of some middle-class cause such as the factory system, stressing working-class deference, reliability, and so forth.[102]

[101] PP 1834, xix. 168; 1831–2, xv. 155; Ginswick 1983: i. 39; Razzell and Wainwright 1973: 298; Parker 1853.

[102] Chadwick 1828; McCullough 1827; Bowen 1835: *passim*; Raumer 1836: ii. 247;

In keeping with what I have said about urban codes, London, perhaps with some other towns, was at the van of this chronology. There
was however one rather formidable opponent of the comment attest-
ing to a change in the moral colouration of the metropolitan working
class in the years 1800–20. In several widely noticed publications in
the 1790s and the first two decades of the nineteenth century, the
London magistrate and penal theorist Patrick Colquhuon argued
from quantitative data that crime was on the increase in the capital.
He gave prostitution a prominent position in his case, and generally
regarded the crime figures as an index of the decay of working-class
morals. Colquhuon's picture, despite its numerical trappings, was
vigorously attacked by some writers and dissented from by the occasional fellow magistrate (though it was acknowledged to have been
influential, and it perhaps inhibited recognition of working-class
moral improvement in London).[103] His figures on prostitution were
certainly wrong, as was later generally recognized, but his perception
of a rising crime-rate was shared by many national commentators in
the next generation. Crime has a doubtful connection with morality,
and statistics of crime are a notoriously unreliable indicator—
especially at a time of rapidly changing penal and police arrangements. Modern assessments of the facts have tended (together with
the most unflustered of the nineteenth-century analyses) to agree that
crime objectively increased for at least part of the early decades of
the century and did not decline unequivocally until about 1850, but
that violent crime was decreasing from the start of the period (a conclusion that may be drawn even from Colquhuon's alarmist
figures).[104]

There were also many attempts in the nineteenth century to feed
criminal statistics into the debate about the moral influence of urbanization and industry. The best modern wisdom on the question
inclines to favour those who claimed that the new industrial town
fostered crime, with apparent confirmation of higher rates in

Foreign Quarterly Review, 38 (1837), 338–57; Ferri di San Costante 1804: i. 145; J. Mill 1826;
W. B. Adams 1832: 47; Guizot 1862: 174; Channing 1874: 178, 305; Grant 1837: i. 294–6;
Simmons 1849: *passim*; J. D. Milne 1857: 154–60; *Eclectic Review*, NS 12 (1856), 130–47.

[103] Ludlow and Jones 1867: *passim*; Lawson 1887: 62; Glyde 1850: 51; Betham-Edwards
1898: 65; 'Working Man' 1858: 49; PP 1816, v. 77; 1840, xi. 208; W. Weir 1842; *Sports,
Pastimes, and Customs* 1847: 15–16; Radzinowicz 1956: iii. 219–46; Feltham 1802: 276–80;
PP 1839, xix. 15.

[104] Tobias 1967: 41, 122, 127; Rudé 1971: 97; Plint 1851: *passim*; Radzinowicz and Hood
1986: 113–15. See also Philips 1977: 284–5.

Lancashire. A rare case of a sophisticated study of criminal data which bears directly on sexuality is a modern survey of London court cases involving violence between working-class men and women in the period: there was a marked decline from around mid-century in such cases which, though partly due to more official vigilance and stringency, must be attributed also to autonomous new standards of respectability. Evidence emerges in the courtrooms of, for example, antagonism to obscene language in front of children in even the poorest families.[105]

For the London working class Francis Place cited certain specific institutions (in addition to the obvious case of prostitution) whose alleged decay or reform indicated that moral standards had changed. What is known of the later history of these confirms that Place pushed the timing of his moral revolution back too far, but was right to be calling attention to such a phenomenon by the 1830s. Bullock-running was a violent street recreation which Place suggests died out around the turn of the century, but it is recorded as still occurring in the 1820s. Place was not the only commentator to treat the sport as diagnostic of working-class moral standards, however, and there are direct contradictions in the claims about its prevalence at this date. Nearer to sexuality are the Cock and Hen clubs, again alleged by Place to be reduced to a small residue, but still attested in the 1820s and 1830s, and even, not very convincingly, in the 1850s (though they seem, over time, to have lost their 'pairing off' aspect, and have faded into the Free and Easy, or mixed sex musical evening).[106]

Place dwells at some length on the improvement of the London tea gardens, establishments on the immediate fringe of the city which were resorted to especially on a Sunday and which in his youth, he says, had harboured much drunkenness and casual sex. Sunday behaviour is a subject so infested with stereotypes that the contemporary descriptions must be treated very cautiously. Foreign visitors came to England even more primed to be stupefied on an English Sunday than they were to be amused by English prudery. Two of

---

[105] Gatrell and Hadden 1972; Tomes 1978.

[106] 'Two Citizens' 1828: 120, 128; *Town* (1837), 1; *Yokel's Preceptor* c.1855: 1; 'Working Man' 1858: 30-1, 36; PP 1816, v. 151, 167; 1849, xvii. 228. The bawdy song collections of the 1830s (see p. 164) often claim to be publishing Cock and Hen material, and see the frontispiece illustrating such a gathering in *The Regular Thing* (London, ?1833). For a mid-century fictional description of a very uncouth Cock and Hen club in Brighton, one of few survivors of an institution 'common all over the country thirty years ago', see Lindridge 1850: 93.

them described the tea gardens as dourly restrained in the first years of the century, while a domestic commentator at the same period found them purged but with the survivors still conforming to Place's young experience. From the 1790s there is a description which certainly suggests that the tea gardens were centres for casual sex but, confusingly, the women involved are said to be chiefly genteel prostitutes, and the prevailing atmosphere refined.[107] It does seem that the worst offenders among the gardens were suppressed and made more decorous around the turn of the century, and by about 1830 the average tone of these institutions was judged to be better. A few gardens survived and prospered well after the mid-century and, more important, while the general demeanour of the gardens was respectable there appears still to have been a definite core of hard-drinking customers (alongside those drinking moderately with their families), and a relaxed sexual code. Even hostile witnesses give the impression that the sexual pairing was by way of picking up rather than prostitution, and concede that a girl could visit a garden without opening herself to unwelcome advances.[108]

IV

Meanings

As the century advanced and working-class Londoners went on further-flung outings—into the country, along the river, or down to the resited Crystal Palace—they still (though to an extent that was much contested) used them as an opportunity to get drunk and pick each other up. One of the keynotes of all such material on the London working-class Sunday is the coexistence of the genteel and the lax. In the case of river excursions to Richmond, it was said, gentility prevailed on the outward leg of the trip and laxity on the return journey, once enough liquor had been drunk by 'those spruce youths, so modest in the morning'.[109] In this sense the topic of Sunday recreation,

---

[107] Baert 1800: iv. 179; Defauconpret 1817: i. 60; Malcolm 1810: i. 333; ii. 408; *Modern Sabbath* 1794: 27, 65, 74, 84, 105–6.

[108] George 1925: 305; Wroth 1896: *passim*; *Tea-Gardens and Spas* 1880: 8; Angelo 1828: i. 284; 'The Tea-Garden', *London Magazine*, 6 (1822), 136–40; Wade 1829: 148; Bulwer 1970: 200; J. Richardson 1855: i. 20; Colman 1850: i. 227; Beggs 1849: 109–11; J. E. Ritchie 1857: 152; 'Old London Tea-Gardens', *London Society*, 40 (1881), 94–7; H. Wood 1843: 190; Prémaray 1851: 311; Hillocks 1865: 85–92; Timbs 1855: 16. See also Hollingshead 1895: i. 24.

[109] Bailey 1987: 27–8; Howitt 1838: ii. 314–17; *Social Science* 1861: 143; Ludlow and Jones 1867: 250; PP 1854–5, x. 428–95; 1854, xiv. 331–547; Barret-Ducrocq 1991: 104.

with the convention of 'Sunday best' in all aspects of personal appearance, brings to a head a problem about the understanding of working-class moral codes which I have hitherto set aside, though I have guarded against its effects as far as possible. Only occasionally does the available evidence about working-class morality relate directly to sex, and I have inevitably been dependent on estimates of a phenomenon which is at once broader and more superficial, namely, working-class 'respectability'. How reliable is respectability as a guide to sexual codes?

The issue cuts both ways. On the one hand there can be no doubt that observers leapt too readily to adverse conclusions about the sexual morality of the working class on the strength of certain appearances. They applied inappropriate standards of decorum in speech and personal address, to conclude, for example, that certain kinds of swearing, or conventions of behaviour between young people, denoted sexual licence. And 'morality' tended to come in a package: so that drunkenness, in particular, is thought to denote every other kind of laxity also, including sexual. In fact drinking codes were not necessarily coupled to other codes in working-class thinking, both in the sense that working-class élites bent on respectability could dissent from the middle-class antagonism to drinking, and that abstinence could be a fervent moral cause with working-class groups and individuals with unstrict attitudes to Sunday observance and premarital intercourse: Allen Clarke, the Lancashire Labour man, recalled that the male half of an unmarried couple in his street was noticeably less drunken and violent than some of his censorious neighbours.[110] I shall explore in the second volume of this study the ideological background to such paradoxes.

Conversely, working-class sexual codes can be misjudged in an affirmative direction. The packaging effect could work in reverse, or observers could be deceived—inadvertently when they imagined that they saw tokens of restraint and high-mindedness in a working-class individual's demeanour, or deliberately when such appearances were put on for middle-class consumption. The most interesting possibility for misunderstanding of this second sort is that respectable appearances were authentic but that, for the working class, they bore a different relationship to attitudes and standards. In the case of middle-class prudery I have argued that appearance and reality must

[110] Crossick 1978: 153; Razzell and Wainwright 1973: 34; Allen Clarke ('Ben Adhem'), *Liverpool Weekly Post*, 26 May 1934, p. 2.

be strongly correlated, indeed that the distinction is to some extent
artificial, and the notion of a totally hypocritical prudish demeanour
very improbable. But if the use of 'ribald' language by a group of
workers, or considerable physical intimacy between them, should not
be interpreted, by middle-class lights, as tokens of sexual licence, it is
also possible that respectable behaviour in a working-class context
will not have the meaning it bears in a middle-class context. This is
an especially important possibility in view of the emphasis I have
placed on attempts at domestic privacy and segregation, and other
kinds of domestic respectability. It is necessary to interpret such features of working-class life cautiously, and not to suppose automati-
cally that they had the sort of connection with ideas of sexual
restraint and orderliness which they would have had in a middle-
class setting. We must respect the impressions of 'Walter', lusting
after a forewoman in a Glasgow dyeing works and guessing 'she was
one of those, who . . . worked well at her business, and was a valuable
servant, but who when not working thought more about fucking than
anything else': 'there are plenty of such, both men and women in all
working classes, [who] . . . know how to get the fullest sexual pleasure
out of life, without lapsing into mere animals of lust, idleness, and
debauchery'.[111]

'Sunday best', one may suppose, could lead very readily to such
wrong signalling. The foreign observers of English working-class
recreation on a Sunday may have seen dourness too readily, and may
have applied a measure of respectability calibrated abroad rather
than in England, but their sense of working-class orderliness on
Sunday is emphatic and goes back to a time when even Francis Place
would probably have agreed that working-class sexual standards
were quite lax. In 1789 the 'modesty' and 'reserve' of the rows of
young couples taking a Sunday stroll in Highgate struck a French
visitor as reminiscent of the French provinces 150 years earlier. The
'robust apprentice' put on 'the language of decency' with his Sunday
suit, according to the *Scourge* in 1812. By 1867, in the jocular words
of a London journeyman engineer turned writer, 'no man can
remember, nor is there the slightest tradition pointing to a time when
working men did not take a pride in having, and look upon as necessary to the proper enjoyment of Sunday, that outward and visible
sign of working class respectability, a Sunday suit'. But though the

[111] *My Secret Life* 1966: 1250.

working class was thus becoming literally confusable with the bourgeoisie in their Sunday garb it is clear from the rest of this account of
a working-class family Sunday (from the illegal pre-lunch visit to a
pub, for example) that theirs is far from being the same ideal as the
respectability of the middle classes. This writer in fact consistently
makes a distinction between the very large, autonomously
respectable sector of the working class and the small number of
would-be-genteel working families.[112]

One of the most beautiful illustrations of the general point occurs
in an anecdote by Alfred Russel Wallace, co-announcer of the theory
of evolution by natural selection. It is in fact so rich in observations,
expected and less expected, that it deserves quoting in full. Wallace
is describing the joinery workshop of a master-builder off the
Hampstead Road, in which he idled away much time as a teenager in
the late 1830s.

My general impression is that there was very little swearing among them,
much less than became common thirty years later, and perhaps about as
much as among a similar class of men today. Neither was there much coarseness or indecency in their talk, far less indeed than I met with among professional young men a few years afterwards. One of the best of the workmen
was a very loose character—a kind of Lothario or Don Juan by his own
account—who would often talk about his adventures, and boast of them as
the very essence of his life. He was a very good and amusing talker, and
helped to make the time pass in the monotony of the shop; but occasionally,
when he became too explicit or too boastful, the foreman, who was a rather
serious though very agreeable man, would gently call him to order, and repu-
diate altogether his praises of the joys of immorality. But I never once heard
foul language as was not uncommonly used among themselves by men of a
much higher class and much more education.[113]

Published in 1905, this illustrates how weak the sense of the
Victorian as a historical bracket still was at this date. The story also
very interestingly implies the autonomy of working-class sexual
respectability in the recollection that 'professional young men a few
years afterwards' were more indecent in their speech than the workmen—but it is thoroughly disconcerting in its belief that the habits of
the latter were to *deteriorate* in the next thirty years. In fact, these
two claims put together suggest that Wallace has not allowed for the

[112] Cambry 1789: 68–9; *Scourge*, 4 (1812), 188–9; T. Wright 1867: 206–17; Tyng 1847: 27;
Reid 1983.
[113] Wallace 1905: i. 80.

extent to which the men in the joinery shop were protecting the ears
of the middle-class lad who was hanging around them: I imagine that
Wallace heard more obscenity in later years, from colleagues and
working men alike, partly because he was by then an adult. It may be
that the foreman also had his teenage auditor in mind when he
sought to tone down the content of the working-class Lothario's
stories. The fact is, however, that the young Wallace heard and
understood anecdotes with a very transgressive gist, so the striking
record stands: of a working-class culture in which linguistic codes
operated independently of moralism about sexual behaviour.

It is hard to escape from middle-class over-readings of both the
negative and positive sort, rare to find a calm, noticing picture of a
working-class setting such as Edwin Waugh offers of the Lancashire
town of Heywood on a Saturday evening in June: a human landscape
with factory workers and country visitors strolling the streets on their
various errands. Mayhew, who noted how the intensely faithful
costermonger couples—young and middle-aged alike—enjoyed ribald 'larking and joking', was one of the few writers who could live
with such paradoxes of working-class ways.[114] The overheard language of the working class was a supposed index of moral laxity particularly cherished by hostile commentators: adverse conclusions
would follow as night follows day if the reader could hear how the
girls and boys leaving the factories in London in the 1870s, Leeds in
the 1840s, Preston in the 1830s, and Manchester in 1816 talked to
each other. Poor nineteenth-century poor! It was hard to satisfy lis-
teners for whom nicknames with rude adjectives attached (as
bandied by male factory workers in the 1820s) were 'filthy language',
or who condemned agricultural labourers because they never chatted
about 'the Giver'.[115]

As a Sadler committee witness more sensibly observed, 'a great
deal of loose slang-talk' did not imply 'actual guilt'—and the official
reception of this kind of allegation in parliamentary inquiry was generally sceptical.[116] Sometimes there is simply alleged a 'boldness and
impudence' in the demeanour of factory hands, or an 'indecency of
. . . appearance' in that of miners, and one may suspect that claims
about objectionable language were often just thrown in as part of the

[114] Waugh 1855: 194–5; Mayhew 1861–2: i. 21.
[115] Greenwood 1876: 143; *Toilers in London* 1883: 11; Dodd 1842: 33; *Moral Reformer*, 1
(1831), 4; J. E. White 1816: ii. 212; Parker 1853; Simmons 1849: 9.
[116] PP 1833, xxi. 118; 1843, xiv. 575; 1842, xv. 180.

process of wild overinterpretation of working-class behaviour, as they clearly seem to have been in this risible account of girls in a Liverpool dance-hall: 'Every motion of the body, every expression of the face, almost every word they utter, is indicative of unbridled lewdness . . . Their language as they whirl past us . . . is disgusting'.[117] Sharp ears indeed!

By contrast, some writers interpret the uncouthness of the industrial workers positively—finding in the 'rude indifference', and 'coarse familiar expressions' which dismay 'superficial observers', evidence that 'the servility of the country' was dead and a more equal relationship with the masters achieved. More fancifully, indeed fantastically, the factory-worker's face is 'blackened by smoke, yet radiant with the light of intelligence'.[118] But the great mass of affirmative readings of working-class demeanour rely on conventional tokens of respectability. It has recently been suggested that when they thought they were discovering a respectable worker middle-class observers were generally the victims of a deliberate deception—of a 'role enactment' performed by the subject, and dropped the moment the observer's back was turned.[119] Working-class individuals were certainly conscious enough of what the bourgeoisie liked to see (it would be odd if they were not) to operate the 'respectable lurk' and the 'cleanly lurk' as full-time begging techniques in London. A Manchester educationalist recommended that middle-class observers should disguise themselves as workers if they wanted to know what immoral and obscene language schoolchildren naturally used (this is perhaps just an ingenious variation on the doubtful motif of the overheard workers' conversation).[120]

---

[117] Huntington 1871: 16; Seeley 1844: 56; Shimmin 1856: 34. On the Liverpool journalist Hugh Shimmin (who was actually of working-class origins) and his observations see Walton and Wilcox 1991: 29 and *passim*.

[118] Sargant 1857: 302, 383; Felkin 1839a; Head 1836: 185.   [119] Bailey 1979.

[120] PP 1835, vii. 800. Related to this is the influence of new mechanisms for public order in the 19th cent. There seems to have been general agreement that most working-class neighbourhoods, whether in Manchester, Merthyr Tydfil, or London, were extremely quiet at night. Sometimes this is treated as evidence of the respectability of the inhabitants (perhaps not running to sexual restraint, however), but other witnesses emphasize the influence of the police, especially in London (and the police are known to have given a large proportion of their effort to disciplining street life). On the other hand, there are many tributes to the quietness of the London streets and the decorum of the London workers in public before the creation of the Metropolitan Police in 1829 (W. C. Taylor 1842: 17; Ginswick 1983: iii. 18; Colman 1850: ii. 102; Verne 1989: 78; C. Knight 1864: i. 121; ii. 5, 25; W. Ware 1851: 108; Trabaud 1853: 57; Davey 1983: 6; F. M. L. Thompson 1988: 331; Nougaret 1816: i. 30; Geiger 1932: 171; Malcolm 1810: ii. 415; J. E. White 1816: i. 321; Campe 1803: i. 81; Gautier 1845: 181).

Crude deception of middle-class observers is probably much too simple a model for most displays of working-class respectability, however. 'Role enactment' there may have been, but often of a kind that influenced the actors as much as the spectators, as the following anecdote would imply:

A manufacturer had always thought of his mechanics as men with greasy jackets, smirched faced, and mouths full of ribaldry. On the opening of a new factory, he gave an evening entertainment to all his people. Their conduct astonished him. He found that with their Sunday clothes they put on a civilised demeanour; that they could behave with propriety, dance, sing comic songs void of offence, and laugh at them.[121]

There was no concealment, according to this account, of working-class ribaldry and general uncouthness from middle-class eyes. Rather, this demeanour was adopted without embarrassment in one situation and abandoned as inappropriate in another. The degree of Circean transformation implied here does go somewhat beyond plausibility. A man cannot change his sense of humour with his clothes: an adequate account of working-class sexual culture must either judge that the response to 'comic songs void of offence' here was in some measure an affectation, or shape itself in such a way that it is intelligible for the ribald and the non-ribald to coexist in working-class humour. If the workers described here were merely pretending to enjoy the comic songs on offer at the boss's party, but not in order to curry favour with him, an alternative motive readily suggests itself: that such behaviour, along with all the physical comforts and pleasures they were temporarily enjoying, gave these men the satisfaction of a sense of enhanced social status.

Certainly this seems to have been part of the impulse to working-class domestic respectability. Though middle-class observers were inclined to interpret a well-furnished and well-kept home as a moral phenomenon it is sometimes strongly implied in their descriptions that the acquisition and ostentation of as many domestic luxuries as possible were among the chief motives involved. This comes across in glimpses of the crammed and proudly displayed adornments of some working-class homes (which have their echo in some accounts of working-class girls' dress), but more tellingly in the way domestic comfort often went along with a hand-to-mouth family economy, in

---

[121] Sargant 1857: 390.

which the answer to bad times was pawning the valued clock rather than money saved.[122] Consumerism was surely a component of nine-teenth-century working-class respectability, and its neglect by mid-dle-class witnesses one of their misreadings of working-class life. Modern historians have probably also neglected to consider how much 'Victorianism', in the sense of physical genteelness, was actively stimulated by new commercial agencies, by the men manu-facturing and marketing utensils, ornaments, furnishings, jewellery, and so forth—just as the manufacturers and entrepreneurs who encouraged a demand for contraceptives have been neglected.

Still, social aspiration does not seem to be the whole truth about the abruptly sanitized sense of humour of the factory-workers men-tioned above, for obscenity in working-class entertainments was an intrinsically complex phenomenon. Historically the device for low humour which flourished most in the nineteenth century was the *double entendre*. And this kind of humour is well attested where it might be most expected: around the working- and middle-class boundary, and in contexts where the tastes of raffish members of the middle class proper were being catered for. It was a leading element in the comedy of such famous London night-spots as the Judge and Jury show and the dives, Evans's, the Cider Cellars, and the Coal Hole, at least for part of their careers.

But the bawdy in these establishments is surprisingly hard to cate-gorize. The mixture of 'grossness and indecency, expressed and implied' at the Judge and Jury shows probably arose quite naturally from the imitation of real-life divorce proceedings which was the staple of their humour; surviving specimens of Judge and Jury scripts indicate that social satire alone could carry a performance, with obscenity, when it did appear, not becoming very explicit.[123] The main body of surviving song-texts seems to have been aimed particu-larly at middle-class, and perhaps provincial, users—gentlemen 'who came up to see life'. There is much humour about Cockneys, and the smut is either innuendo or obscene language printed with dashes (which would presumably lose its *frisson* if sung: these pieces may only be designed for reading, though they include the performance-

---

[122] Parker 1853; Le Play 1855: 189, 206; Ginswick 1983: iii. 52; Razzell and Wainwright 1973: 28; Mayhew 1861–2: iii. 251.

[123] Yates 1884: 172; *Town* (1841), 1826; Tuckerman 1854: 113–15; *Fast Life* 1859: 162–5. For further discussion of the Judge and Jury phenomenon see the first chapter of my next volume.

dependent—and still popular—'Mike Hunt').[124] But the full range of
songs at the Coal Hole, or those published as Coal Hole productions,
seem to have varied quite widely in their obscenity—from the
candidly dirty ('no double meaning, but plain out'), and the
'Lamentations of a Deserted Penis', to songs that are quite innocent
or do not permit themselves anything beyond a euphemism about
breaking wind (though scatological humour is rare), via those which
are in effect just very warm love-songs. A similar range is to be found
in songs supposed to derive from the Cider Cellars, and at Evans's
up until the 1850s it appears that the entertainment changed at midnight from the clean to songs in which 'a spade was not only called a
spade but something more'.[125]

The combination of *double entendre*, plain coarseness, sentimen-
tality, and the quite unexpected tone of 'deserted penis' in this material suggests that the topic of nineteenth-century obscene
entertainment cannot be reduced to a simple pattern, and in particular that *double entendre* was not just a device for reconciling traditional bawdy and new gentility. There is a fascinating record of the
obscene wedding speeches which were traditionally delivered in a
London printing-works at least down to the late 1830s; here, indeed,
it was the very pride of an artisan élite which sustained sexual non-
respectability, since the humour of these speeches all turned on
'technical expressions peculiar to the trade, endowed for the nonce
with an indecent signification'.[126] *Double entendre* was surely
enjoyed as much for its ingenuity as for its power to assuage guilt:
dirty songbooks were puffed as being '*double entendre* flash and
spreeish', suggesting that euphemism could be rakish, not half-
hearted. Among the contents will be found songs in which indirect-
ness of sexual allusion is carried to the most ingenious extremes.
Conversely, there was no particular embarrassment about switching
into a non-obscene mode in a context of convivial entertainment. All

[124] PP 1854, xv. 336; *Rambler's Flash Songster c.*1865: *passim*; *Paul Pry*, 3 (25 Oct. 1856),
1–2.
[125] L. James 1976: 312, 321–2; PP 1854, xv. 335; 1866, xvi. 189, 203; *Yokel's Preceptor*
1855 *passim*; *Town* (1839), 670; Ashbee 1877: 133–7; Fryer 1968: 28–9, 54–5; Burnand 1904:
i. 170, 176. See also 'F.L.G., the Hon.' 1841: *passim*; A. Smith 1844: i. 244–7; 1861: 17–20;
Timbs 1865: 172. At BL shelfmark c.116.a are obscene song-booklets of the 1830s and 1840s;
among the c.1,000 individual songs will be found 60-odd items said to be performed at the
Coal Hole and/or Cider Cellars. The Johnson collection in the Bodleian also has numerous
song-booklets which illuminate this question: see for example *Coal Hole Companion, Fourth
Collection* and *Laughable Songster*.
[126] C. M. Smith 1853: 256–7.

this complicates the interpretation of more strictly working-class ribaldry, even if it makes the switch from shopfloor obscenity to innocent mirth, cited above, not as odd as it appeared to a middle-class observer.

Genteelness did start to affect the character of working-class nightlife, in the towns especially, quite noticeably from at least the early 1840s. The 'music-saloons' attached to public houses—an important feature of urban recreation and a precursor of the music-hall—were in general granted to have had a distinctly genteel aspect to them, though whether this was made the keynote of a description and attributed to the towering moral qualities of the factory-workers (in Manchester in 1842), or noticed but judged to be outweighed by the demoralizing effect of tobacco-fumes on young girls (Birmingham in 1849), or condemned as a sinister deception (Liverpool in the early 1850s), or merely attributed to an admixture of socially superior customers (Liverpool in the late 1850s), depends on the bias of the observer. In fact each locale of any size had a range of venues of this sort, with a small tail dipping into the disorderly: this has been documented for Leicester by Jeremy Crump. Leeds may have had some of the lowest examples to be found in the big industrial cities, but in 1870 there was only one exception to the rule that the music-saloons of Bradford were not 'immoral in themselves'.[127]

These Bradford operations nevertheless managed to be 'suggestive of immorality'. A universal feature of the genteelness of the music-saloons was certainly singing and other comic entertainment marked by innuendo and a titillating semi-frankness. There are references to this in music-saloons in Stockport and Preston (where an innuendo-rich skit called 'The Spare Bed' was staged), in Leeds (with a comparable piece called 'The Henpecked Husband'), and in Liverpool. Here, in one saloon, a girl-singer made as if to be in search of a single man in the audience (chorus: 'Single young gentlemen, how do you do?'), and there was a character song 'deprecatory of the married state'. In another a man impersonated Lady Godiva in a flesh-coloured costume and sang a naughty song on the subject, and there was a *pose plastique* (a common kind of entertainment in which performers of either sex posed in a stationary tableau, again in flesh-coloured costumes) with three females and a male representing 'a

---

[127] Bailey 1987: 168; Judge 1874: 40–3; W. C. Taylor 1842: 131; Razzell and Wainwright 1973: 319; PP 1852–3, xxxvii. 230, 325; 1866, xvi. 255–7; Shimmin 1858: 142; 1860; Crump 1986; Burnley 1871: 62–3. See also F. B. Smith 1974.

classical subject' (could it be other than the Judgement of Paris?).
This elicited remarks from the audience of 400 or so, 'not of the most
delicate kind, as regarded the development of the female forms
exposed to their gaze'. In Bolton it is recorded that the songs were
innocent, but the accompanying gestures indecent (an allegation by
an avid moralist which was, admittedly, conveniently uncheck-
able).[128]

Again the conventions in force were not straightforward. The classical *pose plastique* in Liverpool had been preceded by a girl singing
'a sentimental song with considerable taste and feeling'.
Unexpectedly, in yet another Liverpool saloon which was divided
into a mixed sex room (the 'House of Commons') and a men only
room ('House of Lords') the same balance of sentimental and *double
entendre* songs was to be heard in both—and the audience of
'decently dressed' and 'decorous' workers at the Apollo saloon in
Manchester responded with the same pleasure to the occasional
risqué song as they did to the general diet of innocent items. Early
music-halls in London were reported to offer both songs full of 'out-
rageously obscene and indecent' innuendo and 'good music in abun-
dance'.[129] Though the tendency of this is towards the genteel it is
difficult to interpret all of it as indicating the impact of gentility in a
middle-class sense. It does seem that the possibility mentioned
above—that 'respectability' had a different meaning, for sexual codes,
in a working-class context from the one it bore in a middle-class
context—applies here. Judging by these descriptions of urban entertainments in the North-West, obscenity was not especially problematic for working-class audiences: in the diet of material and its
reception there do not seem to be evinced tensions between avidity
for the obscene and embarrassment about it, and the *double entendres*, the flesh-coloured costumes, and so on, are not, or not precisely, signs of moral taboo.

It could suit the prejudices of middle-class witnesses so to con-
strue such devices. This was a route by which a generally favourable
estimate of working-class morality could be retained despite the evidence of proletarian dirty-mindedness. 'I am satisfied', said one
observer of a penny gaff in Shoreditch, 'that the majority of women

[128] Dodd 1842: 182; Clay 1858: 42; PP 1852–3, xxxvii. 325; Shimmin 1856: 34, 37;
Morning Chronicle, 2 Sept. 1850, p. 5; Poole 1982: 56. See also *My Secret Life* 1966: 555.
[129] *Morning Chronicle*, 2 Sept. 1850, p. 5; Ginswick 1983: i. 81–2; J. E. Ritchie 1859:
235–6; also Hillocks 1884: 179.

. . . did not "take" the jokes' (which were 'unquestionable *doubles entendres*, as gross as any in Shakespeare'). If the widely differing descriptions of the London penny gaffs, the cheap working-class theatres, are all accurate there was an untidiness and inconsistency, by middle-class lights, about sexual codes in these establishments also. In some of them boys and girls were segregated: in others not. Some are reported to have staged fairly obscene entertainments with probably only a slight element of euphemism and innuendo (Mayhew's interesting description of the dirty songs and sketches at a gaff is not entirely clear about this); at others the songs themselves were clean, but with accompanying 'hinted indecencies'.[130]

Perhaps different theatres catered for different tastes. Working-class sexual codes were undoubtedly heterogeneous, but that cannot explain the catholic nature of the entertainment at the music-saloons if the audiences were as unanimously cheerful as they are reported to have been. In fact the evidence is that these audiences sank their differences of respectability when they resorted to a saloon; William Acton was forcibly struck by the 'elbowing of vice and virtue', the 'curious amalgamation' of prostitutes and married women and sweethearts, in a London audience.[131] Elbowings of vice and virtue, as noticed by Acton, have been cited earlier in connection with the new genteelness of prostitutes in the nineteenth century and the prevalence of quasi-prostitution. It must also be stressed, however, that working-class conventions made it possible for thoroughly moral individuals to consort with the thoroughly lax without stigma. Middle-class misunderstanding of this, and generally of the freedoms of behaviour which were compatible, for young working-class people, with sexual probity, undoubtedly led to many wrong assessments of their morality.

Even if Acton was right in labelling a third of the girls in the Holborn Casino as prostitutes there remained a large innocent majority who behaved and dressed similarly. In Bradford, 15-year-old girls, identified by a knowledgeable observer as not prostitutes, or not yet, danced cheek-to-cheek, in a state of dreamy abandon. Liverpool dance-halls were perhaps more segregated into moral and immoral varieties, but the former could still strike the hostile

[130] Rands 1866: 277; Greenwood 1981: 45, 48; Schlesinger 1853: 273; Mayhew 1861–2: i. 41–2; Doré and Jerrold 1872: 167. See also PP 1854: xv. 541; 1866: xvi. 41–2, 275–6; Hollingshead 1895: i. 22–4; *Graphic*, 5 (1872), 127.
[131] W. Acton 1870: 54.

commentator as the thin end of the wedge because of the freedom
with which the young consorted in them: 'the girls here do not
remove either bonnets or mantles, cloaks or veils, but just turn in
from their walk, or . . . from their work, to spend an hour or two
dancing with the male friends who may have brought them, or who
they meet here'. The freedom of resort is also striking in this account:
the ease and spontaneity of the 'turning in' to a dance-hall for a spell
of dancing with a new or an established partner. Even in works of
moralistic advice the issue was not whether the young should have
this kind of freedom, but simply whether it was wise to exercise it in
the dance-hall:

MIND WHERE YOU PICK HER UP . . . If you ask whether a concert hall, a dancing saloon, a casino, a theatre, is a good place to pick up a wife we should say,
certainly not. But if you find a young woman in the habit of attending a bible
class, a mechanics' institute lecture, or such like places, then she is very
likely a suitable person.[132]

Accordingly it was normal for couples to walk out unsupervised at
night on first acquaintance, and to kiss and cuddle quite publicly. In
the South Wales mining districts—at least among the Irish community in the 1880s—it was possible to kiss a girl in the street as soon as
she had agreed to go out, and girls could make the first approach to
boys. This was a community with high moral standards—no divorce
or 'bawdy talk in the young men's conversation'—but it could have
been thoroughly misjudged by an unsympathetic observer. In general, alarmed middle-class descriptions of working-class boys and
girls associating freely and intimately in public, whether it be on the
outskirts of Sheffield 'for the purpose of promiscuous intercourse' or
on the pavements of Blackfriars to 'practice in public ways all the
preliminaries to sexual intercourse' or lying and cuddling in Hyde
Park, have to be distrusted.

We have come full circle, back to the bourgeois over-reading of
working-class demeanour in a negative sense. Of the two kinds of
misinterpretation, negative and positive, this is surely the more considerable—even if working-class respectability was not always what
it seemed to be. The 'promiscuous intercourse' witnessed in Sheffield
might often have been platonic, in fact, for young Yorkshire people
are known to have gone out together, as couples, in a purely friendly
spirit. When relationships did become romantic the boy made the

[132] Burnley 1875: 164–6; Shimmin 1856: 49; Kirton 1870: 27–8.

running: 'a girl who can be so independent as to tell her lover to his face that she is fond of him, is regarded as a bold-faced hussy'. Much the same probably goes for visits to public houses by young working-class men and women as deplored by Engels (paraphrasing a factory commissioner), but actually described by him rather touchingly ('forty to fifty young people . . . each lad beside his lass'), and certainly in a way that is inconsistent with the allegation that pubs were used as places for casual encounters by young couples, followed by intercourse in upstairs rooms. Some Lancashire youth (by the last decades of the century at least) were restrained by sheer bashfulness from taking advantage of situations which would have filled certain middle-class commentators with the worst apprehensions: like the two boys who could not bring themselves to cross the road and walk down the local lovers' lane with two girls who, in hopes, kept up their promenade for almost four miles.[133]

To say that Engels's 'unbridled sexual intercourse' between young workers is a bourgeois fantasy is not to deny that the habits of young couples could have led by other routes to pre-marital sex. The demographic evidence confirms this, with its high levels of pre-nuptial pregnancy and rising illegitimacy rate for the central decades of the century. But the first is a phenomenon known for certain only from country districts, where illegitimacy levels tend also to be higher. The account offered in Chapter 2, of illegitimacy as an aspect of courtship, seems especially applicable to rural behaviour in view of the evidence for conventions of courtship in these areas which easily led to, or even included, complete intercourse. Most of the stories about this concern the old practice of 'bundling' (courtship in bed) as still practised in Wales, apparently until 1870 at least, but traditions of waiting until a girl is pregnant before marrying, for instance, are alleged elsewhere. Easy-going attitudes towards pre-marital intercourse, and illegitimacy, seem to be recorded more commonly by commentators on the working class in the country: I do not know of a case of an urban woman, for example, reported as expressing indifference to the stigma of bastardy. In London, working-class families of many types are recorded as trying to conceal the fact of an illegitimacy from siblings and outsiders. By contrast, there is evidence associated with pre-nuptial pregnancies and illegitimacies in rural Kent

[133] Lawson 1887: 14; T. Wright 1867: 227; Keating 1916: 14, 100, 178; PP 1843, xiii. 179; *Scourge*, 4 (1812), 79; Remo 1888: 218; Blatchford 1931: 55–6; Engels 1973: 213; A. A. Cooper 1843: 11; Allen Clarke ('Ben Adhem'), *Liverpool Weekly Post*, 23 June 1934, p. 2.

(for example, the high rate of subsequent marriage to new partners by unmarried mothers) pointing to a tolerant culture in this region.[134]

According to the hypothesis of 'courtship intensity', the lower illegitimacy levels in the cities should be attended by less sexual activity in courtship. It has been calculated, from one of the very few glimpses of courtship intercourse behaviour in the town, that London female servants who became pregnant—chiefly in relationships which were probably intended to lead to marriage—had had intercourse seldom: on average four times. This group is recorded as being rather severe on sexual transgressions by their peers, in some cases more severe than the employers were. The impression to be derived from the working-class autobiographies of the period, also, is that there was 'a high and increasing degree of sexual self-control' before marriage, especially in urban areas.[135] All this indicates that working-class respectability, although not exactly the same phenomenon as bourgeois respectability, did have a correlate at the level of sexual practices.

V

The Real Victorians

It is time, in fact, to ask what condition the hypothesis of the 'Victorian' is left in, after the survey conducted in the last two chapters—bearing in mind what was claimed at the beginning of Chapter 2 about the prospects of moralistic sexual attitudes being reflected in the evidence about practices. Some kind of set-back in the processes of courtship and marriage occurred in the early nineteenth century in England. If this reflects a refraining from sexual intimacy, of the kind thought of as 'Victorian', then Francis Place's dating for the rise of sexual moralism is as good as our modern one—for the set-back in courtship and marriage occurs in the first twenty years of the century. This would be admittedly a minor resetting of the conventional clock: more significant is the broad social base of the phenomenon that seems to be indicated by the general if patchy growth of a new working-class respectability.

---

[134] *Blackwoods*, 66 (1849), 333; PP 1870, xiii. 43, 52; Gaskell 1833: 28; Razzell and Wainwright 1973: 33–4, 57; Kay 1850: 528–9, 575–7; *Morning Chronicle*, 17 Nov. 1849, p. 5; Barret-Ducrocq 1991: 168–9; Reay 1990.

[135] Gillis 1983; Barret-Ducrocq 1991: 102, 174; Burnett 1982: 254.

Then courtship and marriage start to enjoy an increasing vigour again, though probably less so in upper- and upper-middle-class circles. Illegitimacy rates also rise fast, so the tendency is towards greater sexual intimacy, but probably with marriage as the governing ideal. Prostitutes were available for urban men as a sexual outlet, but the numbers of street prostitutes (to whom working-class clients would chiefly have resorted) actually tend to decline as a proportion of town populations. Courtship by contrast was increasingly intimate, sometimes transgressive, and in marital intercourse opportunities to decouple procreation from pleasure were welcomed more and more. The considerable numbers of men from higher ranks who continued to decline this sexual career resorted on the whole to genteel prostitutes.

But it must be recognized that from soon after the mid-century the demographic record is muffled by the onset of contraception, so that the illegitimacy figures are now uninformative about pre-marital sexuality. Marriage shows signs of losing its cultural vigour, and at the middle-class level other kinds of affectionate liaison were at least part of young people's awareness, perhaps to the point of practical exploration (though signals become harder to read because of the phenomenon of 'parasexuality'). Lower in the social scale marriage may also objectively have weakened its hold on youthful sexuality, so that gradually the ethic of sexual restraint which I have outlined above is eroded, and eventually becomes a subject of nostalgia. Already by 1859 some young working-class Londoners are allegedly articulating a quite developed libertine ideology to undermine the morality of young girls of their class—'about love being "supreme", marriage "a humbug", desire "active love", and so forth'. By the 1880s in Leeds the practices of fifty years earlier, when young people would meet in a group to play old-fashioned games, 'then separate and walk sedately homewards', seemed remote.[136]

So certain interesting possibilities about the timing and character of the 'Victorian' emerge from the behavioural record. For a better understanding of the second aspect—of the constituency for nineteenth-century sexual moralism and its code—it is also necessary to examine the beliefs involved in this episode. These are of various sorts. There are biological beliefs specific to sexuality, but also beliefs with a much wider compass: beliefs about the whole make-up of

---

[136] *Social Science* (1861), 67; Cudworth 1886: 84. See also C. Shaw 1977: 206–7.

human nature, about the right form of society, and about religion. These different beliefs may harmonize in their implications for human sexual conduct, or be dissonant. The question to be asked is: how did beliefs flow together to create the moralism which characterizes English sexual culture in, approximately, the period 1800 to 1860? I shall turn to the wider ideological setting in the next volume. In the remaining two chapters of this volume I look at nineteenth-century medical and demographic ideas specific to sexuality.

I investigate the very large literature which Michel Foucault has dubbed a 'discursive explosion', and I devote space to the three topics which Foucault identifies as novel preoccupations in this literature: pubescent children, the 'uterine' female, and population control. Foucault's stress on the ever-growing torrent of published opinion on sex in the eighteenth and nineteenth centuries leads him to reject the 'repressive hypothesis'. According to him, there are more affinities than points of difference between the repressive sexual discourse of 1800 and the anti-repressive sexual discourse of 1900. It will be seen that Foucault does not doubt the repressive hypothesis because he doubts that men's and women's sexuality was repressed: rather he shifts attention away from the matter of behaviour altogether, to focus on 'sex' (as opposed to 'sexuality', 'bodies', and 'pleasures') in the sense of the topic or subject of a certain domain of discourse. Understood in this way, sex was certainly not repressed in the English nineteenth century (in fact the point, like much in Foucault, emerges as something of a platitude when expressed in a straightforward way).

Foucault's manœuvre here constitutes, if not an argument in the ordinary sense against the possibility of making historical connections between beliefs about sex and sexual practices, then at least an argument by example to this effect: a deliberate eschewing of the whole question of linkages, by an influential cultural historian. In a sense Foucault's 'Introduction' to his projected *History of Sexuality* therefore belongs with the sceptical lines of thought I have listed in the 'Can Sexual Moralism be Detected?' section of the previous chapter. But because its scepticism is in such a different vein I have postponed mentioning it until now. Its scepticism about linkages is also much less compelling than any of the other varieties because it depends wholly on one's acceptance of the need to shift attention from 'sexuality' to 'sex' in thinking about this aspect of the culture of the last three centuries. This shift of attention is not argued for by

Foucault: it is simply performed. He leaves the field of bodies and pleasures perfectly intact as a subject of historical inquiry, with its linkages to belief, if one only chooses, contrary to his example, to investigate it. I have seen fit so to do.

Chapter Four

❦❦❦❦❦❦❦❦❦

CARNAL KNOWLEDGE

❦❦❦❦❦❦❦❦❦

I

Doctors and Patients

ON 13 June 1888, at a meeting of the British Gynecological Society, Robert Lawson Tait—one of the most famous surgeons of his era—described a series of patients on whom he had performed hysterectomies or ovariotomies. All ten patients had been operated on while they were still unmarried virgins. All had subsequently married, and the point of interest addressed by Lawson Tait in his paper was the quality of the women's sexual response in marital intercourse, as described by their husbands. It was another shot in a long-running controversy in which Lawson Tait had already been one of the chief skirmishers. The Liverpool gynecologist Francis Imlach was sued in 1886 by a patient, Mrs Casey, for having operated to remove her acutely inflamed ovaries, together with the Fallopian tubes (this variant of ovariotomy was actually known as 'Tait's operation'). Imlach was already the subject of a local medical Committee of Inquiry concerning his use of ovariotomy, and before the trial started there was considerable discussion of the case in the medical press. The trial itself (where the jury found in Imlach's favour) saw several medical witnesses called on either side; and the subsequent heated debate in the *Lancet* and elsewhere ran on for five years. Lawson Tait contributed prominently, on Imlach's side, in all phases of the affair.[1]

Loss of sexual feelings ('between herself and her husband it had

[1] Moscucci 1990: 160–4; *Casey* v. *Imlach* is reported at length in *Lancet*, 1886(2), 298–303 and *BMJ* 1886(2), 393–5.

made a wonderful change') was not the only grievance alleged by Mrs Casey, but most of the medical witnesses seem to have been asked for their opinion on this feature of the case. Tait denied in the courtroom that ovariotomy could affect a woman's sexual feelings, and he denied it again in his Gynecological Society paper.[2] Of seven husbands married to women without ovaries two reported a 'distinctly aggressive' sexual appetite in their wives, and three a 'perfectly satisfactory' or 'well-developed' one; two others found their wives' sexual drive to be 'satisfactory', and just one reported 'little desire for intercourse'. One of the hysterectomized wives was 'as complaisant as a woman can be' (though only after a first year of marriage in which she had been 'very averse'); the remaining two exhibited 'decided sexual receptivity' and 'a sexual competency which her husband regards as satisfactory'. Tait was confident that these results showed that female sexual feelings were not dependent on the womb or its appendages, and he referred to the 'strangely contradictory evidence given in a court of law recently' on this question. In the discussion of his paper the speakers generally agreed with Tait's interpretation of the facts, but one sceptical gynecologist 'suggested that women might simulate orgasms out of a natural desire to retain the affections of their husbands'.

With this remark a good deal that is damaging to modern clichés about the Victorian understanding of sexual function precipitates out of the Casey affair and its aftermath. It becomes unmistakable that female sexual feeling in the fullest sense, of orgasm, was at issue in this episode. Moreover this full version of a woman's sexual response was evidently understood and regarded as a good by both parties in an ordinary marriage of the period. It appears that a wife's orgasm was very important for a Victorian husband, and even that a woman who had not experienced orgasm might have known enough to simulate one convincingly. The very vocabulary in which the latter possibility is expressed is disconcertingly that of our own day: 'women might simulate orgasms'. (In the usage of the day 'orgasm' certainly denoted a climax, it should be said. The term was not as common in the medical or lay vocabularies as it is today, but 'Walter' in *My Secret Life*, for example, uses it occasionally about both male and female satisfaction.)[3]

In addition to seeing off certain howlers about the subject, the

[2] *British Gynecological Journal*, 4 (1888), 310–17, also *BMJ* 1888(1), 1387.
[3] *My Secret Life* 1966: 2076, 2109.

whole episode can point towards some authentic questions concerning Victorian ideas on human sexual function. It appears that professional wisdom in this area was far from unanimous, and that differences between doctors flowed from different underlying pictures of the whole mechanism of sexual desire and response. For example, Lawson Tait described in his paper only cases in which the womb or ovaries had been lost *before* any experience of intercourse, because where the operation had been done post-maritally 'retention of the sexual appetite . . . would mean nothing at all': it could have been 'developed' by sex in marriage. It is interesting to ask what was the nature of the two-tier model of a woman's sexual feelings which seems to be in mind here.

Some historians have recognized the need to go beyond the mere reiteration of supposed Victorian doctrines about isolated aspects of sexual behaviour, and to enquire into the physiological models which produced them. But scarcely any have asked how unanimous were nineteenth-century notions about sexual function, or, where there was disagreement, who believed what. Medical writings are, inevitably, almost the only evidence about such beliefs. Occasionally, as in the remark about simulated orgasms just cited, they give a glimpse of lay thinking, but usually all that is directly expressed is a doctor's view of some aspect of sexual structure or function. It is none the less important to try to interpret such statements in terms of the lay public's belief; the question of what doctors thought, *per se*, is of parochial interest. And for this purpose we need to bear in mind the organization and circumstances of the medical profession in the nineteenth century. The game of quote and counter-quote, of offering medical utterances, selected without regard for context, as an index of general beliefs in the period, can be played indefinitely: for almost every point of view in the literature, concerning the heterosexual realm at least, the antithesis may also be found. The important task is to decide *which* medical utterances are instructive as to the thinking of ordinary, non-medical nineteenth-century men and women.

In fact the range of professional opinion elicited in the Imlach trial was not quite as wide as Lawson Tait's remark might suggest (even though one surgeon went rather beyond him, and declared that sexual desires could be *more* intense after ovariotomy). No medical witness claimed that the operation always and immediately killed these impulses: on the most pessimistic views, the effect took a year to appear, or was only seen in 50 per cent of cases. It would be pleasing to report, for the general argument of the present study, that these differences of opinion coincided with visible differences in the status of the doctors involved. The English medical profession was a politicized profession, especially in the years before the Medical Reform Act of 1858 but also thereafter, with the fellows of the two Royal Colleges resisting reforms which were very generally desired by general practitioners. No one who deposed for Mrs Casey seems to have been a College fellow, and two FRCSes deposed for Imlach. But the latter were in a mixed company of ordinary practitioners and hospital specialists (Imlach himself was an MRCS and surgeon at a women's hospital).

There are examples of high-profile medical figures in the nineteenth century with active political affiliations: very notably the Cobbettian Thomas Wakley, editor of the *Lancet* and Radical MP for Finsbury. Lawson Tait was said to be 'a Liberal of "the advanced type"'.[4] But there is evidently a difficulty in defining the clinical equivalent of the politically—or even the medico-politically—'progressive', and there are especial dangers for the modern observer trying to do this for nineteenth-century sexual medicine. For which *is* the progressive side in a controversy such as the ovariotomy debate of 1886? To decouple a woman's sexuality from her reproductive capacities, as Imlach, Tait, and others were doing in their physiological theory, tends to grant her right to sexual pleasure for its own sake. But it may also be argued that in their practices these gynecological surgeons were assuming quite illegitimate powers over a woman's physical being (as indeed the opponents of ovariotomy argued throughout the tortured history of this technically momentous innovation).[5] Lawson Tait seems not to have consulted his patients about their sexual responses, but only their husbands. Feminists of the day could have seen evidence here to support their conviction that affirmative attitudes towards female pleasure really served the sexual interests of men.

Other issues may seem less equivocal: we tend to assume that it is 'progressive' to doubt the ill effects of masturbation, to deplore sexual abstinence, and to favour birth control. But the logic of beliefs about sex in the period, to be unravelled in this chapter, was such that not

[4] J. F. Clarke 1874: 18–24; *Biograph and Review*, 3 (1880), 240.
[5] Outstandingly well discussed by Dally 1991: 135–56. See also Longo 1979.

all these positions, or at least not all versions of them, were repudiated by reactionary medical writers. And writers of an opposite tendency did not, by any means, universally accept them. For the time being the complexity of the situation can be indicated by mentioning that Dr George Drysdale, the one declared sexual liberationist of the nineteenth century in Britain and the only candid medical advocate of birth control for most of the Victorian years, took as bleak a view of the evils of masturbation as anyone.

But if different medical dogmas about sexual function cannot readily be correlated with conservative or reforming elements in the medical profession is it possible to associate these dogmas with different levels of medical sophistication? From the very beginning of the nineteenth century the old division of the profession into physicians, surgeons, and apothecaries was becoming much less significant than the modern distinction between hospital-based medical men (consultants, who had bread-winning outside practices, and their trainees and assistants) and 'general practitioners' (the term was in common use by the early 1820s).[6] It was a hierarchy of specialized experience and academicism, above all because of the rapidly expanding role of hospitals as centres of medical education. A consultant at one of the large London teaching hospitals would have been by the mid-century already at a great distance intellectually from most of his provincial GP colleagues. In addition to the benefits of the correlated investigation and treatment of large numbers of patients, systematized for a teaching curriculum, there was a small, slowly growing corpus of pure medical science feeding into the consultant's skills from domestic and foreign researchers. Specialized clinical work could also be done by more lowly practitioners, it is true, and small clinics devoted to particular diseases, to which these doctors were often attached, lent an authority to their more academic work which was sometimes deserved, and sometimes—especially in the field of sexual disorders—not.

One implication of these developments is that there were big disparities in the medical sophistication of nineteenth-century doctors which are not reflected in their formal qualifications, and only partly reflected in the posts they held. The level at which they pitch their writings (and these are our main evidence for their beliefs) is of course very revealing, and throughout this chapter I shall seek to

[6] I. Loudon 1986: 1.

judge how academically minded particular medical authors were from the internal evidence of the texts they wrote. It will become clear how slowly certain fundamental discoveries in sexual physiology permeated through the profession: in effect, how long the mass of practitioners and their patients in the nineteenth century continued to share ideas about sexual function which strictly speaking were obsolete. It is significant that Lawson Tait, as late as 1888, saw all the opinion which linked Mrs Casey's loss of sexual feeling with her ovariotomy as expressions of the 'popular' belief about the female sexual appetite, although they all came from qualified medical witnesses.

The great mass of the medical profession with whom the lay public chiefly had contact (that is, the roughly 90 per cent of doctors who were GPs)[7] was not alert, or did not choose to be alert, to the latest laboratory or dissecting-room discoveries about the processes of ovulation, menstruation, and fertilization, for example. As a result, GP wisdom was relatively akin to lay belief, both systems amounting to much the same mixture of classically derived and late-Renaissance doctrines. Moreover there were powerful inducements, at least until the 1860s, for GPs to respect lay prejudices. One of the great blunders in the historiography of this subject has been the notion that nineteenth-century doctors formed a monolithic, paid-up, secular priesthood, which was both willing and able to interfere moralistically with the sexuality of its patients. For example, a recent study[8] has assumed that as soon as the doctrine of spontaneous ovulation was proposed by certain medical scientists in the 1830s and 1840s it became the orthodoxy of the whole profession, a weapon in the hands of all medical practitioners with which to enforce on lay women a belief that they should not seek to have orgasms. A cursory survey of the literature would have shown, in fact, that spontaneous ovulation took decades to become a generally received doctrine among medical men.

This probably reflects an important truth about the power relations of the lay public and doctors in the period. At least until the last third of the century the profession was oversubscribed, and often seriously underpaid, and in these conditions there was little reason for doctors

[7] I. Waddington 1984: 42.

[8] Laqueur 1986. Laqueur 1990: ch. 5 however appears to take a different view. An important general statement of the ascendancy of patient over doctor (though not based on the economics of the profession) is Gay 1984: 315–17.

to dole out unfamiliar sexual ideas, let alone unwelcome moralistic advice. 'We must not expect', wrote Robert Dale Owen in 1840, 'that physicians will risk at once their reputation and their fortunes in order to tell us, that . . . we should reject the morality which now prevails'. There may have been something of a paid-up priesthood at the very top of the profession (though its income came mainly from private practice, and the lay governors of hospitals, in particular, controlled consultants in a way unthinkable today), but a great number of nineteenth-century medical men were in a condition of strict dependence on lay approval. In the sexual-medical domain this dependence seems to have been especially marked, because of the readiness with which middle-class women compared and changed doctors: a witness at the Imlach trial, J. H. Aveling, is one of several doctors who complained publicly about their ascendancy. Dependence of this sort had certainly been more the rule in the eighteenth century, and the period did eventually see the emergence of the practitioner as the autonomous and dominant party in medical treatment, but it is none the less wrong to project back on to the Victorian medical profession our modern experience of the doctor's status. 'Victorian general practitioners', in the words of a modern expert, were 'without freedom or authority . . . the servants of their employers and their patients'.[9]

This is not to deny that many doctors were uneasy about or even antagonistic to their patients' sexuality. At a time when male patients tended to request treatment for self-diagnosed sexual disorders, and female patients perhaps (though the evidence here is less certain)[10] to expect a new thoroughness in gynecological investigation, some doctors were disconcerted or alienated by the requirements being made of them. They could find men's and women's admissions about irregular sexual habits 'disgusting', 'sickening', and 'repulsive', something it was 'natural' to want to ignore, or at least a regrettable necessity of their work which was 'debasing in its tendencies' and called for 'strong principles in ourselves'. Some felt that it would be right to err on the side of severity about masturbation even if its harmful effects were in doubt. Doctors may have deterred talk about the

[9] I. Loudon 1986: 218–22, 258–61, 265–6; I. Waddington 1984: 35–6, 148–9; Peterson 1978: 90–8, 123, 129, 133–4, 139–50, 221; Owen 1840: 9; Bynum 1992.

[10] G. Drysdale 1868: 158–9, 214, 229; Whitehead 1847: p. xv; W. Jones 1839: 95; 'Fellow of the Royal College of Surgeons' 1857: 6; Graham 1834: passim; C. West 1856: i. 9; Branca 1975: 62–4; Tilt 1852: 176; Donnison 1977: 70.

subject from patients (sometimes referring them instead to a suitable book), and the *BMJ* wanted to keep even the technical vocabulary of venereal disease to a minimum in consultations with women patients.[11]

There was a heated controversy in the period over the use of the vaginal speculum, which there is no room here to describe, but this was a debate entirely within the profession, and brings into audibility some very moralistic medical voices. Some doctors may have tried to avoid making a vaginal examination of any sort except in pressing cases.[12] An even more acrimonious conflict—again not encompassable here, though it will be referred to a little more fully in the last chapter of this study—was that concerning male midwives. Moralistic abuse about the motives of male doctors who attended pregnancies, and those of their patients, had been a feature of this controversy since its early days in the eighteenth century. The debate was not confined to medical participants, and the medical men who opposed male midwifery were by definition not active in obstetrics, or were reformed offenders, but the severe and alarmist attitudes they voiced would presumably have affected what practical dealings with the sexuality of women patients they did have. Inhibitions of this sort were probably felt much more with middle- and upper-class, paying patients than in hospital practice, and the detached (not to say cold) attitude of hospital doctors and their students to the mass of working-class 'material' available in the big hospitals would surely have run to the patients' intimate anatomy and physiology. But there is evidence that even here genital examinations were, by comparison with French hospital practices, mindful of delicacy.[13]

It is hard to form an impression of the spirit in which education about sexual and genital topics was conducted in the hospitals. Sir James Paget recalled how his midwifery teachers at Barts around the latter 1830s (who included Conquest and Locock) used to tell stories that were 'obscene, some very nasty'. He thought the habit died out later, and it is certain that even at this early date the *Lancet* was orga-

[11] E. Waddington 1853; J. Adams 1851: 49; C. Ritchie 1851; Johnson 1860; B. Bell 1793: i. 224; Courtenay 1839: 27; *National Reformer*, 29 (1877), 266; Black 1872: 305; 'Syphilology for Ladies', *BMJ* 1869(2), 442–3.

[12] *Medical Times*, 21 (1850), 425–8; Lee 1858: 9; 'Fellow of the Royal College of Surgeons' 1857: *passim*; *Lancet*, 1850(1), 701–5, and subsequent correspondence; Black 1872: 228; Roe 1852: *passim*; J. H. Bennett 1845: p. xv; C. M. Clarke 1821: ch. 3.

[13] Peterson 1978: 174; C. West 1856: i. 12; G. Drysdale 1868: 214, 262; *Lancet*, 1832–3(1), 587–91; 1850(1), 702–5 (Acton's contribution).

nizing a campaign against the 'frivolous, absurd, indecent' clinical teaching style of Sir Anthony Carlisle. But Shepherd Taylor, a student at Kings in the 1860s, frequently noted in his diary how his teachers would make dirty jokes (of the 'the artery goes in and out, as it were' variety) even on non-sexual topics. These were evidently not mere embarrassed reactions to awkward parts of the curriculum, and they seem to have gone down well with the students even if the latter also felt or affected to feel a certain 'disgust'. On the other hand the distinguished physician Lionel Beale, who taught at the same hospital, urged on colleagues that 'in our lectures to medical students . . . [it was] not necessary or desirable to do more than make general reference' to sexual-medical topics. Lay opinion by this time, as represented by the *Westminster Review*, found medical students at Cambridge to be 'more pure-minded and modest than most men of the same standing'.[14]

One of the most intriguing questions about the moral attitudes of nineteenth-century doctors to their patients' sexuality is the nature of the advice they gave to unmarried men about pre-marital intercourse. Practitioners who felt strongly that unmarried men should be chaste often complained that many of their colleagues were giving the opposite advice, namely, recommending sexual release with prostitutes or mistresses, but it is hard to check the accuracy of this. After 1855 it may be George Drysdale who was in these men's sights, or rather the anonymous but avowedly medical author of *Natural, Sexual and Physical Religion* (later *The Elements of Social Science*) who certainly did advocate regular use of the sexual organs, from puberty onwards, by both sexes in free non-marital unions. Robert James Culverwell, though a doctor on the fringe of professional respectability, had written to the same effect, more darkly, in the previous decade.[15]

How many invisible Drysdales and Culverwells were there? Drysdale himself is oddly inconsistent, in the *Elements*, on the question of how many of his colleagues, how explicitly, were giving their patients the kind of counsel he approved. One Edinburgh practitioner had the courage to endorse the *Elements* as a work which 'should be very extensively advertised'. Given the currency of the notion that sexual abstinence could be damaging, and the almost

[14] S. Paget 1901: 50; J. F. Clarke 1874: 284–93; S. T. Taylor 1927: 10, 45, 69, 84; Beale 1887: 90; *Westminster Review*, NS 56 (1879), 207.

[15] Culverwell 1849: 14–15.

universal belief that masturbation was inadvisable, or worse (both topics are discussed later in this chapter), it should have been inevitable that many doctors endorsed male pre-marital intercourse. On the other hand, the same beliefs were held to very much the same extent about women, and we do not hear that practitioners were recommending the same line of conduct for female patients. Persuasive glimpses of doctors who did explicitly tell male patients to resort to pre-marital intercourse are rare and indirect, but when these are put together with the very frequent complaints about the practice (while making allowance here for hostile exaggeration), it seems likely that there were many consulting-rooms in which relations with prostitutes or mistresses were cheerfully regarded. As a kind of sequel to such attitudes, one doctor tells directly how he recommended to a patient with a potency problem in marriage that he should fantasize about an earlier mistress when making love to his wife.[16]

In other words the medical profession was probably so divided in its policy on this issue that it would be quite wrong to speak of a sexual-moral orthodoxy about male pre-marital intercourse being delivered by doctors to the lay public. On another subject, the ill effects of masturbation and sexual excess, there was much more agreement among medical men, but in this case, as will be argued shortly, a moralistic prejudice among doctors was matched by an equivalent prejudice among their patients. There was one issue on which doctors were virtually unanimous, and yet also out of tune with the tendency of lay attitudes: birth control by means of physical devices. I have already argued that the fertility decline of the last third of the century should be explained mainly in the way it was explained by historians until recently, that is, as a result of the use of condoms, pessaries, sponges, and douches. If I am right, the episode is a striking proof of the failure of doctors to exert moral hegemony over the lay public.

W. J. Linton commented in 1839 on the medical profession's refusal to acknowledge artificial birth control. The doctors' silence could not be due to ignorance, he thought: it is 'a remedy, with which they must be acquainted, since it is commonly applied on the conti-

---

[16] G. Drysdale 1868: 81, 91, 162–3, 504; *National Reformer*, 1 June 1861, p. 6; *British and Foreign Medico-Chirurgical Review*, 21 (1858), 403; *Lancet*, 1836–7(1), 390; 1843–4(1), 440–2; 1879(2), 422; Courtenay 1839: 70; Humphry 1864; *Westminster Review*, NS 56 (1879), 203.

nent'. Linton's surmise must have been broadly correct: as mentioned in Chapter 2, some contraceptive measures were simple applications of medical devices, and the *Lancet* of 1823 had been sufficiently cognizant of Francis Place's birth-control propaganda to condemn it as 'beneath our notice'. But one's confidence about this may come under a certain strain as the century advances, and then reaches a period when large numbers of couples are unmistakably restricting their fertility (probably by artificial techniques), and there is still scarcely a reference to birth control by a doctor to be found. Textbooks are virtually silent about it; studies of fertility from a statistical point of view ignore it when it seems most inescapably relevant. Michael Ryan's attack on birth-control practices in the 1830s is the most explicit and extensive for a long time: thereafter allusions in the medical literature are vague and fleeting, where they are not so ambiguously couched as to be uncertain.[17]

When the subject finally achieves some visibility in the 1860s it becomes apparent that there may have been a genuine element of ignorance among doctors about new physical techniques of contraception, and that medical opposition to such procedures was very nearly, but not quite, universal (confirming what the *Lancet* confidently took to be the case). It seems that some medical men—almost incredibly, for others were deploring under their noses the sale of contraceptive pessaries—really believed that continental practices (which Linton had thought must enlighten them) amounted to coitus interruptus and sodomy.[18] William Acton in *The Functions and Disorders* had been conventional in avoiding all mention of birth control, and he was criticized for this omission by an 1862 reviewer, who knew of 'nothing *sacred* . . . in either spermatozoa or ova'. In the storm provoked by the Dialectical Society debate of 1 July 1868, at which Lord Amberley had implied that doctors should assist in the business of population control, there is heard the occasional medical voice in favour of contraception—even on the grounds of its enhancement of marital sexuality. But by and large the professional reaction to this event was furiously indignant, with Amberley's words being felt as nothing less than an insult to doctors. The profession's anxiety to put distance between itself and birth control at this period

---

[17] *National*, 29 June 1839, p. 365; Peel 1965; F. B. Smith 1979: p. 296; *JSSL* 14 (1851), 79; Duncan 1866: *passim*; *North British Review*, 47 (1857), 441–62; Mann 1855: 124; 'Woman in her Psychological Relations', *Journal of Psychological Medicine*, 4 (1851), 8–50.

[18] *Lancet*, 1869(2), 209; *Medical Press and Circular*, 1869(2), 43–4, 375; 1870(1), 460, 464.

was so great that the celebrated American-born gynecologist
J. Marion Sims would not use condoms even to collect sperm from
his patients for analysis, and the *Lancet* inserted a long editorial note
after a letter from Charles Drysdale, vehemently repudiating his
views.[19]

Charles Drysdale's statements in these years are perhaps themselves revealing of the depth of medical inhibitions about contraception. He was the brother of the more radical and notorious but far
less visible George Drysdale, and went on to found the second
Malthusian League. In the late 1860s he was unwearying in his
attempts to spread the message of population reduction, in a general
form, in lectures and contributions to the press. But he remained at
this period extraordinarily and, one must say, dishonestly evasive on
detail. Faced with repeated challenges to clarify the methods by
which the French had held down family size he claimed not to have
any 'documents' to help him understand the phenomenon. The
Medical Press and Circular, which seems to have been tacitly sympathetic to Drysdale and which he used more than any other journal at
this date as a channel for his views, was also less than forthright: it
recognized that 'modern science' could make marriage affordable for
all, but treated Lord Amberley's speech as if it were about 'abortion
and prostitution'—an interpretation shared by no other section of
medical opinion, but which enabled the *Press and Circular* to join
with them in indignant repudiation of Amberley's invitation to the
profession.[20]

It is difficult to explain the violent fastidiousness of the medical
response to contraception up until the 1870s. Fastidiousness about
the sexual and genital *per se*, which seems only to have been felt by a
minority of doctors, probably had little to do with it. Marion Sims
may have found condoms repugnant, but he was no prude: in treating
sterile couples he would virtually hover outside the bedroom door in
order to take a vaginal smear as little as 'four or five minutes after the
act' (the coition itself must have been a very deliberate and unembar-
rassed act under these circumstances).[21] Some of the medical attacks
on birth control mention the moral or religious offence of interfering

---

[19] *London Medical Review*, 3 (1862–3), 141–7; *Medical Press and Circular*, 1869(1), 265–6
and sequels; 1869(2), 504–5; *Medical Times and Gazette*, 1868(2), 148, 244; *Lancet*, 1869(2),
215; 1870(2), 658; *BMJ* 1868(2), 113, 465–6, 492–4. See also Himes 1936, 248; Stopes 1922:
14.

[20] *Medical Press and Circular*, 1868(2), 210–11; 1869(1), 546–7; 1870(1), 437.

[21] J. M. Sims 1866: 351.

with reproduction, and this may really have weighed with some doctors: others, however, were urging that the safe-period and extended lactation were solutions to the problem of large families,[22] so a planned frustration of reproductive processes was not taboo. It may well be that most doctors hated the idea of mechanical operations with condoms, pessaries, and douches in the genital region and in the course of love-making, and I shall discuss the affirmativeness of doctors about sexual arousal and fulfilment later in this chapter. But some of them must, in their personal lives, have been incorporating artificial contraception successfully into sex, and it does seem that it was above all as *doctors* that the medical profession found an involvement with birth control repellent.

To give advice about, and prescribe for, birth control was to act outside the therapeutic realm, at least on a narrow definition of therapy. Moreover, it was to depart from therapy in the direction of endorsing sexual pleasure, and perhaps of assisting non-marital sex. This resembled what the quack sexologists—members of a fraternity always bitterly resented by the medical establishment—were offering with their cures for sexual debility and female frigidity. Some quacks offered birth-control devices among their other curative wares, and the whole culture of contraception involved the advertising and retailing of services and products in a manner profoundly alien to the cherished protocols of legitimate medical practice. These considerations did not necessarily surface: when Henry Allbutt, who had been the first English doctor to attach his name to detailed published advice on contraception, was struck off the medical register in 1887, it was the encouragement he had given to immorality which swayed the General Medical Council, according to its minutes. But Allbutt was conspicuously commercial and quack-like in his operations, a doctor who announced and sold his own birth-control products through cheap pamphlets.[23]

Quack medicine is very significant for the understanding of qualified medical practice in the nineteenth century, perhaps above all in the area of sexual disorders. It must always be remembered that the nineteenth-century practitioner, in competing for patients and thus patient-approval, was up against not only his own peers but all the non-qualified men trying to make a living out of patent medicines, herbal and dietary remedies, water and electrical cures, and so

[22] C. Loudon 1836: *passim*; *Medical Press and Circular*, 1869(2), 414.
[23] Micklewright 1962.

forth. In the sexual domain he was competing with them for the lucrative and possibly expanding middle- and lower-middle-class market, for it was at this group that the quack specialists in sexual disorders especially made their pitch. This is apparent from the character of the testimonial letters (whether true or false) which they printed in their literature, from the social standing of the few patients who can be identified, and from the price of quack or quasi-quack pamphlets, medicines, and consultations: Brodum's Nervous Cordial cost 5s. 5d. for the smallest bottle, Abercrombie's Genital Nervine Solution 7s. 6d. a bottle, Senate's Balm of Mecca 7s. a packet, Perry's Cordial Balm of Syriacum and the more famous Balm of Gilead from Solomon half a guinea, Henery's electric belt £2 and La'mert's bargain package £10—while £1 or a guinea was the standard consultation fee, with actual treatments for 'spermatorrhoea' sometimes costing hundreds of pounds.[24]

These operators invested heavily to reach their potential patients, in the manufacture of pamphlets (these seem to have been printed by the tens of thousands, and some at least were just mailed randomly to middle-class recipients), and in advertisements in a host of weekly papers and all the leading dailies (except, after the 1830s, *The Times*), where it was worth the quacks' while to soothe proprietorial consciences by paying a very large premium. The dozen or so most profitable concerns probably spent between £1,000 and £2,000 a year on advertising.[25] It should be said, however, that quacks and fringe-doctors further down the market also traded greatly on sex, and were no less ready to arouse anxieties about the effects of masturbation.[26]

The spectacle of such lucrative rewards from entrepreneurial, sub-scientific medicine was too much for some struggling orthodox practitioners. Two of them, Robert James Culverwell and Robert Abercrombie, have left accounts of how the hard facts of life as a young GP with a family forced them to cross over into the world of sex-advice and consultancy and of patent cures by water and electricity.[27] In the case of Culverwell, who seems to have been the more

[24] Bynum 1992; Courtenay 1865: 27; *Lancet*, 1857(2), 150–3; 1861(1), 620; 1863(1), 505; 1864(2), 504; 1865(1), 98–9; W. Acton 1857a: 92.

[25] *Scourge*, 2 (1811), 299; Grant 1842: i. 22; *Lancet*, 1845(2), 563–5; 1851(1), 72; 1861(1), 582–3; 1865(1), 277; 1866(1), 492–3; *Medical Press and Circular*, 1870(1), 464; Courtenay 1865: 2; F. B. Smith 1974; Culverwell 1852: 42.

[26] I. Loudon 1987: Fox 1884: 202–3 (the anti-onanism remedy given in this popular herbalist text could have been made up for about 2s. from the ingredients offered for sale).

[27] Peterson 1978: 244–6; Culverwell 1852: *passim*.

bullish of two, the result was a very quick transformation of his personal finances from a running deficit of £100 a year to something like prosperity, and later to affluence. Another career which started legitimately but moved towards the borderline with the illegitimate was that of J. L. Milton, the author of an endlessly republished booklet on spermatorrhoea; though this was attacked in the medical press, and almost brought about the collapse of another, respectable Milton venture—St John's Hospital for skin diseases—Milton managed to stay within the pale.[28] A shadier character was Richard Dawson, whose claimed affiliation to another small establishment, the 'Institution for the Treatment of Calculus, Diabetes, and the Various Diseases of the Genito-Urinary System', as well as his degrees, came under fierce scrutiny in the *Lancet* after he had allegedly killed a patient. But this journal had published a paper by him on spermatorrhoea, which Wakley later regretted (as did the Royal Medical and Chirurgical Society a paper it commissioned from Dr Harry Lobb).[29]

These men were not distinctive just because they had genuine medical qualifications, however: they believed that their backgrounds in legitimacy still distinguished them from ordinary quacks, whatever their enemies might feel about the matter, and their activities were indeed somewhat different. In an age when it was not an offence to claim a university degree dishonestly—and, if necessary, degrees could be bought from continental and American universities[30]—it is rather surprising that quacks on the whole do not seem to have concocted medical qualifications for themselves (though 'Dr' A. F. Henery, it emerged in court, was really plain Mr Wray). Several quacks did have genuine medical degrees. They all tried, to a varying extent, for a colouration of medical science in their literature (and stole the names of famous doctors for their medicines), but their discourse is always a blatant appeal to the anxieties of their readers behind the backs of their legitimate counterparts, sometimes of the most crudely manipulative sort.[31]

[28] *Dublin Quarterly Journal of Medical Science*, 18 (1854), p. xvi; B. Russell 1963: 2–3, 22–5.

[29] Dawson 1848: 176–8; *Lancet*, 1845(2), 563–5; 1861(1), 582–3 and sequels; Lobb 1880: pp. ix–xi. On Lobb see also Peterson 1978: 252–3. On the internal evidence of another series of articles in the *Lancet* (1840–1(2), 779–85 and sequels) J. R. Smyth was also at the edge of legitimacy (possible further examples are Drs S. Mason and Shadrach Jones).

[30] Belcher 1872: 5–7.

[31] *Lancet*, 1864(2), 503–5, 620; Jordan and Co. 1842; Perry and Co. 1841; C. L. Hunt n.d.; Solomon c.1810.

Even it men like Solomon and Senate had acquired their MDs with a sincere intention of being legitimate practitioners, they obviously very quickly and completely seceded from orthodox medicine. By contrast the quasi-quacks sought to be published in a respectable way as well as popularly, struggled to avoid losing College membership, offered elaborate confirmation of their medical qualifications, and went to the courts to defend their respectability.[32] Above all, they tended to strike a more respectable-looking balance in their pamphlets between self-promotion and medical instruction than the pure quack. Early in the period there may have been some genuine dissent from the profession's embargo on doctors' marketing of their own remedies, but thereafter the quasi-quacks were notably decorous. Where they did offer a patient cure it was likely to be reserved for mention in an appendix (to avoid 'soiling my pages by trumpeting forth the marvellous properties of certain lotions') or to be innocent of the vulgarity of an alluring name (an intriguing possibility in the case of Dr Yeoman's suppositories for sexual debility).[33]

Goss's publications, in particular, featured careful illustrations of sexual anatomy and the physiology of conception and pregnancy. A qualified doctor's knowledge, even what he had learnt as a medical student, was a commodity which commanded a price—again, perhaps a higher price than his orthodox clinical services. In 1837 an MRCS described sympathetically how a GP colleague had been forced to give popular lectures on sex, genuinely knowledgeable lectures, it was said, though the style was 'scarcely moral' and of the 'warmest' (Culverwell gave similar lectures at about this date: indeed he may be the subject of this anecdote).[34] This lecturer used illustrations and models, while at Kahn's famous anatomical museum in the West End the emphasis was on a large display of exhibits, accompanied by a lecture. The latter was generally a standard piece of spermatorrhoea propaganda, the exhibits were often prurient, and the Kahn Harley Street practice was quackery. But one of the two Kahn brothers was a qualified doctor (with a continental degree), the museum did contain embryological exhibits (and in one at least of its West End manifestations had ladies-only sessions and a female lec-

---

[32] Peterson 1978: 246; Dawson 1848: 176–8; De Roos 1840, La'mert 1852, and Culverwell 1852, *passim*, give details of qualifications; 'Horace Goss', who was qualified, but as R. T. Crucefix, also editor of *The Freemasons' Quarterly Review*, sued the *Medical Adviser* for libel; on La'mert see also L. Hall 1991: 55–6.

[33] Brodum 1795: ii. 130–4; De Roos 1840: 48; Yeoman 1854: 82–4.

[34] *Town*, 1 (1837–8), 130–1; Culverwell 1852: 58.

turer), and it put out an apparently respectable *Atlas of the Formation of the Human Body*.[35] There were several other anatomical museums in London, also offering single-sex instruction for women, and more in the provincial cities and towns, some of which survived well into the twentieth century.[36]

Other doctors exploited their medical knowledgeability more honourably. Richard Reece, a doctor with an eye like Culverwell's for any entrepreneurial opening, founded a popular medical magazine, the *Monthly Gazette of Health*, in 1815. He made provision for sexual disorders, but in a fairly unalarmist supplement on the subject in volume 3. Some of the most prominent books on sexuality in the century, despite having a much more academic appearance than the quack and quasi-quack literature, are clearly aimed at a lay readership, and may have proved lucrative. John Roberton's *On the Generative System*, several of Ryan's publications (he admits in the preface that *The Philosophy of Marriage* is intended partly for a general readership), and Acton's *The Functions and Disorders of the Reproductive Organs* are all examples of much reprinted books in this vein. The lay readership was up to reading the *Lancet*, after all,[37] and anyone who has investigated the area will have come across textbooks with their sexual material torn or cut out—by or for the sake of lay readers. Allen Clarke, as a young man in Lancashire in the 1880s, learnt about sex from books of physiology in the public library. 'Walter', who passed himself off as a doctor for some of his more difficult seductions, and who uses a medical vocabulary of some sophistication, prided himself on his knowledge of reproductive processes and structures.[38] But it was difficult for the popular authors to be quite free of vulgarity, quackish or otherwise. Roberton was later published by the somewhat sleazy Joseph Stockdale (and was keen to promote cantharides as a cure, in opposition to more orthodox opinion). Ryan often strikes a prurient note.

It is something comparable in Acton's *Functions and Disorders* (a

---

[35] Hibbert 1916: 41; brochure for Kahn's 'Anatomical and Pathological Museum' (before 1857); Kahn 1856; S. T. Taylor 1927: 16; *Lancet*, 1857(2), 150–3; F. B. Smith 1979: 296; undated advertisement in BL 1880.b.31.

[36] *Saturday Review*, 18 (1864), 680–1; advertisement for 'Anatomical Representation of a Female Figure' in BL 1880.b.31; *Porcupine*, 1 (1860), *passim*; *New Statesman*, 65 (1963), 317–18; Courtenay 1865: 8; Peterson 1978: 254; L. Hall 1991: 58–9; *Catalogue of J. W. Reimer's Gallery* 1853.

[37] Smyth 1844: 233.

[38] Allen Clarke ('Ben Adhem'), *Liverpool Weekly Post*, 16 June 1934, p. 2. See e.g. *My Secret Life* 1966: 1195, 1705.

'warmness' like that of the doctor lecturing in 1837), which inclines a modern authority on nineteenth-century London practitioners to call him 'perhaps the cleverest quack of his generation'.[39] But this is to simplify a complex book. Though no pioneering medical scientist, Acton evidently had a genuine intellectual curiosity about his subject, and could surmount preconceptions (he was struck, for example, by the thoroughly healthy appearance of many of the subjects in a collection of photographs of catamites). He gives the impression of having been a humane clinician: in fact his claims about the physical effects of masturbation and sexual excess are considerably less fantastic than those made by George Drysdale about the evils of abstinence. Acton addresses the first edition of *Functions and Disorders* of 1857 (which had grown out of his academic study, *A Practical Treatise on Diseases of the Urinary and Generative Organs*) to professional colleagues, and only incidentally to lay readers. Certainly as the text changes (the major revision is made in the third edition of 1862, but there are many subsequent modifications) the book becomes increasingly adapted to a lay readership. But I believe that only after a time did Acton properly grasp this potential of his theme, which he signalled by dropping the reference to a chiefly medical audience.

It is true that Acton's posture in relation to the lay public (with whom the book was an outstanding success) was always in a sense quackish. *Functions and Disorders* is, very importantly, entirely about male sexuality, and it is to a great extent about men's sexual anxieties, of the sort the quacks exploited so efficiently. Even in its first version the book was tuned in to the mentality of the many patients who had consulted Acton with fears of impotence, guilt about masturbation, and so forth: 'I believe I know the hints which some who read it will require'. While there is much hostility to quacks in *Functions and Disorders*, Acton is also frequently in the position of rescuing for medical respectability doctrines and clinical conditions which have been 'pooh-poohed' (his term) by his colleagues because of their association with quackery. The popular content of Acton's book has an additional aspect, quite distinct in its tendency, for which it is more celebrated today. *Functions and Disorders* is a work of moral, and moralistic, advice, which has much to say even about topics—such as the financial and social considera-

[39] Peterson 1986; *London Medical Review*, 3 (1862–3), 141–7.

tions affecting a decision to marry—which the author acknowledges to be 'hardly my province'. Because Acton's starting-point is always medicine the book becomes a uniquely elaborate attempt to combine ideas about male sexual physiology (about the secretion and storage of semen, in particular) with counsel about a man's pre-marital and marital career, in a single theory of continence and restraint. The theory has a certain cogency (chiefly by means of the notion of the 'semi-continent' male, which I shall mention later), and it would appear from the text that it was found unpalatable by a significant proportion of Acton's readership.[40]

Acton's medical science remains unsophisticated, and in the ambit of traditional and popular physiology: he tinkers with theories of the formation of semen, but does not wholly lose touch with the belief that it is a fraction of the blood. *Functions and Disorders* in this sense is part of Lawson Tait's 'popular' system of ideas about sexuality, roughly shared by lay public on one hand and journeyman practitioners and quacks on the other. There was recognized to be a vacuum of sexual information, into which the profession at all levels stepped: 'Every one connected with medicine, even to the midwives and nurses in our hospitals, affects to talk knowingly upon sexual matters . . . This . . . is favoured by the profound ignorance and secret curiosity of the public on sexual matters.' But, the more subject to commercial pressures the agencies of lay medical instruction were, the less disruptive of old lay assumptions their offering was, even though there might be an appearance of state-of-the-art physiology. Women visiting Kahn's museum in response to the new lay curiosity about 'the mysterious function of reproduction', which was allegedly in the air, would have noticed Item 262, an illustration of an ovary with an impressively scientific-sounding explanation. But the gist was that 'ova *sometimes* detach themselves during menstruation, or as a result of onanism' (my italics). There is a concession to new knowledge, but with a venerable physiological truth—of ovulation as the equivalent of male ejaculation—remaining essentially intact. An anatomical museum which toured mainly in the north of England did not even envisage (by 1853 at least) that 'falling ova' might occur except at the time of copulation.[41]

If the lay public in nineteenth-century England is not thought of as the passive congregation of a secular priesthood, the medical and

[40] W. Acton 1857*a*: pp. v, 85; 1865: 48–9, 67–8, 86, 100; 1875: 97, 184, 196–7.
[41] G. Drysdale 1868: 221; M. Ryan 1837: 2; *Catalogue of J. W. Reimers's Gallery* 1853.

194 CARNAL KNOWLEDGE

submedical literature can be used with some confidence to arrive at a
picture of lay belief. Even when medical opinion on sexuality appears
to be antagonistic to the interests of the lay public the latter may in
fact be ascendant: 'some of the anxieties that medical men imposed
on their patients were . . . anxieties they had first absorbed from
those who consulted them'.[42] On the face of it there is no living to be
made out of telling young men that, if they have masturbated in the
past, they may have contracted a 'seminal weakness' which can lead
to impotence and severe illness. The buoyant revenues of the quacks
show how wrong this is. Of course the quacks ruthlessly encouraged
and manipulated such beliefs in their patients, but the patients came
half-way to meet them. One gentleman was so angry to be told by a
legitimate doctor that his sexual disease was imaginary that he strode
off and spend £300 fruitlessly at a quack establishment. The quack or
semi-quack literature made keen self-diagnosticians out of patients:
faced with an orthodox practitioner, 'many will even at once say that
they have reached such and such a stage of nervous debility, and will
produce their favourite author to show chapter and verse'. Patients
(among whom doctors and medical students may have figured
significantly) performed daily minute self-examinations, looking for
the 'smallest visible spot' of discharge. Much quack-business was
done by correspondence (visits by the postman to London quack
headquarters were said to be more notable than visits by patients),
and in these cases the 'consultation' amounted to little more than the
patient's written description of his symptoms, with a diagnosis sometimes explicitly requested by the doctor. Both Abercrombie
and Henery stressed the element of self-cure which they were offering.[43]

The fact is that masturbation-pathology probably came and went
with a tide of lay belief about the matter. It was invented in the eighteenth century by the sensationalistic *Onania*, and died at the beginning of the twentieth for no better reason. No doctors recanted: there
was no announcement from the medical profession that masturbation-pathology was discredited. Indeed Freud had declared his belief
in 1896 that masturbation could cause neurosis. According to Peter
Gay, he actually wished to counter a growing leniency towards the

[42] Gay 1984: 317. But see also Gilbert 1975.
[43] W. Roberts 1872: 155; Harvey 1865: 47; Gascoyen 1872; *London Medical Gazette*, 1
(1843), 586; 2 (1843), 315–17; Bird 1857: 378; Culverwell 1847*b*: 206, 139; *Hooper's* 1864:
659.

practice.[44] But even his authority could not stem a sea change in lay opinion.

Even the moralism of nineteenth-century sexual medicine, which may strike a modern observer as thoroughly disagreeable, had its consoling and encouraging aspects. All quacks and most doctors promised a cure for impotence (in addition, quacks stressed that theirs was less painful than the cauterization favoured by some doctors). The converse of pre-marital fears of impotence may have been—after a course of 'treatment' had worked its psychosomatic effect—a vigorous performance on the wedding-night. Quacks and doctors recommended 'moderation' in sexual intercourse: not more than once or twice a week, often less. This sounds restrictive, but it is only so in tone, not in effect: surveys show that the average frequency of intercourse in modern marriage falls at the top of this range. It is surely less stressful for a couple to imagine that sex once a week represents virtuous self-restraint than for them to fear that such a rate falls short of the normal achievement.

II

Women's Sexuality

The most notorious of Victorian statements about sex, William Acton's remark that 'the majority of women . . . are not very much troubled with sexual feeling of any kind', must be seen for what it is: a remark, in a chapter on 'Impotence', from a book aimed at male readers. Its corollary is that 'no nervous or feeble young man need, therefore, be deterred from marriage by any exaggerated notion of the duties required of him' (it is a measure of Acton's affinity to the quacks that if the last few words were replaced by a reference to a nervous tonic or an electrical belt the sentence could have come from their literature). The famous words are not even consistent with Acton's implied or stated views on female sexuality elsewhere in *Functions and Disorders*: when he writes of the 'efficiency' of the penis, for example.[45]

As a claim about a woman's sexual response Acton's remark is, as far as I know, without a parallel in the sexual literature of the day (while it is quite common to find writers mentioning the existence of

[44] Gay 1984: 308.   [45] W. Acton 1857a: 27; 1865: 95, 112–13; 1872: 75–6, 183–4.

female frigidity as a matter of some surprise).[46] As a claim about a woman's sexual appetite (and it may, with a little strain, be read as no more than this) the remark is perhaps not completely isolated, though I know of only one other explicit formulation to this effect. Thomas Girdwood commented in 1844 that a woman's sexual appetite is 'slightly developed', but this was said in the context of equating women's menstruation with 'heat' in animals. Girdwood was denying that the female in our species is compelled by sexual needs at this time to the extent that animals are. And for Girdwood to have made the connection between menstruation and being on heat at all is actually something of a tribute to his sense of a woman's libido. In doing so he tacitly (and oddly) rejects an obvious consequence of a theory of menstruation which he had astutely saved from oblivion, namely John Power's remarkable pioneering statement of the principle of 'disappointed pregnancy'—a principle we now know to be correct.

But Girdwood was not alone in illogically asserting the doctrine of menstruation as the sequel to non-conception and at the same time the doctrine of menstrual libido, even though the former should have rendered the latter anomalous. In general the long-unshaken nineteenth-century belief that women are most fertile, and (according to the mass of writers, including the very moralistic) most interested in sex at the time of menstruation, was based on the analogy with animals. Other writers argued that women could be aroused by a man's dress and smell in the instinctual, overwhelming fashion of birds and beasts, or that women differed from animals in feeling desire at *all* times, though most intensely at the fertile part of the month, or that the human menstrual discharge was a kind of safe release of animal impulses.[47]

It was sometimes said that women are less urgent in their sexuality than men, but quite a number of writers recognized (and a few lamented) the effect of social convention in this, especially premaritally. Anyway, so strong was a woman's response supposed to be that a powerful distaste for intercourse—as in a brutal seduction or a rape—was commonly said to be no bar to sexual arousal once contact

---

[46] M. Ryan 1831: 48; Goss 1853: 56; Nichols 1873: 102; Henry and Co. 1852: 55; Greg 1862; *Old Maids* 1835: 66–7. Also P. Robertson 1982: 176.

[47] Girdwood 1844; Culverwell 1847a: 162, 196; Power 1821; 'Woman in her Psychological Relations', *Journal of Psychological Medicine*, 4 (1851), 8–50; W. B. Carpenter 1876: 959; *Duties of Parents* 1872: 53; G. R. Rowe 1844: 27–8. Also Baly and Kirkes 1848: 58.

with the genitalia had occurred.[48] Female orgasm is ubiquitous in the literature. A textbook published in Britain contained an American doctor's claimed *per vaginam* witnessing of the phenomenon: 'five or six successive gasps' of the mouth of the womb. It could be believed that women experienced orgasm in response to the menstrual flow, or in mere conversation with a lover, or just from a touching of the cervix, or in defecation. The effect on it of the thickness of a man's penis, and of contact with semen, was discussed, as was the ancient issue of the relative pleasure experienced by the two sexes. It was commonly asserted that sexual excess was less deleterious for women than for men, but sexual deprivation more so (the subject of sexual continence and its supposed ills will be taken up later in this chapter).[49] The intriguing questions about the topic in the nineteenth century are what a woman's orgasm was supposed to amount to physiologically, and what value attached to it as a result—and, of course, who held which beliefs on these two matters.

Everyone, it may be supposed, realized that orgasm in a woman usually required stimulation of the external female genitalia, but there is some evidence that popular wisdom was not always aware of the importance of the clitoris. At any rate, a hoary allegation to this effect first made by eighteenth-century opponents of man midwives was still being voiced in the controversy sixty years later.[50] And a presumption by doctors that 'females have not as much knowledge of the clitoris as we have' was perhaps quite general among gynecologists in the mid-1860s, when Isaac Baker Brown was censured by a heavy majority of his colleagues in the Obstetrical Society for his use of clitoridectomy—since the verdict hinged, technically at least, on whether patients and their husbands grasped the consequences of Brown's treatment.

It was open to Brown to argue that he was not removing all capacity for sexual pleasure by excising the clitoris, but simply thwarting masturbation (this being the rationale of his operation), and he did indeed urge in his own defence that the seat of sexual feeling was not

[48] Duncan 1884: 92; Tait 1877: 49; M. Ryan 1837: 12; W. Thompson 1825: 64; *British Gynecological Journal*, 2 (1886–7), 505; Moodie 1858: 41.

[49] Flint 1876: 890; M. Ryan 1831: 9, 53; 1847: 151; *Lancet*, 1866(2), 667–9; De Roos 1840: 70; Nichols 1873: 84; Kitchener 1812: ii. 327; Owen 1877: 63–4; Culverwell 1847a: 91, 162, 229; 1847b: 42, 55; T. Bell 1821: 139, 193; Gaskell 1833: 80; Greg 1891: 73; 'Le Plus Bas' 1859: 481; *Medical Press and Circular*, 1870(1), 465; J. Davenport 1875: 17, 22, 73.

[50] *Junonesia* 1838: 143.

confined to the clitoris. This was not as good a counter-argument
with all his critics as it might appear. Brown was trying to deal with
epilepsy and other disorders supposedly caused by 'irritation of
the pudic nerve', and those of his opponents who accepted the
masturbation–epilepsy nexus tended to claim precisely that this exci-
tation could take place by means other than clitoral stimulation—so
that his operation was objectionable chiefly as being useless. (Their
position was perhaps the strangest of all to modern eyes; there were
those who simply doubted the link with nervous disorder—as I shall
mention later.) Charles West, some years earlier, implied that lesbian
prostitutes habitually stimulated other parts of the genitalia.[51] All in
all, while some doctors regarded it as an article of medical knowledge
that orgasm was impossible for a woman in the absence of a clitoris,
there were others, even specialists, whose sense of its importance
was not apparently any greater than that attributed to lay men and
women.

The latter were not exactly in a climate of ignorance about the
organ. For those who failed to identify its role through sheer untu-
tored experience there were many promptings to knowledge. The
traditional authorities, from classical times, all emphasized the
clitoris, and it is clearly indicated in the illustrations in nineteenth-
century popular medical texts, and its homology with the penis
explained. 'Walter' learnt of its existence, in a hazy way, from the
venerable popular medical manual 'Aristotle's Masterpiece'.[52] A good
deal could be learnt about the clitoris at Kahn's. But such perceptions were probably very commonly qualified by the belief that for a
woman the sites of sexual arousal and fulfilment were significantly
dispersed not only beyond the clitoris but beyond the external genitalia, and even in a sense not located in the latter at all.

This dispersal of a woman's sexuality can, on the face of it, be readily interpreted as the result of an emphasis on woman as a child-
bearer. Her sexuality is understood in terms of her capacity to
reproduce, and therefore associated with her uterus. Then, by the
workings of the doctrine of 'uterine physiology', her sexuality is dispersed even more broadly in her physical being. According to the
uterine theory the existence and condition of the womb and ovaries

---

[51] *Lancet* 1865(1), 485–7; 1866(2), 114, 667–9, 697–8; 1867(1), 425–41; C. West 1856: ii.
228. Cf. Atthill 1871: 28.
[52] *My Secret Life* 1966: 30. But see also Blackman 1977.

have an influence on a woman's whole physical and psychological being far greater than that exercised on men by the testes. By the amplifying logic of the theory, a woman's capacities for sexual arousal become a global aspect of her being, to the fore in most of her physical, social, mental, and other functions. There was probably also at work in this constellation of attitudes another perception, however, according to which a woman is characterized by her capacity for sexual pleasure. This perception is certainly restrictive in its view of a woman's being, like the reproductive model of femininity, but it does grant an intrinsic value to her eroticism, and in a sense dignifies it uniquely. For in practice the idea of the global eroticism of women, the thought that they are more broadly and continuously erotic than men, often appears without any reference to uterine doctrine; and if the link between this tier of female sexuality and female genital pleasure, via the uterus, is supposed to exist, it is often elided. Arguably even the doctrine of the reproductive orgasm in women (the belief that a woman must experience orgasm in order to conceive, which I discuss shortly)—though it may appear to be a very obvious example of the casting of women as childbearers—dignifies female eroticism. According to this doctrine it is the sheer pleasurable intensity of the woman's orgasm which is functional reproductively: on the man's side reproductive ability is only enhanced by the 'vigour' with which he has intercourse, and by moderation in its frequency.

In academic medical circles in the nineteenth century uterine physiology seems to have been a widespread doctrine, but not an unchallenged one. It was perhaps always cast in terms of alleged nervous structure, with the womb and ovaries supposedly more richly connected than any other organ to the rest of the body, and the 'uterine' thus somehow bulking larger in the activity of a woman's nervous system (so old ideas of the uterine origins of hysteria can readily be accommodated). Thomas Laycock gave a classic exposition of this model in the *Treatise on the Nervous Diseases of Women* (1840), but at much the same date the theory was also frankly derided as one that could 'amuse' but not 'enlighten'. This in turn caused indignation, and it is possible to trace through the following years a story of professional disagreement on the issue. Practitioners keen to boost the new specialism of gynecology argued that all sorts of symptoms were due to organic disease of the womb. It is not clear whether other doctors were convinced by these novel claims, but it does seem that the uterine aetiology of hysteria, though a much more venerable doctrine, was never secure, even with the top authorities, and by the 1880s had lost ground.[53]

Popular medical authors, however, often take up the theme of the presiding power of a woman's reproductive physiology, and the eroticism of her general nature (greater than a man's) that was supposed to result. 'A woman of sensibility, who would preserve her chastity, must guard her bosom well' ('exquisitely fine wrought formations' which are 'electrified, as it were' by touch) because of its nervous linkages with her generative organs, which are the 'metropolis of the whole economy'. But popular and professional utterances (including those of Florence Nightingale) are also united in sometimes simply assuming that sensuality is a feminine trait, without reference to the womb—either explicitly or, as in the allusions to the special female capacity for sexual 'excess' cited above, by implication.[54] Feminists such as Anne Dryden, following Mary Wollstonecraft, in effect agree with this account, though they think women's eroticism is a pernicious result of her social subordination. And outside the medical domain altogether the idea occurs, sometimes in bizarre forms, that a woman's physiology colours the most rarified elements in her nature: not only her capacities for 'tenderness and sympathy' but even her immortal being. The strange doctrines of certain Swedenborgian individuals in the 1840s and 1850s about 'sex in the world to come' and Nature as 'a system of nuptials' (ideas I give more attention to in the next volume) could lead to strikingly voluptuous accounts of the female soul.[55]

A much more precise, mundane, and practically significant pair of beliefs emerging from this network of attitudes about women's reproductive and sexual functions is, first, that the main site of a woman's sexuality is her womb and its appendages, and, second, that she must experience an orgasm in order to conceive. Quite simply, these were probably the prevailing beliefs of lay men and women in England in the nineteenth century, and of many of their doctors (though with the latter there was also very often a kind of half-awareness of the fallacy of the second doctrine).

---

[53] *Medico-Chirurgical Review*, 29 (1838), 381; F. W. Mackenzie 1851; C. Ritchie 1851; Conolly 1833; R. B. Carter 1853: *passim*; *Lancet*, 1879(2), 423.

[54] W. Jones 1850: 2; Walker 1840: 134; T. Bell 1821: 140; Nichols 1873: 102; P. Barker 1888: 13; Whitehead 1847: 31; *Lancet*, 1886(2), 315; 'Le Plus Bas' 1865: 61; Nightingale 1860: ii. 403.

[55] Dryden 1844: 178–80; Culverwell 1847b: part 2, p. 13; Parsons 1842: 43–5; Strutt 1857: 26–8.

Imlach v. *Casey* has already illustrated how a working-class couple (Mr Casey was a labourer for a shipping firm) and practitioners below the top rung of the profession could hold in 1886 that the ovaries and Fallopian tubes were, fundamentally, the organs of sexual appetite. Semi-popular writers from at least the 1820s had been teaching that an 'inert' uterus, or divided Fallopian tubes, caused frigidity.[56] Lawson Tait's more accurate (if poorly grounded) belief seem to have met extraordinary resistance among doctors. As early as 1828 it was reported that ovariotomy and hysterectomy did not necessarily affect female libido, but neither this, nor the fact that French physiologists were known to be less decided on the matter, prevented the respected physiological lecturer Herbert Mayo continuing flatly to assert the opposite. Doctors who were aware of the facts probably also argued to themselves that the external genitalia, once stimulated, could harbour libido: hence Lawson Tait's selection of cases for his 1888 paper.[57]

Conversely, it was held that a woman's sexual desires and activities could produce changes in the uterine organs. On one hand, uterine adhesions and other disorders of the internal genitalia were attributed to too much sexual stimulation. On the other hand it was supposed that love could enlarge the ovaries, and if 'ungratified' make them inflamed—and that a husband's failure sexually to satisfy a young wife might cause a 'hypertrophy' of the womb (various ills which were alleged to flow from female chastity will be mentioned shortly).[58] But the most intriguing consequence of this kind of thinking was the notion that ovulation was caused by orgasm. The way in which the medical profession abetted this apparently universal lay belief, to the point of virtual self-contradiction in some instances, is a striking testimony to the disinclination of doctors to acknowledge and familiarize their patients with medical discoveries which were antisensual in tendency.

The age-old idea that women, in some sense, ejaculate seed like men was apparently confirmed right at the end of the eighteenth century by Haighton's work on rabbits, but it was soon to collapse as

[56] Good 1829: v. 24; M. Ryan 1831: 48.

[57] *Lancet*, 1828–9(2), 98, 215, 644; 1836–7(2), 463–6; Mayo 1827: 361; 1837: 386; Blundell 1837: 274; Ashwell 1844: 709; *Medico-Chirurgical Review*, 19 (1833), 468; Churchill 1874: 47. See also *Lancet*, 1858(2), 6.

[58] *Medico-Chirurgical Transactions*, 8 (1817), 505; M. Ryan 1837: 155; Ashwell 1844: 708; La'mert 1852: 90; Copland 1844–58: iii. 444; Graham 1834: 123; C. Drysdale 1866: 14, 41; PP. 1831–2, xv. 487; *Lancet*, 1849(1), 339; C. West 1856: i. 95–6.

scientific doctrine. By the 1820s an awareness of the experiments of the celebrated German physician Blumenbach, and certain native researches, had made a quite different view—that women ovulate spontaneously whether or not they have sex—at least as persuasive with many doctors, including of course specialists. In the early 1840s the matter was virtually clinched by further German work, and spontaneous ovulation was endorsed by the most eminent and knowledgeable British authorities.[59]

It is perhaps not surprising that versions of the orgasmic theory of ovulation continued to be asserted (or at least made room for) in the academic literature through the 1820s and 1830s, and at the same time in popular and quack medical writing (sometimes, indeed, with an apparently increasing confidence). It is more than plausible that married women continued to believe that a 'sensation of animal gratification' was necessary if they were to conceive.[60] Much less to be expected is the persistence with which doctors *after* the mid-1840s found some role for a woman's sexual response in conception. Academically minded medical men were emphatic that ovulation was spontaneous, and the idea made its way more or less quickly into the big, standard textbooks, but even in the 1860s, 1870s, and 1880s there can be found in the professional literature concessions, of varying completeness, to the older view. It finally wagged its tail academically in the theory that the relative sex-drive of partners in intercourse will determine the sex of offspring.[61]

The more non-technical the treatment of the subject the more definite authors were that a woman's reactions are significant for conception. James Copland's *Dictionary of Practical Medicine*, though massive enough, and the subject of well-attested admiration within the medical profession, was perhaps directed at an audience which could include lay readers. Copland is quite definite that orgasm is

---

[59] Haighton 1797; Home 1819; Mayo 1827: 367; Bostock 1824–7: iii. 37–9; Blumenbach 1820: 364–71; Power 1821: 12–14; Wharton Jones 1843; J. Paget 1844; *London Medical Gazette*, 1844(2), 254; 1845(1), 510; Baly and Kirkes 1848: 44–5, 59.

[60] Barry 1839: 2nd ser. 316; *London Medical and Surgical Journal*, 5 (1830), 322–4; 7 (1835), 237; Todd 1836–9: 447, 451; D. D. Davis 1836: i. 492; *Lancet*, 1841–2(1), 735; Mayo 1837: 394; T. Bell 1821: 193; M. Ryan 1837: 143–4; Good 1829: v. 21, 142–3 (cf. 1822: iv. 325–6); Copland 1824: 681 (cf. later citations below); *Medical Adviser*, 2 (1824–5), 292; Perry and Co. 1841: 60.

[61] C. West 1854: 7; J. M. Sims 1866: 197; Duncan 1879: 124; 1884: 96–100; Granville 1860; Baly and Kirkes 1848: 601; Todd 1858: 552; Hilles 1860: 293; *Lancet*, 1867(1), 28–9; 1880(2), 650–2; W. B. Carpenter 1876: 961; A. Milne 1871: 37–9, 151.

necessary for conception 'in most cases'.[62] More obviously popular writers, at least into the 1870s, have a way of riding two horses on the question: ovulation occurs anyway, but sexual arousal somehow helps as well. The semi-quack Horace Goss (alias Dr Crucefix) rather brazenly asserted, like Kahn's museum, that modern medical science had proved that ovulation occurred during intercourse.[63]

It was an unusual feature of Goss's practice that his wife was available to give advice on female disorders, including frigidity (though De Roos also claimed to be able to restore a woman's response, and Lawson Tait was often consulted about it). There is good evidence that lay women in the nineteenth century accepted not only the link between excitement and fertilization but also its corollary: that voluntary or involuntary absence of orgasm would be a bar to conceiving. 'Walter', and all his partners as far as is reported, assume unquestioningly that orgasm opens the route to conception (he is on one occasion delighted to be able to conclude that a prostitute's pleasure was genuine from the fact that she becomes pregnant). Marion Sims, bent on more scientific treatment of sterility, deplored 'the false philosophy' which had 'gained almost universal credence', that there should be 'exhaustive satisfaction to both parties at the same moment' to ensure conception. Married couples continued to believe, into the 1880s, that female 'desire and pleasure are essential elements in fecundity', and to doubt that a wife could be pregnant when a husband had failed for some reason to arouse her to orgasm.[64] The sad reality of a Victorian married woman's sex-life which modern prejudice has created, of joyless inhibition and ignorance, is quite unhistorical, but it must give way to a reality which may sometimes have been sadder: of women fearing and regretting sexual pleasure because they above all wished to avoid having another child. A perusal of Copland, or advice from a GP with Copland on his shelves, would have encouraged them in their lamentable error: 'It is generally understood by females of all ranks in society, that indifference during intercourse, or suppression of the orgasm will prevent impregnation, and, although they are sometimes deceived in this respect, yet their inference is correct in the majority.[65]

[62] Copland 1844–58: ii. 323, iii. 445; J. F. Clarke 1874: 324–5, 419.

[63] Sturt 1854: 71; Nichols 1873: 109–14; Ruddock 1865: 61; G. Drysdale 1868: 254; Goss 1853: 3, 21.

[64] De Roos 1840: 55; *My Secret Life* 1966: 569; 571, 693, 1692, 1779, 2090; Tait 1877: 47; J. M. Sims 1866: 369–70; Courtenay 1854: 142; Duncan 1884: 96. See also Ruddock 1865: 64.   [65] Copland 1844–58: ii. 323.

To our ideas the notion that women ovulate every time they have an orgasm is bizarre; so far has popular medical wisdom swung in an opposite direction that most individuals today would be surprised to hear that modern physiological theory still finds some assisting role for conception in female arousal.[66] In the nineteenth century only the medical specialists had reason to be aware of the great (and counter-intuitive) difference between male and female sexual function in this respect. The old idea was assisted by the belief that women produced a distinct secretion at orgasm (which even Lawson Tait seems to have accepted): who was to say that this secretion did not contain a multi-tude of living agents such as the microscope had revealed in male semen? 'Walter' in *My Secret Life* frequently calls a woman's vaginal moisture 'spermatic', and once refers to the joint effusion of partners as the 'juices which reproduce their kind'. Female masturbation must cause ovulation just as readily as the stimulus of intercourse, and the evidence of ovulation in virgins was coped with—in Kahn's museum and elsewhere—by the assumption that they had masturbated, or at least were especially 'amorous'.[67]

However, perhaps because the ovaries and their activity were not as unequivocally associated with secondary sexual traits as were the testicles, the fact of supposed ovulation does not usually seem to have been invoked as a ground for condemning female masturbation.[68] Masturbation could damage a woman's internal genitalia but—as we have seen—so could other kinds of 'excess'. Indeed in general female masturbation was not singled out for condemnation at this period in the elaborate and persistent fashion that male masturbation was. It was well-recognized as a phenomenon (although the consensus was probably that women masturbated less then men). Quack doctors and popular medical authors inveighed against it (claiming a blunting of sexual response to be among its ill effects, just as they warned men of impotence), but it was rarely at the centre of their attention—and quack resourcefulness did not run to offering cures for it.[69]

Belief in a pathology of female masturbation was more current at a higher level in the profession. I shall discuss shortly how an emphasis on nervous rather than material effects came to be distinctive—even self-consciously distinctive—of the legitimate medical approach to

[66] *New Scientist*, 14 Aug. 1993, p. 27.

[67] Tait 1877: 50; *My Secret Life* 1966: 893; Good 1829: v. 27; J. Davenport 1965: 102.

[68] For a rare case see Brodum 1795: ii. 61.

[69] Brodum 1795: ch. 22; Perry and Co. 1841: 16; De Roos 1840: 55; Nichols 1873: 84.

male masturbation, and this line of thought had an obvious applica-
bility to the other sex. Many specialists seem to have believed that
nervous disorders in women, ranging from epilepsy to schizophrenia,
were due to masturbation. But the extent of this belief should not be
exaggerated. The idea that masturbation could be the sole cause of
insanity, and of insanity of a specific sort, did not crystallize until the
early 1860s, and within about twenty years was on the wane. Early
supporters of the theory, like Henry Maudsley, seem quickly to have
modified their attitude, coming to view insanity as almost always a
cause of masturbation, rather than vice versa (though neurosis was
still a possible effect). In the great controversy over Baker Brown's
clitoridectomies the link between masturbation and nervous or
mental disease was simply denied by some doctors, with Charles
West roundly declaring that he had never known a case of epilepsy,
hysteria, or insanity to be caused by masturbation (a view to which
Lawson Tait lent his authority some years later).[70]

While both these men incidentally argued that the ill effects of
male masturbation had also been exaggerated, it would be unthinkable at this period for two doctors of their eminence to have dis-
counted the latter quite so emphatically. The masturbating layman
received a more unequivocal message from the upper ranks of the
profession about his habit than did the masturbating lay woman. In
addition—and this was no doubt more influential on his attitudes—a
barrage of voices from lower down the medical hierarchy were
confirming some or all of his fears about the damage he was inflicting
upon himself.

III

Masturbating Men

The élite medical hostility to male masturbation is particularly striking because a towering authority of the previous century (indeed, one
of the greatest figures in the history of British surgery), John Hunter,
was well known to have doubted if the practice did any harm at all.
Hunter even suggested that intercourse might have *more* potential
for harm, especially if it was performed with a loved and loving

---

[70] R. P. Ritchie 1861; Hare 1962; Maudsley 1866; Gay 1984: 299; *Medical Press and
Circular*, 1870(1), 465; *BMJ* 1865(2), 705; *Lancet*, 1866(2), 114, 560–1; A. Milne 1871: 26;
Tait 1877: 51. For an earlier controversy see *Lancet*, 1859(1), 344 and *passim*.

woman rather than 'with common women or such as we are indifferent about'.[71] No nineteenth-century medical authority I know of, whether remembering Hunter or not, dared to go this far with the great man. A few voices (and they do include Sir James Paget) were unconvinced of any difference between masturbation and intercourse in respect of the damage they could cause, and doubt was expressed about particular kinds of damage, but this seems to be the extent of the articulated scepticism about masturbation's ill effects for men. In addition, there was a widespread antagonism in the non-popular medical literature to the way quacks harped on masturbation, and a lively awareness of the extent to which men became prey to imaginary masturbatory disease. So no doubt there was a good deal of humane effort in legitimate consulting rooms to reassure and encourage wretchedly anxious patients. But there was always, it seems, a common ground between quack and respectable doctor of residual assent to the evil of male masturbation—as I shall bring out in discussing 'spermatorrhoea'. We do hear of 'many sensible people' and the occasional 'distinguished doctor' doubting if male masturbation was harmful, but if they existed they did not publish their doubts.[72]

Hunter's basic argument appears irresistibly commonsensical to the modern reader. He simply observes that if male masturbation were as deleterious as it is claimed to be, and given the extent of the practice, there should be wholesale disease among the male population. There are some points to be made on behalf of the Victorian medical men who ignored this logic, however. To start with, Hunter was an isolated voice attacking an orthodoxy about masturbational pathology which had already been in place for two generations, and he was reproached for his views in his own day: the Victorians emphatically did not invent the idea that masturbation is harmful. Also, Victorian doctors may not have found the argument from the frequent incidence of masturbation convincing (especially in so far as they took a rather less dire view of its malignancy than the quacks). A survey of male TB patients in 1863 found significance in the fact that 18.2 per cent admitted to having masturbated in the past: the figure is not so much interesting in itself as it is for indicating what was con-

[71] Hunter 1810: 213.
[72] *Lancet*, 1826–7(2), 78–9; 1843–4(1), 68; Peterson 1986; Beddoes 1802: 40; Blackwell 1884: 33; W. Acton 1857a: 58.

sidered a high level (there were admittedly much higher rates of masturbatory activity reported from some public schools).[73]

Lastly, the link between masturbation and some of the nervous varieties of disorder which the medical profession tended to stress was not without observational foundation. A modern historian of the concept of masturbational insanity has granted that 'acuteness of observation' led to the identifying of the hebephrenia, or youthful schizophrenia, which was supposed to be due to masturbation. There was irony in the fact that bromide suppresses the symptoms of epilepsy and also reduces the sex-drive. On a broader front, it was a correct observation that an irregular sex-life (in which masturbation would have seemed to be an element) was correlated with General Paralysis of the Insane. The connection of the latter with syphilis, though also recognized as a possibility, was not compelling in the absence of a more detailed pathological understanding than was available.[74]

Nevertheless the question implicitly asked by Hunter subsisted: what made male arousal and ejaculation worse if they were brought about solitarily than if they were brought about with a partner? Some quacks did not even bother to go into the matter, perhaps confident that their readers were not in a mood to take solace from this difficulty. The various medical authors who did seek a rationale for the special status of masturbation were not impressive on the subject. There was always the problem that masturbation had to be presented as a defective kind of sexual activity, but also as a kind of 'excess'. Some writers argued that masturbation could be, and was, indulged in more frequently or at greater length (and that it might thus become more addictive). Others (perhaps mindful, like Hunter, of the plausible opposite view: that a man will rather try for an inordinate performance in a passionate relationship) denied this: it was the absence of 'reciprocal enjoyment, and the interchange of nervous emanations', of 'inspiration' to balance the 'expiration', which, mysteriously, made the difference. Related arguments were that any stimulus other than that of a beloved partner's body plus a surplus of semen, and in particular a wholly mental stimulus, brought about an unhealthy kind of arousal, or that there was a damaging lack of fulfilment in masturbation (perhaps itself a cause of frequency). It

[73] B. Bell 1793: i. 224; *Dublin Quarterly Journal of Medical Science*, 35 (1863), 11–47; Hare 1962; *Journal of Education*, 4 (1882), 85–6.

[74] Hare 1962; *BMJ* 1871(2), 493–6; Blandford 1871: 60; Sankey 1866: 181–2.

was commonly argued that masturbatory sex meant youthful and therefore damagingly premature sex, but this attack on the practice evidently had only a restricted force. Even the 'posture' of the masturbator was invoked as a significant point of difference about this kind of sexual activity.[75]

This is fairly obviously a catalogue of rationalizations for a prejudice, but it does not include any claims about the distinctiveness of the ejaculate produced in masturbation. Careless or cynical authors, fudging the difference between excessive intercourse and masturbation, had a great deal to say about semen and the dangers of its overproduction. More respectable authorities tended to shun this approach, in part precisely because it was the hallmark of the quack operator in this field. For example, the entrepreneurial Dr Richard Reece, who was on the border with illegitimacy and keen not to cross it, joined in the expressions of professional contempt for the old-fashioned and 'empirical' notion of the semen as a precious substance. Late in the century, and in another country, the American physician G. Stanley Hall claimed to have analysed chemically the vital ingredient lost in masturbation, but there were no such eccentricities in Britain.[76] The main tendency of official opinion was to replace the popular emphasis on material losses to the system due to masturbation with explanations in terms of 'nervous' effects—the more quackish of the legitimate practitioners again following suit here. This was in line with a general shift in the period from a physical to a mental masturbation-pathology. Some doctors who still accepted that the loss of ejaculate was important distanced themselves from old dogmas about seminal loss by focusing on the prostatic or other non-testicular secretions.[77]

I shall term the traditional, officially repudiated view of semen the 'haematic' theory. In the theory there are two links between semen

[75] M. Ryan 1831: 32; *Lancet*, 1844(1), 640–1; 1864(2), 667–8; 1866(2), 560–1; Brodum 1795: ii. 50–3; Curling 1843: 47; J. Adams 1851: 50; La'mert 1852: 46–7; Pratt 1872: 12; 'The Psychology of the Reproductive Functions', *Journal of Psychological Medicine*, 2 (1849), 1–30; 'Genuine Disciple' 1815: 14; Copland 1844–58: iii. 442; Blackwell 1884: 33; Kitchener 1812: i. 35; Henery 1861: 34; Solomon *c*.1810: 197; Senate 1810: 32–43. See also Curtis 1840: 18–19.

[76] Reece 1818: 10; Neuman 1975; 'The Psychology of the Reproductive Functions', *Journal of Psychological Medicine*, 2 (1849), 1–30; W. Roberts 1872: 154; Black 1872: 180.

[77] Gascoyen 1872; Curling 1843: 46; Black 1872: 175, 218–19; *British and Foreign Medico-Chirurgical Review*, 1 (1848), 34–68; Culverwell 1847a: 80; Lobb 1880: *passim*; 'Court Physician' 1876: 48, 55; Macdonald 1967; *Lancet*, 1856(2), 215–17; Humphry 1864; J. Adams 1851: 53.

and blood. To start with, the semen is held to be a rare faction of the blood (usually put at one part in forty) which is extracted in the testicles. The high demand it makes on the system in its manufacture is in itself supposed to make its expenditure debilitating, but there was an optional annexe to the theory whereby the semen was *re*absorbed into the bloodstream if not ejaculated. This allegedly had an invigorating effect on the male constitution including, in some versions of the theory, the maintenance of the secondary sexual characteristics—and was thus a further reason for frugality in ejaculation. This model of seminal function, which derives from Hippocrates, was standard in nineteenth-century quack and vulgar medical writing right through to the 1880s (and was sometimes expressly said to be an instance of ancient medicine being more accurate than modern), while it does not seem to have appeared in the mainstream professional literature after the late 1820s.[78] However not all legitimate doctors with an entrepreneurial or popular orientation felt the need to express their solidarity with official doctrines in the manner of Richard Reece, mentioned above. Some qualified authors of works of instruction and advice which were aimed at or at least accessible to the lay reader (including Acton—from the time of the more lay-oriented third edition of the *Functions and Disorders*—and Copland) stayed loyal to the haematic theory, and consequently it even made its way into the *Lancet* as late as 1841.[79]

Given the inconsistencies of attitude in these lower tiers of the profession, as well as actual havering on the matter in the writings of semi-quacks such as Culverwell and Abercrombie, it is hard to make a judgement about lay beliefs concerning seminal function. A generalized anxiety about sperm-loss was probably common, but in their strict form the haematic ideas may have been obsolete with the lay public by the 1870s except in some rural areas, or as a piece of rather picturesque sexual lore. 'Walter', as I have observed in an earlier chapter, uses the haematic vocabulary on occasion, but in a way that suggests that he does not accept its full, literal implications.[80]

The official medical rejection of the haematic theory was a victory for intuitive biochemistry over intuitive arguments about the workings of the male sex organs. A rudimentary understanding of the

[78] Fox 1884: 202; Henery 1861: 73; Bostock 1824–7: iii. 9.

[79] Pratt 1872: 11; W. Acton 1862: 152; Smyth 1844: 176 (previously *Lancet*, 1840–1(2), 779–85); Copland 1844–58: iii. 447; Courtenay 1839: 42.

[80] Culverwell 1847b: 45; Abercrombie 1864: 12; 'Court Physician' 1876: 57; J. Davenport 1875: 68.

composition of the two fluids led specialists to deny the old association of blood and semen: and the logic of the old theory was that
ejaculating an ounce of semen had the same effect as losing two
pints of blood, which seemed preposterous. It is natural to applaud
the new attitude for being on the right track and, in some respects,
more reasonable. But the haematic doctrine contained at least one
sensible element, which the new thinking had to ignore: it was
undeniable that the activation of the testis at puberty coincided with
the masculinization of a boy's whole physiology, yet the new wisdom
denied that the one known secretion of this organ was important for
the general system. The discovery of the sex-hormones in this century shows that this could have turned out to be unwarranted.
Nineteenth-century believers in the need to conserve semen could
have pointed to another known fact, that the more frequently a man
ejaculates the smaller the number of sperm his semen contains (and
high levels were accepted as desirable even by those who denied
that the sperm were fertilizing agents). But one of the oddest features of sexual debate at this period is that the sperm-count never
plays a significant role in it.[81] The anti-traditionalists perhaps
believed that the male secretion was still fertile at low sperm levels,[82] but the known link between rate of ejaculation and the sperm-
count should have been gratefully seized on by anxiety-mongering
traditionalists, as reinforcing old perceptions of the value of the
semen. That it was not is perhaps a token of how fraudulent was the
scientism of even the quasi-quacks.

So there was less unanimity among the nineteenth-century lay
public and their practitioners on the status of a man's semen than
there was on the fact of the reproductive orgasm in women. On the
former question new attitudes among the medical élite found more of
an echo in what some popular writers said, and what some GPs and
their patients probably thought. This uncertainty in beliefs might
have had an impact on what *was* very widely accepted, namely,
that male masturbation was an evil. But at a crucial juncture the
nineteenth-century medical élite, somewhat against the grain of its
habitual thinking, allowed the quacks and the more quackish practi-

---

[81] *Lancet*, 1834–5(2), 100; J. Wilson 1821: 92; 'The Psychology of the Reproductive
Functions', *Journal of Psychological Medicine*, 2 (1849), 1–30; Milton 1887: 47; 'Court
Physician' 1876: 23; Black 1872: 175. Cf. however W. Acton 1865: 95.

[82] J. M. Sims 1868; *Lancet*, 1841–2(1), 555.

tioners to dictate the broad assumptions of sexual medicine. The issue on which the élite failed to take a stand (sometimes, one may divine, with misgivings) was the so-called disease of 'spermatorrhoea'. As a result a pathological category of the shakiest sort, which none the less possessed a terrible power to depress and frighten males of all ages, appeared to be comprehensively ratified by the medical hierarchy (see Appendix).

As a masturbation-disease spermatorrhoea shared with other so-called disorders of this type a horribly ineluctable aetiology. A quack who listened to a worried young man's symptoms and then asked with a bogusly solemn face whether he masturbated was betting on a fairly sure thing. But spermatorrhoea was distinct from other masturbation-diseases in its Catch 22 symptomology, which helped to make it cruelly difficult for a male patient to doubt the diagnosis. The overt tokens of the disease were phenomena which nowadays it seems very perverse to yoke together: nocturnal emissions, premature ejaculation, and impotence (in addition there are references in the literature to visible diurnal discharges without erection, which are perhaps best put down to sexually transmitted disease, or to imagination).

To modern ideas, the first two signs are evidence of an active and healthy sexual apparatus, and are positively incompatible with the third. In the last century—and this is the central point to grasp about spermatorrhoea—the unintended flux of semen involved in wet dreams or premature ejaculation showed that the sexual apparatus was diseased. The analogy, frequently drawn, was with mucous and other secretions from inflamed organs elsewhere in the body. Masturbation had put the seminal tract into an 'irritable' condition and an excessive flux was the result (though there was some division of opinion as to whether this inflammation increased the seminal secretion, or simply made it harder to retain). By the same thinking masturbation and nocturnal emissions were connected as cause and effect, and not as alternative operations of the sexual apparatus. Potentially there was an awkwardness here for the pathological interpretation of nocturnal emissions, in that a man might observe that they diminished in frequency or ceased once he started to masturbate. But the symptoms of spermatorrhoea were regarded as a more-or-less delayed sequel to masturbation, a time bomb waiting for the past masturbator. A man who gave up masturbation to avoid this pathological outcome would perhaps then experience exactly the symptoms which showed him that his renunciation had come too late.

So one may see that many male sexual careers would appear to exhibit the effects of spermatorrhoea. A man who wanted to renounce masturbation but failed might have a problem of potency through his anxiety about this. As I have just mentioned, a man who renounced masturbation but remained celibate might well show the dangerous symptom of nocturnal emissions. A man who renounced masturbation and had intercourse might still fear the effects of his past habit, and thus bring on the impotence he was anxious about, or, if prone to ejaculate early, would again detect the consequences of earlier vice. In addition to this insidious logic concerning a patient's overt history and symptoms there was in the quack and legitimate theory of the disease, as this became more sophisticated in the nineteenth century, an element of hidden symptomology which meant that a diagnosis of 'spermatorrhoea' could *always* be made if the patient had masturbated, and the practitioner were sufficiently unscrupulous. For nocturnal emissions and incontinent ejaculation were not the only means by which the spermatorrhoeal flux was supposed to be discharged: it could escape unnoticed by the patient, either in his urine or as a damp exhalation. Indeed this was an important additional bridge between the two kinds of overt symptom, at first glance so difficult to reconcile. The vague idea of an irritable 'weakness' which prevented erection could be helpfully supplemented by the claim that the patient had been losing semen involuntarily in much larger quantities than he was aware of: in effect, he was approaching his sexual partner as poorly equipped as a man who had just had intercourse several times.

The microscope was the obvious means of identifying sperm in urine, and it is clear that some quacks quite simply performed bogus microscopic analyses of their patients' urine—the 'microscope humbug' part of the 'spermatorrhoea dodge'.[83] Given the extent of consultation by post this was all too easy: the only reason for a quack to be cautious was the occasional false sample sent in an effort to expose him. Quackish qualified men like Dawson and out-and-out quacks like Henery made considerable play with the notion that spermatorrhoea was an entity at the cutting edge of medical science, a disease of the microscope age (as long as the instrument was in suitably expert hands, of course).[84] Conversely, those writers who were at

---

[83] Courtenay 1865: 65, 771.   [84] Dawson 1845: p. vii; Henery 1861: 74–80.

least partial sceptics about spermatorrhoea tended to query whether sperm did appear in urine at all commonly, and whether there could be such a thing as an unconscious diurnal emission of semen. But the more respectable spermatorrhoeal practitioners had a way of side-stepping this challenge: they played down the role of the microscope, or denied—to the irritation of colleagues—that it was infallible, or even went sanctimoniously on the attack themselves ('histology and chemistry . . .[are] scientific relaxation from the serious business of healing disease'). Even William Acton, who was not dishonest, and duly stressed the power of the microscope to discriminate different urethral discharges, is ultimately rather evasive on the importance of sperm in the urine.[85]

The oddity of the idea that an escape of semen showed the genitals to be operating other than satisfactorily was also noticed by the more sceptical writers—either in the quite common recognition that a certain frequency of wet dreams was healthy, or more explicitly. And it was even urged that nocturnal emissions and impotence were quite distinct conditions, which should not be classified under the single heading of 'spermatorrhoea'.[86] It is likely that most doctors had a much richer sense of the causes of male impotence than it suited the spermatorrhoeal quacks to peddle; consulting their own intuitions, as men, about the matter would surely have helped them to this, and John Hunter's amusing remarks about the psychological element in impotence were well known.

The divergent character of the main symptoms of spermatorrhoea did in fact prompt a certain amount of nosological rejigging, which nowadays seems almost as comic as it is sad. It was claimed that the disease had 'two stages', with an initial overproduction of semen leading to possible underproduction in the second stage, or alternatively 'sthenic' and 'asthenic' forms, to embrace various kinds of discharge as well as impotence (and elsewhere only 'atonic' impotence was held to be spermatorrhoea-related). One early author changed his general classification from 'seminal emission' to 'morbid stricture of the seminal vesicles' because of the alleged frequency with which one condition passed into the other.[87] To others it seemed

[85] J. Adams 1851: 53; Black 1872: 191; Courtenay 1865: 90; Gascoyen 1872; A. Smith 1871: p. 10; Ranking 1843–4; *Lancet* 1843–4(1), 152–3; Milton 1855: 5; W. Acton 1865: 192.

[86] B. Bell 1793: i. 220; Gascoyen 1872; 'The Passions' *Journal of Psychological Medicine*, 3 (1850), 141–64; Courtenay 1839: 70; 1858: 27–8.

[87] B. Bell 1793: i. 224–31; M. Wilson 1856; Good 1829: v. 126; Roberton 1817: 61.

appropriate to distinguish premature ejaculation, for which the term 'spermaspasmos' was suggested, from the other symptoms—perhaps to be called 'spermorrhoea' (which itself had 'atonic' and 'entonic' forms, depending on the degree of arousal involved). It was proposed by an author who did not believe in constant, inconspicuous seminal loss that the whole constellation of symptoms be renamed 'spermorrhagia'—a suggestion taken up by a colleague who *did* believe in this, so that 'spermatorrhoea' could be reserved for it.[88]

In contrast to these futile attempts to make a flawed pathological category coherent there was a body of widely read literature from quacks and less finicky medical popularizers in which nocturnal emissions, premature ejaculation, unspecified urethral discharges, and failure of erection were coolly packaged up as one disease, 'fundamentally the same'.[89] One cannot doubt that for many lay males this entity became terribly real, a phobia instead of a medical phantom. There is some direct evidence that this was the experience of the poet Arthur Hugh Clough, in his Oxford days. A large asterisk crops up every now and then in his diaries, clearly encoding sexual events, and it appears from some of the contexts of its use that Clough was referring to *both* masturbation and nocturnal emissions with this symbol. He often records that he is upset by behaviour of the asterisk sort ('this catastrophe'); in October 1839 he consulted a surgeon about the problem, after a conversation with his father. At very much the same date a brilliant Edinburgh undergraduate, George Drysdale, seems to have been driven to severe depression, and perhaps a suicide attempt, by fears that masturbation had wrecked his mind.[90]

'Spermatorrhoea' is a reproach to the nineteenth-century medical profession intellectually, and also in respect of the orthodox 'treatment' of the condition. Lallemand was insistent on the value of cauterizing the urethra, which meant depositing silver nitrate at the prostatic portion of the canal. Lallemand's reasoning, if it may be called such, was that this improved the 'tone' of debilitated ducts, but some English doctors who followed him may have adopted the procedure just because it was deterringly painful. There seems little doubt that cauterization *did* hurt and was at least temporarily injuri-

[88] Erichsen 1869: ii. 700; Good 1829: v. 90; Black 1872: 163; 'Court Physician' 1876: 73–4.
[89] Henery 1863: 17.
[90] Kenny 1990: 120–2. I shall discuss the evidence concerning Drysdale in the next volume.

ous: Lallemand freely conceded as much—though his English trans-
lator denied it—and there were admissions by some English doctors
using cauterization that it could be extremely painful and traumatic.
Among medical men it was acknowledged to be a controversial
aspect of a disease which otherwise, as we have seen, the profession
tended not to quarrel with; several practitioners not known to be
sceptical about spermatorrhoea attacked cauterization, while those
who believed the disease had been overrated sometimes alleged very
severe outcomes, including death.[91] A lay victim told in the *Lancet* of
the 'torture' of the procedure, and speculated that it would drive
patients into the arms of quacks. Some quacks, De Roos for example,
did cauterize, but more commonly, ever since the days when 'seminal weakness' had been treated in a similar fashion by some doctors,
the quacks were able to crow over the horrors of cauterization and
the greater eligibility of their own methods. Some of the men on the
fringes of legitimacy weighed in with the equivalent message in their
literature, or resorted clinically to less drastic urethral interventions
then their Lallemandian superiors—though this did not protect
Dawson from being publicly accused of giving a patient a fatal cysti-
tis. Given the extent to which impotence was irrationally bound up
with the notion of a dangerous seminal flux it is not surprising that
some of the non-orthodox cures on offer for this disease were more or
less candidly aphrodisiacs.[92]

IV

Celibacy versus Marriage

Impotence, indeed, is a component of 'spermatorrhoea' which it is
crucial to stress if we are to grasp the full meaning of this strange
medical phenomenon (and to see, incidentally, that it had a benign or
at least non-punitive side to it). In its English version the disease
was a much less serious one than Lallemand had made it out to
be, and, more importantly, it was less serious than other alleged

---

[91] Lallemand 1847: pp. xvi–xvii, 328; Holmes 1875: 802; Curling 1843: 419; *Lancet*,
1852(1), 89–91; 1861(1), 582–3; *Edinburgh Medical and Surgical Journal*, 21 (1824), 322;
Humphry 1864; Black 1872: 249; Bird 1857: 379; W. Roberts 1872: 156; Courtenay 1858:
37, 57.
    [92] *Lancet*, 1843–4(1), 330; 1861(1), 582–3; Hodson 1795: p. vi; Kahn 1856: 60; 'Court
Physician' 1876: 182; Milton 1855: 5; 1887: 5; Yeoman 1854: 86–7; Roberton 1817: *passim*;
Solomon *c.*1810: 197.

consequences of male masturbation. Professional opinion in the nineteenth century had gone against its own grain in conceding that seminal loss mattered in the instance of spermatorrhoea, but it retained its
antagonism to the haematic theory of seminal function. So legitimate
practitioners did not allege that this disease caused systemic damage
of the kind that was often said to arise from masturbation via 'nervous'
mechanisms. And the quacks, of course, were not in the business of
diagnosing incurable disease, which inclined them likewise to offer a
restricted account of spermatorrhoea's field of operations. Standard in
quack rhetoric are the lurid descriptions—as alarming in their desired
effect in the same measure as they are titillating—of loving, voluptuous young brides driven to adultery by sexual frustration.

According to all parties on the medical side, in other words, spermatorrhoea was a disease which produced *genital* dysfunction primarily. So the emergence of 'spermatorrhoea' in the nineteenth
century represents a tendency which is the opposite of what is commonly taken to be the distinctive tendency of the period: it amounts
to a reduction of claims made for the pathological effects of masturbation. How much weight should be given to this fact depends on the
relative importance of spermatorrhoea compared with other kinds of
supposed masturbational disorder in the thinking of professional and
lay people, and one can only speculate as to which category of disease loomed largest in their minds. What is certain is that 'spermatorrhoea' and 'seminal weakness' composed the one nineteenth-century
addition to a stock of wisdom about masturbational disease (apart
from the short-lived idea of masturbational insanity), which otherwise
dates from the early eighteenth century.

For most men there is just one kind of genital dysfunction of
significance, and it is a fair guess that anxiety about 'spermatorrhoea',
in the minds of the majority of patients, came down to the question,
'will I be impotent because I have masturbated?' In its strange, even
barbaric way the disease was a reflex of concern for satisfactory intercourse. That patients should have felt such a concern is hardly surprising, but on this score they would have found a much more
sympathetic attitude in their practitioners than might be imagined.
Moreover this very affirmative medical attitude to heterosexual
desire and its satisfaction extended equally to women. 'More of the
mutual respect of the sexes' has sprung from an 'integrity of the
reproductive organs and functions . . . than the purists of the present
day imagine', said a *Lancet* editorial of 10 January 1857—thus indi-

cating that the 'purists' had not made much headway into the medical profession.

It was a natural if not strictly necessary corollary of uterine physiology that sexual abstinence was damaging for a woman. No doctor in the country—again, according to the *Lancet*—would have judged that a chaste woman could be healthy: the editors agreed that it was damaging for a woman to suppress her drives. The professional belief in the 'ravages' that could be caused by enforced chastity was often echoed by more popular medical authors, who said it could cause hysteria, of course, but also cancer and syphilis, and generally shorten a woman's life. Once a woman was married it was especially dangerous, according to some doctors, for her to be aroused but cheated of fulfilment by her husband's withdrawal (though partly because semen was supposed to have a healthy action on her organs).[93] There were also plenty of medical voices, at the professional and popular levels, recommending sex for men, though here the emphasis fell rather differently. Sex is less of a medical necessity for men: it is, rather, a splendid, God-given natural function (one to 'glory in', said the *Lancet*) which can promote health, but will only lead to relatively limited disorders such as atrophy of the testicles, or other forms of impotence, if not exercised.[94]

If such views were the whole truth, and the only truth, about medical and lay attitudes to the human sex-drive in the English nineteenth century the period would be unfamiliar to the point of absurdity. There would be no place at all for doctrines of sexual restraint beyond the usual wisdom about the evils of 'excess', and it is certainly not the purpose of this book to argue that Victorianism, in the sense of a positive valuation of such restraint, is an illusion. For example, while Protestant nineteenth-century England was certainly mistrustful of celibacy there were many writers, especially of a feminist inclination, who defended the figure of the 'Old Maid' against traditional calumnies. How is this to be reconciled with the undoubtedly strong medical conviction of the dangers of female chastity? Indeed, how are the latter to be reconciled with utterances from the

---

[93] *Lancet*, 1864(2), 667–8; 1869(1), 333–4; 'The Passions', *Journal of Psychological Medicine*, 3 (1850), 141–64; Dick 1858: 20–1; M. Ryan 1831: 54; T. Bell 1821: 141–3; Ruddock 1883: 116; Goodell 1879: 440; Routh 1879: 545. See also the 1872 complaint by a wife in a divorce suit that her husband's use of a condom had endangered her health, in Hammerton 1992: 110.

[94] Black 1872: 267; *Lancet*, 1858(1), 459–60; 1843–4(1), 399–400, 478–9; Dick 1858: 19; M. Ryan 1837: 126; 1831: 12; J. Russell 1833: 163–4; Beatty 1833–5; Yeoman 1854: 74.

heart of popular medical orthodoxy such as Edward Tilt's 'chastity permits the more perfect improvement of the mental faculties; it ensures the strength of the yet immature constitution'?[95] And there is a clash also with social fact. As my second chapter mentions, marriage rates rose in the nineteenth century over several decades, but not enough to prevent large numbers of individuals remaining single (and in some groups nuptiality may not have increased at all). Did this happen despite a belief in the institution, or was it partly expressive of attitudes towards marriage?

One very noticeable aspect of the semi-medical and lay literature of marriage is its eroticism. There can be no doubt that marriage was commonly looked to by both parties as an opportunity for very rewarding sexual pleasures, as several modern commentators on the period have recognized, none more than Peter Gay in *The Education of the Senses* (1984). On the woman's side this is, of course, strongly implied by what has already been said about beliefs concerning the female genitalia and orgasm. Some popular authors had written indulgently about women who had been driven into adultery, sex with strangers, and prostitution by frustration inside and outside marriage, and a minority vein in serious writing about fallen women held that some of them were respectable women driven by thwarted desire.[96] Even quite prim advice-literature in the period can recognize that women are 'made to love, and to be loved', that the unmarried girl can never be distracted from the 'the mighty influence' of the passion, and that this 'powerful engine' must not be played with lightly, so that marriage should not necessarily be postponed beyond her teens. And the familiar quack talk of sexually disappointed wives had its echo in the family magazines:

Is she certain that something better than his manly graces and tender promises makes her willing to trust her happiness to her keeping? Oh, it is fearful to awake from the brief dream of passion . . . The young man who now kisses your cheek so tenderly . . . will not be always thus . . . those manly limbs, now so full of energy, will totter beneath the burden of disease.

Equally, on the male side, imagery deriving from the physiology of sperm-production can crop up with remarkable blatancy in high-minded texts about marriage:

[95] Tilt 1852: 176.
[96] Branca 1975: 126; Neuman 1975; Culverwell 1847a: 39; Lawrence 1811: p. xvi; *Crim-Con Gazette*, 2 (1839), 171; 'Le Plus Bas' 1859: 67; 1865: 9–16; W. B. Ryan 1862: 83; C. Drysdale 1866: 37–8.

Too often an attempt is made to teach a young man that he must not think of marriage . . . Why should he not think of it . . . let him lay up for himself a fund of happiness during his time of probation; for reservoirs of joy accumulate in every man's heart, if they are not allowed to dribble and leak away in small rivulets of unworthy indulgence . . . There is a hurry and throb of Man's and Woman's hearts . . . not because of their hurry and throb impure . . . Nay, if the bridegroom lacks a man's strong passion towards his bride, *then* there would be a reason to suspect impurity.[97]

The joint outcome of these views, the 'hurry and throb' of the matrimonial couch, was also endorsed across a wide range of texts. Medical popularizers advised that marriage *was*, in essence, sex ('love emanates from sexuality'); intercourse should be reasonably frequent and, when performed, performed with abandonment. But the same erotic message is discernible in much more decorous writing about married love:

Look at a young husband and wife a month or two after their marriage; and—if they have 'married for love', and are otherwise worthy young people—you catch life at its flower.

The marriage of the loving young is by the direct blessing of GOD, and is the only realisation of the complete ideal of a lovely human life.

The *Medical Adviser*, suggesting that married couples would sometimes sleep better in separate beds (during hot weather, for example), was jocularly quick to reassure the 'thousands' of potentially indignant female readers that 'we do not mean eternal separation. Heaven and all earthly happiness forbid!': the shortest summer night 'should not be wholly passed alone'. This is vulgarly done, but the basic assumption it makes about the bedroom is shared by one of the most solemn and anti-sensual of advice manuals.[98]

So the evidence is that marriage was regarded very positively as a locus for sexual fulfilment, and by implication that foreign observers who noticed how keen the English were on the institution—especially English girls—were seeing an effect of this. But in this case the considerable numbers of unmarried nineteenth-century men and women should represent a large pool of sexual unhappiness, or they would do if no form of sexual union other than marriage was

---

[97] S. Lewis 1840: 74–8; I. Taylor 1818: 134; 'Marriage', *Halfpenny Journal*, 4 (1864–5), 303; *Ethics of Love* 1881: 63.

[98] M. Ryan 1837: 139, 195–6; Culverwell 1847b: 16–20; 'Young Husbands and Wives', *Temple Bar*, 16 (1869), 498–506; 'The Young Wife', *London Review*, 2 (1861), 38–9; 'Marriage Beds', *Medical Adviser*, 1 (1824), 358–9; *Duties of Parents* 1872: 46.

generally available in the period. It was certainly William Thompson's indignant belief about the plight of women in his day that they were quite unjustly offered only one route—marriage—to the fulfilment of their natural sexual needs, while to the bachelor 'the gratification of every sexual desire is permitted'.[99]

It would be naïve, of course, to take the popular medical literature (that about spermatorrhoea, for example) at face value when it addresses the 'married' and speaks of 'marriage' as its ideal—as it generally makes a point of doing. But this literature does at least seem to be mainly addressed to *couples*, to readers who actually or potentially belong to some kind of affectionate hedonistic union, and not on the whole to casually promiscuous bachelors such as Thompson describes. If concubinage and stable prostitutional relationships were at all common in the period Thompson's indignation on behalf of unmarried women would be misplaced. It could be argued that this popular literature, with its predominantly pro-sensual stance, its offers of devices to enlarge the penis and its advice about 'the enjoyment of the orgasm simultaneously' interspersed with its warnings about masturbation and excess, reflects the values of a sexual underworld of this sort.[100]

But as I mention in my second chapter, while there is certainly evidence for the existence of such transgressive stable unions in the period, among the middle and upper classes they do not seem to have been widespread. So it is probable that the attitudes chiefly reflected in the popular literature are indeed those of the people its authors claim to be writing for: men and women planning to marry, or already married. To judge from a song performed at the Cider Cellars in the 1830s, it was convincing to claim that marital sex could be just as abandoned as illicit sex, if not more so:

> I love, oh, how I love to ride,
> My hot, my wheedling, coaxing bride,
> While every throb, and every heave,
> Does near of senses her bereave,
> And she takes the *staff of life* in hand,
> 'Till she makes each pulse and fibre stand!
> I love her C——! I love her C——!
> And on it I will ever be,

[99] Haussez 1833: i. 47; Taine 1957: 78; Malot 1862: 197–8; W. Thompson 1825: 61.
[100] Culverwell 1847a: 42; Goss 1857: 49.

> In spite of every randy whore
> I'll kiss my luscious bride the more![101]

In other words, Thompson's plea on behalf of unmarried women would seem exactly to the point. They were being excluded from a union in which sexual pleasure was expected and sought by both parties (with the encouragement of much literature to this effect, high and low), and which was the only such union available to them.

There were by modern standards also large numbers of unmarried men in nineteenth-century England. Many achieved an outlet for their drives with prostitutes but, given the erotic image of marriage projected by so many writers, should these bachelors also be thought of as men denied what they regarded as a sexual good? There was a very common perception at the time that middle-class men were deliberately refraining from marriage. It is impossible to assess the truth of this belief, but it is quite likely that nineteenth-century English bachelors—who after all were considerably outnumbered by unmarried women—actively declined to marry. To what extent might they have had values antithetical to the pro-sensual beliefs about sexuality and marriage, in medical and lay circles, which I have sketched earlier? This takes us back to the matter of an alternative wisdom concerning sexual needs and fulfilment, which could provide arguments on behalf of quite severe sexual restraint.

At the medical level one such piece of wisdom, relating to female sexual function, crops up in Lawson Tait's 1888 paper and in the arguments of some like-minded doctors: that women may acquire or at least develop their sexual appetite through sexual activity. A related belief is that the onset of female puberty may be advanced or retarded by external influences, such as climate and, importantly, sexual stimulation (it is chastity in the sense of delayed sexual awakening in puberty which is actually being praised by Tilt in the quotation above). The whole theory was scrupulously investigated and exploded by John Roberton in 1851 but, as he complained, it was widely believed by doctors.[102] Both these doctrines are consistent, though not quite comfortably consistent, with the belief that a woman's sex-drive is powered by the uterus and its appendages, which may be damaged, along with other aspects of her physical being, if it is thwarted.

---

[101] 'The Bride', *The Comic Songster* (London, ?1836), 28–9, ll. 13–22.
[102] Roberton 1851: 1–165.

There was a more direct clash of views over male libido. Some doctors flatly dissented from the doctrine, cited above, that abstinence caused physical disorders in men. There was a long and quite fierce debate on the matter—one of the most interesting items in the whole literature of English nineteenth-century sexual beliefs—in the *Lancet* in the winter of 1843–4. The original issue was the truth of Lallemand's claim that continence was one cause of spermatorrhoea, but the debate widened to include other possible kinds of damage (among English Lallemandians, apart from George Drysdale, there was always a tendency to play down this side of the theory and play up masturbation and excess). Those who were prepared to defend male abstinence were in a minority in this instance, but there is some evidence that their views gained ground in the period: at least it was recalled as a matter of some wonder in the early 1860s how it had been 'gravely argued round the dissecting-room fire of former days that connexion was absolutely necessary to prevent atrophy of the testicles'.[103]

While the enemies of male continence argued from the analogy with other organs that disuse would lead to deterioration of the genitals (George Drysdale was the most insistent on this organ-entails-use theme) those in the opposite camp held that genital function was a remarkable exception to the usual rule: 'the functions of the testicle . . . may be suspended for a long period, possibly for life; and yet its structure may be sound and capable of being raised into activity'. 'Activity' of the testicle was understood by such writers to include the production of semen in more than minimum quantities, and there follows the important corollary that spermatogenesis is in some measure dependent on sexual wishes and behaviour. Indeed the crucial division in nineteenth-century physiological theory, as far as questions of male sexual ethics are concerned, is between the view that the spontaneous processes of the testicle stimulate sexual desire and activity, and the view that the causal link operates (at least above a certain low level of spermatogenesis) in the opposite direction. The second kind of thinking can readily be extended to the onset of all testicular function, at puberty—so that this epoch is allegedly capable of the same plasticity in the male as in the female.[104]

[103] Ranking 1843–4; *British and Foreign Medico-Chirurgical Review*, 1 (1848), 34–48; *London Medical Review*, 3 (1862–3), 141–7.

[104] Curling 1843: 40, 45; Beale 1887: 42; Humphry 1864; W. B. Carpenter 1865: 567; 'Court Physician' 1876: 22–3, 32; J. Wilson 1821: 130–1. See also *Lancet*, 1843–4(1), 328, 437–40.

An important variant of this view is Acton's theory of 'semi-continence' (though Acton actually changes his mind as to the physiological reality underlying this moral concept, as I shall explain shortly). His scheme, in essence, reconciles an austere code for illicit sex with a more lenient one for licit sex by the proposal that the pains and damage allegedly suffered by unmarried men as a result of sexual frustration only arise if they have awakened their otherwise calmly dormant libidos through the 'semi-continence' of sexual thoughts or mild sexual activity. This is very like the belief about female libido that Lawson Tait entertained, but is unusual in being applied to the male in such a strong version. For Acton is definite that a complete sexual continence, a 'voluntary paralysis of the reproductive organs', is achievable without discomfort or damage by the male, as long as his copybook remains unblotted, mentally and physically, from the very start of his sexual adulthood. The converse of this is that the properly conducted loss of chastity by the male, in marriage, leads to a condition of sexual need, with an associated possibility of damage from its frustration.[105]

All this medical reasoning is predicated on the idea that the potential for sexual self-control is, so to speak, wired into male physiology: a man's genital function is actually the physical representation of a moral fact, of the power to assert 'his superiority to the brute creation and the dignity of his character'.[106] This claim—and its counter-claim, that physiology indicated the need for regular male sexual release—were carried through in considerable empirical detail by nineteenth-century medical writers. Attention focused on the seminal vesicles, the structures which lie at the end of the extensive pathway from the testis to the urethra, that is, adjacent to the penis itself. John Hunter, again casting a long shadow over nineteenth-century sexual medicine, had claimed that these organs did not serve as reservoirs for sperm but housed only a secretion of their own. Hunter himself believed that the testicles could act as a reservoir for sperm, but in the subsequent debate this was lost sight of and the question of what the seminal vesicles contained became at the same time the question whether or not there was a spermatic reservoir. The abundant evidence about nineteenth-century opinion on the matter—whether in the form of comment on the standing of Hunter's theory, or in the form of fresh pronouncements—is rather contradictory, and

[105] W. Acton 1857a: 7–8; 1865: 27, 30, 48–7; 1870: 196–7. See also Farley 1982: 126.
[106] Curling 1843: 48.

I have not been able to decide whether there was an orthodoxy among doctors.[107] A writer of the day, whichever view of the seminal vesicles his moral opinions inclined him to adopt, could fairly claim to have support from some reputable authority or other in the profession.

If there is a spermatic reservoir, continuous and spontaneous secretion of sperm by the testis becomes entirely feasible, since the reservoir would explain how it is that men can ejaculate with a frequency of their own choosing. Sexual desire, which has to be a result rather than a cause of such a secretion, probably results from some kind of filling or overfilling of this reservoir. Morally speaking, it thus seems right for a man to ejaculate when he wants to, since this urge is the natural outcome of a process inevitable in a healthy system. Moreover, if it is by means of this reservoir that man is granted the power he has, unlike animals, of copulating whenever he chooses it would seem to give him a licence to do just this.

But it was possible to concede the existence of a spermatic reservoir and decline to be led to this conclusion. To start with, it might be that the testicle's secretion was none the less still subject to psychological influence. Then the reservoir would acquire a very different moral tendency, as a kind of buffer between sexual arousal and sexual activity, between 'the frequent excitement of the passions and the gratification of them denied in a civilised state of human society'. And, even if this reservoir did indicate that the testicle secreted spontaneously, the capacity to ejaculate at any chosen time which it afforded could be nature's way of permitting a man to refrain—rather than a signal that he need not.

Writers who followed this line of argument had to confront the question of what happened to unejaculated sperm. For old-fashioned believers in the haematic theory of semen and its beneficial reabsorption this was not a difficulty, rather the reverse. But most doctors had a contempt for this theory, and settled for occasional nocturnal emissions—which all but the most dogmatic of the spermatorrhoeaists recognized as acceptable. Acton, interestingly, changed his view on seminal secretion and the seminal vesicles between the first and third

---

[107] Bostock 1824–7: iii. 7–8; Kirkes 1848: 612–13; Copland 1824: 679; Guy 1832: 17; Brinton 1853: 626; J. Wilson 1821: 122–31; *Lancet*, 1856(2), 300–2; 1834–5(2), 401–5; 1841–2(1), 555; *London Medical and Surgical Journal*, 6 (1835), 610; Davy 1838; W. B. Carpenter 1865: 565 (and cf. 1876: 949–50); Todd 1836–9: 458; G. Drysdale 1868: 63; Milton 1887: 47; Good 1829: v. i. 9–10, 130; Black 1872: 164–75; 'Court Physician' 1876: 16; J. T. Carter 1887.

editions of *Functions and Disorders*, announcing in 1862 his acceptance of continuous secretion and reservoir-like vesicles (though
secretion is still under voluntary control in the sense that its onset is
triggered by sexual activity at or above the threshold of 'semi-
continence'). He was intellectually consistent enough to accept reabsorption also as a corollary (though he interprets nocturnal emissions,
at a moderate rate, as an additional healthy means of disposal of
sperm).[108]

To what extent was medical thinking about female and male abstinence and indulgence, with its tensions and contradictions, echoed in
the thinking of lay people? There are many lay voices, of many different types, who endorse the belief that a woman can seriously or even
fatally damage her health if her sexual needs are not fulfilled. But it is
also easy to find versions of the belief that a woman's sexuality
depends on sexual activity for its full development: that her desire for
sex is awakened by intercourse, and that her capacity for pleasure is
increased by it (especially if she 'strive' to achieve pleasure, as she
should), or even just by social contact with men. Francis Place
believed intercourse was 'absolutely necessary' for a woman's figure
to develop. He also thought that intercourse, with its aftermath, was
essential for female health, but several writers were prepared to
argue that there was nothing physically or mentally defective about
lifelong women celibates, or 'Old Maids'.[109] The outstanding statement of personal anti-matrimonial convictions by a woman of the day
is Mary Smith's *Autobiography* (1892). This indicates interestingly
how a dedicated (if occasionally hesitating) code of chastity could find
various ideological props in nonconformist religion and, later, in feminist work.

It was something of a commonplace for observers of England's
working class to claim that crowding, physical and sexual exposure,
the warmth of the factories, and so forth accelerated the onset of
puberty in both sexes.[110] Male and female sexual drives were also

[108] *London Medical and Surgical Journal*, 8 (1836), 267; Black 1872: 191; J. Wilson 1821:
130–1; Davy 1838; Brodum 1795: ii. 30; W. Acton 1857a: 40–3; 1862: 150–2; 1865: 141–2;
1875: 125–7.
[109] Wakefield 1833: i. 104–5; Haughton 1841: 115; Greg 1857, 1850; 'Le Plus Bas' 1859:
481, 516–18; 1865: 81; T. Bell 1821: 196–7; Kitchener 1812: i. 268, 329; Wade 1859: 372;
British Library, Place Collection, vol. 41, 'Observations: On a Bill to Amend the Poor Laws,
July 1827'; Himes 1930: 310, 330–1.
[110] Gaskell 1833: 68; PP 1842, xv. 33; Ginswick 1983: i. 31; Engels 1973: 176, 210, 249;
Mayhew 1861–2: i. 477.

sometimes spoken of in the same breath by lay commentators who had a general sense that the human physique needed sexual activity, but what of male sexual release more specifically? There seems to have been no inhibition felt by perfectly respectable writers in declaring that sex was good for a man's health and deprivation damaging, and this is several times reported as an almost universal, tacit belief of the society. It might have been—indeed, given the avidity with which sexual-medical advice was devoured, it surely was the case—that this belief could take quite a sophisticated physiological form, with it being a 'popular adage' that a man must not allow the 'seminal fluid . . . to stagnate in its receptacles'.[111]

But this does not actually correspond to any medical dogma of the day, quack or legitimate, and reports in this vein tend to be hostile in their approach, so they should be treated cautiously. It is tempting to say that such accusations from moralistic commentators about a lax code in the male public indicates some kind of gulf between the two parties, even if not exactly the one alleged. But this may be wrong. Moralism needed a soil to thrive in just as the masturbation-anxiety exploited by quacks did. The belief that his sexual physiology was such that he could lead a chaste life if he tried was surely real and influential for many a nineteenth-century English bachelor. He would have felt encouraged on one hand by a moralist such as Francis Newman, who told him that his wet dreams were a God-given safety valve, and by non-technical statements from some medical writers to the effect that the more advanced a man was culturally and intellectually the easier it was for him to subdue his sexual drives. Even the most unthinkingly hedonistic undergraduates at Cambridge in the 1840s—who assumed that a man could only be chaste through 'extraordinary frigidity of temperament or high religious scruple'—conceded the physiological first premiss of Actonian moralism: they believed that a man could row better if he refrained from sex.[112]

I have sought to maintain from the start of this chapter that lay opinion determined the tendency of medico-sexual ethics in the nineteenth century. In the thinking of doctors individuals with very diverse sexual codes could have found scientific reinforcement for their wishes or practices. On balance medical thought about sex was

---

[111] *Medical Press and Circular*, 1870(1), 211–12; *British Controversialist*, NS 1 (1859), 44; Wade 1859: 291; Varley 1884: 16–17; Miller 1859: 18; Kitchener 1812: i. 278–95.

[112] Newman 1869: 23; Good 1829: v. 118; Todd 1836–9: 443; Bristed 1852: ii. 40–1.

pro-sensual in tendency, but it was still a broad church. A distinction must be drawn, however, between two very different kinds of recourse to support from medical wisdom, and the ethical corollaries drawn. Some of the physiological doctrines I have referred to were for all intents and purposes beliefs about others, not oneself. The notion that the age of puberty is influenced by external stimuli cannot have any effect on the life·of the person who believes this, apart from very obliquely reinforcing a sense that person may have of the plasticity of his or her libido. But as an idea about other men and women, in the working class perhaps, this particular belief could appear to have great practical significance.

Here nineteenth-century sexual physiology touches hands with, and is really no more than an annexe to, the other main kind of intellectual inquiry that underlay the sexual-moral ideas of the period: the analysis of social phenomena. On the face of it physiology did have an important supportive role in the thinking of nineteenth-century sociological and statistical researchers, who liked to square their ideas with human sexual function. In historical perspective it can be seen that the two approaches—from the sperm and ova upwards, and from the population facts down—had little in common. In particular, while medical wisdom could nourish a variety of sexual codes for the self, sociological evidence was consistently taken to bolster anti-sensual codes for others. Because personal sexual fulfilment was not at stake, the power relations as between expert and lay thinking were more evenly balanced in the sociological domain, and opinion was more unanimous on behalf of the possibilities of sexual continence.

Chapter Five

QUANTIFYING SEXUALITY

I

'Conclusive Facts'

This modern notion of averages introduces a habit of thought
and a state of feeling which set off the present age from all that
have preceded it . . . something *unique* in the history of the
world.[1]

THERE is a host of innovations in nineteenth-century England
which at once make this contemporary perception plausible,
exaggerated though it may sound: the establishment of the census in
1801; the founding of numerous statistical societies and the first government statistical department in the 1830s; civil registration in 1837;
the greatly increased use by government of Royal Commissions
of Inquiry, many of them on social issues; the on-going activity of
permanent governmental boards and commissions; the powerful
operations of the National Association for the Promotion of Social
Science in the 1850s and 1860s (usually called the Social Science
Association); and innumerable ramifications from all this. Some of
these activities would not count as statistics in the modern sense, and
are closer to the original sense of the term as meaning 'the study of
the state', but that is very much the tendency of nineteenth-century

[1] Cyples 1864.

statistical inquiry and what makes it relevant in this book. Statistics meant virtually the same as a celebrated formula of the day, 'the condition of England question', and all the aspects of the nation's life which I have surveyed in Chapters 2 and 3—marriage, fertility, sexual standards—were to some extent investigated by the Victorians themselves.

The statistical movement's history was, however, not a simple one of increasing strength and prosperity, and its centre of gravity was never quite at the political centre of gravity. Of the spawn of local statistical societies in the 1830s only two, Manchester and London, survived for more than a few years (and the latter was itself founded out of dissatisfaction with the inadequacies of the statistical section of the British Association for the Advancement of Science). So modest does the scale of regional work become in the mid-century that the famous investigations of Booth and Rowntree in the 1880s have the air of being more novel than they were. The parliamentary Royal Commission was a most striking phenomenon in the English nineteenth century, but in its period of greatest expansion, around the mid-century, the proportion of Commissions addressing social questions actually declines.[2]

Many factors which cannot be detailed here were responsible for the falterings in the grand march of nineteenth-century society's self-scrutiny.[3] One very important thread which runs through this story is the constant pressure against 'pure' statistics, in the sense both of the mathematical theory of the subject, and of the compilation of raw fact. This was apparent at all levels, but especially when statistical investigation was in the hands of small bodies or individuals.[4] Practically, indeed politically, oriented social enquiry did in due course have its triumph through the Social Science Association. This was founded in 1856, and soon became an organization with a large membership and a major influence on national policies for some twenty-five years. Brougham was the first president, and on the council sat some formidably powerful politicians as well as members of the non-political élite. The avowed aim of the Association was to formulate solutions for social problems and seek their expression in legislation through sympathetic MPs. It was a kind of huge, publicly

---

[2] Chadwick 1965: 27; Elesh 1972; Abrams 1968: 19; Clokie and Robertson 1937: 78 and *passim*.

[3] For some of these see Elesh 1972; Cullen 1975: 104, 146; Abrams 1968: 18, 32–6.

[4] See Briggs 1973; E. P. Thompson 1967; Goldman 1983; Hilts 1978.

visible think-tank, not formally linked to any party but in practice very reflective of Gladstonian Liberalism. At various times it was called an 'outdoors', 'unofficial', 'supplementary', and 'amateur' parliament.[5]

The practical aims which gave such an important colouring to the countless Victorian investigations of the condition of England were very mixed in character. In its short career the Bristol Statistical Society quickly homed in on the problem of poverty in the city, because of the need for a person to find out 'what his duties to the poor are' in the new 'artificial and complicated state of things when a nation manufactures for half the world'. But in the same context of economic novelties the work of the Manchester society, which had been partly founded by industrialists, betrayed an intention to defend the factory system and blame the ills of the industrial proletariat on urban conditions. Liverpool merchants organized a survey of working-class conditions at the behest of the local free trade lobby, which duly demonstrated the evils of monopoly. And in the 1830s and 1840s part of what was perceived to be troubling about the working class was the possibility that it would become restive, socialistically and jacobinically. In the later wave of activity represented by the Social Science Association there is a tendency towards lamentation over the moral shortcomings of the lower classes. Even when it is not being judgemental, sometimes when it is being authentically compassionate, this middle-class research can be oddly detached from its material, as if the slums and other miseries of the period both did and did not exist. Philip Abrams, in his fine sketch of the subject, points out that the early surveys were usually derivative, bent on 'the correlation of institutional statistics' from schools, law-courts, and employers. As I have mentioned in a previous chapter, descriptions of working-class life are often bizarrely devoid of a sense that middle-class visitors could be observed as well as observe (with Mayhew an honourable exception).[6]

How deep did the statistical attitude go in the nineteenth century? Statistical inquiry was certainly not cordoned off as a professional specialism, as it is today. The amateur statisticians were often clergymen: Robert Malthus—though he stands out in terms of historical reputation—is in this respect a familiar type, forerunner of many clerical contributors to the London Statistical Society's proceedings.

---

[5] Goldman 1986; Abrams 1968: 44–50; McGregor 1957; Rodgers 1952.
[6] Ashton 1934: 11; Finch 1842: p. iv; Abrams 1968: 20, 36, 40–1; Cullen 1975: 135, 142–7.

Clergyman-statisticians can be detected in their larval stage as they discordantly combine the rhetoric of quantification with that of the pulpit. For the Catholic journal *The Rambler*, reviewing an account of Protestant city missionary work, the admixture could have been stronger: 'we find a lamentably meagre allowance of facts and statistics buried in a mass of what are meant to be edifying reflections and quotations from Methodist hymns'.[7] An enthusiasm for statistics could infect the ordinary man, or woman, such as Florence Nightingale (if she is ordinary). Even middle-brow women's magazines occasionally print statistical tables, while figures on prostitution and other social problems appear in Elizabeth Barrett Browning's *Aurora Leigh* (see Book VIII, l. 414), and enumerative language becomes a striking trope in Victorian topographical writing on towns.[8] The human subjects of enquiry—for the most part the working class—were generally well-disposed towards their investigators, and only occasionally justified fears of recalcitrance.[9]

From the beginning of the period there is a proverbial wisdom about the fallaciousness of statistics, which might have been expected to militate precisely against the policy-oriented tendency of these studies at this period, but almost the reverse seems in fact to have occurred. Carlyle opens the second chapter of *Chartism*, which is entitled 'Statistics', by citing the 'witty' politician who said that you can prove anything with figures. But his treatment of the subject, as it unfolds, is by no means hostile to this new agency in public policy, or even to its capacity for tendentiousness. 'Statistics, one may hope,' says Carlyle, 'will improve gradually, and become good for something', and by the last phrase he does not mean simply 'become practical' but also something like 'become the vehicle of preconceptions', for—to return to his words—'conclusive facts are inseparable from inconclusive except by a head that already understands and knows'. In *Frasers* a few years later there appears another seeming complaint about statistics—by the anonymous 'A Grumbler'—in which the argument takes much the same surprising turn: 'No man with an ounce of brain in his head sets to work to amass figures, unless goaded to do it by some opinion of which he would test the truth and soundness'. Asa Briggs has noted how both Dickens and

---

[7] e.g. Blackburn 1827, Ainslie 1836, Guthrie 1859: *passim*; Northcote 1853.

[8] e.g. *Bow Bells*, 2 (1864), 573; J. E. Ritchie 1857: 1–11. Shimmin 1856: 34, 49 implausibly counts 58 dancers on the floor at two *different* Liverpool dance-halls.

[9] Drake 1972: 20–2; Harrison 1982: 277–91.

Wordsworth, who were opposed to statistics in a pure form, drew the conclusion that they should be supplemented (in Wordsworth's view, by assistance from the 'imaginative faculty'), rather than abolished. The main response of lay intellectuals generally to statistics seems to have been an apprehension that the science would be trivial and arid, unanimated by beliefs and concerns.[10] Individual statistical claims are sometimes challenged for prejudice, but there is scarcely any generalizing of the doubt. By the mid-century W. R. Greg was an isolated voice, not apparently echoed until 1870, in warning how 'the purpose of forming or proving a theory', ubiquitous in statistics, can lead to a 'coaxing' of the facts.[11]

And there was a great deal that was cavalier, a rich display of the Carlylean prior 'understanding' and 'knowledge' in the worst sense, in the statistical arguments which were offered to the Victorian public. I have mentioned in Chapter 2 the grotesque disparity between alarmist and less alarmist estimates of the scale of English prostitution (the former sometimes achieved by such blatant devices as counting in all unmarried mothers, plus women speculated to have failed to conceive outside marriage). Prostitution seems to have induced a particularly careless approach to figures, and individual texts can be plainly self-contradictory on prostitute numbers or life-expectancy. One foreign visitor, Friedrich von Raumer, was utterly contemptuous of the confidence with which absurd totals of prostitutes were issued, and got the degree of distortion exactly right: 'who has counted them? and who knows whether an "0" may not be safely struck off?'[12] I have also emphasized earlier the bias in surveys of working-class housing that was achieved by the deleting of the less miserable cases.[13] This was done quite explicitly, and out of an honourable wish to focus on working-class needs, but the stress on a restricted slum component in urban accommodation is less honourable when it is helped along by imagery of the criminal poor 'shrunk like snails deeper into their shells'.[14]

[10] 'A Grumbler', 'Statistics', *Frasers*, 52 (1855), 91–5; Briggs 1973; T. M. Porter 1986: 40. On Dickens's response, and other aspects of this whole issue, see the very stimulating discussion by Kent: 1989.

[11] Goede 1807: i. 142; B. Scott 1884: 6–9; *The Times*, 24 Feb. 1858, p. 12; Vaughan 1843: 227; Beggs 1847: 15; Radzinowicz 1956: iii. 219–46; Knox 1857: 20; Greg 1850, 1854–5; Sargant 1869–70: *passim*.

[12] *British Controversialist*, NS 1 (1859), 107; *Female's Friend* (1846), 81, 87; Kirwan 1963: 14, 180, 182; Ainslie 1836: 17, 57; Raumer 1836: ii. 24; 1842: i. 115.

[13] e.g. Felkin 1839*b*.   [14] W. Weir 1842.

Regarding sexuality, it is not difficult to find in the literature quite candid statements of what *must* be the case for social groups under certain conditions, and would never, presumably, be contradicted by the statistical evidence. For Shaftesbury the proposition that crowding led to sexual laxity was 'as clear, simple, unmistakeable as any proposition in Euclid'. The prostitution expert Ralph Wardlaw called the demoralizing effects of factory work an '*a priori*' truth, deducible from 'the present state of human nature'; for another commentator it was 'an inevitable result', apparent to mere commonsense. For the membership of the Social Science Association spelling out intuitions on this point was apparently socially scientific enough: 'the eye lets into the heart corrupt imaginings, and the heart broods over what the eye sees, till it becomes familiar with sights and sounds which alarm the conscience no longer, and renders the fall of virtue easy'. The self-confirming feeling of such doctrines is assisted by the imagery deployed: moral corruption spreads by contact like contagious disease, or like fire 'will rage more fiercely' in confined conditions, or is analogous to 'fermentation or putrefaction in a heap of organic matter'; slum-dwellers not only resemble snails but also animals copulating in the zoo and 'swine' or 'cattle in the shambles'.[15]

Some writers frankly dispense with statistics in view of the power of intuitive verities: 'let anyone walk certain streets of London, Glasgow, or Edinburgh, of a night, and, without troubling his head with statistics, his eyes and ears will tell him at once what a multitudinous amazonian army the devil keeps in constant field service'. Perhaps the extremely confused state of the prostitution estimates made such gestures of indifference to dull enumeration particularly tempting in this area: 'nor are statistical tables required: the fact speaks for itself, is proved by the swarms of prostitutes to be met with in every town'; 'we are not among those who believe . . . in the infallibility of statistics . . . you may enumerate the houses of ill-fame which disgrace a city, but you do not thereby reveal the degrees of social vice and virtue that prevail in it'; 'it would appear almost a work of supererogation to quote figures to prove that prostitution prevails to an enormous extent'.[16] One can sympathize with

[15] Wohl 1977: 203; Wardlaw 1842: 103; *British Controversialist*, 5 (1861), 258–9; *TNAPSS* (1861), 788, (1869), 542; Symons 1849: 32; Seeley 1844: 30; PP 1840, xi. 82; W. B. Adams 1833; Hillocks 1865: 221.

[16] Miller 1859: 5; Wakefield 1833: i. 76; 'Our Social Morality', *Taits*, 21 (1854), 603–10; *Sanitary Review and Journal of Public Health*, 3 (1857), 328.

observers who urged that it was as necessary to have a qualitative account as a quantitative one, an account of 'the life within the outward life that the Blue Books speak of', and it was a fair argument that illegitimacy figures may have been kept artificially low, as an index of non-marital sexuality, by abortion and infanticide. But often the latter point seems to be introduced simply as a permission for falling back on moralistic assertion. With sufficient ingenuity it was always possible to deduce a negative verdict from the data about the working class: according to the *Saturday Review* in 1858 more accommodation for labouring families would actually mean more incest, because the children, conscious that their parents were occupying one bedroom 'for their own use', would seek 'to take . . . the same advantage' in a second bedroom.[17]

The well-known slum worker Thomas Beames is amusingly frank about the statistical rigour of his audience:

Gentle reader, I first thought of giving thee some statistics on these points . . . but then I recollected that the most perfect collection of reports ever placed within the reach of the political economist—the Poor-law Annual Reports—are now being sold for waste paper. I had a vision of thee shutting the book in despair.

But statistics in a suitably digestible form were obviously felt to add something, sometimes a considerable amount, to claims about sexual behaviour. There was still satisfaction in finding that 'experience has proved, what indeed *a priori* reasoning would have induced us to believe' about laxity in the slums, or that the data on rural and urban morality are 'the exact results which might have been expected'— and some point, it seemed, in furnishing histograms in seven colours while at the same time disclaiming 'statistical nicety'. 'Statistics are not to be despised' (though presumably they otherwise might be) when they confirm 'what experience everywhere tells us in a language not to be misunderstood'. Conversely, where statistics are not available it is trusted that they would have supported a certain intuition.[18] There is a fantastic, fetishistic precision in some of the amateur work: 'we easily ascertain the absolute [*sic*] amount of crime and immorality in each of the districts—St John's contains nineteen and a

[17] Robinson 1862: i. 7; Symons 1849: 39; Bulwer 1970: 121; Greg 1831: 25; J. S. Smith 1850: 67; 'Another Great Social Evil', *Saturday Review*, 5 (1858), 343–4. See also Thornton 1846: 67.
[18] Beames 1850: 9; Glyde 1850: 46; Worsley 1849: 118; Symons 1849: 31; Gillies 1847; W. Scott 1856; Clay 1857; Alison 1844.

half percent, St Simon's fifteen . . .'. William Logan subdivides the prostitutes of Glasgow, in terms of their original motivation, into distinct groups some of which are as small as a twelfth of the total, so that one twelfth were 'indolent and wayward', another twelfth 'urged by mothers', and so on. While it is hard if not impossible to find a case of a statistical author admitting that the figures utterly contradict his intuitions it was quite common for writers to use statistics to deride the intuitions of their opponents. This is particularly a strategy of those speaking up for the moral superiority of the town over the country: 'how these practical masses of figures in blue-books spoil our romances' about 'fields and hamlets' is a common occasion of satisfaction.[19]

II

Home Truths

I freely admit that this Victorian ambivalence about statistics has a very familiar air to it. The Victorians were a little more ingenuous than us in betraying their unreasonableness on the subject, rather more absurd in their contempt for figures when they did not suit their prejudices and deference to them when they did, but the state of mind is very recognizable a century later. Most of us would admit, if we are honest, that we too treat public statistics as convenient props for our prejudices, and often have a poor recollection of them, because at bottom we do not know what *would* count as a large or a small aggregate in a particular context. We can add or drop the odd nought (just as the Victorians often did for levels of prostitution) without any real sense of damage to our convictions.

A considerable further inducement to lay sloppy-mindedness about statistics in the nineteenth century was the tendency, which I have mentioned, of this material to be information about *others*: specifically, information about the working class presented to a middle- and upper-class readership. There were exceptions; in two instances 'condition of England' information was felt to come closely home to this readership. The first of these is an overall, theoretical aspect of the statistical approach—the one such aspect, in fact, which seems to have aroused some systematic public controversy. In the

---

[19] Hume 1858: 24–5; Logan 1843: 11; Dixon 1850: 301; Milner 1856: 111–12.

opening chapter of his *History of Civilisation in England* (1857) Henry Thomas Buckle announced that he was undertaking a new kind of 'philosophic history', 'equivalent, or at all events analogous' to natural science. This scientific historiography would rely crucially on the accumulation of large amounts of quantitative data: 'the most comprehensive inferences respecting the actions of men . . . rest on statistical evidence, and are expressed in mathematical language'. Buckle's *History*, as is well known, is about national morality, and it is the way he proposes to link morality with the 'comprehensive inferences', or generalizations, from the statistical data that is the really startling feature of his programme.

According to Buckle, the various uniformities which show up in the aggregated conduct of individuals in a society warrant an extreme conclusion about individual moral responsibility: that personal 'volition' does not cause a person's actions. Instead, 'large and general causes' must lie behind our actions as members of a society. In the case of marriage, though we have the illusion of 'a connexion with personal feelings', we actually go to the altar or registry office, or refrain from doing so, because of economic facts, chiefly discernible in the price of corn. Nor is this just a way of saying that our decisions are more calculating than we like to admit: according to Buckle, in such a case we are genuinely unaware of our reasons for acting. This line of thought, which was a development of the ideas of the French statistician Quetelet, was one of the most discussed features of a very discussed book, and by its nature potentially relevant to the personal experience of Buckle's readers, though pitched in terms of the nation at large.

I shall suggest shortly that at the latter tier of interpretation Buckle's thought struck a chord with professional commentators and ordinary educated individuals, especially those of a progressive cast of mind. At the personal level Buckle's account of sexual behaviour did seem hard to swallow. An obvious demurring line, taken by several writers, was to agree that marriage rates are correlated with economic facts, while denying that this impugns individual conscious volition: the statistics representing a harmony between large numbers of individuals in their conscious decisions. The influential Herbert Spencer was certainly somewhere on this middle ground. Nevertheless, Spencer concedes a good deal to the Buckle doctrine of an illusory sense of responsibility for our actions when he accepts that it is an individual's *inclination* to marry which is picked up in the statistical trends: 'whether he will marry or not, no one can say; but it is possible to say, if not with certainty still with much probability, that after a certain age an inclination to marry will arise'. 'Very widely-spread repugnance' there may have been to the personal implications of Buckle's argument, but perhaps only because it made explicit 'views which are very prevalent', especially 'in the form of a vague sentiment'. Some years before Buckle, there was jocular comment on how economic and demographic statistics were 'revealing the hitherto hidden laws which rule that charming mystery of mysteries . . . matrimony'. As far as I know, only one commentator asked the simple but devastating question: are Buckle's statistics correct?[20]

There was one practical feature of the national statistics which seemed sharply relevant to the sexual careers of the middle class and their betters. It took black-and-white form in the census results of 1851, the first in which the marital status of the population was investigated. Previous estimates of the numbers of married and single men and women were derived from the annual record of marriages, interpreted by analogy with other countries, and for the period of the last census in 1841 it was guessed in this way that of the nearly four million women aged between 15 and 45 more than two million (or almost 55 per cent) were unmarried.[21] When reliable figures became available for 1851 the level of significant female celibacy was shown to be less high than might have been feared: some 29 per cent of women aged over 20. At the same time the Registrar General commented on another topic which had caused anxiety but on which statistics had actually been available for many years: the total proportions of the sexes in the population. Though more male children are born than female the proportions tend to level out; in the English population the trend had gone too far and had produced what the Registrar General frankly called an 'unnatural' shortage of men aged over 20—which he attributed to excessive male mortality plus permanent or temporary removal abroad. This second phenomenon in fact had little relation to the first, since the excess of adult women amounted to some 400,000 while the numbers of bachelors

[20] Drummond 1860: *passim*; 'Statistical Averages and Human Actions', *Temple Bar*, 15 (1865), 495–504; Leslie 1879: 10; H. Spencer 1873: 56; Abrams 1968: 71; Venn 1866: 361; F. K. Hunt 1850; Sargant 1869–70: 166–8.

[21] Annual Reports of the Registrar General, *Sixth* (1844) pp. vi–x; *Eighth* (1848) pp. xv–xviii; *Ninth* (1848), pp. vi–vii. It is an indication of the dearth of information on this question that until the 1851 census commentators were harking back to Granville's small 1825 survey of working-class pregnant women for information on marriage chances (PP 1825, iv. 455).

and spinsters were just about equivalent, at around 1.7 million. Clearly, the level of female celibacy had more to do with a failure of men and women to agree to marry than with a lack of potential husbands.[22]

Complaints about an English shunning of marriage go back to at least the first decade of the century, but they are invariably made in relation to the middle and upper classes. They represent, in other words, the fears of the social élite about its own behaviour, 'a great panic about celibacy', which the classless aggregates of celibate individuals that eventually appeared in the early 1850s could not have confirmed or disconfirmed (in the annual reports in the 1840s, cited above, the Registrar General had actually stressed that the overall year-by-year marriage rate was buoyant).[23] These apprehensions always tended to be shadowed, and probably bolstered, by the sense of a sheer surplus of women—which, again, was irrationally but tellingly seen as a problem of the higher social grades. The several schemes mounted for the relief and support of genteel spinsters from the 1830s no doubt fed on a more or less undifferentiated blend of the two anxieties, and in the formal and informal propaganda for emigration projects for single women (which had a way of focusing on middle-class needs) the Englishman's reluctance to marry, the ready prospects of finding a husband in the antipodes, and the demographic excess of women are variously emphasized. This propaganda was reflected in steeply rising proportions of unmarried emigrants to destinations such as Queensland, an increase made up largely of women.[24]

By 1864, if we can trust the jocular columnist 'Orlando Pepys', modern girls had taken to advertising boldly in the press for husbands because they were aware of the 'unpleasant fact' that for every one of them 'there are . . . four or five rival angels'. This does not correspond to any of the statistics (five unmarried women for every four bachelors would have been near the truth) but attests to a continuing hazily numerical anxiety about women's marriage prospects. While harder-headed women writers in the years after the 1851 census, such as Harriet Martineau, confined themselves to the problem of

[22]   But cf. Anderson 1984.

[23]   *Remarks on a Late Publication* 1803: 27–9; Ingram 1808: 79–82; Morley 1862.

[24]   Hammerton 1979: chs. 1 and 2 *passim*, 105–8, 115–16; Wakefield 1833: *passim*; Sidney Herbert, 'Advertisement' for 'Fund for Promoting Female Emigration', *The Times*, 6 Dec. 1849, p. 6; Neale 1972: 133–6; Woolcock 1986: 42–4. Cobbe 1862*b* sees clearly that the scale of spinsterhood is not just due to relative numbers of the sexes.

women's employment, and feminists wanted the emigration idea to be kept distinct from matrimony, there were several prominent statements by women regretting the existence of a vaguely quantified but large body of single girls.[25]

This, the most active phase of the debate, was initiated and taken to a fascinating extreme by W. R. Greg.[26] He touches on the celibacy figures in the census as early as 1854 (when they were first published), enlarges in 1857 on the serious damage, medical and other, caused by this 'growing social gangrene', and in his most celebrated intervention, of 1862, uses domestic and foreign census figures with extraordinary literalness to argue for the biological rarity of female frigidity. Only 6 per cent of women are 'utterly devoid of the *fibre feminin*', he concludes; thus there are over one million sexually susceptible but unmarried English women whose condition is a physical and emotional tragedy. Greg's essay is the most fine-spun attempt to translate into statistical terms the widespread medical intuitions about a woman's need for sex outlined in the last chapter. Other studies had tried to establish a more direct route to a similar conclusion, for men and women alike, via the relative mortality of the married and celibate. It is striking that William Farr, the dominant figure in the official demography of the era, though in effect concluding from the statistics that celibacy has little bearing on mortality, cannot manage a more downright dissent from popular wisdom than this: 'it is held generally that the suppression of a physiological function is prejudicial to health, which our tables confirm, and at the same time qualify'.[27]

III

Environmentalism

If middle- and upper-class England was careless with the statistics which affected itself it was downright cavalier with those concerning the mass of the population. But the very bias with which this public approached the sexuality of others is instructive. Statistical informa-

---

[25] *Household Journal*, 1 (1864), 152; Martineau 1859; Hammerton 1979: 130–1; Oliphant 1858; Greenwell 1861–2; Mulock 1858: 2–3 and *passim*; A. Ritchie 1861. Cf. Combermere 1863: 278–86. For a review see Worsnop: 1990.

[26] See the various entries for Greg in the bibliography.

[27] 'Le Plus Bas' 1865: 81; *Lancet*, 1837–8 (2), 562–3; Farr 1859.

tion about the English nation was of two general types: demographic and environmental. Of the two issues I have already touched on, the celibacy problem is wholly a matter of demographic data, data that was fresh but not radically new in conception. Buckle's statistical fatalism combined the novel demonstration of certain demographic regularities with environmental explanations for them. In the nineteenth century the power of statistics to report on the environment threw an emphasis on this aspect of the world which was quite new, and opened the prospect of control and influence undreamt of by any civil authority in the past. Here is William Farr again, celebrating this prospect, specifically in relation to the working class: 'We obtain data about a governed class whose deportment is offensive, and then attempt to alter what we guess are relevant conditions of that class in order to change the laws of statistics that the class obeys . . . The *we* who know best change the statistical laws that affect *them*.'[28]

Middle- and upper-class opinion of all shades accepted in some measure the power of the environment to alter working-class sexuality. There was a spectrum of experimental conditions running from the psychological to the purely physical. At the extreme psychological end of the spectrum lay the influence which the provisions of the new Poor Law regarding paternal liability were supposed to exert on the inclination of working-class males to have casual intercourse.[29] The equivalent protests, of pre-1834, about the tendency of the Poor Law's provisions to promote *female* sexual licence had consistently presupposed that working-class women totted up the amount of financial support a family of illegitimates would bring in. It was obviously necessary that a man should know what rights the new law gave a woman in the courts before he felt freer to risk fathering a bastard, but the older, more moralistically pessimistic approach to the matter shows signs of giving way to a new environmentalism, with the connection between new legal conditions and a raised level of male incontinence becoming less mediated: 'you are giving the reins to the most pernicious vices that can pervade domestic society . . . "Cry

[28] Quoted in Hacking 1990: 118–19.

[29] The liabilities of the father were decisively reduced by the terms of the Amended Poor Law Bill; and even with the modifications made for the eventual Act, and in further amendments of 1838 and 1844, the mother had an arduous and humiliating task in proving paternity. There is no evidence to support middle-class anxieties about bastardy as female-driven before 1834 or as male-driven after 1834 (see Reiss 1934: 118, Henriques 1967, Rose 1986: 24–8, Blaug 1963).

havoc! and let slip"'.[30] Pitched a little closer to environmentalism in a physical sense is Benjamin Love's proposal of 1838 that moral probity in the Manchester working class could be boosted by a system of annual graduated 'premiums' to deserving families, funded out of a special local tax.[31]

I leave aside for the moment the countless appeals to the power of education to determine moral standards, including sexual, since the aptness of the term 'environmentalism' here needs some discussion. Environment in an uncontroversial sense comes obviously to the fore in the very general confidence that housing conditions would make or break the sexual morals of a family. I have given several examples of this assumption being so strong as to contradict the evidence of commentators' own senses. To turn assumption into reality model housing was created by several mill-owners and rural landowners for their workers. Most opinion at the time seems to have believed that a yet more powerful influence on morality was the broad environment: town or country. One must not overstate the novelty of the bias towards an environmental explanation of moral phenomena shown here: the town–country contrast as a key to moral contrast is one of the most ancient motifs in European culture. In so far as Victorian commentators attack the towns or defend the country they are, moreover, attaching values in the traditional way, however fresh the detail of the argument. The power of the old antithesis is evinced, it might be said, in the very starkness of the distinction between the two social conditions as it strikes Victorian observers. It is only seldom that their attention is drawn by what must have been common, at least to our thinking, namely environments intermediate between urban and rural, or showing an interplay of the two. Examples are William Howitt on the hand-loom villages of Lancashire and their 'desolating' effect on the rural community, and Henry Worsley more generally on how the power of the cities has destroyed old patterns of social organization in the country.[32]

These writers do also point to what is novel and interesting in the generality of Victorian comment on the town–country question, however. To start with, they have both in some sense given up on traditional rural virtue: the more conservative Worsley because of a perceived deterioration (he is still nostalgic for the old 'cottier population . . . nestled like birds under the manorial eaves'), but Howitt

[30] 'Vestrian' 1834: 22; also *The Times*, 8 May 1857, p. 10, Rose 1986: 27.
[31] Love 1838: 30–6.   [32] Howitt 1838: i. 257, 286–90; Worsley 1849: 25, 62–8.

because he feels that rural society, lacking a bourgeoisie, never had the necessary moral robustness to withstand the impact of greater urbanization (his ideal is of a rural population which sounds rather like Francis Place's new urban working class). Favourable estimates of rural sexual morality which positively argue their case, as opposed to asserting it as the corollary of an attack on the towns, seem to be rare, and tend to be woolly: things are better if society is 'distributed into families and hamlets, all over the country'; the 'more agricultural' its occupations 'the more intense and elevated the moral and religious feelings'; 'the influences of rural life are more pure, and young people generally form marriages of inclination'. Philip Gaskell, one of the most intemperate critics of industrial urban licence, concedes that pre-marital sex is 'almost universal' in the country (the difference being that marriage does usually follow).[33]

It is as if the new environmental moralism, seeking to correlate measurable external phenomena and fluctuating internal drives, cannot find much in the rural situation to support a positive account of the agricultural workers' morality. By contrast, overcrowding in rural accommodation is often adduced on behalf of a negative estimate: the real moral import of those rustic cots, it is claimed, is no better than that of the Manchester cellars. There are some bizarre attempts to press distinctive and measurable features of the countryside into service as moral indicators. The countryside has hills, the town does not: hence the attempt, by one of the period's most eccentric amateur statisticians, to show that crime rates in the county of Worcestershire are inversely correlated with hilliness. There are more small freeholders in the country than the city: hence the attempt to show the favourable moral influences of 'subdivision of the soil' (in effect, a lament that the urban worker is not a 'yeoman').[34]

The town, especially if it is a big commercial and industrial city, offers a range of palpable and measurable features (or ones that can be made to sound measurable) which have a prima facie claim as moral indicators. The links which the friends of the Victorian city sought to forge between morality and environment were not necessarily predictable and uninteresting. One of the first attempts really to assess the new phenomenon of the city, *The Age of Great Cities* by the congregationalist and educationalist Robert Vaughan, offers an intriguing cluster of features of the economic, social, and working

---

[33] *Moral Reformer*, 1 (1831), 8; Holland 1839: 25; Child 1835: ii. 205; Gaskell 1833: 28.
[34] 'Le Plus Bas' 1859: 516–18; Macqueen 1831: 4; Bentley 1842: *passim*; Barton 1850.

conditions of urban life—relative prosperity, competitiveness, better communications, and so on—which might have a salutary moral effect, some of which imply a considerable reversal of conventional wisdom. Perhaps Vaughan's most unexpected idea is that the break-down of old patterns of deference, both to social superiors *and* within the family, is a corrective to immorality, and the general line of argument is echoed by other commentators:

habits of vagabondism and vice are as powerfully recommended by the stag-nation of small, as well as by the stir of large communities. There is a spirit of enterprise and an air of life, pervading the great gatherings of men—of free-dom from cramping servility . . . which is favourable to the wholesome devel-opment of the mind.

One may find moral paradoxes more extreme than Vaughan's: 'in towns . . . there are many opportunities for crime . . . but most men overcome the temptations, and are raised in the moral scale by solici-tations repelled'.[35]

The factory is one of the cardinal experimental environments in the Victorian theory of moral formation. On one side are the friends of the factory with a broad range of approving descriptions of its moral spirit: it is orderly and regular; it removes the worker from a vitiated domestic and social scene, taking him or her into a superior 'household'; here an ineluctable vigilance and control can be exer-cised by the employer; it is an Edenic environment combining 'per-fect despotism with perfect freedom'; in fact the workers themselves are the main source of authority and control.[36] From the opposite camp two complaints came with a tiresome frequency: that the employment of women in the factories, in so far as they were moth-ers, destroyed family morality and, in so far as they were young girls, depraved morals via physical contiguity with men, light dress, heat, and so forth. The latter thinking shades into some cases of Victorian environmental moralism at its most dogmatic and strange. The tem-perance pioneer Joseph Livesey believed that the mere noise of machinery tended to 'bear down within the sphere of the brute', but it is Philip Gaskell—whose views are of a piece with contemporary thought, but also too extreme and sexually obsessed to deserve their later celebrity—who produces the most grotesque allegations of

[35] Vaughan 1843: 271, 283–6, 296; Milner 1856: 98–9; Sargant 1869–70: 123.

[36] Plint 1851: 34, 141; E. Potter 1856: 13–14; Baker 1850: 15; 'The Factory System and Factory Legislation', *British Quarterly Review*, 1 (1845), 117–57; Wheeler 1836: 192; *TNAPSS* (1869), 609; W. C. Taylor 1842: 119, 235; Felkin 1839a; Ure 1835: 420–1.

sexual physiology directly affected by factory conditions. Heat, physical proximity, and actual or potential sexual indulgence arouse sexual drives prematurely and even accelerate the onset of puberty: factory girls' breasts—in one of Gaskell's most prurient pieces of so-called evidence—acquire a maternal character ('large and firm and highly sensitive') very early and deteriorate by the time of motherhood.[37]

Gaskell was a doctor, drawing on that strain in the contemporary understanding of female sexual physiology which lent support to his environmentalism. Immoral company or physical crowding in the home, it is sometimes claimed, did not just arouse lust but actually brought sexual drives into being.[38] Human biology enters the cohort of environmental factors in a quite different way in the notion that personal morality has a genetic basis. Though most familiar as a late nineteenth-century, 'eugenicist' attitude, such thinking is already quite explicit from Herbert Spencer in the 1860s, and William Farr, in his long involvement through the middle years of the century with government statistics, can be seen to shift progressively towards a 'biological' mode of thought.[39] In an informal way these doctrines were always current in prejudices about race and morality: for some writers the 'Celt' (meaning chiefly Irish and Welsh) was a factor that overrode all other influences.

Nowhere is the gamut of environmental determinants of morality brought together and assessed more compendiously—and, it must be admitted, impressively—than in the work of Joseph Fletcher, lawyer, inspector of schools, and honorary secretary to the Statistical Society of London. His three papers to that body in 1847 and 1849 on 'Moral and Educational Statistics of England and Wales' are documents which no student of the period can afford to ignore.[40]

Fletcher's enormous array of basic data is displayed in the first of these, and analysed and retabulated from various points of view in the second and third. He offers a county-by-county breakdown of the population under seven main kinds of heading: density, class and occupation, wealth, education, age of marriage, illegitimacy, and crime, but these categories are both richer and more jejune than might be expected. There are four different measures of wealth (real property, realized property, savings, pauperism), but for age of

---

[37] *Moral Reformer*, 2 (1832), 42; Gaskell 1833: 63–73, 138; see also Ginswick 1983: i. 31.
[38] 'Le Plus Bas' 1859: 517; Wakefield 1831: 18–19; T. Wright 1873: 52.
[39] Abrams 1968: 74; Hilts 1970.
[40] See Fletcher references in bibliography. On Fletcher's career see Cullen 1975: 142.

marriage only the proportion of males marrying under 21 is recorded, and the analysis of education is entirely a matter of numbers signing the marriage register with marks, so that this aspect of working-class life is very inflexibly regarded. Fletcher is of course highly constrained in all this by the limitations of the civil data officially collected (which at this date only looked at age of marriage in terms of numbers of minors, for example), but he finds these data illuminating none the less. Together with the grouping of the counties under broad economic activities, such as 'agricultural and mining' or 'mining and manufacturing' (with some glance at the 'Celtic' component in Wales and Cornwall), and the division of each group into counties of 'most instruction' and 'least instruction', the whole arrangement is a vivid expression of environmentalist thought.

Fletcher is mainly concerned to prove (somewhat in the teeth of the evidence) the key role of 'education' in moral statistics. For us the main interest of his analysis is the handling of the sexual data, which shows very explicitly what he assumed about sexual drives—or, more accurately, the twin strands in his assumptions. Although the notion of the plasticity of the human libido was widely canvassed at the level of social analysis (and with somewhat less confidence at the level of physiology), it would be wrong to suggest that opinion was consistent, or views unanimous, on this doctrine. The literature is indeed not lacking in explicit or implied accounts of sexual drives as constant in energy, and therefore varied only in expression—of various 'safety valve' phenomena, in other words. Women allegedly suffer illness, and perhaps are even driven to prostitution, by thwarted sexual needs. Prostitution in general, it is said, is greatly boosted by the male avoidance of marriage—and concubinage is entirely an outcome of this.

Some of these safety-valve effects will show up as different measurable elements in the statistics, and to measure the real level of sexual activity they can be aggregated. This was done informally by those commentators who treated 'wives, courtesans, and concubines' as equivalent and interchangeable categories: 'all . . . exist—all contribute to the fabric of Western society'.[41] Fletcher performs the same addition sum formally, in a striking move in the retabulation of his data. He *combines* the illegitimacy and 'improvident [i.e. youthful] marriage' totals, to give a single index of 'the incontinence of

---

[41] Walker 1840: 284; see also 'Le Plus Bas' 1865: 84.

youth' for each region, on the assumption that this incontinence simply finds a 'legitimated channel' in early marriage. He stresses how
consistently the two levels, area by area, 'check into' one another
(that is, correlate inversely). He even goes so far as to suggest that in
some regions where both figures are low an invisible alternative
'channel'—such as 'professional vice' in London or concubinage in
the mining districts—is having an effect. On the other hand he does
also admit real differences between the incontinence levels of various
regions. Warwickshire is genuinely low in both illegitimacy and early
marriage rates: this particular instance, Fletcher concedes, may be
due to more spacious working-class accommodation in the
Birmingham area, but in general he is satisfied that there is 'a large
and steady balance on the combined result in favour of instruction' as
the cause of variation.

Fletcher's particular procedure is not representative, but the
attempt to strike a balance of some sort—to cater somehow for conservation and variation of sexual energies—is very characteristic of
the period. The *Morning Chronicle* visitor to the North-West, at the
same date, calculates intuitively somewhat in Fletcher's way: the factory system has 'a peculiar forcing effect upon the physical energies
of youth', but early marriage saves many of Manchester's young
people from vice. On the other hand another statistician, reporting to
the Statistical Society of London on illegitimacy some fifteen years
after Fletcher, treats the early marriage figures in the precisely opposite sense, as a possible index of the 'prudence' of youth, which might
therefore vary *directly* with illegitimacy levels.[42]

To the modern reader, this approach may seem thoroughly
Victorian, and Fletcher's at least half-way towards an enlightened
modern treatment of sexuality. Ironically, however, the newest analyses of nineteenth-century fertility and nuptiality have yielded the
very Victorian hypothesis of 'courtship intensity', as explained in
Chapter 2. It seems that young people in the period did indeed tend
to adjust the total level of their sexual activity, and not just divert
their incontinence from one channel to another.

But if Fletcher's key variable is education, is it right to think of his
explanation of the variability of sexual continence, region by region,
as 'environmentalist'? This is not just a quibble about terms, but a
most important issue concerning the conceptual roots of nineteenth-

[42] Ginswick 1983: i. 31; Lumley 1862.

century anti-sensualism. Philip Abrams cites tellingly the image
which G. W. Hastings, first secretary of the Social Science
Association, resorted to as 'the type of the great work before us':
Hastings likened the ideal society to 'a well-run reformatory school',
exhibiting 'moral and religious discipline, combined with good sanitary arrangements, and a proper union of industrial and intellectual
education'.[43] This is certainly a kind of environmentalism, but, one
might protest, in a very Victorian key, with an anti-environmental
agenda not well hidden.

The immediately striking, and disagreeable, aspect of Hastings's
analogy is the suggestion that most English men and women are
somehow delinquent, and that even a benevolent government must
be in a severe if not antagonistic relationship to the mass of society.
This is the first respect in which it seems odd to grant that Hastings
is really an environmentalist. We are accustomed to thinking of concepts of morality which put an emphasis on circumstances as lenient
or benign, whereas Hastings's analogy sounds harsh. But there is a
confusion here. Environmentalism is intrinsically benign only in the
sense that it does not blame the individual for his or her bad behaviour. There is nothing in this point of view which rules out the possibility that the circumstances which conduce to good behaviour are
stringent or even painful—though it tends to be our modern assumption, in so far as we are environmentalists, that kindliness, comfort,
and so forth, bring out the best in people.

But there is a more serious possible objection to interpreting
Hastings's 'well-run reformatory school' trope as environmentalist in
its implications. Is not the idea of 'reform' precisely antithetical to
environmentalism, because it indicates that it *is* character, and not
conditions, which must be blamed? Here it is important to draw
attention to something else about Hastings's analogy which may
seem odd to the modern reader, namely, its coupling of the idea of a
change in individual moral nature with the generally rather mechanical procedures by which this is supposed to be brought about.
Nowadays we would doubt if better sanitation could achieve anything analogous, in the general society, to the turning of a juvenile
delinquent into a law-abiding citizen: conversely, we would judge
that while 'education' might be an important route to such a reformation it would have to be in a more personal and flexible vein than the

[43] Abrams 1968: 49.

education apparently foreseen by Hastings. And 'religious discipline' almost sounds to us like a contradiction in terms.

The belief in sanitation is unmistakably environmentalist, in a way we have no difficulty in recognizing. Our problem here, indeed, might be that this belief is almost too naïvely confident about the efficacy of circumstances. But it is the close conjunction of 'sanitary arrangements' with 'industrial and intellectual education' which mainly suggests that the latter will be a mechanical affair, some kind of Gradgrindish learning by rote of practical knowledge. In other words, education is being conceived of in an environmentalist spirit here, as a passive, impersonal feature of the 'reformable' individual's circumstances. By the same token, 'reform' does not imply what it may seem to imply, a direct interference with personal character. Thus there is left plenty of room for the operation of that characteristic agency in nineteenth-century moralism, self-help.

To read Hastings's words in this way appears to create yet another objection to an environmentalist interpretation of them, however. It seems natural to regard the environmentalist moral stance as antithetical to, and exclusive of, belief in individual free will as the determinant of behaviour, good or bad. 'Environmentalism' and 'voluntarism' are polar opposites, perhaps. Historically this may have been the case, and if it is also a conceptual truth then a great deal of Victorian moral thought is certainly not environmentalist, for in this thought there is often a heavy emphasis on the power of individuals to decide how they will behave.

But, while a view which says that individual choice is the only determinant of behaviour is certainly incompatible with the belief that circumstances entirely explain behaviour, there are many intermediate positions, and in practice few people would adhere to either of the extreme views. It is fair to call a position 'environmentalist' which gives a preponderating weight to circumstances, and it seems to me that that was the case with the generality of Victorian social moralizing. More precisely, circumstances are perceived to be the dominant influence on behaviour in two senses: first, the right circumstances are always a necessary, even if not a sufficient condition, for good behaviour; second, circumstances usually are a sufficient condition for bad behaviour.

There are, I admit, considerable difficulties about squaring such a theory of Victorian 'weak environmentalism' with the judgements of contemporaries, and of historians of the period. John Stuart Mill, recording in the *Autobiography* his father's 'fundamental' conviction of 'the formation of all human character by circumstances . . . and the consequent unlimited possibility of improving the moral and intellectual condition of mankind by education', says that of all James Mill's beliefs 'there is none which is more contradictory to the prevailing tendencies of speculation, both in his time and since'.[44] Coming from such a quarter, this is a judgement it seems rash to doubt. But John Stuart Mill was active in the Social Science Association and there is, at least, the appearance of a considerable overlap between the belief (correctly) ascribed to James Mill by his son, and the statement of aims by the Association's secretary of which I have made so much. A rich and important new book, Martin Wiener's *Reconstructing the Criminal*, which is the fullest discussion to date of the questions involved here, sees Benthamism—with its conviction that individuals will choose the behaviour which most conduces to pleasure—as a crucial influence making for a 'voluntarist' notion of crime in the first half of the nineteenth century.

This links with the confusing matter of the extent to which working-class moral shortcomings, including crime, were attribute to flaws in character. It has been said that Chadwick's Sanitary Condition report of 1842 made the decisive break with an older tradition in which working-class morals (and therefore circumstances also) were alike blamed on irretrievable defects of the working-class character, and that the 'liberal instinct' in Bradford until about this date (in this case traced not to Benthamism but to Nonconformity) was also that the working man must be blamed. But one advocate of such a view was defensively conscious that it was 'not a popular . . . doctrine' by 1836. By contrast, the veteran Marxist Ernest Bax thought that 'the average *bourgeois* mind of England of the fifties and sixties' perceived the working class as 'a lot of idle, worthless rascals'. If he is right, a good deal of the descriptive evidence I have cited in the third part of the previous chapter must be very untypical of middle-class opinion.[45]

How can the social-moral attitudes of the period have produced such conflicting assessments? No doubt many bourgeois did continue to believe that the working class were radically flawed in character; and even among the spokesmen of a broadly environmentalist approach there may have been a measure of instability or insecurity

---

[44] J. S. Mill 1989: 95–6.
[45] Chadwick 1965: 59; Koditschek 1990: 528; Wheeler 1836: 201; Bax 1918: 202–8.

attending environmentalist convictions, such that traditional perceptions of innate working-class depravity could suddenly reassert themselves. But chiefly, I think, the contradictions in the record arise from the conceptual latitude of weak environmentalism, which made it compatible with a varying emphasis on the will-power of individuals, for example, or with different degrees of rigour and amenity in the hypothetical environment.

Patrick Colquhoun, really the founding father of the kind of social comment which is at issue here, may have been genuinely undecided as to whether the working class was responsible for its own depravity, or had it visited upon them. He certainly aroused conflicting perceptions—so characteristic of the whole area—about his position. His views were called 'methodistical' by the *Monthly Magazine*, and attacked as an insult to the working class by radicals, including the environmentalist and Benthamite Francis Place. But Bentham admired his work. At the heart of Colquhoun's analysis of working-class ills is the concept of 'indigence'; in some contexts this is spoken of as a condition which society should try to alleviate to reduce crime, but elsewhere Colquhoun represents it as flowing, commonly, from what has been called 'a formidable catalogue of twenty-six defects and limitations of human personality'.[46]

A figure who was much more certainly an environmentalist, but who seems also to have kept the possibility of intrinsic working-class depravity simmering at the back of his mind, is James Kay-Shuttleworth. It is interesting to trace his disillusion, as recorded in a series of papers he reissued in 1862, with his earlier confident environmentalism. A deeply honourable man, Kay-Shuttleworth was by 1861 dismayed that thirty years of sanitary improvement in Manchester had done nothing to dent the terrible figures for child mortality in the city; he now felt forced to the view that environmental improvement had simply served to 'unmask' a residual moral depravity, 'the habits of an unlettered sensual population' (ironically, within a decade the mortality figures in Manchester started to respond strongly to new health measures). Even here, however, there are concessions which keep environmentalism importantly intact: Kay-Shuttleworth has a lot to say about the contribution of the 'semi-barbarous' Irish of Manchester (and 'race' was often a drainage-point for surviving anti-environmentalist views at this time), while

[46] Radzinowicz 1956: iii. ch. 9; Phillips 1817: 146–7; George 1925: 403–4; Poynter 1969: 200–7.

'unlettered' implies the importance of education—that activity whose mechanical efficacy was so trusted by the Social Science Association.[47]

John Clay, chaplain to Preston prison and indefatigable collector of moral statistics from this site, was sufficiently outspoken in support of the notion of innate working-class depravity that he attracted disapproving comment in his own day. 'In the tendencies and habits of many of our artisans and labourers, there must be something deeply wrong', argued Clay, because levels of crime and immorality rose in good times. But he was not consistent on the relationship between prosperity and vice, for like several other commentators he was pro-factory in the strong sense: factories save the working man from the moral dangers associated with other kinds of industrial labour, and the 'regularity' of the system has its concomitant moral effect. For Clay the advocate of the factory-system the Preston strike was morally damaging (street prostitution increased, for example), but for Clay the scourge of innate working-class depravity the workers showed their best qualities under the hard conditions of unemployment.[48]

More common is the spectacle of attacks on particular versions of environmentalism which tend to obscure the underlying common ground, weakly environmentalist, which the attacker and the attacked share; moreover this consensus crops up well beyond the frontiers of middle- and upper-class opinion, running deep into the articulated opinion, at least, of the working class. The considerable but none the less qualified displeasure aroused by Buckle's claim that our perceived motives are not what determine whether we marry (for example), is a case in point. Most of Buckle's critics were only arguing for a limited extension of the power of volition in human behaviour (the importance of environmental factors much stressed by Buckle, such as diet and climate, is widely accepted in the period). Especially in so far as the personal message of Buckle's determinism could be set on one side, and a message about social policy concentrated upon, there were commentators who embraced it with some warmth. They mentioned that Buckle was not completely sound on the role of conscious human choice, but found the tendency of his argument—towards the view that 'human actions are governed by great general laws', and

[47] Kay-Shuttleworth 1862: 149–53.
[48] Clay 1855a: 34–5; 1855b; 1857. See also Clay 1840; 'Criminality Promoted by Distress', *Economist*, 14 (1856) 672–4.

subject to causality like any other empirical phenomenon—to be salutary none the less.[49]

The complexion of these judgements is distinctly progressive: the voices include those of Mark Pattison and John Stuart Mill. Buckle's most vociferous critics were reactionaries such as Lord Acton and his professorial opposite number at Oxford, Goldwin Smith, and James Fitzjames Stephen.[50] Especially notable is the long attack on Buckle's determinism by the conservative philosophical writer William Cyples. Cyples is absolutely explicit that, in human sexual behaviour, the inclination to marry is not affected by economic factors, only thwarted: 'Mary and John may postpone their marriage when the loaf rises from eightpence to ninepence, but they don't suspend their loving—we even question whether the kissing stops till the loaf goes back to eightpence'.[51] An inverse relation between marriage and illegitimacy rates is only a short logical step from here. Cyples is the author of the remark quoted at the head of this chapter. It seems that he would have counted as part of the completely novel 'state of feeling' created by statistics the belief that our very sex-drives are under the control of impersonal circumstances.

It was observed late in the century that the 'kernel' of Buckle's thought on the law-bound nature of human behaviour was actually not unfamiliar, having been 'vigorously pressed on the public mind by Robert Owen in the previous generation'. Though in a very different social register, the determinism of Robert Owen resembled Buckle's 'statistical fatalism' in the sense that it was an extreme doctrine which other democrats attacked, almost but not quite throwing out the baby of environmentalism with the bathwater of the denial of free will. In his anti-Owenite mood Robert Lowery, the Chartist and teetotalist, sounds as if he regards intrinsic moral flaws in the working-class character as the main target of reform: the Owenites, he says, 'overlooked the fact that the times are as men make them . . . ignorance and vice are impotent to work out heavenly visions' (William Lovett was also prepared to make it his chief argument against Owenism that men and women are 'imperfect'). But Lowery's tune is very different when it comes to defending the working class against accusations from *above* that it is depraved: 'in consideration of all moral action, we must not only know the act but also all the

[49] Vaughan 1858; Sandars 1857; Pattison 1857; J. S. Mill 1862: bk. vi, ch. 11.
[50] Stephen 1858; J. E. D. Acton 1907; G. Smith 1861: 12–19.
[51] Cyples 1864.

modifying and often complex influences which produced the result before we can judge'.[52]

The teetotal movement tended to attack Owenism and its belief that man is the creature of circumstance—and it has been pointed out that Owenism itself, keen on temperance too, did not invoke environmentalist arguments to explain working-class drinking. In an important sense, teetotalism and the 'pledge' (an act of individual resolve which is accounted adequate to surmount all circumstantial pressures) are plainly anti-environmental in spirit. But it is interesting that by the standards of moralists with a really developed sense of human depravity and the need for salvation—namely the Clapham Sect and other Evangelicals—the teetotal principle was too melioristic. It is another telling observation of Philip Abrams that the Social Science Association resorted with a betraying readiness to drinking as a single, underlying explanation of working-class ills. The figure of the drunken working man—on the assumption that he might have been an industrious, dutiful, principled, prudent individual—seems to express both the considerable plasticity of our moral nature, and its capacity to be controlled by quite crude physical factors. Teetotalers, for all their emphasis on a quasi-religious act of renunciation, were moved by the same vision: 'for them the world was not a vale of tears but a place in which man, by his efforts at improving himself and his environment, can attain genuine happiness'.[53]

There was of course no shortage of voices inside and outside the working class urging the importance of those 'efforts'. In so far as many men with a firm conviction of the injustice of the class system were also committed self-improvers (men like Rowland Detroisier, for example) there was no incompatibility between believing in external and in internal remedies. I shall touch in the next volume on the ambiguities attending the thought of Samuel Smiles, who is normally regarded as a man who always left the moral ball in the working-class court. But self-improvement *was* sometimes yoked to an explicit reduction or doubting of claims made about the role of environment, even by working-class writers. A prominent case is Timothy Claxton, an early activist in the Mechanics' Institutes movement, and his rhetoric is instructive. Even when the oppressed condition of the working class is granted, says Claxton, 'making this and every allowance, I do wish to enforce the still more important and quite as

[52] J. M. Robertson 1895: 291; Harrison and Hollis 1979: 40, 69.
[53] Harrison 1971: 173, 185; 1982: 143–4; Abrams 1968: 38–41.

obvious fact, that an immense proportion of this degradation is the stupid and disgraceful fault and crime of those who submit to it; it is their voluntary option to live like brutes'. But what is the key to escape from moral degradation? All would change for the working class, 'if they respected themselves as *men should*' (Claxton's italics). So, at the heart of this self-improving, anti-environmentalist creed lies the conviction that the basic nature of the working man is unflawed. In such utterances the period's frequent collocation of 'self-respect' and 'respectability' emerges as much more than a patterning of like-sounding concepts.[54]

'True, we know, alas! that we all carry within us the seeds of depravity and sin, but it is remarkable that sin itself seems subject to some general laws as yet unknown'.[55] In this confrontation of sin and statistics it is sin that has lost out and become a husk of itself, depleted of its central meaning by the vigorous young principle of 'general law'. The author here is the Congregationalist minister Edwin Paxton Hood, and it is significant that mere lip-service to an older moral system has encroached so far in such a quarter. But did the religious notions of 'depravity and sin' not retain, for all that, great authenticity and vitality in the English nineteenth century? I have cited the Evangelicals for their hostility to the melioristic notions of salvation represented by teetotalism, and it is here—in the culture of the Clapham Sect and Methodism—that one would look for the stewardship of doctrines of human depravity which are directly inimical to environmentalism.

On almost any account of the nineteenth-century English mentality the role of Evangelicalism is so important that if its moral colouration was solidly anti-environmentalist, then the century cannot have been pro-environmentalist. In fact the picture is complicated. In the next volume I shall devote considerable space to the activity whereby Evangelicalism chiefly engaged systematically with sex, namely, prostitute rescue work. The central device in this work was the penitentiary, a closed institution of the type which Michel Foucault has rightly identified as distinctive of the Enlightenment, and not native to the Christian tradition. The full range of Anglican Evangelical philanthropy and proselytizing involved scores of organizations, and for many of these philanthropy was the exclusive project. Moreover

[54] Claxton 1839: 47–8, 53.   [55] Hood 1850: 162.

several of these groups conceived their philanthropy in a new, modern, and scientific vein.

The Philanthropic Society, for example, was devoted to the cause of educating the children of criminals: the choice of material was by way of an 'experiment' to prove that education could overcome background. But most striking is Sir Thomas Bernard's Society for Bettering the Condition and Increasing the Comforts of the Poor, also founded expressly to confound an old hypothesis (that the poor have themselves to blame, and should be dealt with by the law) and to test a new one: 'the society has ventured to submit to the consideration of the public, whether the same object may not be attained by encouragement, by kindness, by management'. Southey was evidently aware of how Bernard's project broke with its Christian origins on human sinfulness, but he contrived to come down on its side none the less:

The individual Christian . . . will ever bear in mind a humiliating sense of the evil propensities of fallen humanity . . . But it is the business of governments to regard the bright side of human nature; the better they think of mankind the better they will find them, and the better they will make them.

George Jacob Holyoake claimed that Bernard was the ideological ancestor of the Social Science Association. Southey and Holyoake seem to me to have placed the right emphasis in their assessments of the Bettering Society, but as with so much in this area a variety of readings is possible, and still offered by historians.[56]

Wilberforce was a member of the Philanthropic Society, and both he and his fellow Clapham Sectarian Thomas Gisborne played some part in the work of the Bettering Society. On the other hand Wilberforce, in particular, was involved in almost every Evangelical group, and these bodies certainly interested him less than did the Vice Society. In that sense Anglican Evangelicalism was in its early phase, and centrally, condemnatory and punitive in its approach to popular morals. But the picture changed greatly in the next thirty years, with an immensely prestigious wing of the movement— working largely via the Christian Influence Society, which was an indirect descendant of the Bettering Society—urging that the route to working-class moral reform lay through improved conditions. Part

---

[56] R. Young 1789: *passim*; Gray 1906: 278–9; *Society for Bettering the Condition and Increasing the Comforts of the Poor*, 2 (1800), 11; Southey 1832: i. 198; Holyoake 1888: 36; Poynter 1969: 91–8; Hilton 1988: 91–2, 99–100.

of the role of Evangelical city missionaries was to provide the ammunition for secular agencies working for sanitary reform, and other environmental goals.[57] It would be wrong to assume a simple link to sexual environmentalism, since one of the great figures in the Christian Influence movement is Michael Sadler, who emerges as an enemy of restraint of libido in the Malthusian controversy, described in the next section. But the terms of Anglican Evangelical social theory readily permitted the view that individuals would become more temperate and orderly in their sexuality if their circumstances improved.

There was also a notable involvement from a very different quarter in both the Philanthropic and the Bettering Societies: Bentham was on the committee of the former, and Count Rumford, arch projector of scientific social schemes, was an important influence in the latter. Such benign convergences of utilitarian and Evangelical social designs, in a context of tackling working-class conditions rather than working-class character, anticipate developments noted by the historian Trygve Tholfsen in the 1840s and 1850s.[58] Tholfsen's belief that utilitarianism became mellower, and an important force for a more environmentalist treatment of working-class ills, is roughly in line with the argument of Martin Wiener's impressive study of changing notions of the criminal in the period, which I have mentioned already. But Wiener would certainly wish to deny that either utilitarianism or Evangelicalism could have been influences of this sort in the first half of the century. He agrees that the two movements collaborated, ideologically, but to a very different effect:

Although want and mistreatment were acknowledged as contributing factors, crime was essentially seen as the expression of a fundamental character defect stemming from a refusal or an inability to deny wayward impulses or to make proper calculations of long-run self-interest.

But this is a complex definition of the notion of 'defect'. I think that Wiener's account of how it was implemented in the criminology of the day indicates that the perception of the criminal, in the early nineteenth century, fell within the range of what I have called 'weak environmentalism'.

For the defect was apparently neither fundamental in the sense of being the ultimate truth about the personality of a criminal, nor incorrigible: 'the effort at mass character reform that the law aided

[57] D. Lewis 1986: 151–64.   [58] Tholfsen 1976: 132–3.

insisted upon the existence of a popular capacity to stand back from impulse . . . It was a capacity sometimes undeveloped, sometimes damaged, but, it was insisted, it was there to be called upon and encouraged.' This strikes me as an accurate description of the unfamiliar version of environmentalism which held sway in the last century, and therefore as a welcome endorsement, from an exceptionally knowledgeable historian, of my own sense of the logic of nineteenth-century moralism. It also means that the appearance of a discontinuity during the period, of a watershed at mid-century or thereabouts, is an illusion, an artefact of the process of quarrelling allies which I have already described (Martin Wiener in fact concedes that the supposedly novel environmentalism of the years after 1860 had its roots in 'the early Victorian period' and 'the appearance of the science of statistics'). The new inclination was there from the start of the century, indeed at least from the 1790s and the Bettering Society: to lift the burden of moral culpability from the shoulders of individuals and transfer it to the conditions of their existence.[59]

IV

The Case of Robert Malthus

The trail of environmental moralism leads well beyond the middle- and upper-class paternalistic meliorism of the Social Science Association, and even deep into working-class opinion itself, although the working class was the main focus of environmentalist analysis and policy. Francis Place's list of the 'good-producing' factors in the working-class world around 1800, which I quoted in the first chapter, is actually an excellent example of the baggy notions of environmental circumstance to be found in the period. It shows that this kind of thought had an early currency and, to the extent that Place was a Benthamite, that classic utilitarianism had an intrinsic environmentalist potential. All this is confirmed by other evidence I have brought forward—which also tends to show that even low church and Nonconformist social policy sometimes worked from environmentalist premisses.

But on the whole the evidence is so unsystematic—the issues so heterogeneous, the discussion so sporadic, and the concepts so

---

[59] Wiener 1990: 46–8, 162–4. See also Radzinowicz and Hood 1986: 49–64, 172–8.

ambiguous—that there might appear to be no way of determining more precisely how much of the ideological map of the period this environmentalism occupied, let alone in the special case of environmentalist ideas about sex. Fortunately, there was one relevant episode in which a wide range of commentators, most of them with known ideological affiliations, all discussed the same topic, with some conceptual rigour and over several decades. Moreover, their debate was inevitably about sex, for the subject they were all interested in was Robert Malthus's *Essay on the Principle of Population*.

The publication of the *Essay*, with the attendant controversy, is a crucial moment in early nineteenth-century English culture and throws up an extraordinarily rich body of evidence. There were six editions of the *Essay* in Malthus's lifetime, but the first of these, from 1798, is so different from the rest as scarcely to count as the same book. And all the subsequent editions, of 1803 and after, though broadly identical, were revised and supplemented by the author, often with a view to addressing the arguments of other writers on the population question. This secondary literature, which has been very fully documented by modern scholars,[60] ran broad and deep. It embraced a diverse group of authors, from the utterly unknown to the very celebrated, and had a striking tendency to exfoliate in attack and counter-attack. In the case of the MP Michael Sadler's contribution to the debate, and Macaulay's *Edinburgh Review* assaults on this, the process went to no fewer than five stages, as well as exciting comment from other parties; the final document in the Macaulay–Sadler exchange is a pamphlet by Sadler with the remarkable title *A Reply to an article in the Edinburgh Review (No. CIV) entitled 'Sadler's refutation refuted'*.

The Malthusian literature also abounds with ideological markers, above all because of the number of prominent individuals, with known beliefs and affiliations, who contributed to it. The tally includes great literary figures of the period (Coleridge, Shelley, Byron, and others), MPs from left and right, extra-parliamentary theorists and activists of all hues, a future Archbishop of Canterbury, and *parti-pris* writers for the magazines. But for a variety of reasons the response to Malthus in the first third of the nineteenth century is also replete with ideological paradoxes. Some of these are uninformative, but others are very illuminating, all the more so because of the

[60] Eversley 1959: *passim*; K. Smith 1951: *passim*; Banks and Glass 1953; Boner 1955: *passim*; P. James 1979: chs. 2, 3, 4, 11; J. A. Field 1931: 1–86.

appearance of contradiction.

In this volatile era individual creeds were often in transition. It is hard to say whether Robert Southey's vehement dislike for Malthus, for example, should be put down to Southey the young democrat—as a modern student has judged—or to Southey the middle-aged reactionary (it could certainly be uttered in the same breath as Southey's most extreme anti-jacobinism).[61] In Southey's case matters are complicated by his heavy dependence in his Malthus campaign on the coaching of Samuel Taylor Coleridge, another, less extreme renegade to reaction. Southey unblushingly complained when Coleridge, ever the non-achiever, failed to provide him with a complete crib for his *Annual Review* attack on Malthus. He did use Coleridge's few marginalia in the *Essay* verbatim, however, including a crucial formulation about the equivalence of lust and hunger being 'a faith which we should laugh at for its silliness, if its wickedness had not pre-excited abhorrence'.[62]

William Cobbett was another man in a state of ideological flux at the time, identifying himself increasingly with English working-class interests. He was less embarrassed than others about making visible changes of tack, and he was able to praise the 'luminous principle' of Malthus in the *Political Register* only months before he acclaimed Hazlitt's great assault on the *Essay* in the same periodical.[63] Cobbett was also being pulled in different directions by different aspects of the complex doctrine that was Malthusianism. His ambivalence is simply more transparent than that of his contemporaries, and I shall enlarge shortly on the strange ideological cross-currents of Malthusian theory.

Even without these cross-currents the theory might have tended to decouple individual response from ideological affiliation because of the stress it placed on claims about the human sex-drive. In modern demographic thinking the human sex-drive plays only a small part: two of the main determinants of population growth, rate and age of marriage, are recognized to depend importantly on the age and sex distribution of the population, and in addition there are possibly variations in biological fertility between different societies. In Malthusian theory sexual drives loomed very large. It was supposed that sexual needs would force up the numbers marrying, and force

[61] Carnall 1960: 62; Southey 1812.

[62] G. R. Potter 1936; Curry 1939; 1965: i. 350; Coleridge 1956: 1026–7; Southey 1804.

[63] Kegel 1958; *Political Register*, 9 (1806), 65; 11 (1807), 397.

down their age at marriage, without limit unless certain 'checks' came into play.

Once population questions were couched in terms of personal sexuality in this fashion there was a natural tendency to neglect the arithmetic necessary to show that population *would* grow given specific numbers of marriages and births. There seemed to be enough warrant for this assumption in an individual's capacity to reproduce more than once. One commentator straightforwardly glosses Malthus's 'principle of population' as 'i.e. the sexual appetite, and the desire for marriage'. Another uses an almost erotic vocabulary to urge the tendency of population to outstrip resources: 'to recollect the mere properties of the procreative principle, is sufficient for removing all doubt of this pressure . . . the vigour of the procreative principle is not less than its ardour'.[64] Southey actually complained that the *Essay* was effectively so obscene in its concerns that it 'ought not to have been written in English'. Several participants in the controversy do frankly 'recollect the properties of the procreative principle', in the sense that they adduce their own experiences of love and marriage.[65] Malthus himself does this, in broad terms, in a memorable passage at the beginning of chapter 11 of the 1798 *Essay*. Cobbett has two long autobiographical sections in the anti-Malthusian chapters of his *Advice to Young Men*. Hazlitt introduces a celebrated description of Sarah Walker, the lower-middle-class girl by whom he was sexually obsessed, in the *Reply*.

The last example is an especially teasing piece of evidence about the link between the Malthusian emphasis on the libido and the ideology of Malthusian writers. Since the latter were naturally led to consult their own experiences, to introspect their own sexuality, by the Malthusian approach, there was a good chance, on the face of it, that the verdicts they delivered would be at odds with their other beliefs: you might hate Malthus on the Poor Laws, perhaps, but feel forced into reluctant panic about the 'principle of population' because of your sense of your own sexual proclivities. Malthus's modern biographer suggests that Coleridge reacted to Malthus as vehemently as he did because he was 'obviously unbalanced' by his own marital unhappiness.[66] Hazlitt's deployment of his memories of Sarah Walker appears, by contrast, to be a case of the triumph of moral convictions over private sexuality. Her image is invoked 'because it may

---

[64] Ingram 1808: 16; *London Review*, 1 (1809), 358–9.

[65] Southey 1812; see also *Malthus Re-examined* 1868: 21–2.   [66] P. James 1979: 103.

in some measure account for my temperate, tractable notions of this passion, compared with Mr Malthus's. It was not a raging heat, a fever in the veins'. The reader who knows Hazlitt's furious, febrile *Liber Amoris* may well be surprised, and perhaps impressed, by this denial. At a deeper level, however, Hazlitt's 'temperate' stance on the libido could indeed have had autobiographical roots: in the manuscript origins of *Liber Amoris* there is evidence that Hazlitt was inhibited from consummating the relationship with Sarah by anxieties about his own sexual prowess.[67]

For the rest of this chapter and for much of the next volume—which is about the sexual creeds of individuals of various ideological persuasions—I shall proceed on the assumption that nineteenth-century writers were not on the whole rationalizing their private experience when they made judgements about the sex-drive, though I am conscious that personal factors were likely to have had more impact on judgements in this area than in most areas of moral or political discussion. Some of the ironies and paradoxes to be found in sexual controversy in the period may be due to this mechanism, but it would be absurdly reductive to explain all such effects in this fashion. The Malthusian episode offers many striking ironies which evidently have nothing to do with the theory's approach to personal sexuality—perhaps most notably the association that grew up in people's minds between artificial birth control and Robert Malthus, although the latter abominated the former.

The whole Malthusian philosophy participated fascinatingly and unexpectedly, as Harold Boner has so well brought out in *Hungry Generations* (1955), in the shift from old doctrines about a self-depraved working class to the new environmentalism. John Stuart Mill said of the publication of the *Essay on Population* that 'though the assertion may be looked upon as a paradox, it is historically true, that only from that time has the economical condition of the labouring classes been regarded by thoughtful men as susceptible of permanent improvement'.[68] More specifically, Malthus's *Essay* participated in a crucial movement whereby an essentially revolutionary picture of human sexuality (according to which the latter was embraced in the new conviction that social arrangements had a supreme influence, and that limitless human improvement could be wrought by a change in arrangements) came to prevail in the social thought of

---

[67] Hazlitt 1807: 231; see above p. 129.   [68] Quoted in P. James 1979: 109.

the Victorian years. The doctrine had by now lost its revolutionary edge, but was still strongly associated with the progressive mentality.

This was deeply against the odds, not only because this view of sex had been held by an isolated and to some extent discredited minority when the *Essay* was first published, but also because one of Malthus's main purposes had been to give such thinking its death-blow. Malthus's relationship to his main antagonist, William Godwin, was, however, very peculiar, and involved an element of positive support for the latter's views. Whether this was crucial in securing the triumph of Godwinian ideas of sexuality among Victorians is a moot question, for Godwinian themes also acquired a taint for some people by their association with Malthus. Indeed the story of the different versions of the *Essay*, their link with Godwin's pronouncements, and the public reaction to the results, seems at times like a story which should be told by the immunologist rather than by the historian of ideas.

The 1798 *Essay* is a short octavo volume in which an ambitious range of political, economic, and metaphysical topics are worked into a novel and arresting pattern; the handling is informal but energetic and even witty. Malthus argues, as a self-evident matter, that the unrestricted rate of increase of human population is much greater than any feasible rate of increase in the food-supply. Therefore it must be supposed that past and present populations have been held down by limiting agencies, and Malthus proposes two categories of 'check': 'positive' ones, which have reduced human numbers through the death of children and adults, and 'preventive' ones, which have reduced the numbers born. Among the positive checks are disease, war, famine and infanticide; among the preventive are abortion, non-procreative forms of intercourse between couples, and prostitutional sex. At another level of description, in terms of their effects, the whole range of checks can be classified as 'vice', or 'misery', or both. According to Malthus, these inescapable truths render futile all prospects of a major improvement in human societies, such as late-eighteenth-century writers had hoped for and the French Revolution had tried to achieve. To make men more virtuous and less miserable would be to lift the checks on population, whose explosive expansion would soon entail the return of disease, war, prostitution, and so forth.

The much longer quarto version of the *Essay* which appeared in 1803 is emblematic of the nineteenth-century discovery of statistics, but also of their hollowness. The book is expanded by an enormous display of anecdotal and official evidence relating to population in past and present societies. Coleridge commented in the margin '350 pages to prove an *axiom*! to illustrate a self-evident truth', and Godwin was later to analyse its structure as 16 pages enunciating 'the whole doctrine' followed by 698 pages of fact undermining it.[69] But neither writer quite puts his finger on the unsatisfactoriness of Malthus's new display of data.

Coleridge comes nearest to the heart of the matter when he says (though not disapprovingly) that the theory is like an axiom: for its core doctrine is so constructed that *no* evidence could count against it. It is important to grasp, what many of Malthus's critics misunderstood, that the 'checks' are supposed to have operated already, and for time immemorial, in almost every society that has existed. Hence—by a logic which resembles that of a descendant theory, Darwin's theory of evolution—whatever pattern offers itself in the data of a country's population will be catered for by the theory. Either that population is stable (or shrinking, presumably, but this is not much dealt with), in which case it is being successfully 'checked'; or it is expanding, in which case it is deemed to be in the unusual and fleeting situation (such as Malthus claimed for the North American settlement) of having surplus agricultural resources.

This is exactly Malthus's procedure in interpreting his great array of information, and it corresponds to the history of the theory. As a matter of biographical fact, the reading and travelling from which Malthus gathered his data was undertaken after the first edition of the *Essay*. He was confident that this *post hoc* research would bolster his case:

being certain that a theory so adverse to all rooted prejudices and received opinions of mankind, was not likely to make its way by argument alone, however logically supported, he was anxious for the sake of truth as well as of public happiness to collect from every quarter of the habitable world all the prominent facts which could fairly be supposed to bear upon the question.

Malthus, in the fashionable Baconian idiom of the day, denied that he had formed hypotheses in advance of the facts, but the commentator who sensed that he had violated Bacon's rule, to be influenced more by 'the beauty of a theory' than by 'the discovery of truth', was making a correct guess.[70]

[69] G. R. Potter 1936; Godwin 1820: 26.   [70] P. James 1979: 72; Comber 1808: 5–7.

Malthus's main target as a deluded utopian political theorist was William Godwin, whose great exposition of non-violent anarchism, *An Enquiry concerning Political Justice*, had been published in 1793. Malthus was aware that Godwin's particular brand of perfectibilism contained, inadvertently as it were, an element which would disable the pressure-of-population argument against social advance. Godwin, who was an exceptionally warm advocate of the pleasures to be derived from thinking, reading, discussion, and other activities of the mind, not only believed that any normal human being should value intellectual pleasures over sensory ones but also, implicitly at least, that sexual drives would weaken as society progressed.[71]

Malthus dismissed this possibility in chapter 11 of the 1798 *Essay*, on the grounds that there had been no sign of such a shift 'in the five or six thousand years that the world has existed', but in 1803 he dropped the section and—though he certainly continued to regard the Godwinian decaying sex-drive as both impossible and undesirable—he did in this version of the *Essay* make an important explicit concession to progressive views in a new category of 'preventive check', which he termed 'moral restraint'. This denoted a prudential postponement of marriage which was not accompanied, in the meanwhile, by any other form of sexual outlet: an entirely chaste (or 'moral') delaying of procreative intercourse. It disrupted the old two-tier classification of the checks, because here was a check which involved neither vice nor misery, except in respect of the discomfort caused by sexual abstinence.

Intriguingly, it seems likely that Malthus introduced this modification of the theory at the behest of Godwin himself. At least, there survives a letter from Malthus to Godwin which makes it clear that the latter had written to urge the importance of 'prudence . . . as a check to population' (it is part of the oddity of the relationship that the two men met and corresponded politely at this period).[72] Malthus sounds sceptical about Godwin's idea, but he does not object that it would lead to vice (he mentions that it would require a 'foresight of difficulties'), so it is probably the 'moral' postponement of marriage which is at issue in this exchange: postponement of marriage with resort to pre-marital outlets had anyway been dealt with in the 1798 *Essay*, so Godwin's point could hardly have been about prudence in this form.

[71] Godwin 1793: bk i, ch. 5, bk viii, ch. 8; 1797: 241–2.
[72] Kegan Paul 1876: i. 321–5; P. James 1979: 68.

Godwin also urged publicly on Malthus the important role of moral restraint, though not in this phrasing, in his first published response to the *Essay*, entitled the *Thoughts occasioned by Dr Parr's . . . Spital Sermon* of 1801. Godwin calls moral restraint 'the check from virtue, prudence or pride', and it is likely that he was making a genuine attempt to argue Malthus into a change of heart because the whole treatment of the latter in this document is still very courteous, indeed complimentary. Coleridge, in a marginal note in his copy in the British Library, found some of this puzzling: 'Strange, that G. should so hastily admit principles so doubtful in themselves, and so undoubtedly dreadful in their consequences', and the *British Critic* denounced the *Thoughts* for its 'Malthusian' tendencies.[73] Whether consciously or not, Malthus did in 1803 modify the central argument of the *Essay* along Godwin's lines, and astute contemporaries noted that the author was 'clearly a convert to the Godwinian doctrine', conceding 'everything which he has controverted' and 'all for which Mr Godwin had originally contended'. Southey observed that Godwin had been knocked down in public opinion not even by a pop-gun, but by its wind: 'the pellet has missed him'.[74]

Godwin himself never claimed that he had influenced Malthus. The two men were still dining companions in 1805, and for many years there was a silence between them on population matters. When this was broken by Godwin in 1820 he attempted a slashing attack on Malthus, frankly galled and disappointed by the continuing success of the *Essay* in its various editions. Godwin's *Of Population* was answered by a cruelly personal review in the *Edinburgh*, almost certainly by Malthus himself. Even at this stage Godwin did not make capital out of Malthus's concession of moral restraint: as one commentator noted, he wrote as if the revised form of the *Essay* had 'never appeared. There is a perpetual confusion in his head between the years 1820 and 1798'.[75] But Godwin had made it clear in the *Of Population* that he now regarded the alterations made by Malthus as superficial, 'mere sacrifices at the shrine of decorum'. Moreover, his response to the population issue was now deeper and more complex than a simple appeal to the efficacy of prudence. Godwin must count as the pioneer of a more modern approach to fertility, in which the

[73] Godwin 1801: 73; *British Critic*, 18 (1801), 189–90.

[74] Coleridge 1956: 1026–7; *Monthly Review*, 94 (1821), 117; Southey 1804.

[75] P. James 1979: 378; Godwin 1820: p. v; Rosen 1970; *Remarks on Mr Godwin's Enquiry* 1821: 8.

prospects of population growth are related to demographic facts. He sketched this line of argument in 1801 and enlarged on it in 1820, to be followed quickly by a disciple, Piercy Ravenstone. By 1822 Godwin was even perceived, again, to have reneged on his former views.[76]

The new mechanism of 'moral restraint' was never a success with Malthus's critics. They called it variously a 'snivelling interpolation', an 'Aaron's serpent' which had swallowed up the other checks, an attempt to restore the credit of the 'insolvent firm of his philosophy', and 'one of the most whimsical facts to be found in the history of authorship'. Godwin was not the only man to accuse Malthus of paying mere lip-service to the idea of a chaste postponement of marriage, or of being less than confident about the efficacy of this mechanism in restraining population.[77] The evidence of Malthus's own text is confusing on this question. It is possible, in fact, to find some implied acknowledgement of the notion of moral restraint even in the 1798 version of the theory, whether in connection with the sexual 'apathy' of some primitive peoples or, in more Godwinian mode, with the impact of 'improved reason'. Malthus's own aggrieved protest against Godwin in 1821 that he had set real store by moral restraint in later versions of the *Essay* is borne out at least by the scale of its discussion in book iv. Malthus does offer accounts of how a loving but chaste engagement could give real satisfactions, promoting 'a brighter, purer, steadier flame' of married passion and feelings of 'romantick pride' in sexual self-control. He writes enthusiastically of the old maids of modern society and the prestige they should be accorded (so much so that the passage was derided by some critics and later deleted).

But it is characteristic of Malthus's rhetoric in this area that he switches into the feminine gender when he wants to make sexual abstinence non-problematic. Above all, when he is forced to state the real contribution that he foresees moral restraint making to the control of population in the future he is hesitant, and no more than wishful. This is consistent with one feature of his position which is quite firm, and anti-Godwinian: he never budges from his conviction that sexual drives are basically invariant. He makes a clear distinction

---

[76] Godwin 1820: 512; Ravenstone 1821: 25–44, 120; *New Monthly Magazine*, 4 (1822), 541.

[77] Howe 1932: 357–61, 408–10; Ensor 1818: 19; Scrope 1831; *Monthly Review*, 94 (1821), 115, 118; Sadler 1830a: i. 317.

between two effects which the Godwinian school had a habit of elid-
ing, namely, sexual self-control arising from a calculation of
unwanted consequences, and a true decay of libido. Malthus was
even prepared to argue on occasion that sexual drives could be
enhanced by a climate of rational restraint: 'in European countries,
where . . . manners have imposed considerable constraints on this
gratification, the passion . . . rises in force'. In the last resort it is hard
to avoid the impression that for Malthus the invariance of the sex-
drive was not just a descriptive but also an ethical truth:

It is clearly the duty of each individual not to marry till he has the prospect
of supporting children; but it is at the same time to be wished, that he should
retain undiminished his desire of marriage . . . It is evidently therefore, regulation and direction that is required with regard to the principle of population, not diminution or alteration.

Here, characteristically resorting to a masculine grammar, Malthus
allows his moral distaste for Godwinian anti-sensualism actually to
override the great message of the calamitous effects of population
growth.[78]

While the introduction of moral restraint into Malthus's system did
not make it as thoroughly inconsistent as some of his critics alleged it
is not surprising that the long, hybrid argument of the *Essay* in its
1803 and subsequent versions provoked wildly divergent interpretations. It is here that the *Essay* becomes a unique instrument for trac-
ing the ideological affiliations of different attitudes to sexuality and,
specifically, sexual continence. The 1798 *Essay* had received little
attention, and the great bulk of contemporary comment on Malthus
relates to the revised version of the theory, with the proposal that
young people should marry only when their finances permit, and
until then refrain from sex, prominently in place.

One critic, interestingly, did choose to write as if 'moral restraint'
were only a minor extension of the theory. Horace Twiss, who was a
Peelite Tory MP and opponent of the Reform Bill, took the view that
the prudential check may 'be or be not attended, during the period of
restraint, by a conduct strictly moral as to sexual intercourse', and he
ventured to answer on behalf of Malthus the objection that his policies would thus connive at immorality:

[78] Malthus 1970: 81, 148; 1963: 139; 1803: 10, 351, 384, 386, 488–9, 492–3, 496–7, 550–1;
J. A. Field 1931: 36; Senior 1829: 64–5.

We might . . . say, to a man the most religious and virtuous in the whole kingdom, whose son should be about to marry, without the means of maintaining a family, 'Sir, if your son can be brought to abstain from this indiscreet marriage, shall you regret the dissuasive, because during his celibacy, there is a chance of his allowing himself some incorrect gratification?'[79]

This is the true voice of an old-fashioned, latitudinarian morality, not ashamed to recommend compromise, indeed rather priding itself on its lack of doctrinal strictness and its low estimate of human nature. In the Victorian years the *Saturday Review* is the main heir of this temperament, and it is tempting to suppose that Twiss has expressed the working code of many people who were convinced by Malthus. This seems to be a wrong assumption. Certainly Twiss is out of tune with the other published comment on Malthus, friendly or hostile, all of which discusses 'moral restraint' in its full sense. On the face of it, a lenient view of pre-marital hanky-panky was as much against the spirit of the times as resistance to parliamentary reform.

The strange and illuminating disagreements over the Malthusian code of restraint are best introduced by a pair of examples. 'Simplex' is an unidentified author, but evidently a Scottish Calvinist and a member of the sect known as Sandemanians or Glassites (Michael Faraday is the most famous of all Sandemanians). Malthus's doctrine of abstinence struck Simplex as being profoundly immoral, given that 'the mutual propensity of the sexes is . . . as truly a part of the constitution of human nature as man's desire for food when hungry, or drink when thirsty'.[80] As I have mentioned, Coleridge—and Southey following him—reprobated in the strongest terms the view they attributed to Malthus that 'lust is a thing of physical necessity equally with the gratification of hunger' ('Shame upon our race', said Coleridge, 'that there lives the individual' who could even suggest as much). However it is Hazlitt who runs down and tries to destroy the supposed Malthusian analogy of lust and hunger most thoroughly, in one huge bravura paragraph on the variability of sexual behaviour in different cultures.[81] These writers have responded to the hybrid character of the *Essay*. Simplex, we may say, has seen the Godwinian Malthus; and Coleridge, Southey, and Hazlitt the Malthusian Malthus. Each of these readings reflects the thinking of a particular ideological grouping in the dispute.

[79] Twiss 1809.   [80] 'Simplex' 1808: 228.
[81] G. R. Potter 1936; Hazlitt 1807: 123–41.

Simplex lays much stress on the imperative claims of the sexual appetite (*ninety-nine* of *one hundred* of the human species will find the *must-be* of Mr M. a *physical impossibility*'), but his Calvinism is not in abeyance when he does this. The Sandemanian doctrine admittedly had an antinomian cast, and the sect's worship was modelled on the primitive Christian love-feast, with kissing included, but there is no note of sexual unorthodoxy in Simplex's argument. He cites the opening of the fourth chapter of Paul's first epistle to Timothy to prove that 'forbidding to marry' is a 'doctrine of devils'. He interprets the 'burning' which is the unacceptable alternative to marriage in Corinthians in a literal, hell-fire sense. The fates of Onan and the citizens of the plain are taken to show that even violating the Malthusian code of restraint by masturbation will have fearful consequences. On the other hand, the mortality Malthus tell us will flow from uncontrolled sexual gratification is found consonant with Christian ideas of death.[82]

The only protests against Malthusian chastity of comparable strength also come from religious voices within or close to fundamentalist Nonconformity. William Keir, another Scot of apparently Calvinist convictions, agreed that moral restraint was a diabolical teaching: Malthus was like Satan seducing Eve, and the code in Eden was that it was not good for man to be alone. As this will suggest, such writers could be oddly unmindful of the Fall when they discussed sex, though in Keir's case it was a vivid enough doctrine elsewhere, invoked by him when he treats the 'positive checks' as part of the punishments meted out to rebellious mankind at Genesis 3: 14–19.[83]

The sense of man the miserable transgressor, afflicted with pain, disease, and death until redeemed by Christ, seems to have dropped entirely from Michael Sadler's vision of human sexuality, but his remarkable unqualified rejection of moral restraint in *Law of Population* springs nevertheless from the dissenting end of the English religious spectrum. Sadler, the pioneer of the campaign to control child labour in the factories, was a Tory MP of an Evangelical persuasion, with youthful links to Nonconformity. According to him, chastity is only possible for a few frigid individuals, for religious zealots under extreme conditions of discipline, and for young people reining back their desire with 'the prospect of its timely gratification':

<hr>

[82] 'Simplex' 1808: 205, 211, 223–6, 229–31.   [83] Keir 1807: 99–104.

otherwise 'it contradicts nature, reason, scripture, and common sense'.

The list of authorities is comprehensive, and probably one that any ideologically middle-of-the-road English man or woman of the day would have been happy to invoke. There is superficially a good deal of the Deist about Sadler, because he was making a conscious attempt to use a broadly acceptable language, and arguments which did not hinge on 'the inspired volume', 'God', and 'direct interference', as opposed to 'natural theology', 'nature', and 'secondary causes'. He is able to invoke the great William Paley in support of the view that the male libido is imperious and unmodifiable. But there is also an exuberant and almost visionary quality about Sadler's feeling for a providential divine agency in nature, and his readers varied in the degree to which they found a sense of direct divine control, or more orthodox natural theology, in his account of population mechanisms. Sadler's answer to the population problem was that God had contrived things so that human fecundity diminishes as communities become more dense: hence the pernicious Malthusian check of moral restraint will actually decline in importance as population grows.[84]

In assessing the mainstream Anglican response to Malthusian restraint it is important to be aware that Malthus started with several strikes against him, theologically. The 1798 *Essay* had concluded with two consciously heterodox metaphysical chapters, putting forward an account of man's earthly existence which denied the immortality of the soul in the conventional sense. The reactionary *British Critic* welcomed the dropping of this material in 1803, but was now doubtful about the new check: 'we cannot agree with his ideas of extending the period, and even the habit, of celibacy . . . unless monastic institutions for the female sex were revived . . . this would be accompanied with a very great increase of vice'. Religious alarms about planned celibacy were bound to be potent in Protestant Britain, and were certainly a ground for some of the dislike of Malthusian restraint. But above all there was the feeling that Malthus's system of checks, though the author made a valiant and probably heartfelt attempt to square it with God's benign concern for mankind, did impeach divine providence. Sadler's is the most

---

[84] Sadler 1830a: i. 318–24; ii. 584, 629–30; 1830b: 7; J. Wilson 1830; Macaulay 1830; G. Young 1832: 49; Paley 1785: ii. 352; also Turner 1837: 46–9, *Taits*, 21 (1854), 65–9.

personal and spiritual of the major responses along these lines, while
that by the historian Sharon Turner is the most grandly and serenely
complacent about the benign tendency of virtually every facet of current sexual conduct in his society.[85]

One of the Anglican commentators dismayed by the incongruity of
Malthus's system with 'the received tenets of natural theology' was
the Leicestershire rector Robert Ingram, and it is notable that he
finds an expression of heterodox doubt as to God's providence in one
of the key anti-Godwinian passages in the *Essay*, that in which
Malthus speaks of the 'light and superficial' role of institutions, as
opposed to basic human nature, in driving human population. This is
inconsistent of Ingram, who is a fairly head-on opponent of moral
restraint, because Malthus and Godwin were agreed that moral
restraint, whatever its effectiveness, was the product of institutions.
But it is one of the ironies of the affair that Godwin's version of population mechanisms had some claim to be more 'Christian' than
Malthus's: Godwin in the 1820 *Of Population* freely invokes biblical
authority for the sacredness of humanity and human propagation, and
ten years earlier one pamphleteer had already judged that his theory
was 'founded upon the wise system of christianity'.[86]

It was claimed in 1839, implausibly, that 'not one in a thousand' of
Anglican clergymen approved of 'the Malthusian theory'. If this had
been even approximately true at the beginning of the century it certainly needed reporting, because representatives of the Church—as
one of them complained—were not at all vocal against the *Essay*.
Moreover some influential Anglican opinion was evidently embracing the Godwinian element in Malthus. There had always been political inducements in this direction from the reactionary tenor of
Malthus's views on the working class and the Poor Laws. The attack
on the Poor Laws as an encouragement to improvident marriage in
the 1798 *Essay* was supplemented, in the newly Godwinian 1803 version, by proposals for a vigorous propaganda to modify working-class
attitudes. Here was a bridging-point between two historically widely
separated attitudes: severe religious moralistic reproach of the working class for self-induced ills and the utopian confidence of
the 1790s that men could be swayed simply by a clear statement of
the truth. Even though the working classes had only themselves to
blame they could be 'taught' to improve demographically: 'you are

[85] *British Critic*, 23 (1804), 244; Grahame 1816: 83; Turner 1837: letter xi.
[86] Godwin 1820: 107–8; *Clear, Fair, and Candid Investigation* 1810: 2.

this day called upon solemnly to deliberate, whether you will squander away the most precious moments of your existence in extravagant and sensual pleasures . . . or whether you will deny yourselves a few immediate gratifications'.[87]

Other Anglicans were moving significantly further than this towards Godwin via Malthusian moral restraint. The key influence here, making Malthus 'acceptable to a generation of churchmen', was a future Archbishop of Canterbury, John Bird Sumner. He wrote in 1816, in remarkably Godwinian terms, of how painless the experience of chaste postponement of marriage would be if literature and other intellectual pursuits were brought into play: 'the mind, diverted from one object, turns, without pain or convulsion, to another'. Sumner was on the Church's Evangelical wing, it should be said, though he was not associated with Wilberforce's ginger group and had a reputation for conciliatoriness. He should perhaps be bracketed with the Enlightenment-influenced vein of Evangelicalism, which I have already noted at work in some philanthropy of the period.[88]

Sumner's one-time chaplain when he was bishop of Chester, Henry Raikes, gave lectures to the Mechanics' Institute in that city which represent a striking assimilation of Godwinian ideas into the Anglican promotion of Malthusian thought for the working class (Raikes himself is apparently ingenuous about this, being only aware that the *Essay* of 1798 contained some unwelcome 'paradoxical asperities'). Not only does Raikes tell his rough audience that society's growing 'intellectual refinement . . . withdraws men from the mere sensualities of life' and that 'wherever society is highly cultivated, more men will be found living in voluntary celibacy', but by an impressive sleight he turns the very imperiousness of the sexual appetite, so unequivocal a token of God's intentions for the Calvinist Simplex, into an argument for its suppression: 'That tendency to increase which seems implanted in our nature by a law, which it is not easy to evade, seems likewise intended to force upon our minds the absolute necessity of moral restraint.'[89]

Evangelicalism not just modified but renounced was the background to the Godwinian population theory of that interesting figure, Thomas Southwood Smith. Smith migrated from Evangelical

[87] Campbell/Bannister 1839: 35; Soloway 1969: 93; Malthus 1803: bk iv, chs. 3–8; 'Clergyman' 1820: pp. vi, 20; see also Burdon 1803: 11.

[88] Sumner 1816: ii. 167; Soloway 1969: 93–106.   [89] Raikes 1845: 27, 31–2, 50.

dissenting origins to Unitarianism and close involvement with the *Westminster Review* group of second-generation utilitarians. He is best known as an ardent sanitary reformer. During his period as a Unitarian minister in Scotland he wrote the *Illustrations of the Divine Government*, which can only be described as an essay in theological Godwinism, glowingly optimistic that God's providence has arranged man's circumstances so that utopia will soon dawn. Smith's explanation of population growth reinforces the doctrine of decaying drives with a classic, and remarkably confident, statement of environmentalism. It is also instructive, for an understanding of the nineteenth-century environmentalist temperament, that the 'good producing' factors have a painful or at least stringent aspect—for Smith is prepared to accept Malthus's basic arithmetic and the possibility of consequent suffering:

under a wise and upright administration of affairs, the power of multiplication in man, however extensive, might be rendered the source of an immeasurable increase of happiness over the face of the whole earth . . . Those consequences, therefore, ought in all justice to be referred, not to the principle of population, but to the institutions of society: they do not disprove the wisdom and goodness of the Deity in the appointment of the law . . . Man . . . might render it innoxious, because he can obtain the mastery over the grosser impulses of appetite . . . By a wise arrangement of the circumstances in which he is placed at an early period, and trained to maturity, he might be made to see his own interest so clearly . . . that it should not be possible for him to deviate from the course prescribed by an enlightened regard to his well-being. This opinion is founded on the universally-admitted truth, that man is what the circumstances in which he is placed make him.[90]

At an opposite ideological extreme from Simplex stand the radicals, progressives, and secularists of the era. In the thought of Godwin himself the links between the essential plasticity of the libido and a confidence in vast social improvement simply became clearer, the logic firmer, although he also developed a set of purely demographic arguments against Malthus, as I have mentioned. The second chapter of book vi of Godwin's 1820 *Of Population*, though perhaps indebted in some measure to Hazlitt, is an unabashed affirmation of the essential rationality of man and of his great destiny as a creature completely in control of his passions, collectively and individually.

[90] T. S. Smith 1822: 174–6.

Such utopian thinking about sexuality stirred the imaginations of several now forgotten authors, minor even in their day. The self-taught working-class writer William Manning looked forward to sexual virtue as the free choice of a free people. J. C. Ross was a man so haunted by egalitarian fervour that he did not even bother to explain why an equal society would also have no population problems. One of the strangest of these documents is the *General Statement* by the unknown Samuel Read, in which a Godwinian de-sensualizing process—now somewhat redefined as the progress of 'LUXURY AND REFINEMENT'—is transmuted into a kind of eroticism of the intellect and spirit: 'Luxury and refinement, then, in females . . . while it . . . diminishes in a degree their prolific powers, increases their susceptibility, and enlarges their capacities of receiving and communicating happiness.'[91]

By far the most prominent of the progressive anti-sensualists, after Godwin himself, is of course William Hazlitt. Hazlitt's various articles on Malthus in the ten years from 1807 to 1817—almost all contributions to Cobbett's *Political Register*, and the most significant, first wave, of them gathered as *A Reply to the Essay on Population* of 1807—have a rhetorical brilliance and a sophisticated complexity of tone that sets them apart from all other contributions to the debate. For the modern reader their most memorable element is perhaps the cumulative picture of human sexuality as capable of a great variety of expression depending on cultural circumstances (and not simply as a decaying impulse in an improved society of the future—though Hazlitt believed in that too).

In terms of his contemporary influence the most important argument developed by Hazlitt against Malthus, on Godwin's behalf, may be called the 'Inconsistent Utopia Argument'. Malthus had made great play, first of all in chapter 10 of the 1798 *Essay*, with a thought-experiment whereby a Godwinian utopia—'a society constituted according to the most beautiful form that imagination can conceive, with benevolence for its moving principle . . . and with every evil disposition corrected by reason and not force'—was shown spontaneously to collapse under population pressures within a maximum of thirty years. Hazlitt protested that in a utopia sexual drives could be expected to be as much under the sway of altruistic and rational controls as any other disruptive element.[92]

[91] Manning 1838: 292, 297; J. C. Ross 1827: ii. 218–19; Read 1821: 13–15.
[92] Hazlitt 1807: 48–52; Howe 1932: 332–7, 357–61, 408–10.

The argument was adopted by Southey, De Quincey, and Francis Place, and this is especially significant as all three men perceived themselves as more-or-less distant from Godwin. Southey claimed to regard both Malthus and Godwin as political quacks: their disagreement was like Solomon criticizing Brodum. But he was completely at one with Hazlitt on the 'absurdity of supposing that a community, which . . . had obtained the highest state of attainable perfection, should yet be without the virtue of continence'.[93] The modern reader is bound to feel an enormous weight of assumption in Southey's supposedly self-evident link between 'perfection' and 'continence', and it testifies to a considerable unanimity among those who doubted, and those who trusted in progress, as to what an improved humanity should be like, and what the status of sexuality would be under such conditions. There is an agreement that sexuality is a lower function, an aspect of one's 'animal' nature, and that progress axiomatically means an enlargement of the specifically human qualities of mind and reason.

Similarly De Quincey, who thought that Malthus's theory remained valid as economic doctrine and claimed to be agnostic on the question of whether humans could learn to abstain from sex, betrays his unMalthusian valuation of such an abstinence when he couches the problem as one of 'whether any great change for the better in the moral nature of the man' will occur.[94] Francis Place's position is more complicated, not to say puzzling. I shall mention shortly his advocacy of birth control in response to population problems, which was based on a doubt as to the possibility and even desirability of sexual abstinence. But in an article reliably attributed to him, in the *New Monthly*, Place writes compellingly of how the 'principle of population' may undergo a 'transmutation by the same alchemy, which is to change every other principle of the human character': 'As society advances in civilisation . . . a multitude of passions, habits, peculiarities, and prejudices, grow up and dispute, in the human character, the dominion which is almost exclusively possessed by the simpler and more original (but not therefore the more natural) propensities, when man is in a ruder state'. The two aspects of Place's position are presumably harmonized, if not very comfortably, in his explanation that by the 'principle of population' he does not (contrary to the general usage of the period) mean libido—'the passion

[93] Southey 1804: 295; 1812.   [94] De Quincey 1890: 16–17.

between the sexes in its coarser and more general import'—but 'that modification of it, which induces men to marry'.[95]

The qualified progressives such as Southey did also have a pro-sensual vein in their comment, elicited by the Godwinian Malthus as opposed to the Malthusian Malthus. Overt inconsistency was often avoided by making the complaint one about the unfairness of requiring the working class alone to limit their fertility, but Southey does wriggle rather painfully in the attempt to make out that it is abominable to restrict working-class marriage, as Malthus the 'sow-gelder' wishes, but also important to create the moral and social climate whereby a restriction will occur. The image of Malthus the callous enemy of working-class philoprogenitiveness was particularly appealing to literary men, from Shelley through Leigh Hunt to Dickens, via the more equivocal Peacock. Shelley's vignette of the tyrant Swellfoot summoning 'Moses the sow-gelder' to spay the rebellious pig population, now that 'moral restraint . . . prostitution . . . starvation, typhus-fever, war . . . prison' have failed, is presumably a reference, using Southey's conceit of 1804, to the currently proposed legislation whereby poor relief would be denied for children born after a certain date.[96]

Such attitudes received a powerful reinforcement from the intense regard which was felt for marriage, a very important sentiment at this period and something of a rogue element in the population debate. Marriage was commonly said to be the one consolation left to the poor (Godwin himself writes in this vein), and occasionally claimed to be particularly fine in its working-class version. Affirming the value of marriage was not incongruous in a pro-sensual writer such as Sadler, who has a very remarkable analysis of how romantic love is Nature's way of ensuring that young people will be able to gratify their sexual needs without being deterred by the perception that they are in fact obeying 'the impulse of mere animal indulgence'.[97] But in William Cobbett, for twenty-eight years tribune of the working class and their right to marry against 'Parson Malthus', matrimonialism is an altogether more awkward doctrine.

Cobbett's high valuation of marriage, 'the greatest of all earthly

[95] Place 1821.

[96] Curry 1939; Southey 1816; 1818a; 1818b; Shelley, *Oedipus Tyrannus or Swellfoot the Tyrant* (1820), I. i. 72–9; Leigh Hunt, 'A New Chaunt' (1819); Dickens, *The Chimes* (1844); Peacock, *Melincourt* (1817), ch. 35.

[97] D. Booth 1823: 64; Grahame 1816: 241–5; Godwin 1820: 555; Sadler 1830a: i. 344.

blessings', is frankly rooted, like Sadler's, in overriding erotic needs ('far too strong to be subdued by any apprehensions to which the human heart is liable'), and erotic satisfactions: 'to indulge this passion, to perform this act, is among the rights of nature herself'. By contrast, Cobbett is a great, even prudish, advocate of pre-marital sexual decorum, especially for women, in the central chapters of his *Advice to Young Men* (1830). His ambivalence about a dedicated chastity emerges interestingly in relation to Malthus himself. It compounds the offence of the 'Parson' that he belongs to a church historically founded, according to Cobbett, in opposition to clerical celibacy: the Church of England took a principled stand against an unnatural doctrine, and her clergy should do likewise. But elsewhere Cobbett writes as if the Reformation was a matter of a 'voluptuous . . . sensual fraternity' being unable to maintain the chastity that Paul had required of the priesthood.[98]

Not quite all the progressive contributors to the Malthusian debate believed that sexual continence, suitably defined, was indissolubly linked to human improvement. There was a scattering of voices speaking, or at least verging on speaking, as a later fashion of thought would expect a good progressive to speak: in favour of more sex and less restricted sex. One of the very few notices of the 1798 *Essay* appeared in Joseph Johnson's *Analytical Review*, the outstanding radical literary magazine of these years.[99] Although this periodical had been favourable to Godwin, Mary Wollstonecraft, and Thomas Paine, its reviewer felt obliged to side with Malthus against Godwin on sexuality. Godwin is compared to a religious crank, Richard Brothers, and Malthus's views on a powerful and invariant sex-drive completely endorsed. It is not clear how Malthus's reactionary political solution is regarded, but the reviewer perhaps hints, sardonically enough, that the radical way out of the impasse of population would be to lift the 'vice' embargo on some of the 'preventive checks': 'without intending it . . . we think the author . . . has furnished the best apology for prostitution, that ever was written'. It is, incidentally, a striking indication of the tenor of the whole Malthusian debate that no other writer, as far as I know, draws attention to the flimsy symmetry of Malthus's 'vice' and 'misery' pairing.

William Thompson, the proto-socialist, is significant here as a case

[98] Cobbett 1823: 246, 254–5, 260–2; *Cobbett's Two-Penny Trash*, 9 (Mar. 1831); *Political Register*, 32 (1817), 25–30; 34 (1819), 1022, 1025.

[99] *Analytical Review*, 28 (1798), 119–25.

of a writer who directly dissents from the Godwinian principle of inversely related perfection and sensuality. Godwin is one of the 'intellectual speculators' who, 'conscious of their own powers of restraining and regulating what they regard as the grosser propensities of our nature, proclaim man as capable of attaining happiness by his mental powers alone'. Malthus represents another pernicious extreme, that of the 'mechanical speculators', and Thompson wants a mean between the two, a 'wise *regulation* of . . . appetites and passions'. But that one phrase about 'what they regard as the grosser propensities' is pregnant with an utterly new view of sex and social progress. The note is not sounded again with such confidence until the opening sentence of George Drysdale's *Elements of Social Science*, thirty years later.[100]

Francis Place, as I have mentioned, had a calm, unmoralistic conviction that significant sexual abstinence was impossible, now and in the future, but this is as far as he goes towards a permissiveness on sexual morality. The birth-control measures which he so courageously advocated were designed to enable young people to marry as soon as they wished, thus avoiding the debasing effects of non-marital sex, and indirectly enhancing the whole moral tone of society. A corollary of this is, of course, that early marital fecundity *is* an evil, as Malthus had said, and Place was also prepared to recommend 'abstaining from marriage for even a few years'. But the nature of the evil was primarily moral in Place's eyes, and he disliked the idea of contraceptives used merely to control total numbers.[101]

This seems to be the extent of the pro-sensualist, or at least not firmly anti-sensualist, progressive lobby in the Malthusian discussion—unless one counts in also some obscure egalitarian proponents of population increase.[102] The lobby does join hands in a sense with another, heterogeneous grouping: those whose confidence in the progressive tendency of society as a spontaneous thing was such as to incline them positively to urge the rejection of Malthusian restraint. At its religiosely vaguest this sort of optimism may be found in Sharon Turner, who saw 'no reason to doubt, that . . . our world will become happier in every succeeding generation', so that it could be 'left most generally to the free will of the individuals themselves, to modify, indulge, or restrain their natural inclination'.[103] In a different vein, there is the crankily precise improvement theory of Thomas

---

[100] W. Thompson 1824: pp. iii–vii.
[101] Himes 1930: 165, 174, 314, 325, 327.
[102] See C. Hall 1850: 247; 'Mechanic' 1817: 15–16
[103] Turner 1837: 106, 248.

Doubleday, whose confidence that improvements in diet reduced fertility encouraged him to urge indulgence towards young marriage, and that of a rare medical man in the debate, Thomas Jarrold. Jarrold may conceivably have been inspired by very recent moves in physiological doctrine towards a decoupling of fertility and sexual response. He argues that the enhanced mental life associated with social progress (he has in mind such things as commercial activity, rather than a Godwinian intellectual refinement) reduces fertility, but *not* libido, whose demands may therefore still be freely gratified: 'fecundity is independent of passion'.[104]

These wayward specimens of polemic are mainly interesting for the way they cite social and cultural changes of an arguably progressive sort—but more tangible and certain changes than the Godwinian tokens of advance—as evidence against Malthusian fears about population pressure. For this indicates the route by which Malthusian theory eventually collapsed: the important distinction being that in the effective case against Malthus, as opposed to the eccentric one, materially measurable progress was represented as tending to restrain sexual drives, not as legitimating them. There is in fact a sort of link, in the case of Jarrold's ideas, between one approach and the other. W. E. Hickson, owner and editor of the *Westminster Review*, and then Herbert Spencer in the pages of that journal, are writing at the mid-century about the links between evolutionary development and sexuality in terms which rather annoyingly confound notions of libido and fecundity. Hickson would have it that 'enforced celibacy' is a medical calamity for women, and plainly contra-indicated by our physical make-up, and yet that the growing 'cultivation of the intellectual faculties' will 'moderate the intensity of the passions'. Spencer confines his explicit discussion to the supposed links between mental activity and the sperm-count, but it would be consonant with everything we know about Spencer if he were telling us also that the intellectual has only a moderate sexual appetite.[105]

However the famous and decisive stroke against Malthus, tying up social progress and reduced sexual drives, had occurred over twenty years earlier. In two lectures delivered in Oxford in 1828 the respected utilitarian economist Nassau Senior tersely and effectively advanced what has become known as the 'comfort' theory of popula-

[104] Doubleday 1842: 22 and *passim*; Jarrold 1806: 250–8, 298.
[105] Hickson 1850: 14–16, 62–4; H. Spencer 1852. See also *Malthus: Re-examined* 1868: 53–4.

tion control. Senior in effect related the facts of the present composition of society to its material goods by proposing three categories for the latter: luxuries, decencies, and necessities. Luxuries, or the threat of their loss, were granted to have little chance of competing with the powerful 'instincts, that prompt the human race to marriage'. Necessities were also unimportant in modern England, because there was only very rarely a prospect of actual want for a couple marrying and having children. But decencies—social standing and physical well-being above the level of mere subsistence—were sought in their various degrees by all tiers between the abjectly poor and the very wealthy, and according to Senior the anticipated impact of marriage on decencies exerted an enormous control over marriage rates.[106]

The thought that an increasingly emulative and commercial environment would 'distract' more and more people from marriage had been offered before, as had the claim that the working class was already much influenced by prudential considerations: at an early stage Malthusian moral restraint was being glossed even by admirers as 'the desire of bettering our condition', and a 'hardly perceptible' sacrifice for the modern individual.[107] The main significance of Senior's contribution is that it carries the latter process (namely, the revising of the Malthusian scheme from within) to an influential extreme. Senior was an economist of impeccable credentials, and very respectful of Malthus: there is something almost comic in his efforts to suggest—at the end of a not very harmonious correspondence with the latter attached to the published lectures—that his views are completely in tune with Malthusian theory.

Other men on the controlling heights of utilitarian economics, unshakeably loyal to Malthus though they appeared, were also shifting their ground significantly: McCulloch on moral restraint, for example, and John Stuart Mill on the efficacy of economic assistance to the working class. Mill's associate William Thornton, quick to accuse McCulloch of defection, was himself a defector to full-blown comfort theory.[108] Harold Boner rightly sees it as a fine irony, of the 1830s and beyond, that 'at last the seed planted by Hazlitt had

---

[106] Senior 1829: 25–6.

[107] Weyland 1816: 63, 406, 409; *Remarks on a Late Publication* 1803: 30; *Imperial Review*, 1 (1804), 111–32; *Monthly Review*, 43 (1804), 63, 69; *Edinburgh Monthly Review*, 5 (1821), 549–50. Alison 1840 was probably completed by 1828, or earlier, and is an outspoken statement of such views.

[108] J. A. Field 1931: 42; Boner 1955: 159–60; Thornton 1846: 270.

borne formidable fruit' within, moreover, 'the very citadel of Malthusianism'. But the most intriguing question, for the purposes of our inquiry, is how much the defection from Malthus bore the authentic stamp of Hazlitt's and Godwin's anti-sensualism. There was evidently a broad umbrella of environmentalism uniting comfort theory and the early radical opposition to Malthus: even very quietly restating Malthus as being about 'extent of ground' and 'increase of industry' was to move the theory in this direction. But to what extent had these disloyal admirers assimilated, specifically, unMalthusian ideas on the plasticity of sex-drives?

Much of Hazlitt's assault on Malthus was reissued in the *Political Essays* of 1817. Godwin's long-delayed counter-attack of 1820— though it elicited robust assertions of the invulnerability of Malthus's great theory to such a misconceived, if not senile, attack—did, according to Place and probably Malthus too, make a favourable impression in establishment circles. For what it is worth, the venerable *Monthly Review*, which in 1803 reviewed Malthus warmly, at Godwin's expense, was extremely positive about Godwin's 1820 *Of Population*, while recording the decay of the 'dazzling comet' of Malthus's *Essay*. The *Edinburgh Monthly Review* did not join in the rehabilitation of Godwin, but its deferential treatment of 'some circumstances' Malthus has 'rather overlooked' amounts to a remarkable picture of a Godwinian desensualized future, in which a growing number of men and women engaged in political, artistic, and intellectual life will be permanently celibate: most important, this will occur cheerfully and naturally because of a 'beneficial alteration in some of the passions of men'.[109] People were perhaps particularly likely to be driven into Godwin's arms at this time because of the appearance

---

[109] Boner 1955: 115; *British Critic*, NS 15 (1821), 247–61; Rosen 1970; *Quarterly Review*, 26 (1822), 148–68; Himes 1930: p. viii; Malthus 1963: 128–9; *Monthly Review*, 42 (1803), 337–57, 43; (1804), 56–70, 94; (1821), 113–36; *Edinburgh Monthly Review*, 5 (1821), 535–57. See also Alison 1840: i. 86–93. The *Monthly Review's* articles, incidentally, illustrate well the workings of the paradoxical culture of Malthusian theory: in the ease with which the *Essay* itself, because of its partial incorporation of Godwinian ideas of restraint, permitted even its friends to take up an increasingly anti-sensual position. Already in 1803 the reviewer, Stephen Jones, was representing moral restraint not only as the sole modern mechanism of population control, but also as an easily endured privation which could bring on a 'happy era' in the distant future—positions which are all more or less starkly unMalthusian. In 1821 the magazine clearly saw, as a prologue to its about-face on Godwin, that the introduction of moral restraint in the 1803 *Essay* was an extraordinary capitulation to the very theory it had proposed to destroy, and now Malthus is accused of having not granted the full and encouraging implications of the new doctrine for the future of population.

before Parliament of that hardline Malthusian legislative proposal, Scarlett's 1821 bill to withdraw poor relief from imprudent couples.

Nassau Senior, writing in an extremely conciliatory spirit, does not defect to Godwinism on the variability of sexual drives: these he appears to regard as constant in strength, though always susceptible of control by varying economic circumstances. However the whole logic of 'decencies', of material goods desirable enough to be put before sexual gratification, but not amounting to anything as extreme as sheer wants, works better if sexual drives are conceived as not significantly stronger than other psychological forces. Senior accordingly gives reason a standing which recalls Place, if not Godwin: 'reason, in some degree or other, is as natural to man as passion'.[110] Richard Jones, a theoretically ambitious economist perhaps as well known as Senior in his day, and Malthus's successor at the East India College, delivered his own version of comfort theory in his lectures to students in the 1830s. He too assumes the 'sexual attraction' to be a 'given quantity', but makes its restraint not only natural but positively beneficial, indeed the motor of civilization in its highest sense. Jones is impressed by the importance of love poetry and other chivalric institutions in early societies: the first stirrings of cultural refinement seem to be inseparable from codes of sexual abstinence, 'elicited by the struggle . . . for the means and opportunities of indulging an innocent and holy union between the sexes'.[111]

A final example from this sphere is the Scots academic economist Robert Hamilton, less celebrated than either Senior or Jones, and a man who seems unaware that in favourably expounding Malthus he has transmuted him into a Hazlitt: 'It is . . . an undoubted fact . . . that the rate of increase becomes slower with the progress of art and civilisation'.[112] These professional political economists at the dawn of Victoria's reign, if not exactly endorsing Godwinian doctrines of a variable, virtually extinguishable libido, were certainly giving good grounds for wishing that the latter were correct. Their writings have a wholly different atmosphere from those of Robert Malthus, much as they reckoned to admire him.

[110] Senior 1829: 56.   [111] R. Jones 1859: 102–9.   [112] Hamilton 1830: 352.

V

Carnal Knowledges

Exactly forty years after the first edition of Malthus's *Essay* Carlyle intoned in 'Chartism' that all could see that *laissez-faire* and Malthusianism must part company: it was absurd to tell the working class to tackle population problems by their own decision, as if 'twenty-four millions of human individuals . . . are . . . a kind of character that can take a resolution, and act on it'.[113] This was an exaggeration. There were still men who did not accept that the working class must be prompted to changes in their sexual behaviour by changes in their circumstances. The reactionary Whig MP A. H. Moreton was even continuing to adhere to the 'positive' checks as enunciated in 1798.[114] The environmentalist principle was not omnipotent, but it had a very broad following: Southwood Smith I have quoted as thinking it was a 'universally-admitted truth'.

Its constituency was skewed very much in the direction of progressives, reformers, and meliorists. These were believers in the need and potential for an indefinite amount of improvement in mankind's physical circumstances and political institutions. That this would be accompanied by moral improvement was an extremely attractive additional prospect, in fact a virtually indispensable one. Antisensualism was thus the creed of the forward-looking and the optimistic: it had the aroma of modernity and change about it. This gave it an enormously secure position in the ideology of this transforming but hopeful society. But why should 'moral' mean anti-sensual? The conventional explanation of the anti-sensualism of sexual codes in the Victorian years is that a conservative, religiose moralism achieved a temporary ascendancy in the culture. There is no ready explanation of why this happened (especially if anti-sensualism had the early and broad base I have argued for), whereas there would be no puzzle about the ascendancy of progressive, relatively secular anti-sensualism.

The puzzle is, rather, the anti-sensual element in progressive ideology. But in fact the explanation is not far to seek. The exalted status of rationality in the advanced thought of the eighteenth century had a lasting influence on all radical and reforming creeds in the nine-

---

[113] Carlyle 1899: iv. 201.   [114] Moreton 1836: 150.

teenth. William Godwin, and the triumph of his views on population, is a cardinal example. The loyalty to rationality was sufficiently strong that when libertarian sexual ideas arose within progressive movements the latter suppressed these initiatives quite voluntarily. I shall trace in the next volume such a story among the Owenites. The few libertarian radicals—William Thompson is the most notable in the early years of the century—are bound to catch the eye of today's observer. They do raise in their writings the query which the modern reader is likely to be itching to hear voiced: 'Why must an improved mankind also be a less sensual mankind?' To a Godwin, a Hazlitt, a Coleridge, a Mill, a Lovett, a Holyoake, and to countless other leaders and disciples of progressive thought, the question was preposterous, and the connection between the advance of humanity and its de-sensualizing axiomatic.

The progressive anti-sensualists were certainly helped in their ascendancy by some elements of conservative and religious opinion. But lukewarm, unreflective religious belief was probably no less supportive in its influence than the more militant religious groups. I sketch this variant of the period's anti-sensualism in the next volume, under the heading 'classic moralism'. Religious commitment did actually, in isolated cases, draw believers—Swedenborgians, Irvingites, Princeites, Southcottians—in a pro-sensual direction. In one of the most striking alignments to emerge in the previous discussion, Evangelicals and Nonconformists were strongly opposed to restraint of the sexual drives (though a more modern-minded Evangelicalism was evidently at the same time seeing the attractions of an environmentalist approach to problems of sexual morality, as represented by the prostitute penitentiary for example).

Environmental moralism, as applied to sexuality, did however require the doctrine of a transformable libido, or something like it, and this was a point of weakness. Nineteenth-century environmentalism, as I understand it, did not exclude conscious personal effort as a contributory source of moral improvement, but it would always have been uncomfortable for meliorists to have claimed very much for 'self-help' in the sexual domain. A utopia in which men and women were sexually continent, but only through a denial of drives, was not in the spirit of nineteenth-century social optimism. Malthus's 'moral restraint' proposed just such a voluntary restraint of surviving drives, and it proved unacceptable. By a paradoxical convergence of the efforts of Malthus's enemies, who wanted to replace this doctrine with the Godwinian decay of the libido, and the efforts of his non-conservative friends, who wanted to massage 'moral restraint' into something very like the latter, the idea came to be in the air that sex-drives would be moderate in the properly circumstanced individual (hard-working, mentally active, envisaging or enjoying comfortable domesticity), and would become more temperate in society over time.

As I have mentioned, there was often an element of vagueness about the mechanisms of sexual continence among the neo-Godwinians. Hazlitt's seed bore fruit, but usually without an explicit commitment to plasticity of the libido such as Hazlitt argued for. The very widespread implied allegiance to this doctrine did not hold up in all contexts. I have cited the case of Joseph Fletcher: painter of statistical portraits of the nation's morals and believer in the modifying power of education on moral standards—who nevertheless has not wholly given up the expectation that sexual continence in one quarter will be balanced by sexual indulgence in another. Buckle's *History of Civilisation* was a best-seller, but when Buckle's readers encountered the suggestion that their own inclinations to marry might be unavoidably modified by environmental factors they seem to have jibbed.

If they had turned for advice on the matter to medical authority—to the consulting room or the various kinds of non-technical literature dealing with sexual physiology—they would have received inconsistent messages on the plasticity of human sexual drives, with medical and quasi-medical opinion tilting to the view that for men, and even more for women, the sexual appetite could only be thwarted at the cost of concomitant physical disorders. The division between medical and sociological opinion on sexual drives is reflected in a division of personnel: only a handful of men with medical qualifications contributed to the Malthusian controversy, despite the salience in this debate of human sexual function.

Conversely, doctors writing about sexuality are generally silent about population questions. The notable exception here is William Acton, and arguably the most impressive feature of his *Functions and Disorders* is the attempt to link physiological theory and demography. The book was written, and then rewritten, in the years when facts about marriage in the English population had first become available through the census. Acton's theory of true pre-marital continence renders tolerable the substantial celibacy figures for both sexes. According to the theory, only in so far as the unmarried are 'semi-continent' (that is, visited by sexual thoughts, and aware of sexual possibilities) or worse, do they have sexual drives which it may be damaging to thwart (Acton calculates from the illegitimacy figures that at least one in thirteen unmarried women experience such drives).

Actonian true continence is remarkably like the progressive version of moral restraint which emerged from the interplay of Malthusian and Godwinian ideas on population: voluntary action, self-denial, has a role, but the underlying effect is an objective reduction of sexual appetite (represented, in the male, by a low rate of sperm production), and this is mainly achieved by environmental influences. Acton emphasizes the element of attitude and moral commitment—'voluntary and entire abstinence from sexual indulgences in any form', 'voluntary paralysis of the reproductive organs'—but one cannot *decide* that the activity of the testis will cease or slow down, even in Acton's physiology, except indirectly by refraining from sexual ideas and provocations. Alongside these devices for continence Acton sets a range of physical routines (exercise, diet, cold-bathing) which will spontaneously prevent the development of sexual drives. He actually likens the resulting continent human to sexually neuter members of communal species such as bees—in the awareness that it is diet which controls sexuality in these cases. The image beautifully expresses the modulation of Godwin's utopian anti-sensualism into a scientific key.[115]

Such arguments, to our ideas, give sexuality too exclusively physical a basis. This is indeed, something which makes all nineteenth-century medicine, of whatever shade of opinion, seem alien in a post-psychiatric culture. George Drysdale, insisting that sexual abstinence causes lesions and inflammation in the genital organs, strikes us as no less outlandish than William Acton teaching that sexual appetite can be subdued by diet. There is a crucial psychological dimension to sexual arousal and its absence, we want to protest, which is being ignored in all this. Walter, of *My Secret Life*, was in general much more of a believer in the plasticity of the libido than the facts of his sexual career might lead one to expect, and he is also more receptive than many of his contemporaries to this psychological dimension. He places a remarkable emphasis on the contribution of

[115] W. Acton 1857a: 21–2; 1865: 27, 41, 45, 81–4; 1875: 196.

'idealities' (which we would nowadays call fantasies) to the sexual response: 'the idealities are everything'.[116] This leads him to insist rather strikingly that human sexual pleasures are *not* animalistic, being in fact superior to anything animals can experience: he liked to contradict one of his chief mistresses, who had a habit of saying 'Ain't we beasts?' when recovering from any particularly elaborate and novel piece of coupling. There is a disconcerting overlap—in phrasing at least—between Walter's remarks in this vein and the high-mindedness of certain anti-sensual individuals and coteries I shall take up in the next volume.

Walter's understanding of the mechanisms controlling the libido is more Victorian, more Actonian, when he gives a role to certain strictly physical factors: country diet, for example. Acton is the only medical authority, however, who uses the physicalist logic to do what would appear to be attractive: namely, to provide a physiological reinforcement for progressive doctrines of moral restraint as developed by population theorists. On the medical side of the century's carnal knowledge there was an undertow running against sexual continence. Accounts were offered of male sexual function which sought to wire in a capacity for abstinence, but they were not the last word on the subject; in the case of women, such a theory did not even exist (on the contrary, spontaneous ovulation rather pointed in the direction of unavoidable periodic drives). Coleridge may have abominated the analogy between sexual desire and hunger, but doctors stuck by it, even where female libido was concerned.[117] Acton himself, as I have mentioned, moved in the 1860s to a version of seminal production, storage, and disposal which fitted less comfortably with a code of abstinence than his 1857 theory had done. In other words, it was always on the cards that the worst damage to progressive anti-sensualism would come from medicine, and the threat was realized in George Drysdale's *Elements of Social Science* of 1855. For good measure, Drysdale was also an ardent Malthusian: not in the revisionist spirit of the comfort theorists and other progressives, with their submerged Godwinism, but in the spirit of Malthus himself—for whom the prospect of a desensualized human race was a fantasy, even a nightmare.

---

[116] *My Secret Life* 1966: 2239. See also pp. 1933, 1946, 1949, 1993, 2106.
[117] e.g. Laycock 1840: 71.

Appendix I

✦

ENGLISH CLASSES

OUR knowledge of nineteenth-century social structure derives very largely from the information about occupations contained in the returns of the decennial census, which was instituted in 1801. This instrument steadily improves in accuracy and complexity, and a picture of considerable haziness, for the early decades of the century, gives way to something much clearer— but none the less rather cryptic on the matter of class, so that it is important to bring into play the limited surviving evidence, from outside the census, on nineteenth-century incomes. Some rudimentary information about class was assembled in the 1831 census, but thereafter the increasingly sophisticated enquiries made about occupation took another direction, so it is actually not possible at any period in the nineteenth century to make deductions about English class structure directly from the census, or even from the raw data that lies behind it, namely, the census enumerators' books.

To start with, after 1831 the analysis of occupation was conducted in terms of the physical character of an individual's work (materials, processes, and so on). Using the data of 1831 and 1841 a categorization of England's male adult population into three classes (employing, self-employed, and employed) has been proposed for this period. The suggestion is that about 12 per cent were employers, about 7 per cent self-employed, and about 81 per cent employees. In both rural and industrialized areas (Devon and Lancashire) the proportion of employees to the total was roughly the same (Banks 1978). Then, from 1851 onwards, the occupational information in the censuses is not only not class-oriented, it is classified in slightly different ways on different occasions. Charles Booth was the first investigator to try to impose a uniform system on the census information of the period 1841 to 1881, and his scheme has stood the test of time (C. Booth 1886; W. A. Armstrong 1972). Some information about class does emerge directly in Booth's tables. He has a category 'Property Owning and Independent' in which the total numbers (self-supporting adults plus dependants) drop slightly between 1851 and 1881, from 1.9 per cent of the population to 1.4 per cent. Also reflective of class is his 'Public and Professional Service' category, which rises to a high in 1871 (total numbers are 4.2 per cent in 1841 and 6.2 per cent in 1871). 'Domestic Service', confirming what was suggested above about the earlier part of the century, is an even larger category and also a growing one: the total proportion of the population involved here rises from 7 per cent in 1841 to 8.6 per cent in 1881.

But on the whole there is still a gap to be negotiated between Booth's valuable digest of the data on occupation and social class. The rest of his analysis—divided as it is into bald categories such as 'Agriculture', 'Mining', 'Transport', and so forth—is necessarily but frustratingly opaque on this. A tentative translation into the five classes of modern British social inquiry (in itself a scheme that may not be the most appropriate for Victorian England; see Neale 1968; Royle 1977; Mills 1989) has been performed, giving the percentages in the table. Even if the numerical values in this table are rough and ready the comparisons from decade to decade are presumably reliable, and suggest a surprisingly constant picture for the forty years of Victoria's reign we are concerned with, except in respect of classes IV and V (semi-skilled and unskilled workers). Here, again surprisingly, there seems to be a clear increase in the size of the unskilled workforce, and a clear shrinking of the semi-skilled, a possibility supported by some local studies (Dennis 1984: 190). The latter movement is actually about twice as large as the former, so that the mass of the working class, as a proportion of the whole English male workforce, is getting smaller as Victoria's reign advances. Nevertheless, on this analysis it remains true throughout the period that semi-skilled workers and labourers amounted to around 56 per cent of the adult male population, upper- and middle-class men to around 23 per cent, and craftsmen, clerks, and so forth (the difficult-to-summarize Class III) to around 21 per cent (though it is possible on a more relaxed interpretation of the last category, such as some historians have used, to arrive at figures more than twice as large as this: Dennis 1984: 189).

The suggested percentage for the upper and middle classes corresponds very closely to contemporary calculations by Dudley Baxter (relating to workers and their dependants in 1861) in which occupation is translated into class on the strength of the male income for the job in question. It is also possible to arrive at good estimates of the size of this fraction of English soci-

Percentages of adult males in the five British social classes

	1841	1851	1861	1871	1881
I	9.4	8.5	9.1	9.9	10.9
II	12.3	14.0	13.8	13.5	12.8
III	20.0	20.1	21.0	20.7	21.5
IV	44.1	43.2	41.8	38.4	36.3
V	14.2	14.2	14.3	17.5	18.4

Source: Banks 1978.

ety (and geographically detailed ones, as it happens, for 1860) from income
tax data. Though the salary threshold at which this was levied varied during
the period, in such a way as sometimes to catch better paid clerks and their
equivalents in the tax net and sometimes to let them out, Baxter's 1861 figures for the upper and middle classes seem to match the tax evidence. Also,
there is arguably an indication of a growth of this sector over time—something not clearly apparent in the occupation-based calculations (Baxter 1868
passim; Rubinstein 1988; Best 1971: 81–91). But Baxter's estimates identify a
large proportion of the population as semi-skilled or unskilled (around 65 per
cent, some 10 per cent larger than has been calculated from the record of
jobs). The criterion he applies in achieving this estimate (earnings less than
£1 per week) seems fair, and the only ground on which the figure may be
questioned is whether occupational categories, as used by the 1861 census,
can each be so readily assigned a single level of income. A modern extrapolation from Baxter's figures suggests that this large group of less skilled workers had fallen behind the rest of the population economically since the
beginning of the century (Perkin 1969: 419–20).

The occupation figures simply for London in 1851 (though in this case for
the whole workforce, men and women alike) have been translated into a representation of the capital's class structure (Bédarida 1968; 1979: 56–61). The
result is broadly similar to the national occupation-based (as opposed to
income-based) estimates cited above, but with a difference that is on the face
of it significant. Unskilled labourers only amount to about 12 per cent of
working Londoners, and as a result the proportion of working-class men and
women, skilled and semi-skilled, in the capital is only about half the total relevant population. But the 12 per cent figure may be an underestimate, due to
the greater likelihood with this group that they would escape enumeration
by the census. Another study has suggested that the most degraded of the
unskilled London working class, the casual workers and their dependants,
alone amounted to about 10 per cent of London's population—and that they
were on the increase from 1861 (Stedman Jones 1971: 387–91) (it may be
surmised that there were equivalent possibilities of not being counted, for
the very poorest individuals, at least in the largest of the English provincial
cities). However the same study is not in disagreement on the *total* numbers
of the male and female workforce in London who are semi-skilled or
unskilled (Classes IV and V), which both authors judge to be about 48 per
cent. It seems more likely either that the two interpretations have been
affected by different ways of estimating equivalences of class and occupation,
or that (in keeping with a possibility mentioned above) the proportion of
unskilled workers had increased between 1851 and 1861 in London. Finally,
though, it is interesting that the one sizeable movement detected in the second of these studies is a shrinking in London's Class III population, relatively, between 1861 and 1891, and an expansion of the Class II fraction in
these years.

Appendix II

❧❧❧

WORKING-CLASS HOUSING

LONDON experienced a slight overall rise in numbers per house between 1800 and 1880, which was more marked in working-class districts; in addition there were certainly sharp local increases in density, especially (as contemporaries often observed) when slum areas were 'rookeried out' without any provision of replacement housing. On the other hand the scale of the areas where this effect has been demonstrated is sometimes extremely small, even street-sized. When a good-sized area of classic London working-class dwellings (the East End parish of St George's-in-the-East) was surveyed in 1845 the average number of persons per house was 6.4 even when two streets of superior housing had been omitted (to be compared with a national average at this date of 5.4 per house). In terms of accommodation within the houses the researchers found no multi-occupation of rooms by different families at all (and the latter phenomenon was judged to be confined to a 'few localities', unspecified, elsewhere in the city). Just over a third of the families, the largest group, lived in one room, at an average density of 3.2 persons. There were similar densities in a smaller area of mainstream working-class housing (omitting extremes at both ends) in Marylebone at this date (Wohl 1971; 1977: 22–3; Welton 1869: 85; Stedman Jones 1971: 175–6; Dyos and Wolff 1973: ii. 375; *JSSL* 11 (1848), 193–249; 6 (1843), 44–8).

Outside London also the contemporary investigations tend to focus on the extreme cases. An unusually broad survey of working-class Bristol was performed in the late 1830s, however, covering 20,000 people in 6,000 families. The number of occupants per house, and the proportion of families living in one room, were similar to the St George's-in-the-East figures; it is not possible to calculate the resulting numbers per room from this survey, but 'families' are understood to include unattached individuals, and these account for just over a fifth of the total (and in these Bristol houses about a tenth of the 'families' shared a room) (Fripp 1840).

The slum areas in the big manufacturing towns attracted the most selective surveys, but even these tell a less horrible story than might be feared, given that what is involved is the worst, or nearly the worst, housing which nineteenth-century England had to offer. A group of streets in the Deansgate area of Manchester, housing some 4,300 individuals in 713 houses, yielded a density of 2.46 to a room, with just over a quarter of the families in single room accommodation. Conditions were actually better in a comparable sample of streets from the nearby Ancoats district. A sample of just eighteen houses in Leeds in 1840, which included both dwellings and cheap lodging-houses, yields some appalling images of crowding (such as eleven individuals in one room of 800 cubic feet), but even at the bottom of the Leeds barrel there are many rooms accommodating four or less people (Oats 1864–5 and 1865–6; *JSSL* 2 (1840), 397–424).

Some of the most harrowing accounts of nineteenth-century housing concern the accommodation of agricultural workers and their families; the *Morning Chronicle* reports on rural areas contain particularly vivid examples. But again the real conditions in which most of these families were housed are much misrepresented by the worst instances. In the 1860s densities in the country were found to be much lower than in the towns both nationally and in two randomly selected groups of rural parishes; there were about 4.5 persons per cottage, with an average per bedroom of less than 3. It was noticed, however, that the general level of accommodation was 'indifferent', with fewer families enjoying anything like comfort than in the towns. This finding had been anticipated in the 1840s, when three Rutland villages were compared with various parts of cities, both manufacturing and other. 'Squalid misery' of an urban sort was almost non-existent in the villages, but while about 45 per cent of the rural cottages were deemed 'well furnished' (itself an interestingly high figure) about 55 per cent of the houses surveyed in Manchester and Hull came into this category. And the less demanding standard of 'comfortable' was met by no less than 95 per cent of the Hull houses (and by 72 per cent of those in Manchester) while the two best Rutland villages only had 65 per cent of cottages at this level. 'Thrifty poverty' was judged to be the general characteristic of this rural accommodation (Palgrave 1869; H. J. Hunter 1865: 126–48; Chadwick 1965: 221).

These perhaps surprisingly high figures for decent housing conditions in both town and country (if no more than decent in the latter) are borne out by many further pieces of evidence. In Bury St Edmunds 60 per cent of workers' houses were 'decidedly comfortable' in 1838, and the next year a survey of the handloom-weaving district of Manchester, Miles Platting, found that out of 176 dwellings (which included 11 of the much-noticed cellars) 68 were 'neat and comfortable', with 46 in the 'uncomfortable' or 'wretched' categories, and the rest described as 'neat' or 'just comfortable'. The same researcher had investigated working-class housing more generally in Manchester some years earlier and found almost exactly the same proportion (38 per cent) of no less than 4,000 houses to be 'comfortable' (though unfortunately only two descriptions were employed in this survey, and all the rest of the accommodation is simply classified as 'uncomfortable'). The picture of Hull above is also given some support by a survey, at the same date, of workers' housing in the whole town: 60 per cent of 8,000 houses visited were 'respectable' or 'comfortable' (though this certainly implies that the figure quoted above is misleadingly high—and Hull struck a Danish visitor of the day as a town where even 'misery . . . would look respectable'). The review of Bristol housing already cited also judged that 60 per cent of families were 'clean and respectable'. And in London an exceptionally large investigation of slum housing in Westminster in 1841 found that two-fifths of the accommodation was 'well furnished'. This may seem to be in disagreement with the important St George's-in-the-East survey, which gave this classification to only some 30 per cent of homes, until it is realized what a high standard was being applied in this investigation: to be well furnished meant possessing 'every article essential to comfort, and some even of luxury, such as a piano' (Bremer 1853: 2; Chadwick 1965: 293; Heywood 1839; 1835; *JSSL* 5 (1843), 212–21; 3 (1841), 14–24).

Appendix III

ᑎᕫᕤᕬᐧ

THE MEDICAL STANDING
OF 'SPERMATORRHOEA'

SPERMATORRHOEA was never a completely orthodox and entrenched medical concept in the nineteenth century. Its being so much the stock in trade of quacks did give it a taint for the profession of non-respectability and clinical spuriousness. Most doctors, however sympathetic to the concept, probably agreed that the disease's prevalence had been exaggerated, even greatly so. It was recognized that spermatorrhoea was not used as a disease-term in hospital practice: in tacit dissent from the classic formulation of the disease by the French physician Lallemand, who had regarded it as a clear life-threatening type of disorder, with specific post-mortem features. In the medical literature (and, interestingly, in the quack literature) it is perhaps never approached on quite the same footing as syphilis and gonorrhoea (another divergence from Lallemand, who links spermatorrhoea closely to the latter). It was often, perhaps usually, omitted altogether from textbooks on venereal disease and from those on urology, sometimes even when one of its supposed signs, sperm in the urine, was under discussion (*London Medical Gazette* (1845), 1: 17–19; *Lancet* (1861), 1: 582–3; (1870), 2: 72; (1857), 2: 150–3; (1859), 1: 174; *Medical Times and Gazette*, 14 (1857), 454; Hassall 1859: 23; *British and Foreign Medico-Chirurgical Review*, 1 (1848), 34–48; Parkes 1860: 213).

Such omissions from the academic pabulum were perceived by contemporaries as possibly indicating official scepticism about spermatorrhoea, which is telling. When Marion Sims writes about chronic inflammatory diseases such as urethritis being contracted by men who have had a vigorous premarital sex-life, but makes no reference to spermatorrhoea, the lacuna certainly seems eloquent; as mentioned in Chapter 4, some doctors gave an emphasis to non-testicular secretions, and this could be linked to an implied scepticism about spermatorrhoea. On the other hand, it will happen that a venereologist gives very little attention to the disease, but in what he does say shows that he regards it as a genuine and serious entity, so one must be cautious of making too much of its absences from the literature (Gascoyen 1872; Lallemand 1847: p. v; J. M. Sims 1868; *Lancet* (1856), 1: 289–90;

Aspray 1872: 34; Bayfield 1863 *passim*). And the fact is that spermatorrhoea did make a respectable showing not only in the occasional monograph but also in mainstream academic medical publications. It was taken seriously in Richard Quain's *Dictionary of Medicine*, in *Hooper's Physician's Vade Mecum*, in Robert Druitt's equivalent handbook for surgeons, and in the long-lived, authoritative surgical textbooks of John Eric Erichsen and Thomas Holmes. In keeping with this, spermatorrhoea played some part in the theoretical education of medical students. The *Lancet* published a report of what appeared to be a careful clinical demonstration that sperm in the urine could be treated by cauterization of the urethra, and this is just the most striking of many favourable treatments of the disease in the medical journals (Curling 1843: 407–21; Hassall 1859: 23; Venables 1850: 31; *Lancet* (1861), 1: 582–3; Gascoyen 1872; *BMJ* (1860), 871; *Lancet* (1849), 1: 527–8).

It was the complaint of John Lawes Milton, after forty years of lucratively republishing his book on spermatorrhoea, that there were still doctors 'neither intolerant nor ill-informed . . . who conscientiously believe that spermatorrhoea exists only in imagination'—and Milton's involvement with the subject at first caused a crisis with medical colleagues (see Chapter 4). On another estimate, the number of 'honest practitioners' who believed in the disease was said to be small (the author of this estimate, the pioneering biochemist James Thudichum, was himself a rare case of a doctor who declared a virtually complete incredulity about spermatorrhoea, though as an aside). The private attitude of London hospital consultants towards spermatorrhoea was allegedly sceptical. A modern historian of nineteenth-century medicine, reconstructing the views of Sir James Paget on this question from his more incidental utterances, has concluded that this enormously prestigious figure was also a sceptic (Milton 1887: 6; *Lancet* (1861), 1: 582–3; Thudichum 1858: 269; Peterson 1986).

So did the doubtful security of spermatorrhoea in overt clinical theory actually run to a general disbelief among the profession, not much voiced, but operative in the consulting-room? One can see that a disbelief of this kind was unlikely to be made the subject of professional publication by a doctor of standing. It was undeniably true that 'absolutely there *is*, or there is *not*, such a disease . . . as spermatorrhoea', but few high-ranking practitioners would have agreed that 'if there is, it is ours *to treat it*; if not, it is ours *to expose the fallacy*', as the Glasgow GP Campbell Black urged. This author admitted that it required 'courage' to enter the 'charnel-house of quackery' (Black 1872: pp. viii–ix, 163). One danger implicitly envisaged by him here may have been that of dignifying quack superstitions by even deigning to discuss them; it is plausible that a Sir James Paget could have thought like this.

The danger which Black does mention is that the respectable doctor would be associated with 'imposition' on patients if he investigated spermatorrhoea scientifically. Such a fear only makes sense if it is envisaged that *some* credibility will be left to spermatorrhoea as a disease-entity when the truth about it is out. The fact is that the doctors who did undertake to query this disease head-on all found a residual element of truth in it. Black himself, although he urges with considerable eloquence and humanity the cruelty of inculcating exaggerated fears of the evils of nocturnal emissions, masturbation, and frequent intercourse, is not in doubt that a damaging level of seminal emission can occur. There is also an intense compassion for the victims of sexual hypochondria in the vigorous attacks of Golding Bird and Thomas Chambers, and an admirable hostility to the activities of the sexual quacks in those of Francis Burdett Courtenay. But for all these writers there remained a category of true spermatorrhoea, even if it was an extremely rare condition. The physician Lionel Beale told his students at King's College in the mid-century that the term 'spermatorrhoea' 'ought to be abolished altogether': there was nothing necessarily wrong with sperm in the urine, and great psychological damage could be done by an imprudent doctor—nevertheless, the latter was justified in acting if the presence of urinary sperm was 'constant, and accompanied with other more important symptoms'. Only much later in his career, it seems, did Beale arrive at a downright scepticism about spermatorrhoea. Students at St Thomas', back in the 1820s, were told by Sir Astley Cooper that 'what you hear about seminal weakness, is nothing but absurdity and folly' ('seminal weakness' was the older term for the concept). But he seems to have meant only that gonorrhoea had nothing to do with such a condition: the disorder itself, resulting from debauchery or masturbation, was accepted by this illustrious medical man (Beale 1887: 32–4; *BMJ* (1860), 871; *Lancet* (1824), 4: 421).

The truth is that many doctors were probably drawn into a contradictory state of mind on the question of spermatorrhoea by a variety of impulses: 'some members of the profession . . . without venturing to deny the reality of this class of maladies, when consulted by a patient . . . act as if they either deemed them ideal . . . or else thought it beneath their dignity to undertake the treatment of such disorders'. In an age when laymen were often anxiously on the alert for symptoms of masturbational disease, and when one specialist found that two-thirds of his patients had already been through the hands of quacks, such ambiguous responses from a legitimate doctor would not have dented a man's belief in the reality of spermatorrhoea (Courtenay 1858: 5; A. Smith 1871: 7). No message could really be heard from the qualified practitioners to contradict the propaganda of the quacks.

Astley Cooper's 'seminal weakness' was supplanted by the term 'spermatorrhoea' when the whole topic became conspicuous in the 1840s with the publicizing of the work of the French physician Claude François Lallemand. This occurred most notably through a series of papers (surprisingly low-key) by Benjamin Phillips in the *London Medical Gazette* between 1842 and 1845, and through Ranking's paper of 1843 in the *Lancet*, with the subsequent correspondence (which reveals that Lallemand's ideas, first published in French in 1836–42, had already influenced a number of British doctors). A translation of an abridged version of Lallemand's *Les Pertes seminales* then appeared in 1847, and spermatorrhoea was on the British medical agenda for the rest of the century. The strange tenacity of the concept in legitimate medical circles in Britain may in fact be chiefly due to this serious French treatment. Lallemand's work reads nowadays like the production of a madman, but the author was a competent medical scientist (he contributed elsewhere to the accurate understanding of spermatogenesis), and in an age when almost all pathology was a matter of syndromes—with hardly any reliable knowledge of actual processes—the grotesque constellations of sexual history and symptoms which are Lallemand's 'cases' were not obviously unscientific.

It is important to realize that the general idea of 'seminal weakness' had a venerable history, however. 'Gonorrhoea', a term coined in the sixteenth century, indicates in its etymology exactly the same concept as 'spermatorrhoea'. 'Seminal weakness' had been given great respectability by John Hunter's description of involuntary diurnal discharges, and although the disease was never discussed under this heading to the same extent as 'spermatorrhoea' was to be, his description was often reverted to by doctors and quacks alike. Courtenay's assertion that until the 1840s all these disorders had been considered psychosomatic seems exaggerated. Medical popularizers, incidentally, had familiarized the lay public with the notion of seminal weakness in the early decades of the century (J. Hunter 1810: 218–20; Roberton 1817: 61–73; M. Ryan 1831 *passim*, 1837 *passim*; R. Thomas 1822: 502). In keeping with his views on the innocuousness of masturbation Hunter did not attribute seminal weakness to this practice, and for Lallemand masturbation was only one of several causes of spermatorrhoea, though a greatly emphasized one. But to all intents and purposes both conditions are part of the history of masturbation-pathology. There was just one maverick, George Drysdale, who adhered loyally to Lallemandian teaching on the causes of spermatorrhoea in its full form. Although some English followers of Lallemand took an almost Hunterian view of the dangers of self-abuse, doctors could not bring themselves to be more thoroughly Hunterian and look upon spermatorrhoea as simply an inflammatory disease, not linked to masturbation specifically, and devoid of moral colouration. The quacks, of course, were unrelenting in exploiting the extra dimension given to masturbation anxiety by seminal weakness/spermatorrhoea. In the lay mind, in fact, spermatorrhoea probably had an almost exclusive link with masturbation: patients allegedly told their doctors they had the disease as a 'euphemistic way' of confessing their habit (*London Medical Gazette* (1845), 1: 17–19; *Lancet* (1856), 2: 215–17; (1861), 1: 582–3).

Bibliography

ABERCROMBIE, ROBERT, *A Popular Treatise on the Anatomy, Physiology, Pathology, and a New Treatment of Specific Diseases of the Genital Organs in Males* (London, 1864).

ABRAMS, PHILIP, *The Origins of British Sociology* (Chicago, 1968).

ACTON, JOHN E. E. D., 'Mr Buckle's Thesis and Method', in John Neville Figgis and Reginald Vere Laurence, eds., *Historical Essays and Studies* (London, 1907), pp. 305–23.

ACTON, WILLIAM, *The Functions and Disorders of the Reproductive Organs* (1st edn. London, 1857*a*; 3rd edn. London, 1862; 4th edn. London, 1865; 6th edn. London, 1875).

—— *Prostitution* (1st edn. London 1857*b*; 2nd edn. London, 1870).

—— *Prostitution*, ed. Peter Fryer (London, 1968).

—— 'Observations on Illegitimacy in the London Parishes of St Marylebone, St Pancras, and St George's Southwark', *JSSL* 22 (1859), 491–505.

'A.D.', 'Conversations of an American with Lord Byron', *New Monthly Magazine*, 45 (1835), 193–203, 291–302.

ADAMS, JOHN, *The Anatomy and Diseases of the Prostate Gland* (London, 1851).

ADAMS, WILLIAM BRIDGES, ('Junius Redivivus'), *The Rights of Morality: An Essay on the Present State of Society, Moral, Political, and Physical, in England* (London, 1832).

—— 'On the Condition of Women in England', *Monthly Repository*, 7 (1833), 217–31.

ADAMS, W. E., *Memoirs of a Social Atom* (London, 1903).

AINSLIE, ROBERT, *The Present State and Claims of London* (London, 1836).

ALISON, ARCHIBALD, *The Principles of Population* (Edinburgh, 1840).

—— 'Causes of the Increase of Crime', *Blackwoods*, 56 (1844), 1–14.

ALLEN, ANNIE WINSOR, 'Victorian Hypocrisy', *Atlantic Monthly*, 114 (1914), 174–88.

ALLEN, GRANT, 'The Girl of the Future', *Universal Review*, 7 (1890), 49–64.

—— 'The New Hedonism', *Fortnightly Review*, 66 (1894), 377–92.

ALLEN, ZACHARIAH, *The Practical Tourist* (Providence, 1832).

ANDERSEN, J. A., *A Dane's Excursions in Britain* (London, 1809).

ANDERSON, MICHAEL, 'Marriage Patterns in Victorian Britain', *Journal of Family History*, 1 (1976), 55–78.

—— 'The Social Position of Spinsters in Mid-Victorian Britain', *Journal of Family History*, 9 (1984), 377–93.

—— 'The Social Implications of Demographic Change', in F. M. L. Thompson ed., *The Cambridge Social History of Britain 1750–1950* (Cambridge, 1990), i. 1–70.

ANDREWES, GEORGE, *The Stranger's Guide; or the Frauds of London Exposed* (London, ?1810).

ANGELO, HENRY, *Reminiscences of Henry Angelo* (London, 1828).

ANGIOLINI, LUIGI, *Lettere sopra l'Inghilterra* (Florence, 1790).

ANICHINI, P., *A Few Remarks on the Present Laws of Marriage, Adultery, and Seduction, in England* (London, 1836).

ANSELL, CHARLES, *On the Rate of Mortality . . . and other Statistics of Families in the Upper and Professional Classes* (London, 1874).

ARCHENHOLZ, JOHANN WILHELM VON, *A Picture of England* (London, 1797).

ARMSTRONG, ALAN, *Stability and Change in an English Country Town* (London, 1974).

ARMSTRONG, W. A., 'La Population de l'Angleterre et du Pays de Galles (1789–1815)', *Annales de Démographie Historique* (1965), 135–89.

—— 'The Use of Information about Occupation', in E. A. Wrigley, ed., *Nineteenth-Century Society* (Cambridge, 1972), 191–310.

ASHBEE, HENRY SPENCER, *Index Librorum Prohibitorum* (London, 1877).

ASHTON, T. S., *Economic and Social Investigations in Manchester 1833–1933* (Manchester, 1934).

ASHWELL, SAMUEL, *A Practical Treatise on the Diseases Peculiar to Women* (London, 1844).

ASPLAND, ALFRED, *Crime in Manchester* (London, 1868).

ASPRAY, CHARLES OWEN, *Diseases of the Reproductive Organs in the Male Sex* (London, 1872).

ATTHILL, LOMBE, *Clinical Lectures on the Diseases Peculiar to Women* (Dublin, 1871).

AUSTIN, WILLIAM, *Letters from London Written during the Years 1802 and 1803* (Boston, Mass., 1804).

AVOT, MADAME M. D', *Lettres sur l'Angleterre* (Paris, 1821).

BABBAGE, CHARLES, *A Chapter on Street Nuisances* (London, 1864).

BADCOCK, JOHN, ('John Bee'), *Living Picture of London, for 1828* (London, 1828).

BAERT, ALEXANDRE, BARON DE, *Tableau de la Grande Bretagne* (Paris 1800).

BAILEY, PETER, '"Will the Real Bill Banks Please Stand Up?"', *Journal of Social History*, 12 (1979), 336–53.

—— 'Champagne Charlie: Performance and Ideology in the Music Hall Swell Song', in J. S. Bratton, ed., *Music Hall* (Milton Keynes, 1986), 49–69.

—— *Leisure and Class in Victorian England* (Oxford, 1987).

—— 'Parasexuality and Glamour: The Victorian Barmaid as Cultural Prototype', *Gender and History*, 2 (1990), 148–72.

BAKER, FRANKLIN, *The Moral Tone of the Factory System Defended* (London, 1850).

BALLARD, JOSEPH, *England in 1815* (Boston, Mass., 1913).

BALY, WILLIAM, and KIRKES, WILLIAM SENHOUSE, *Recent Advances in the Physiology of Motion, the Senses, Generation and Development* (London, 1848).

BANKS, J. A., *Prosperity and Parenthood* (London, 1954).

—— 'The Social Structure of Nineteenth Century England as seen through the Census', in Richard Lawton, ed., *The Census and Social Structure* (London, 1978), 179–223.

—— and GLASS, D. V., 'A List of Books, Pamphlets, and Articles on the Population Question, Published in Britain in the Period 1793 to 1880', in D. V. Glass, ed., *Introduction to Malthus* (London, 1953), 84–112.

BARKER, PRISCILLA, *The Secret Book* (Brighton, 1888).

BARKER, THEO, and MICHAEL DRAKE, *Population and Society in Britain 1850–1980* (London, 1982).

BARLEE, ELLEN, *A Visit to Lancashire in December, 1862* (London, 1863).

BARRET-DUCROCQ, FRANÇOISE, *Love in the Time of Victoria* (London, 1991).

BARRY, MARTIN, *Researches in Embryology* (London, 1839).

BARTLETT, DAVID W., *What I saw in London* (Auburn, NY, 1852).

BARTON, JOHN, 'The Influence of Subdivision of the Soil on the Moral and Physical Well-being of the People of England and Wales', *JSSL* 13 (1850), 63–77.

BATESON, MARY, 'Social Life', in H. D. Traill, ed., *Social England*, vi (London, 1896), 488–500.

BAX, ERNEST BELFORT, *Reminiscences and Reflexions of a Mid and Late Victorian* (London, 1918).

BAXTER, R. DUDLEY, *National Income* (London, 1868).

BAYFIELD, SAMUEL J., *On Syphilis, Gonorrhoea and Stricture of the Urethra* (London, 1863).

BEALE, LIONEL S., *Our Morality and the Moral Question* (London, 1887).

BEAMES, THOMAS, *The Rookeries of London* (London, 1850).

BEATTY, THOMAS EDWARD, 'Impotence', in John Forbes, Alexander Tweedie, and John Connolly, eds., *The Cyclopaedia of Practical Medicine* (London, 1833–5), ii. 594–604.

BÉDARIDA, FRANÇOIS, 'Londres au milieu du xixe siècle', *Annales* (1968), 268–95.

—— *A Social History of England 1851–1975* (London, 1979).

BEDDOES, THOMAS, *Hygeia or Essays Moral and Medical* (Bristol, 1802).

BEERBOHM, MAX, '1880', *Yellow Book*, 4 (1895), 275–83.

BEGGS, THOMAS, *Three Lectures on the Elevation of the People* (London, 1847).

—— *An Inquiry into the Extent and Causes of Juvenile Depravity* (London, 1849).

BELCHER, HENRY, *Degrees and 'Degrees'* (London, 1872).

BELL, BENJAMIN, *A Treatise on Gonorrhoea Virulenta, and Lues Venerea* (Edinburgh, 1793).

BELL, THOMAS, *Kalogynomia* (London, 1821).

BENNETT, JAMES HENRY, *A Practical Treatise on Inflammation, Ulceration, and Induration of the Neck of the Uterus* (London, 1845).

BENNETT, JOHN, *Letters to a Young Lady* (London, 1789).

BENNETT, W. J. E., *Crime and Education* (London, 1846).

BENTLEY, JOSEPH, *State of Education, Crime, etc. etc.* (London, 1842).

BESANT, WALTER, *Fifty Years Ago* (London, 1888).

BEST, G. F. A., *Mid-Victorian Britain* (London, 1971).

BETHAM-EDWARDS, M. B., *Reminiscences* (London, 1898).

BEVAN, WILLIAM, *Prostitution in the Borough of Liverpool* (Liverpool, 1843).

BIRD, GOLDING, *Urinary Deposits* (5th edn. London, 1857).

BLACK, D. CAMPBELL, *On the Functional Diseases of the Renal, Urinary, and Reproductive Organs* (London, 1872).

BLACKBURN, JOHN, *Reflections on the Moral and Spiritual Claims of the Metropolis* (London, 1827).

BLACKER, J. G. C., 'The Resort to Divorce in England and Wales 1858–1957', *PS* 11 (1957), 188–233.

BLACKMAN, JANET, 'Popular Theories of Generation', in John Woodward and David Richards, eds., *Health Care and Popular Medicine in Nineteenth Century England* (London, 1977), 56–88.

BLACKMORE, JOHN, *Midnight Cruizes* (London, 1854).

BLACKWELL, ELIZABETH, *The Human Element in Sex* (London, 1884).

BLANC, LOUIS, *Letters on England* (London, 1867).

BLANCHARD, SIDNEY H., 'Courtship', *Belgravia*, 23 (1874), 511–15.

BLANDFORD, GEORGE FIELDING, *Insanity and its Treatment* (Edinburgh, 1871).

BLATCHFORD, ROBERT, *My Eighty Years* (London, 1931).

BLAUG, MARK, 'The Myth of the Old Poor Law and the Making of the New', *Journal of Economic History*, 23 (1963), 151–84.

BLOUET, PAUL ('Max O'Rell'), *John Bull's Womankind* (London, 1884).

BLUMENBACH, JOHANN FRIEDRICH, *The Institutions of Physiology*, ed. John Elliotson (1st edn. London, 1815; 3rd edn. London, 1820).

BLUNDELL, JAMES, *Observations on Some of the More Important Diseases of Women* (London, 1837).

BLYTHELL, DUNCAN, 'The History of the Poor', *EHR* 89 (1974), 365–77.

BONER, HAROLD A., *Hungry Generations* (New York, 1955).

BOOTH, CHARLES, 'Occupations of the People of the United Kingdom, 1801–81', *JSSL* 49 (1886), 314–435.

—— 'The Inhabitants of Tower Hamlets', *JSSL* 50 (1887), 326–91.

BOOTH, DAVID, *A Letter to the Rev. T. R. Malthus* (London, 1823).

BOSTOCK JOHN, *An Elementary System of Physiology* (London, 1824–7).

BOULTON, JAMES T., ed., *The Letters of D. H. Lawrence*, i (Cambridge, 1979).

BOWEN, JOHN, *A Letter to the King* (London, 1835).

BOYER, GEORGE R., and WILLIAMSON, JEFFREY G., 'A Quantitative Assessment of the Fertility Transition in England, 1851–1911', *Research in Economic History*, 12 (1989), 93–117.

BRANCA, PATRICIA, *Silent Sisterhood* (London, 1975).

BREMER, FREDERIKA *England in 1851* (London, 1853).

BRIDGES, J. A., *Victorian Recollections* (London, 1919).

BRIGGS, ASA, 'The Human Aggregate', in H. J. Dyos and Michael Wolff, eds., *The Victorian City* (London, 1973), i. 83–104.

BRINTON, WILLIAM, trans., *G. G. Valentin, A Text Book of Physiology* (London, 1853).

BRISTED, CHARLES ASTOR, *Five Years in an English University* (New York, 1852).

British Association for the Advancement of Science: Reports (London, 1834–40).

BRODUM, WILLIAM, *A Guide to Old Age or a Cure for the Indiscretions of Youth* (London, 1795).

BROOKE, RICHARD, *Liverpool as it was during the Last Quarter of the Eighteenth Century* (London, 1853).

BUCKLE, HENRY THOMAS, *History of Civilisation in England* (London, 1857).

BUDGETT, J. B., *The Ethnology of London* (London, 1865).

BULWER, EDWARD LYTTON, *England and the English* (Chicago, 1970).

BURDON, WILLIAM, *Advice Addressed to the Lower Ranks of Society* (Newcastle, 1803).

BURNAND, FRANCIS C., *Records and Reminiscences* (London, 1904).

BURNETT, JOHN, *A Social History of Housing 1815–1970* (Newton Abbot, 1978).

—— *Destinies Obscure* (London, 1982).

BURNLEY, JAMES, *Phases of Bradford Life* (Bradford, 1871).

—— *West Riding Sketches* (Bradford, 1875).

BURR LITCHFIELD, R., 'The Family and the Mill: Cotton Mill Work Patterns and Fertility in mid-Victorian Stockport', in Anthony S. Wohl, ed., *The Victorian Family* (London, 1978), 180–96.

BURT, THOMAS, *An Autobiography* (London, 1924).

BURTON, RICHARD F., *The Book of the Thousand Nights and a Night*, i (n.pl., 1885).

BYNUM, W. F., 'Medical Values in a Commercial Age', in T. C. Smout, ed., *Victorian Values* (Oxford, 1992), 149–63.

CAIRD, MONA, *The Morality of Marriage* (London, 1897).

CAMBRY, JACQUES, *De Londres et ses environs* (Amsterdam, 1789).

CAMPBELL, ALEXANDER, and BANNISTER J. T., *Socialism: Public Discussion between Mr Alexander Campbell and Rev. J. T. Bannister* (Coventry, 1839).

CAMPE, JOACHIM HEINRICH, *Reise durch England und Frankreich* (Brunswick, 1803).

CARDIGAN AND LANCASTRE, COUNTESS OF, *My Recollections* (London, 1909).

CARGILL, WILLIAM, 'Educational, Criminal, and Social Statistics of Newcastle-upon-Tyne', *JSSL* 1 (1839), 355–61.

CARLYLE, THOMAS, *Critical and Miscellaneous Essays* (London, 1899).

CARNALL, GEOFFREY, *Robert Southey and his Age* (Oxford, 1960).

CARPENTER, EDWARD, *Love's Coming of Age* (Manchester, 1896).

—— *My Days and Dreams* (London, 1916).

CARPENTER, W. B., *A Manual of Physiology* (4th edn. London, 1865; 8th edn. London, 1876).

CARR, J. COMYNS, *Some Eminent Victorians* (London, 1908).

CARRIER, N. H., 'An Examination of Generation Fertility in England and Wales', *PS* 9 (1956), 3–23.

CARTER, JAMES T., 'Seminal Vesicles', *Glasgow Medical Journal*, 27 (1887), 332–4.

CARTER, THOMAS, *Memoirs of a Working Man* (London, 1845).

CARTER, ROBERT BRUDENELL, *On the Pathology and Treatment of Hysteria* (London, 1853).

Catalogue of J. W. Reimers's Gallery of all Nations, and Anatomical Museum (Leeds, 1853).

CHADWICK, EDWIN, 'Life Assurances', *Westminster Review*, 9 (1828), 384–421.

—— *The Sanitary Condition of the Labouring Population of Great Britain*, ed. M. W. Flinn (Edinburgh, 1965).

CHANDRASEKHAR, S., *'A Dirty, Filthy Book'* (Berkeley, Calif., 1981).

CHANNING, WILLIAM, *Correspondence of William Ellery Channing DD and Lucy Aikin*, ed. Anna le Breton (London, 1874).

CHILD, MRS D. L., *The History of the Condition of Women* (London, 1835).

CHURCHILL, FLEETWOOD, *On the Diseases of Women* (6th edn. Dublin, 1874).

CLARKE, CHARLES MANSFIELD, *Observations on those Diseases of Females which are Attended by Discharges* (2nd edn. London, 1821).

CLARKE, J. F., *Autobiographical Recollections of the Medical Profession* (London, 1874).

CLAXTON, TIMOTHY, *Hints to Mechanics* (London, 1839).

CLAY, JOHN, 'Annual Report of the Rev. John Clay', *JSSL* 2 (1840), 84–103.

—— *Chaplain's Thirtieth and Thirty-first Reports on the County House of Correction at Preston* (Preston, 1855a).

—— 'On the Effect of Good or Bad Times on Committals to Prisons', *JSSL* 18 (1855b), 74–9.

—— 'On the Relation between Crime, Popular Instruction, Attendance on Religious Worship, and Beer-houses', *JSSL* 20 (1857), 22–32.

—— *Chaplain's Thirty-Second and Thirty-Third Reports on the County House of Correction at Preston* (Preston, 1858).

A *Clear, Fair, and Candid Investigation of the Population, Commerce, and Agriculture of this Kingdom* (London, 1810).

CLELAND, JOHN, and WILSON, CHRISTOPHER, 'Demand Theories of the Fertility Transition: An Iconoclastic View', *PS* 41 (1987), 5–30.

'A Clergyman of the Established Church', *Sermons . . . Written Chiefly with the View of Illustrating the Principles Delivered by Mr Malthus* (London, 1820).

CLOKIE, HUGH McDOWALL, and ROBERTSON, J. WILLIAM, *Royal Commissions of Inquiry* (Stanford, Calif., 1937).

COBBE, FRANCES POWER, 'Celibacy v. Marriage', *Frasers*, 65 (1862a), 228–35.

—— 'What Shall We Do with Our Old Maids?', *Frasers*, 66 (1862b), 594–610.

—— 'The Nineteenth Century', *Frasers*, 69 (1864), 481–94.

COBBETT, WILLIAM, *Twelve Sermons* (London, 1823).

—— *Advice to Young Men* (Oxford, 1980).

COLERIDGE, SAMUEL TAYLOR, *Collected Letters of Samuel Taylor Coleridge*, ed. Earl Leslie Griggs (Oxford, 1956).

COLMAN, HENRY, *European Life and Manners* (Boston, Mass., 1850).

COLQUHUON, PATRICK, *A Treatise on the Police of the Metropolis* (1st edn. London, 1796; 6th edn. London, 1800).

COMBER, W. T., *An Inquiry into the State of the National Subsistence* (London, 1808).

COMBERMERE, VISCOUNTESS, *Our Peculiarities* (London, 1863).

CONOLLY, JOHN, 'Philosophical History of Hypo-chondriasis and Hysteria', *Foreign Quarterly Review*, 12 (1833), 110–30.

COOPER, ANTHONY ASHLEY, *Moral and Religious Education of the Working Class* (London, 1843).

COOPER, FRANCIS, *Report to the Local Board of Health on the Sanitary Conditions of Southampton* (Southampton, 1851).

COOPER, JAMES FENIMORE, *England* (London, 1837).

CORDEROY, EDWARD, 'Popular Amusements', *Lectures Delivered before the Young Men's Christian Association, in Exeter Hall, from November, 1856, to February, 1857* (London, 1880), 329–76.

COPLAND, JAMES, ed., B. A. RICHERAND, *Elements of Physiology* (London, 1824).

—— *A Dictionary of Practical Medicine* (London, 1844–58).

CORRY, JOHN, *The English Metropolis: Or, London in the Year 1820* (London, 1820).

'A Court Physician', *Reproductive Disorders Spermatorrhagia Exhausted Brain etc.* (London, 1876).

COURTENAY, FRANCIS BURDETT, *A Practical Essay on the Debilities of the Generative System* (London, 1839).

—— *On True and False Spermatorrhoea* (2nd edn. London, 1854).

—— *On Spermatorrhoea* (London, 1858).

—— *Revelations of Quacks and Quackery* (2nd edn. London, 1865).

CRAFTS, N. F. R., 'Average Age at First Marriage for Women in Mid-Nineteenth Century England and Wales: A Cross-section Study', *PS* 32 (1978), 21–5.

—— and IRELAND, N. J., 'A Simulation of the Impact of Changes in Age of Marriage during and before the Advent of Industrialization in England', *PS* 30 (1976), 495–510.

CRAPELET, G. A., *Souvenirs de Londres en 1814 et 1816* (Paris, 1817).

CROSSICK, GEOFFREY, *An Artisan Élite in Victorian Society* (London, 1978).

CRUMP, JEREMY, 'Provincial Music Hall: Promoters and Public in Leicester, 1863–1929', in Peter Bailey, ed., *Music Hall* (Milton Keynes, 1986), 53–72.

CUDWORTH, W., *Condition of the Industrial Classes of Bradford and District* (Bradford, 1886).

CULLEN, M. J., *The Statistical Movement in Early Victorian Britain* (Hassocks, 1975).

CULVERWELL, ROBERT JAMES, *On Single and Married Life* (London, 1847*a*).

—— *Lecture to Young Men on Chastity and its Infringements* (London, 1847*b*).

—— *The Solitarian* (London, 1849).

—— *The Life of Dr Culverwell* (London, 1852).

CURLING, T. B., *A Practical Treatise on Diseases of the Testis* (London, 1843).

CURRY, KENNETH, 'A Note on Coleridge's Copy of Malthus', *PMLA* 55 (1939), 613–15.

—— ed., *New Letters of Robert Southey* (New York, 1965).

CURTIN, MICHAEL, *Propriety and Position* (New York, 1987).

CURTIS, J. L., and Co., *Manhood: The Causes of its Premature Decline, with Directions for its Perfect Restoration* (London, 1840).

CUSTINE, A. L. L. DE, *Mémoires et voyages* (Paris, 1830).

CYPLES, WILLIAM, 'Morality of the Doctrine of Averages', *Cornhill*, 10 (1864), 210–24.

DALLY, ANN, *Women under the Knife* (London, 1991).

DANA, RICHARD, *Hospitable England in the Seventies* (London, 1921).

DAUNTON, M. J., *Home and House in the Victorian City* (London, 1983).

DAVENPORT, JOHN, *Curiositates Eroticae Physiologiae* (London, 1875).
—— *Aphrodisiacs and Anti-aphrodisiacs*, ed. Alan Hull Walton (London, 1965).
DAVENPORT, WILLIAM H., 'Sex in Cross-Cultural Perspective', in Frank A. Beach, ed., *Human Sexuality in Four Perspectives* (Baltimore, 1977), 116–63.
DAVEY, B. A., *Lawless and Immoral* (Leicester, 1983).
DAVIS, DAVID D., *The Principles and Practice and Obstetric Medicine* (London, 1836).
DAVIS, GRAHAM, 'Beyond the Georgian Facade: The Avon Street District', in S. Martin Gaskell, ed., *Slums* (Leicester, 1990), 144–85.
DAVIS, JAMES EDWARD, *Prize Essay on the Laws for the Protection of Women* (London, 1854).
DAVY, JOHN, 'Observations on the Fluid in the Vesiculae Seminales of Man', *Edinburgh Medical and Surgical Journal*, 5 (1838), 1–15.
DAWSON, RICHARD, *An Essay on Marriage* (London, 1845).
—— *An Essay on Spermatorrhoea* (4th edn. London, 1848).
DEANE, PHYLLIS, and COLE, W. A., *British Economic Growth 1688–1959* (Cambridge, 1967).
DEFAUNCONPRET, A. J. B., *Londres et ses habitans* (Paris, 1817).
DELFAU, GERARD, *Jules Valles l'exil à Londres (1871–1880)* (Bordas, 1971).
De Londres et des Anglais (Paris, 1817).
DENNIS, RICHARD, *English Industrial Cities of the Nineteenth Century* (Cambridge, 1984).
DE QUINCEY, THOMAS, 'Malthus on Population', in David Masson, ed., *Works* (Edinburgh, 1890), vii. 11–19.
DE ROOS, *The Medical Adviser* (47th edn. London, 1840).
DESQUIRON DE SAINT-AGNAN, A. T., *Tableau descriptif, moral, philosophique et critique de Londres, en 1816* (Paris, 1817).
DICK, ROBERT, *Marriage and Population: Their Natural Laws* (London, 1858).
DIXON, W. HEPWORTH, *The London Prisons* (London, 1850).
DODD, WILLIAM, *The Factory System Illustrated* (London, 1842).
DOLBY, THOMAS, *An Address to the Magistracy and Parochial Authorities of London, Westminster and Southwark and other Populous Cities* (London, 1830).
DONNISON, JEAN, *Midwives and Medical Men* (London, 1977).
DORÉ, GUSTAVE, and JERROLD, WILLIAM BLANCHARD, *London: A Pilgrimage* (London, 1872).
DOUBLEDAY, THOMAS, *The True Law of Population* (London, 1842).
DRAKE, M., 'The Census, 1801–1891', in E. A. Wrigley, ed., *Nineteenth-Century Society* (Cambridge, 1972), 7–46.
DRUITT, ROBERT, *The Surgeon's Vade Mecum* (1st edn. London, 1839; 9th edn. London, 1865).
DRUMMOND, ROBERT BLACKLEY, *Free Will in Relation to Statistics* (London, 1860).
DRYDEN, ANNE RITCHIE, *Can Women Regenerate Society?* (London, 1844).
DRYSDALE, CHARLES, *Prostitution Medically Considered* (London, 1866).
DRYSDALE, GEORGE, *The Elements of Social Science* (5th edn. London, 1868).
DUCOS, B., *Itineraire et souvenirs d'Angleterre et d'Écosse* (Paris, 1834).

DUNCAN, J. MATTHEWS, *Fecundity, Fertility, Sterility and Allied Topics* (Edinburgh, 1866).

—— *Clinical Lectures on the Diseases of Women* (London, 1879).

—— *On Sterility in Woman* (London, 1884).

The Duties of Parents: Reproductive and Educational (London, 1872).

DYOS, H. J., and WOLFF, MICHAEL, *The Victorian City: Images and Realities* (London, 1973).

ELDERTON, ETHEL M., *Report on the English Birthrate Part 1. England North of the Humber. Eugenics Laboratory Memoirs*, 19 and 20 (London, 1914).

ELESH, DAVID, 'The Manchester Statistical Society: A Case Study of a Discontinuity in the History of Empirical Social Research', *Journal of the History of the Behavioural Sciences*, 8 (1972), 280–301, 407–17.

ELLIS, HENRY HAVELOCK, 'The Changing Status of Women', *Westminster Review*, 128 (1887), 818–28.

—— *Studies in the Psychology of Sex*, ii (Leipzig, 1899 = vol. i, Philadelphia, 1900), vi (Philadelphia, 1910).

—— 'The Love-Rights of Woman', *Little Essays of Love and Virtue* (London, 1922), 102–15.

—— 'Women and Socialism', *Views and Reviews, First Series: 1884–1919* (London, 1932), 1–18.

ELLIS, S. M., ed., *The Letters and Memoirs of Sir William Hardman* (London, 1925).

ENGELS, FRIEDRICH, *The Condition of the Working-Class in England* (London, 1973).

ENSOR, GEORGE, *An Inquiry Concerning the Population of Nations* (London, 1818).

ERICHSEN, JOHN ERIC, *The Science and Art of Surgery* (5th edn. London, 1869).

ESCOTT, T. H. S., *Social Transformations of the Victorian Age* (London, 1897).

The Ethics of Love (Walsall, 1881).

EVANS, POLLY, *Memoirs of Madam Chester of Manchester* (London, 1865).

EVERSLEY, D. E. C., *Social Theories of Fertility and the Malthusian Debate* (Oxford, 1959).

FARLEY, JOHN, *Gametes and Spores: Ideas about Sexual Reproduction 1750–1914* (Baltimore, 1982).

FARR, WILLIAM, 'Influence of Marriage on the Mortality of the French People', *TNAPSS* (1859), 504–13.

Fast Life (London, 1859).

'FATHER NORTH', *The Mysteries of London* (London, 1844).

FAUCHER, LEON, *Manchester in 1844* (London, 1844).

—— *Études sur l'Angleterre* (Paris, 1845).

FAYET, AUGUSTE NOUGAREDE DE, *Lettres sur l'Angleterre* (Paris, 1846).

FELKIN, W., 'An Account of the Situation of a Portion of the Labouring Classes in the Township of Hyde, Cheshire', *JSSL* 1 (1839*a*), 416–20.

—— 'Moral Statistics of a District near Grays Inn, London, in 1836', *JSSL* 1 (1839*b*), 541–2.

'A Fellow of the Royal College of Surgeons', *The Speculum: Its Moral Tendencies* (London, 1857).

FELTHAM, JOHN, *The Picture of London* (London, 1802).

FERRI DI SAN COSTANTE, G. L., *Londres et les Anglais* (Paris, 1804).

FIELD, JAMES ALFRED, *Essays on Population* (Chicago, 1931).

FIELD, JULIAN OSGOOD, *More Uncensored Recollections* (London, 1926).

Fifty Years of London Society 1870–1920 (London, 1920).

FINCH, JOHN, *Statistics of the Vauxhall Ward, Liverpool* (Liverpool, 1842).

FINNEGAN, FRANCES, *Poverty and Prostitution* (Cambridge, 1979).

FISKE, STEPHEN, *English Photographs by an American* (London, 1869).

'F.L.G., THE HON.', *The Swell's Night Guide* (London, 1841).

FLACK, I. HARVEY, *Lawson Tait 1845–1899* (London, 1949).

FLEISCHMAN, RICHARD K., *Conditions of Life among the Cotton Workers of Southeastern Lancashire, 1780–1850* (New York, 1985).

FLETCHER, JOSEPH, 'Moral and Educational Statistics of England and Wales', *JSSL* 10 (1847), 193–233; 12 (1849a), 151–76, 189–335.

—— *Summary of the Moral Statistics of England and Wales* (London, 1849b).

FLINT, AUSTIN, *A Text-book of Human Physiology* (London, 1876).

FONTANE, THEODOR, *Journeys to England in Victoria's Early Days* (London, 1939).

—— *Theodor Fontane. Von Dreissig bis Achtzig. Sein Leben in seinen Briefen* (Munich, 1970).

FONTRÉAL, A.-D. DE, *A travers Londres et l'Angleterre* (Paris, 1875).

FORD, CLELLAN S., and BEACH, FRANK A., *Patterns of Sexual Behaviour* (New York, 1951).

FORNEY, JOHN W., *Letters from Europe* (Philadelphia, 1867).

FOUCAULT, MICHEL, *The History of Sexuality*, i. *An Introduction* (London, 1981).

FOX, WILLIAM, *The Working Man's Model Family Botanic Guide or Every Man His Own Doctor* (10th edn. Sheffield, 1884).

FRIEDLANDER, DOV, 'The Speed of Urbanization in England and Wales', *PS* 24 (1970), 423–43.

—— 'Demographic Responses and Socioeconomic Situation: Population Processes in England and Wales in the Nineteenth Century', *Demography*, 20 (1983), 249–72.

—— and MOSHE, ELISHU BEN, 'Occupations, Migration, Sex Ratios, and Nuptiality in Nineteenth Century English Communities: A Model of Relationships', *Demography*, 23 (1986), 1–12.

FRIPP, C. BOWLES, 'Report of an Inquiry into the Condition of the Working Classes in the City of Bristol', *JSSL* 2 (1840), 368–75.

FRYER, PETER, *Mrs Grundy: Studies in English Prudery* (London, 1963).

—— *The Man of Pleasure's Companion* (London, 1968).

GALTON, FRANCIS, 'The Relative Supplies from Town and Country Families, to the Population of Future Generations', *JSSL* 36 (1873), 19–26.

GARNETT, RICHARD (with Edward Garnett), *The Life of W. J. Fox* (London, 1910).

GARRETT, EILIDH M., 'The Trials of Labour: Motherhood versus Employment in a Nineteenth-century Textile Centre', *Continuity and Change*, 5 (1990), 307–54.

GASCOYEN, GEORGE G., 'On Spermatorrhoea and its Treatment', *BMJ* 1872(2), 67–9, 95–6.

GASKELL, PETER, *The Manufacturing Population of England* (London, 1833).

GATRELL, V. A. C., and HADDON, T. B., 'Criminal Statistics and their Interpretation', in E. A. Wrigley, ed., *Nineteenth-Century Society* (Cambridge, 1972), 336–96.

GAULDIE, ENID, *Cruel Habitations* (London, 1974).

GAUTIER, THEOPHILE, *Zigzags* (Paris, 1845).

GAY, PETER, *The Bourgeois Experience*, i. *Education of the Senses* (Oxford, 1984).

GEIGER, E. G., *Impressions of England 1809–10* (London, 1932).

'A Genuine Disciple of Hippocrates', *The Enemy of Empiricism* (London, 1815).

GEORGE, M. DOROTHY, *London Life in the XVIIIth Century* (London, 1925).

GILBERT, ARTHUR N., 'Doctor, Patient, and Onanist Diseases', *Journal of the History of Medicine*, 30 (1975), 217–34.

GILLIES, MARY LEMAN, 'An Appeal to the Better Order of Men, on behalf of the Women of the Factory Districts', *People's Journal*, (1847), 131–4.

GILLIS, JOHN, 'Servants, Sexual Relations and the Risks of Illegitimacy', in Judith L. Newton, Mary P. Ryan, and Judith R. Walkowitz, eds., *Sex and Class in Women's History* (London, 1983), 114–39.

—— *For Better, for Worse* (Oxford, 1985).

GILLY, W. S., *The Peasantry of the Border* (Berwick-upon-Tweed, 1841).

GINSWICK, J., ed., *Labour and the Poor in England and Wales 1849–51*, i–iii (London, 1983).

GIRDWOOD, G. F., 'On the Theory of Menstruation', *Lancet* 1844(2), 312–16.

GITTINS, DIANA, 'Inside and Outside Marriage', *Feminist Review*, 14 (1983), 22–34.

—— 'Between the Devil and the Deep Blue Sea', in Judith Friedlander, Blanche Wiesen Cook, Alice Kessler-Harris, and Carroll Smith-Rosenberg, eds., *Women in Culture and Politics* (Bloomington, Ind., 1986).

GLASS, DAVID V., 'Changes in Fertility in England and Wales 1851 to 1931', in L. Hogben, ed., *Political Arithmetic* (London, 1938), 161–212.

GLYDE, JOHN, *The Moral, Social and Religious Condition of Ipswich in the Middle of the Nineteenth Century* (Ipswich, 1850).

—— 'Localities of Crime in Suffolk', *JSSL* 19 (1856), 102–6.

GODWIN, WILLIAM, *An Enquiry Concerning Political Justice* (London, 1793).

—— *The Inquirer* (London, 1797).

—— *Thoughts Occasioned by the Perusal of Dr Parr's Spital Sermon* (London, 1801).

—— *Of Population* (London, 1820).

GOEDE, C. A. G., *The Stranger in England* (London, 1807).

GOLDMAN, LAWRENCE, 'The Origins of British "Social Science": Political Economy, Natural Science and Statistics, 1830–1835', *Historical Journal*, 26 (1983), 587–616.

—— 'The Social Science Association 1857–1866', *EHR* 101 (1986), 95–134.

GOOD, JOHN MASON, *The Study of Medicine* (1st edn. London, 1822; 3rd edn. London, 1829).

GOODELL, WILLIAM, *Lessons in Gynecology* (Philadelphia, 1879).

GORE, MONTAGUE, *On the Dwellings of the Poor* (2nd edn. London, 1851).

Goss, Horace, *Woman* (London, 1853).

—— *Man and Woman* (London, 1857).

Gosse, Edmund, 'The Agony of the Victorian Age', *Edinburgh Review*, 228 (1918), 276–95.

Gourbillon, J. A. de, *L'Angleterre et les Anglais* (Paris, 1817).

Graham, Thomas J., *On the Diseases Peculiar to Females* (London, 1834).

Grahame, James, *An Inquiry into the Principle of Population* (Edinburgh, 1816).

Grant, James, *The Great Metropolis* (2nd edn. London, 1837).

—— 'Hints to the Ladies', *London Saturday Journal*, 3 (1839), 46.

—— *Lights and Shadows of London Life* (London, 1842).

Granville, A. B., 'On Certain Phenomena, Facts, and Calculations Incidental to or Connected with the Power and Act of Propagation in Females of the Industrial Classes in the Metropolis', *Transactions of the Obstetrical Society of London*, 2 (1860), 139–96.

Gray, B. Kirkman, *Philanthropy and the State* (London, 1906).

Greaves, George, 'On Infanticide', *Transactions of the Manchester Statistical Society* (1862–3), 1–24.

Green, David R., and Parton, Alan G., 'Slums and Slum Life in Victorian England: London and Birmingham at Mid-Century', in S. Martin Gaskell, ed., *Slums* (Leicester, 1990), 17–91.

Greenwell, Dora, 'Our Single Women', *North British Review*, 36 (1861–2), 62–87.

Greenwood, James, *Low-life Deeps* (London, 1876).

—— *The Seven Curses of London* (Oxford, 1981).

Greg, William Rathbone, *An Enquiry into the State of the Manufacturing Population* (London, 1831).

—— 'Prostitution', *Westminster Review* 53 (1850), 448–506.

—— 'Curiosities of the Census', *North British Review*, 22 (1854–5), 401–12.

—— 'The Social Sores of Britain', *North British Review*, 47 (1857), 497–532.

—— 'Why are Women Redundant?', *National Review*, 14 (1862), 434–60.

—— *Enigmas of Life* (18th edn. London, 1891).

Grey, Mrs E. C., *Passages in the Life of a Fast Young Lady* (London, 1862).

Griscom, John, *A Year in Europe* (New York, 1823).

Gronow, R. H., *Recollections and Anecdotes: Second Series* (London, 1863).

Guizot, F., *An Embassy to the Court of St James's in 1840* (London, 1862).

Guthrie, Thomas, *The City its Sins and Sorrows* (Glasgow, 1859).

Gutteridge, Joseph, *Master and Artisan in Victorian England*, ed. Valerie E. Chancellor (London, 1969).

Guy, John, *A Popular Treatise on Diseases of the Generative System* (London, 1832).

Habakkuk, H. J., *Population Growth and Economic Development since 1750* (Leicester, 1971).

Hacking, Ian, *The Taming of Chance* (Cambridge, 1990).

Haighton, John, 'An Experimental Inquiry Concerning Animal Impregnation', *Philosophical Transactions of the Royal Society*, 87 (1797), 159–96.

HAINES, MICHAEL R., 'Fertility, Nuptiality, and Occupation: A Study of the Coal Mining Populations and Regions in England and Wales in the Mid-Nineteenth Century', *Journal of Interdisciplinary History*, 8 (1977), 245–80.

—— *Fertility and Occupation* (New York, 1979).

—— 'Social Class Differentials during Fertility Decline: England and Wales Revisited', *PS* 43 (1989), 305–23.

HAIR, P. E. H., 'Bridal Pregnancy in Rural England in Earlier Centuries', *PS* 20 (1966), 233–43.

—— 'Bridal Pregnancy in Earlier Rural England Further Examined', *PS* 24 (1970), 59–70.

HALE, WILLIAM, *Considerations of the Causes and the Prevalence of Female Prostitution* (London, 1812).

HALL, CHARLES, *The Effects of Civilisation on the People in European States* (2nd edn. London, 1850).

HALL, LESLEY, *Hidden Anxieties* (Oxford, 1991).

HAMERTON, PHILIP GILBERT, *French and English, a Comparison* (London, 1889).

HAMILTON, ROBERT, *The Progress of Society* (London, 1830).

HAMMERTON, A. JAMES, *Emigrant Gentlewomen* (London, 1979).

—— *Cruelty and Companionship* (London, 1992).

HANGER, GEORGE, *The Life, Adventures, and Opinions of Col. George Hanger* (London, 1801).

HANSARD, LUKE JAMES, *Remarks in Relation to an Appeal now before Parliament* (London, 1844).

HARE, E. H., 'Masturbatory Insanity: The History of an Idea', *Journal of Mental Science*, 108 (1962), 1–25.

HARRISON, BRIAN, 'Francis Place and the "Drunken Committee"', *History Journal*, 11 (1968), 272–300.

—— *Drink and the Victorians* (London, 1971).

—— *Peaceable Kingdom* (Oxford, 1982).

—— and HOLLIS, PATRICIA, *Robert Lowery Radical and Chartist* (London, 1979).

HARVEY, JOHN, *The Restoration of Nervous Function* (London, 1865).

HASSALL, ARTHUR HALL, *The Urine in Health and Disease* (London, 1859).

HAUGHTON, G. D., *On Sex in the World to Come* (London, 1841).

HAUSSEZ, BARON C. L. D.', *Great Britain in 1833* (London, 1833).

HAWTHORNE, NATHANIEL, *Our Old Home* (London, 1863).

HAYNES, E. S. P., 'Early Victorian Characteristics', *Independent Review*, 2 (1904), 66–71.

HAZLITT, WILLIAM, *A Reply to the Essay on Population* (London, 1807).

—— *Liber Amoris* (London, 1985).

HEAD, GEORGE, *A Home Tour through the Manufacturing Districts of England* (London, 1836).

HENERY, A. F., *Manly Vigour* (London, 1861).

—— *Cure Yourself!* (London, 1863).

HENNEQUIN, VICTOR ANTOINE, *Voyage philosophique en Angleterre et en Écosse* (Paris, 1836).

HENRIQUES, U. R. Q., 'Bastardy and the New Poor Law', *Past and Present*, 37 (1967), 103–29.

HENRY, C. D., and Co., *Life's Renovator* (London, 1852).

HEYWOOD, JAMES, 'Statistics of Manchester', *Report of the Fourth Meeting of the British Association for the Advancement of Science* (1835), 690–1.

—— 'Report of an Enquiry, Conducted from House to House, into the State of 176 Families in Miles Platting, within the Borough of Manchester', *JSSL* 1 (1839), 34–6.

HIBBERT, H. G., *Fifty Years of a Londoner's Life* (London, 1916).

HICKSON, W. E., *Malthus* (London, 1850).

HIGGINBOTHAM, ANN R., '"Sin of the Age": Infanticide and Illegitimacy in Victorian London', in Kristine Ottesen Garrigan, ed., *Victorian Scandals* (Athens, Ohio, 1992), 257–88.

HILLES, M. W., *The Essentials of Physiology* (London, 1860).

HILLOCKS, JAMES INCHES, *My Life and Labours* (London, 1865).

—— *Hard Battles for Life and Usefulness* (London, 1884).

HILTON, BOYD, *The Age of Atonement* (Oxford, 1988).

HILTS, VICTOR L., 'William Farr (1807–1883) and the "Human Unit"', *Victorian Studies* 14 (1970), 143–50.

—— '*Aliis exterendum*, or, the Origins of the Statistical Society of London', *Isis* 69 (1978), 21–43.

HIMES, NORMAN, *Place on Population* (London, 1930).

—— *Medical History of Contraception* (London, 1936).

HIMMELFARB, GERTRUDE, 'Mayhew's Poor: A Problem of Identity', *Victorian Studies*, 14 (1971).

HODSON, JAMES, *Nature's Assistant to the Restoration of Health* (London, 1795).

HOHER, DAGMAR, 'The Composition of Music Hall Audiences, 1850–1900', in Peter Bailey, ed., *Music Hall* (Milton Keynes, 1986), 73–92.

HOLDEN, W. H., *They Startled Grandfather* (London, 1950).

HOLLAND, G. CALVERT, *An Inquiry into the Moral, Social, and Intellectual Condition of the Industrious Classes of Sheffield* (London, 1839).

HOLLINGSHEAD, JOHN, *My Lifetime* (London, 1895).

HOLLINGSWORTH, T. H., 'A Demographic Study of the British Ducal Families', *PS* 11 (1957), 4–26.

—— 'The Demography of the British Peerage', *PS* 18 (1964).

—— 'Illegitimate Births and Marriage Rates in Great Britain 1841–1911', in J. Dupaquier, E. Helin, P. Laslett, M. Livi-Bacci, and S. Sogner, eds., *Marriage and Remarriage in Populations of the Past* (London, 1981), 437–51.

HOLMES, TIMOTHY, *A Treatise on Surgery* (London, 1875).

HOLYOAKE, GEORGE JACOB, *Self-Help a Hundred Years Ago* (London, 1888).

HOME, SIR EVERARD, 'On Corpora Lutea', *Philosophical Transactions of the Royal Society*, 109 (1819), 59–69.

HOOD, EDWIN PAXTON, *The Age and its Architects* (London, 1850).

HOOKER, R. H., 'Is the Birth-Rate Still Falling?', *Transactions of the Manchester Statistical Society* (1897–8), 100–26.

Hooper's Physicians' Vade Mecum (7th edn. London, 1864), ed. William Augustus Guy and John Harley.

HORN, PAMELA, *Ladies of the Manor* (Stroud, 1991).

HOUSMAN, LAURENCE, *The Unexpected Years* (London, 1937).

HOWE, P. P., ed., *The Complete Works of William Hazlitt*, vii (London, 1932).

HOWITT, WILLIAM, *The Rural Life of England* (London, 1838).

HUDSON, DEREK, *Munby Man of Two Worlds* (London, 1974).

HUME, A., *Condition of Liverpool, Religious and Social* (Liverpool, 1858).

HUMPHRY, G. M., 'Diseases of the Male Organs of Generation', in Timothy Holmes, ed., *A System of Surgery*, iv (London, 1864), 539–624.

HUNT, F. K., 'A Few Words about Matrimony', *Household Words*, 1 (1850), 374–7.

HUNT, MISS CHANDOS LEIGH, *A Treatise on All the Known Uses of Organic Magnetism* (London, n.d.).

HUNTER, H. J., *Inquiry on the State of the Dwellings of Rural Labourers*, PP 1865, xxvi. 126–302.

HUNTER, JOHN, *A Treatise on Venereal Disease* (3rd edn. London, 1810).

HUNTINGTON, GEORGE, *The Church's Work in Our Large Towns* (2nd edn. Oxford, 1871).

HUTCHINS, B. L., 'Note on the Distribution of Married Women in Relation to the Birth-rate', *JSSL* 68 (1905), 95–103.

HUTTON, WILLIAM, *A Journey from Birmingham to London* (Birmingham, 1785).

INGRAM, ROBERT ACKLOM, *Disquisitions on Population* (London, 1808).

INNES, JOHN W., *Class Fertility Trends in England and Wales 1876–1934* (Princeton, NJ, 1938).

JAMES, LOUIS, *Print and the People 1819–1851* (London, 1976).

JAMES, PATRICIA, *Population Malthus* (London, 1979).

JARROLD, THOMAS, *Dissertations on Man* (London, 1806).

JOHN, ANGELA V., *By the Sweat of their Brow* (London, 1980).

JOHNSON, ATHOL A. W., 'On an Injurious Habit Occasionally Met with in Infancy and Early Childhood', *Lancet*, 1860(1), 344–5.

JONES, HARRY, *East and West London* (London, 1875).

JONES, RICHARD, *Literary Remains* (London, 1859).

JONES, SHADRACH, *On the Diseases of Men* (London, 1879).

JONES, WILLIAM, *Practical Observations on the Diseases of Women* (London, 1839).

—— *An Essay on Some of the More Important Diseases of Women* (London, 1850).

JORDAN, J., and Co., *Human Frailty* (London, 1842).

JUDGE, HENRY, *Our Fallen Sisters* (London, 1874).

Junonesia; or the Woman Rescued (London, 1838).

KAHN, JOSEPH, *The Shoals and Quicksands of Youth* (100th edn. London, 1856).

KATSCHER, LEOPOLD, *Bilder aus dem Englischen Leben* (Leipzig, 1881).

KAY, JOSEPH, *The Social Condition and Education of the People in England and Europe* (London, 1850).

KAY-SHUTTLEWORTH, JAMES, *Four Periods of Public Education* (London, 1862).

KEATING, JOSEPH, *My Struggle for Life* (London, 1916).

KEGAN PAUL, C., *William Godwin: His Friends and Contemporaries* (London, 1876).

KEGEL, CHARLES H, 'William Cobbett and Malthusianism', *Journal of the History of Ideas*, 19 (1958), 348–62.

KEIR, WILLIAM, *A Summons of Wakening* (Hawick, 1807).

KENNY, ANTHONY, ed., *The Oxford Diaries of Arthur Hugh Clough* (Oxford, 1990).

KENRICK, G. S., 'Statistics of Merthyr Tydvil', *JSLL* 9 (1846), 14–21.

KENT, CHRISTOPHER, 'The "Average Victorian" Constructing and Contesting Reality', *Browning Institute Studies*, 17 (1989), 41-52.

KIRK, NEVILLE, *The Growth of Working-Class Reformism in Mid-Victorian Britain* (London, 1985).

KIRKES, WILLIAM SENHOUSE, *Hand-book of Physiology* (1st edn. London, 1848; 10th edn. London, 1880).

KIRTON, J. W., *Happy Homes and How to Make them* (Birmingham, 1870).

KIRWAN, D. J., *Palace and Hovel* (London, 1963).

KITCHENER, HENRY THOMAS, *Letters on Marriage* (London, 1812).

KNIGHT, CHARLES, *Passages of a Working Life* (London, 1864).

KNIGHT, PATRICIA, 'Women and Abortion in Victorian and Edwardian England', *History Workshop*, 4 (1977), 57–68.

KNODEL, JOHN, 'Family Limitation and the Fertility Transition: Evidence from the Age Patterns of Fertility in Europe and Asia', *PS* 31 (1977), 219–49.

KNOX, ROBERT, ('A Physician'), *The Greatest of our Social Evils: Prostitution* (London, 1857).

KODITSCHEK, THEODORE, *Class Formation and Urban Industrial Society Bradford 1750–1850* (Cambridge, 1990).

KRAUSE, J. T., 'Changes in English Fertility and Mortality, 1781–1850', *EHR* 11 (1958), 52–70.

KUCHEMANN, C. F., BOYCE, A. J., and HARRISON, G. A., 'A Demographic and Genetic Study of a Group of Oxfordshire Villages', *Human Biology*, 39 (1967), 251–76.

LALLEMAND, CLAUDE FRANÇOIS, *A Practical Treatise on the Causes, Symptoms, and Treatment of Spermatorrhoea*, trans. Henry J. MacDougall (London, 1847).

LAMB, ROBERT, *Free Thoughts on Many Subjects* (London, 1866).

LA'MERT, SAMUEL, *Self-Preservation* (London, 1852).

LAQUEUR, THOMAS W., 'Orgasm, Generation, and the Politics of Reproductive Biology', *Representations*, 14 (1986), 1–41.

—— *Making Sex* (Cambridge, Mass., 1990).

LARCHER, L.-J., *Les Anglais, Londres et l'Angleterre* (Paris, 1860).

LAROCQUE, JEAN, *L'Angleterre et le peuple anglais* (Paris, 1882).

LASLETT, PETER, *Family Life and Illicit Love in Earlier Generations* (Cambridge, 1977).

—— 'Illegitimate Fertility and the Matrimonial Market', in J. Dupaquier, E. Helin, P. Laslett, M. Livi-Bacci, and S. Sogner, eds., *Marriage and Remarriage in Populations of the Past* (London, 1981), 461–71.

——, OOSTERVEEN, KARLA, and SMITH, RICHARD M., *Bastardy and its Comparative History* (London, 1980).

LAVER, JAMES, *The Age of Optimism* (London, 1966).

LAW, C. M., 'The Growth of Urban Population in England and Wales', *Transactions of the Institute of British Geographers*, 41 (1967), 125–43.

LAWRENCE, JAMES, *The Empire of the Nairs* (London, 1811).

LAWSON, JOSEPH, *Letters to the Young on Progress in Pudsey during the last Sixty Years* (Stanningley, 1887).

LAYCOCK, THOMAS, *A Treatise on the Nervous Diseases of Women* (London, 1840).

LECOMTE, JULES, *Voyages ça et là* (Paris, 1859).

LEE, ROBERT, *A Treatise on the Employment of the Speculum* (London, 1858).

LE PLAY, M. F., *Les Ouvriers Européens* (Paris, 1855).

'Le Plus Bas', *Our Plague Spot: In Connection with Our Polity and Usages* (London, 1859).

—— *Woman's Rights and Woman's Wrongs: A Dying Legacy* (London, 1865).

LERNER, LAURENCE, and HOLMSTROM, JOHN, eds., *Thomas Hardy and his Readers* (London, 1968).

LESLIE, THOMAS EDWARD CLIFFE, *Essays in Political and Moral Philosophy* (Dublin, 1879).

LESTER, C. EDWARDS, *The Glory and Shame of England* (London, 1841).

Letters from Albion (London, 1814).

LEVINE, DAVID, *Family Formation in an Age of Nascent Capitalism* (New York, 1977).

—— *Reproducing Families* (Cambridge, 1987).

LEWALD, FANNY, *England und Schottland* (Brunswick, 1851).

LEWIS, DONALD, *Lighten their Darkness* (New York, 1986).

LEWIS, SARAH, *Woman's Mission* (1st edn. London, 1839; 2nd edn. London, 1840).

LINDRIDGE, JAMES, *The Merry Wives of London* (London, 1850).

LINTON, ELIZA LYNN, 'The Girl of the Period', *Saturday Review*, 25 (1868) 339–40.

LIVI-BACCI, MASSIMO, 'Social-Group Forerunners of Fertility Control in Europe', in Ansley J. Coale and Susan Cotts Wilkins, eds., *The Decline of Fertility in Europe* (Princeton, NJ, 1968), 182–200.

LOBB, HARRY, *Hypogastria* (3rd edn. London, 1880).

LOCKHART, J. G., *Memoirs of the Life of Sir Walter Scott, Bart.* (Edinburgh, 1837).

LOGAN, WILLIAM, *An Exposure, from Personal Observation, of Female Prostitution in London, Leeds, and Rochdale, and Especially in the City of Glasgow* (2nd edn. Glasgow, 1843).

—— *The Great Social Evil* (London, 1871).

London by Night (London, ?1857).

The London Guide (London, 1818).

London Life as it is (London, 1851).

LONGO, LAWRENCE, D., 'The Rise and Fall of Battey's Operation: A Fashion in Surgery', *Bulletin of the History of Medicine*, 53 (1979), 244–67.

LONGSTAFF, GEORGE BLUNDELL, *Studies in Statistics* (London, 1891).

LOUDON, CHARLES, *The Equilibrium of Population and Sustenance Demonstrated* (Leamington Spa, 1836).

LOUDON, IRVINE, *Medical Care and the General Practitioner 1750–1850* (Oxford, 1986).

—— '"The Vile Race of Quacks with which this Country is Infested"', in W. F. Bynum and Roy Porter, eds., *Medical Fringe and Medical Orthodoxy 1750–1850* (London, 1987), 106–28.

LOVE, BENJAMIN, *Chapters on Working People* (London, 1838).

—— *Manchester as it is* (Manchester, 1839).

LOWNDES, FREDERICK W., *Prostitution and Syphilis in Liverpool* (London, 1876).

—— *Prostitution and Venereal Disease in Liverpool* (London, 1886).

LUDLOW, J. M. F., and JONES, LLOYD, *Progress of the Working Class 1832–1867* (London, 1867).

LUMLEY, W. G., 'Observations upon the Statistics of Illegitimacy', *JSSL* 25 (1862), 219–74.

MACAULAY, THOMAS BABINGTON, 'Sadler's Law of Population . . .', *Edinburgh Review*, 51 (1830), 297–321.

McCARTHY, JUSTIN, 'Novels with a Purpose', *Westminster Review*, NS 26 (1864), 24–48.

McCULLOUGH, J. R., 'Rise, Progress, Present State, and Prospects of the British Cotton Manufacture', *Edinburgh Review*, 46 (1827), 1–39.

MACDONALD, ROBERT H., 'The Frightful Consequences of Onanism: Notes on the History of a Delusion', *Journal of the History of Ideas*, 28 (1967), 423–31.

MACDONOGH, F., *The Hermit in London* (London, 1819–20).

McGREGOR, O. R., 'Social Research and Social Policy in the Nineteenth Century', *British Journal of Sociology*, 8 (1957), 146–57,

MACKENZIE, COMPTON, *Literature in my Time* (London, 1933).

MACKENZIE, F. W., 'On the Relation of Uterine to Constitutional Disorder', *London Journal of Medicine*, 3 (1851), 980–1006.

McLAREN, ANGUS, 'Women's Work and Regulation of Family Size', *History Workshop*, 4 (1977), 70–81.

—— *Reproduction Rituals* (London, 1984).

MACQUEEN, T. POTTER, *The State of the Nation at the Close of 1830* (London, 1831).

MALCOLM, JAMES PELLER, *Anecdotes of the Manners and Customs of London during the Eighteenth Century* (1st edn. London, 1808; 2nd edn. London, 1810).

MALOT, HECTOR, *La Vie moderne en Angleterre* (Paris, 1862).

MALTHUS, THOMAS ROBERT, *Essay on the Principle of Population* (2nd edn. London, 1803).

—— *Occasional Papers of Thomas Malthus* (New York, 1963).

—— *Essay on the Principle of Population*, ed. Anthony Flew (Harmondsworth, 1970).

Malthus Re-examined by the Light of Physiology (London, 1868).

'Man about Town', *Minnie Skittles and Hints on Life in London* (London, 1857).

'The Man in the Club-Window', *The Habits of Good Society* (London, 1859).

MANN, ROBERT JAMES, *The Philosophy of Reproduction* (London, 1855).

MANNING, WILLIAM, *The Wrongs of Man Exemplified* (London, 1838).

MARSHALL, DONALD S., and SUGGS, ROBERT C., *Human Sexual Behaviour* (New York, 1971).

MARTINEAU, HARRIET, 'Female Industry', *Edinburgh Review*, 109 (1859), 293–336.

MARX, KARL, and ENGELS, FRIEDRICH, *Historische-Kritische Gesamtausgabe, Briefwechsel*, s. 3, vol. ii (Berlin, 1930).

MATRAS, JUDAH, 'Social Strategies of Family Formation: Data for British Female Cohorts born 1831–1906', *PS* 19 (1965), 167–81.

MAUDSLEY, HENRY, 'Illustrations of a Variety of Insanity', *Journal of Mental Science*, 14 (1866), 149–62.

MAYHEW, HENRY, *London Labour and the London Poor* (London, 1861–2).

—— *The Morning Chronicle Survey of London and the Poor: The Metropolitan Districts* (Horsham, 1980).

MAYO, HERBERT, *Outlines of Human Physiology* (1st edn. London, 1827; 4th edn. London, 1837).

MEARNS, ANDREW, *The Bitter Cry of Outcast London*, ed. Anthony S. Wohl, (Leicester, 1870).

'A Mechanic', *Observations on the Use of Machinery in the Manufactories of Great Britain* (London, 1817).

MEISTER, HENRI, *Letters Written during a Residence in England* (London, 1799).

MERRICK, G. P., *Work among the Fallen* (London, 1891).

MICHIELS, ALFRED, *Angleterre* (Paris, 1844).

MICKLEWRIGHT, F. H. AMPHLETT, 'The Rise and Decline of English Neo-Malthusianism', *PS* 15 (1962), 32–51.

MILES, DUDLEY, *Francis Place* (Sussex, 1988).

MILL, JAMES, 'State of the Nation', *Westminster Review* 6 (1826), 249–78.

MILL, JOHN STUART, *A System of Logic* (5th edn. London, 1862).

—— *Autobiography* (London, 1989).

MILLER, JAMES, *Prostitution Considered in Relation to its Cause and Cure* (Edinburgh, 1859).

MILLS, DENNIS R., *Aspects of Marriage* (Milton Keynes, 1980).

—— and JOAN, 'Occupation and Social Stratification Revisited: The Census Enumerators' Books of Victorian Britain', *Urban History Yearbook* (1989), 63–77.

MILNE, ALEXANDER, *The Principles and Practice of Midwifery* (Edinburgh, 1871).

MILNE, JOHN DUGUID, *Industrial and Social Position of Women* (London, 1857).

MILNER, THOMAS, *The Elevation of the People, Moral, Instructional, and Social* (London, 1856).

MILTON, JOHN LAWS, *Practical Remarks on the Treatment of Spermatorrhoea and Some Forms of Impotence* (2nd edn. London, 1855; 12th edn.—as *On the Pathology and Treatment of Spermatorrhoea*—London, 1887).

MINGAY, GORDON, 'The Rural Slum', in S. Martin Gaskell, ed., *Slums* (Leicester, 1990), 92–143.

MIRECOURT, EUGÈNE DE, *Nos voisins les Anglais* (Paris, 1862).

MITCHELL, GEOFFREY, ed., *The Hard Way up* (London, 1968).

MITCHELL, JOHN, ('Orlando Sabertash'), 'Courtship and Love-Making', *Frasers* 25 (1842), 144–59.

A Modern Sabbath (London, 1794).

MONTULÉ, ÉDOUARD DE, *Voyage en Angleterre et en Russie* (Paris, 1825).

MOODIE, JOHN, *A Medical Treatise* (Edinburgh, 1858).

MOORE, GEORGE, *Literature at Nurse*, ed. Pierre Coustillas (Hassocks, 1976).

MORETON, A. H., *Civilisation* (London, 1836).

MORGAN, LADY SYDNEY, *France* (2nd edn. London, 1817).

MORLEY, JOHN, 'Marriage in the Nineteenth Century', *Dublin University Magazine*, 59 (1862), 542–53.

MORRISON, C., *An Essay on the Relations between Labour and Capital* (London, 1854).

MOSCUCCI, ORNELLA, *The Science of Woman* (Cambridge, 1990).

MULOCK, DIANA, *A Woman's Thoughts about Women* (London, 1858).

MUNYARD, J. H., *Munyard's Bagatelle* (Yarmouth, 1840).

My Secret Life (New York, 1966).

NADAL, E. S., *Impression of London Social Life* (London, 1875).

NARJOUX, FÉLIX, *En Angleterre* (Paris, 1886).

NASMYTH, JAMES, *James Nasmyth Engineer, an Autobiography* (London, 1883).

NEAD, LYNDA, *Myths of Sexuality* (Oxford, 1988).

NEALE, R. S., 'Class and Class-Consciousness in Early Nineteenth-Century England: Three Classes or Five', *Victorian Studies*, 12 (1968), 4–32.

—— *Class and Ideology in the Nineteenth Century* (London, 1972).

NEUMAN, R. P., 'Masturbation, Madness and the Modern Concepts of Childhood and Adolescence', *Journal of Social History*, 8 (1975), 1–27.

NEVILL, RALPH, *The Man of Pleasure* (London, 1912).

—— and JERNINGHAM, CHARLES EDWARD, *Piccadilly to Pall Mall* (London, 1908).

NEVINS, J. BIRKBECK, 'Enquiry into the Condition of Prostitution', *Medical Enquirer*, 2 (1876), 17–28.

NEWMAN, FRANCIS W., *The Cure of the Great Social Evil* (London, 1869).

—— 'What is Prostitution?', *Miscellanies*, iii (London, 1889), 285–8.

NICHOLS, T. L., *Esoteric Anthropology* (London, 1873).

NICHOLSON, RENTON, *Rogue's Progress*, ed. John L. Bradley (London, 1965).

NIEMEYER, A. H., *Travels in the Continent and in England* (*New Voyages and Travels*, ix; London, 1823).

NIGHTINGALE, FLORENCE, *Suggestions for Thought to the Searchers after Truth among the Artisans of England* (London, 1860).

NORTHCOTE, J. S., 'The Morality and Religion of England', *Rambler*, 12 (1853), 201–17.

NOUGARET, P. J. B., *Londres, la cour et les provinces d'Angleterre, d'Écosse et d'Irlande* (Paris, 1816).

OATS, HENRY CARNE, 'Inquiry into the Educational and other Conditions of a District in Deansgate', *Transactions of the Manchester Statistical Society* (1864–5), 1–13.

—— 'Inquiry into the Educational and other Conditions of a District in Ancoats', *Transactions of the Manchester Statistical Society* (1865–6), 1–16.

O'DONNOGHUE, H. C., *Marriage: The Source, Stability and Perfection of Human Happiness and Duty* (2nd edn. London, 1836).

OGLE, WILLIAM, 'On Marriage-rates and Marriage-ages, with Special Reference to the Growth of Population', *JSSL* 53 (1890), 253–80.

OKEY, THOMAS, *A Basketful of Memories* (London, 1930).

Old Bachelors (London, 1877).

Old Maids (London, 1835).

OLIPHANT, MRS, 'The Condition of Women', *Blackwoods*, 83 (1858), 139–54.

OLMSTED, FREDERICK LAW, *Walks and Talks of an American Farmer in England* (Ann Arbor, 1967).

OUTHWAITE, R. B., 'Age of Marriage in England from the Late Seventeenth Century to the Nineteenth Century', *Transactions of the Royal Historical Society*, 5th ser. 23 (1973), 56–70.

OWEN, ROBERT DALE, *Situations* (London, 1840).

—— *Moral Physiology* (London, 1877).

PAGET, JAMES, 'Report on the Progress of Anatomy and Physiology in the Year 1842–3', *British and Foreign Medical Review*, 17 (1844), 249–78.

PAGET, STEPHEN, ed., *Memoirs and Letter of Sir James Paget* (London, 1901).

PALEY, WILLIAM, *The Principles of Moral and Political Philosophy* (London, 1785).

PALGRAVE, R. H. I., 'On the House Accommodation of England and Wales', *JSSL* 32 (1869), 411–27.

PARKER, JOHN, 'On the Literature of the Working Classes', *Meliora* (2nd ser. 1853) 181–97.

PARKES, EDMUND A., *The Composition of the Urine* (London, 1860).

PARSONS, BENJAMIN, *The Mental and Moral Dignity of Woman* (London, 1842).

PATTISON, MARK, 'History of Civilisation in England', *Westminster Review*, NS 12 (1857), 375–99.

PAULDING, JAMES KIRKE, *A Sketch of Old England, by a New England Man* (*New Voyages and Travels*, viii; London, 1822).

PEARCE, CAROL G., 'Expanding Families', *PS* 27 (1973), 22–35.

PEEL, JOHN, 'The Manufacturing and Retailing of Contraceptives in England', *PS* 17 (1964), 113–25.

—— 'Contraception and the Medical Profession', *PS* 18 (1965), 133–45.

PERKIN, HAROLD, *The Origins of Modern English Society* (London, 1969).

PERRY, R. and L. and Co, *The Silent Friend* (Birmingham, 1841).

PERTHES, JACQUES BOUCHER DE, *Voyage en Angleterre* (Paris, 1868).

PETERSON, M. JEANNE, *The Medical Profession in Mid-Victorian London* (Berkeley, Calif., 1978).

—— 'Dr Acton's Enemy: Medicine, Sex, and Society in Victorian England', *Victorian Studies*, 29 (1986), 569–90.

—— *Family, Love, and Work in the Lives of Victorian Gentlewomen* (Bloomington, Ind., 1989).

PHILIPS, DAVID, *Crime and Authority in Victorian England* (London, 1977).

PHILLIPS, RICHARD, *A Morning's Walk from London to Kew* (London, 1817).

PICHOT, AMEDÉE, *Historical and Literary Tour of a Foreigner in England and Scotland* (London, 1825).

PILLET, R. M., *Views of England* (Boston, Mass., 1818).

PLACE, FRANCIS, 'On the Theories of Malthus and Godwin', *New Monthly Magazine*, 1 (1821), 195–205.

—— *Improvement of the Working People* (London, 1834).

—— *The Autobiography of Francis Place*, ed. Mary Thale (Cambridge, 1972).

PLINT, THOMAS, *Crime in England* (London, 1851).

PONTÈS, LUÇIEN DAVÉSIÈS, *Social Reform in England* (London, 1865).

POOLE, ROBERT, *Popular Recreation and the Music Hall in Nineteenth-Century Bolton, Centre for North-West Regional Studies Occasional Paper*, 12 (1982).

PORTER, G. R., *The Progress of the Nation*, i (London, 1836).

PORTER, THEODORE M., *The Rise of Statistical Thinking 1820–1900* (Princeton NJ, 1986).

POTTER, EDMUND, *A Picture of a Manufacturing District* (London, 1856).

POTTER, GEORGE REUBEN, 'Unpublished Marginalia in Coleridge's Copy of Malthus's *Essay on Population*', *PMLA* 51 (1936), 1061–8.

POWER, JOHN, *Essays on the Female Economy* (London, 1821).

POYNTER, J. R., *Society and Pauperism* (London, 1969).

PRATT, WILLIAM, *A Physician's Sermon to Young Men* (London, 1872).

PRÉMARAY, JULES DE, *Promenades sentimentales dans Londres et le Palais de Cristal* (Paris, 1851).

QUILLER COUCH, ARTHUR, *Studies in Literature: Second Series* (Cambridge, 1922).

RADZINOWICZ, LEON, *A History of the Criminal Law and its Administration from 1750*, ii, iii (London, 1956), v (with R. Hood) (London, 1986).

RAIKES, HENRY, *Two Lectures on Population* (Chester, 1845).

The Rambler's Flash Songster, The Flash Chaunter, The Cuckhold's Nest, The Cockchafer (London, ?1865).

RANDS, WILLIAM BRIGHTY, ('Matthew Browne'), *Views and Opinions* (London, 1866).

RANKING, W. H., 'Observations on Spermatorrhoea', *Lancet*, 1843–4(1), 46–53.

RATCLIFFE, B. M., and CHALONER, W. H., *A French Sociologist Looks at Britain* (Manchester, 1977).

RAUMER, FRIEDRICH VON, *England in 1835* (London, 1836).

—— *England in 1841* (London, 1842).

RAVENSTONE, PIERCY, *A Few Doubts as to the Correctness of Some Opinions Generally Entertained on the Subjects of Population and Political Economy* (London, 1821).

RAWSON, R. W., 'Results of Some Inquiries into the Condition and Education of the Poorer Classes in the Parish of Marylebone, in 1838', *JSSL* 6 (1843), 44–8.

RAZZELL, P. E., and WAINWRIGHT, R. W., *The Victorian Working Class* (London, 1973).

READ, SAMUEL, *General Statement of an Argument on the Subject of Population* (London, 1821).

REAY, BARRY, 'Sexuality in Nineteenth-Century England: The Social Context of Illegitimacy in Rural Kent', *Rural History*, 1 (1990), 219–47.

REECE, RICHARD, *Monthly Gazette of Health*, 3 (1818).

REID, ALISTAIR, 'Intelligent Artisans and Aristocrats of Labour: The Essays of Thomas Wright', in Jay Winter, ed., *The Working Class in Modern British History* (Cambridge, 1983), 171–86.

REISS, ERNA, *Rights and Duties of Englishwomen* (London, 1934).

Remarks on a Late Publication Entitled 'An Essay on the Principle of Population' (London, 1803).

Remarks on Mr Godwin's Enquiry Concerning Population (London, 1821).

REMO, FÉLIX, *La Vie galante en Angleterre* (Paris, 1888).

RÉMUSAT, C. F. M. DE, *La Vie de village en Angleterre* (Paris, 1862).

RENDLE, T. MCDONALD, *Swings and Roundabouts* (London, 1919).

RICHARDSON, JOHN, *Recollections, Political, Literary, Dramatic, and Miscellaneous, of the Last Half-Century* (London, 1855).

RICHARDSON, LEANDER, *As Yankees See us or the Customs of the Cockneys* (Boston, Mass., 1886).

RITCHIE, ANNA, 'Toilers and Spinsters', *Cornhill*, 3 (1861), 318–31.

RITCHIE, CHARLES, 'Clinical Contributions to the Investigation and Treatment of General Disease', *Edinburgh Medical and Surgical Journal*, 75 (1851), 31–85.

RITCHIE, J. EWING, *The Night Side of London* (London, 1857).

—— *Here and there in London* (London, 1859).

RICHIE, ROBERT P., 'An Inquiry into a Frequent Cause of Insanity in Young Men', *Lancet*, 1861(1), 159–61, 185–7, 234–5, 284–6.

ROBERTON, JOHN, *On the Generative System* (4th edn. London, 1817).

—— *Essays and Notes on the Physiology and Diseases of Women* (London, 1851).

ROBERTS, SAMUEL, *Autobiography and Select Remains* (London, 1849).

ROBERTS, WILLIAM, *A Practical Treatise on Urinary and Renal Diseases* (2nd edn. London, 1872).

ROBERTSON, JOHN MACKINNON, *Buckle and His Critics* (London, 1895).

ROBERTSON, PRISCILLA, *An Experience of Women* (Philadelphia, 1982).

ROBIN, JEAN, 'Prenuptial Pregnancy in a Rural Area of Devonshire in the Mid-Nineteenth Century: Colyton, 1851–1881', *Continuity and Change*, 1 (1986), 113–24.

—— 'Illegitimacy in Colyton, 1851–1881', *Continuity and Change*, 2 (1987), 307–42.

ROBINSON, F. W. R. ('A Prison Matron'), *Female Life in Prison* (London, 1862).

RODGERS, BRIAN, 'The Social Science Association, 1857–1886', *The Manchester School of Economic and Social Studies*, 8 (1952), 283–310.

ROE, EDWARD THOMAS, *A Report on the Cause Jackson and Wife v. Roe, Esq M.D.* (Plymouth, 1852).

ROGERS, FREDERICK, *Labour Life and Literature* (London, 1913).

ROSE, LIONEL, *The Massacre of the Innocents* (London, 1986).

ROSEN, FREDERICK, 'The Principle of Population as Political Theory', *Journal of the History of Ideas*, 31 (1970), 33–48.

ROSS, ELLEN, '"Fierce Questions and Taunts": Married Life in Working-Class London, 1870–1914', *Feminist Studies*, 8 (1982), 575–602.

Ross, J. C., *An Examination of Opinions Maintained in the 'Essay on the Principles of Population', by Malthus* (London, 1827).

Routh, C. H. F., *The Moral and Physical Evils Likely to Follow if Practices Intended to Act as Checks to Population be not Strongly Discouraged and Condemned* (London, 1879).

Rowe, D. J., 'Francis Place and the Historian', *History Journal*, 16 (1973), 45–63.

—— 'The North-East', in F. M. L. Thompson, ed., *The Cambridge Social History of Britain 1750–1950* (Cambridge, 1990), i. 415–70.

Rowe, George Robert, *On Some of the Most Important Disorders of Women* (London, 1844).

Rowe, Richard, *Picked up on the Streets* (London, 1880).

Rowley, Charles, *Fifty Years of Ancoats* (Ancoats, 1899).

Rowntree, Griselda, and Carrier, Norman H., 'The Resort to Divorce in England and Wales, 1858–1957' *PS* 11 (1957), 188–233.

Royle, Stephen A., 'Social Stratification from Early Census Returns: A New Approach', *Area*, 9 (1977), 215–19.

Rubinstein, W. D., 'The Size and Distribution of the English Middle Classes in 1860', *Historical Research*, 61 (1988), 65–89.

Ruddock, E. H., *The Lady's Manual of Homeopathic Treatment* (2nd edn. London, 1865; 8th edn. London, 1883).

Rudé, George, *Hanoverian London 1714–1808* (London, 1971).

Rushton, Adam, *My Life* (Manchester, 1909).

Russell, Brian, ed., *St John's Hospital for Diseases of the Skin 1863–1963* (Edinburgh, 1963).

Russell, G. W. E., *Collections and Recollections* (London, 1899), *Second Series* (London, 1908).

Russell, James, *Observations on the Testicles* (Edinburgh, 1833).

Ryan, Michael, *Lectures on Population, Marriage, and Divorce* (London, 1831).

—— *The Philosophy of Marriage* (London, 1837).

—— *Prostitution in London* (London, 1839).

Ryan, William Burke, *Infanticide* (London, 1862).

Sadler, Michael Thomas, *The Law of Population* (London, 1830*a*).

—— *A Refutation; of an Article in the Edinburgh Review* (London, 1830*b*).

St Helier, Lady, *Memories of Fifty Years* (London, 1909).

Sandars, T. C., 'Buckle's History of Civilisation in England', *Frasers*, 56 (1857), 409–24.

Sankey, W. H. O., *Lectures on Mental Diseases* (London, 1866).

Sargant, William Lucas, *Economy of the Labouring Classes* (London, 1857).

—— *Essays of a Birmingham Manufacturer* (London, 1869–70).

Sarrazin, J., *Tableau de la Grande Bretagne* (Paris, 1816).

Sauer, R., 'Infanticide and Abortion in Nineteenth-Century Britain', *PS* 32 (1978), 81–93.

Schlesinger, Max, *Saunterings in and around London* (London, 1853).

Schofield, Roger, 'English Marriage Patterns Revisited', *Journal of Family History*, 10 (1985), 2–20.

SCHOPENHAUER, JOHANNA, *Reisen durch England und Schottland* (Leipzig, 1818).

The Science of Love (London, 1792).

SCOTT, BENJAMIN, *Is London More Immoral than Paris or Brussels?* (London, 1884).

SCOTT, CLEMENT, *The Wheel of Life* (London, 1897).

SCOTT, WILLIAM, 'Breach of Promise and Marriage Morals', *Saturday Review*, 2 (1856), 314–15.

SCROPE, G. POULETT, 'Malthus and Sadler—Population and Emigration', *Quarterly Review*, 45 (1831), 97–145.

SECOMBE, WALLY, 'Starting to Stop: Working-class Fertility Decline in Britain', *Past and Present*, 126 (1990), 151–88.

SEELEY, R. B., *The Perils of the Nation* (London, 1844).

SÉGUR, J. A., *Women: Their Condition and Influence in Society* (London, 1803).

SENATE, E., *The Medical Monitor* (London, 1810).

SENIOR, NASSAU WILLIAM, *Two Lectures on Population* (London, 1829).

SHAW, CHARLES, *When I was a Child* (Firle, 1977).

SHAW, DONALD, *London in the Sixties* (London, 1908).

SHIMMIN, HUGH, *Liverpool Life: Its Pleasures, Practices, and Pastimes* (Liverpool, 1856).

—— *Town Life* (London, 1858).

—— 'The "Road to Ruin" (Licensed)', *Porcupine*, 1 (1860), 56–7.

—— *Liverpool Sketches* (London, 1862).

—— *The Courts and Alleys of Liverpool* (Liverpool, 1864).

SHONFIELD, ZUZANNA, *The Precariously Privileged* (Oxford, 1987).

SHORTER, EDWARD, KNODEL, JOHN, and WALLE, ÉTIENNE VAN DE, 'The Decline of Non-Marital Fertility in Europe, 1880–1940', *PS* 25 (1971), 375–93.

SIKES, HERSCHEL MORELAND, ed., *The Letters of William Hazlitt* (London, 1979).

SILLIMAN, BENJAMIN, *A Journal of Travels in England, Holland, and Scotland* (Boston, 1812).

SIMMONS, G., *The Working Classes* (London, 1849).

SIMOND, LOUIS, *Journal of a Tour and Residence in Great Britain, during the Years 1810 and 1811* (2nd edn. London, 1817).

'Simplex', *An Inquiry into the Constitution, Government, and Practices of the Churches of Christ* (Edinburgh, 1808).

SIMS, GEORGE R., *My Life* (London, 1917).

SIMS, J. MARION, *Clinical Notes on Uterine Surgery* (London, 1866).

—— 'Illustrations of the Value of the Microscope in the Treatment of the Sterile Condition', *BMJ* 1868(2), 465–6, 492–4.

Sinks of London Laid Open (London, 1848).

SLANEY, R. A., *A Plea to Power and Parliament for the Working Classes* (London, 1847).

SLIDELL, A. MACKENZIE, *The American in England* (London, 1836).

SMEETON, GEORGE, *Doings in London* (Southwark, 1828).

SMELSER, NEIL JOSEPH, *Social Change in the Industrial Revolution* (Chicago, 1959).

SMITH, ABBOTTS, *Notes on Spermatic Diseases* (London, 1871).

SMITH, ALBERT, *The Adventures of Mr Ledbury* (London, 1844).

—— ed., *Gavarni in London* (London, 1849).

—— *Sketches of the Day (First Series)* (London, 1856).

—— *The London Medical Student* (London, 1861).

SMITH, CHARLES MANBY, *A Working-Man's Way in the World* (London, 1853).

SMITH, F. B., 'Sexuality in Britain, 1800–1900', *University of Newcastle Historical Journal*, 2 (1974), 19–32.

—— *The People's Health 1830–1910* (London, 1979).

SMITH, GOLDWIN, *The Study of History* (Oxford, 1861).

SMITH, JOHN STORES, *Social Aspects* (London, 1850).

SMITH, KENNETH, *The Malthusian Controversy* (London, 1951).

SMITH, M. B., 'Victorian Entertainment in the Lancashire Cotton Towns' in S. P. Bell, ed., *Victorian Lancashire* (Newton Abbot, 1974), 169–85.

SMITH, ROGER, 'Early Victorian Household Structure', *International Review of Social History*, 15 (1970), 69–84.

SMITH, THOMAS SOUTHWOOD, *Illustrations of the Divine Government* (3rd edn. London, 1822).

SMYTH, JAMES RICHARD, *Miscellaneous Contributions to Pathology and Therapeutics* (London, 1844).

SNELL, HENRY, *Men, Movements, and Myself* (London, 1936).

Social Science: Being Selections from John Cassell's Prize Essays (London, 1861).

Society for Bettering the Condition and Increasing the Comforts of the Poor: Reports (London, 1799–1808).

SOLOMON, SAMUEL, *A Guide to Health* (60th edn. London, c.1810).

SOLOWAY, R. A., *Prelates and People* (London, 1969).

SOUTHEY, ROBERT, 'Malthus's Essay on Population', *Annual Review*, 2 (1804), 292–301.

—— 'Inquiry into the Poor Laws etc.', *Quarterly Review*, 8 (1812), 319–56.

—— 'On the State of the Poor', *Quarterly Review*, 15 (1816), 187–235.

—— 'On the Poor Laws', *Quarterly Review*, 18 (1818a), 259–308.

—— 'On the Means of Improving the People', *Quarterly Review*, 19 (1818b), 79–118.

—— *Essays, Moral and Political* (London, 1832).

SPENCER, ALFRED, ed., *The Memoirs of William Hickey* (London, 1913–25).

SPENCER, HERBERT, 'A Theory of Population, Deduced from the General Law of Animal Fertility', *Westminster Review*, NS 1 (1852), 468–501.

—— *The Study of Sociology* (London, 1873).

Sports, Pastimes, and Customs of London (London, 1847).

STAEL-HOLSTEIN, A. L. de, *Letters on England* (London, 1825).

STEDMAN JONES, GARETH, *Outcast London* (Oxford, 1971).

STEPHEN, JAMES FITZJAMES, 'Buckle's *History of Civilisation in England*', *Edinburgh Review*, 107 (1858), 465–512.

STEVENSON, T. H. C., 'The Fertility of Various Social Classes in England and Wales from the Middle of the Nineteenth Century to 1911', *JSSL* 83 (1920), 401–44.

STOPES, MARIE CARMICHAEL, *The Early Days of Birth Control* (London, 1922).

STORCH, ROBERT D., 'Police Control of Street Prostitution in Victorian London', in David H. Bayley, ed., *Police and Society* (Denver, Colo., 1977), 49–72.

STRUTT, ELIZABETH, *The Feminine Soul: Its Nature and Attributes* (London, 1857).

STURT, THOMAS JAMES, *Female Physiology* (London, 1854).

SUMNER, JOHN BIRD, *A Treatise on the Records of the Creation* (London, 1816).

SWAN, GUIDA, ed., *The Journals of Two Poor Dissenters 1786–1880* (London, 1970).

SYMONS, JELLINGER C., *Tactics for the Times* (London, 1849).

—— *Rough Types of English Life* (London, 1860).

TAINE, HIPPOLYTE, *Notes on England*, trans E. Hyams (London, 1957).

TAIT, ROBERT LAWSON, *Diseases of Women* (Edinburgh, 1877).

TALBOT, JAMES BEARD, *The Miseries of Prostitution* (London, 1844).

TAYLER, WILLIAM, *Diary of William Tayler, Footman*, ed. Dorothy Wise (London, 1962).

TAYLOR, ARTHUR J., ed., *The Standard of Living in Britain in the Industrial Revolution* (London, 1975).

TAYLOR, ISAAC, *Advice to the Teens* (London, 1818).

TAYLOR, SHEPHARD T., *The Diary of a Medical Student during the Mid-Victorian Period 1860–1864* (Norwich, 1927).

TAYLOR, W. COOKE, *Notes of a Tour in the Manufacturing Districts of Lancashire* (2nd edn. London, 1842).

Tea-Gardens and Spas of Old London (London, 1880).

TEITELBAUM, M. S., *The British Fertility Decline* (Princeton, NJ, 1984).

TEXIER, EDMOND, *Lettres sur l'Angleterre* (Paris, 1851).

THIEBLIN, NICHOLAS LEON ('Azamut-Batuk'), *A Little Book about Great Britain* (London, 1870).

THOLFSEN, TRYGVE R., *Working-Class Radicalism in Mid-Victorian England* (London, 1976).

THOMAS, DAVID, 'The Social Origins of Marriage Partners of the British Peerage in the Eighteenth and Nineteenth Centuries', *PS* 26 (1972), 99–111.

THOMAS, EDWARD W., *Twenty-five Years' Labour among the Friendless and Fallen* (London, 1879).

THOMAS, ROBERT, *The Way to Preserve Good Health* (Salisbury, 1822).

THOMASON, DENNY R., *Fashionable Amusements* (London, 1827).

THOMPSON, E. P., 'The Political Education of Henry Mayhew', *Victorian Studies*, 11 (1967), 41–62.

THOMPSON, F. M. L., *The Rise of Respectable Society* (London, 1988).

THOMPSON, WILLIAM, *An Inquiry into the Principles of the Distribution of Wealth* (London, 1824).

—— *Appeal of One Half of the Human Race, Women, against the Pretensions of the Other Half, Men, to Retain them in Political, and thence in Civil and Domestic, Slavery* (London, 1825).

THOMSON, CHRISTOPHER, *Autobiography of an Artisan* (London, 1847).

THORBURN, GRANT, *Men and Manners in Britain* (Glasgow, 1835).

THORNTON, WILLIAM THOMAS, *Over-Population and its Remedy* (London, 1846).

THUDICHUM, J. L. W., *A Treatise on the Pathology of the Urine* (London, 1858).

TILT, E. J., *Elements of Health, and Principles of Female Hygiene* (London, 1852).

TIMBS, JOHN, *Curiosities of London* (London, 1855).

—— *Walks and Talks about London* (London, 1865).

TOBIAS, J. J., *Crime and Industrial Society in the Nineteenth Century* (London, 1967).

TODD, ROBERT B., *The Cyclopeadia of Anatomy and Physiology*, ii (London, 1836–9), v (London, 1858).

Toilers in London (London, 1883).

TOLLY, BARON BARCLAY DE, *L'Angleterre, l'Irlande et l'Écosse* (Paris, 1843).

TOMES, NANCY, 'A "Torrent of Abuse": Crimes of Violence between Working-Class Men and Women in London, 1840–1875', *Journal of Social History*, 11 (1978), 328–46.

TRABAUD, P., *D'Inverness à Brighton* (London, 1853).

TRAILL, H. D., 'The Abdication of Mrs Grundy', *National Review*, 17 (1891), 12–24.

TRANTER, N. L., *Population and Society 1750–1940* (London, 1985).

TREBLE, J. H., 'Liverpool Working-Class Housing, 1801–1851', in S. D. Chapman, ed., *The History of Working Class Housing* (Newton Abbot, 1971) 167–220.

TRISTAN, FLORA, *London Journal*, trans. Dennis Palmer and Giselle Pincetl (London, 1980).

TROLLOPE, FRANCES, *Domestic Manners of the Americans* (New York, 1949).

TRUDGILL, ERIC, 'Prostitution and Paterfamilias', in H. J. Dyos and Michael Wolff, eds., *The Victorian City* (London, 1973), ii. 693–705.

—— *Madonnas and Magdalens* (London, 1976).

TUCKERMAN, HENRY T., *A Month in England* (London, 1854).

TURNER, SHARON, *The Sacred History of the World*, iii (London, 1837).

TWISS, HORACE, 'Answers to Mr Malthus's Essay on the Principle of Population', *London Review*, 1 (1809), 355–413.

'Two Citizens of the World', *How to Live in London* (London, 1828).

TYNG, STEPHEN H., *Recollections of England* (London, 1847).

URDANK, ALBION M. 'Religion and Reproduction among English Dissenters: Gloucestershire Baptists in the Demographic Revolution', *Comparative Studies in Society and History*, 33 (1991), 511–27.

URE, ANDREW, *The Philosophy of Manufactures* (London, 1835).

VALLES, JULES, *La Rue à Londres* (Paris, 1884).

VANDEKISTE, R. W., *Notes and Narratives of a Six Years' Mission* (London, 1852).

VARLEY, HENRY *Lecture to Men* (4th edn. London, 1884).

VAUGHAN, ROBERT, *The Age of the Great Cities* (London, 1843).

—— 'Buckle on Civilisation', *British Quarterly Review*, 28 (1858), 3–43.

VAUX, JAMES HARDY, *Memoirs* (London, 1819).

VENABLES, ROBERT, *Elements of Urinary Analysis and Diagnosis* (2nd edn. London, 1850).

VENN, JOHN, *The Logic of Chance* (London, 1866).

VERNE, JULES, *Voyage à reculons en Angleterre et en Écosse* (Paris, 1989).

'Vestrian', *Illegitimates* (London, 1834).

VICINUS, MARTHA, *The Industrial Muse* (London, 1974).

A View of London (London, 1803–4).

VINTRAS, A., *On the Repressive Measures Adopted in Paris* (London, 1867).

WADDINGTON, EDWARD, 'Masturbation in a Female Apparently without a Uterus', *BMJ* (1853), 672–3.

WADDINGTON, IVAN, *The Medical Profession in the Industrial Revolution* (Dublin, 1984).

WADE, JOHN, *A Treatise on the Police and Crimes of the Metropolis* (London, 1829).

—— *Women, Past and Present* (London, 1859).

WAKEFIELD, EDWARD GIBBON, *Facts Relating to the Punishment of Death in the Metropolis* (London, 1831).

—— *England and America* (London, 1833).

WALKER, ALEXANDER, *Woman Physiologically Considered, as to Mind, Morals, Marriage, Matrimonial Slavery, Infidelity and Divorce* (2nd edn. London, 1840).

WALKOWITZ, JUDITH R., *Prostitution and Victorian Society* (Cambridge, 1980).

—— *City of Dreadful Delight* (London, 1992).

WALL, MARY M., and HIRSCH, JENNY, *Haus und Gesellschaft in England* (Berlin, 1878).

WALLACE, ALFRED RUSSEL, *My Life* (London, 1905).

WALTON, JOHN K., and WILCOX, ALISTAIR, eds., *Low Life and Moral Improvement in Mid-Victorian England* (Leicester, 1991).

WARD, DAVID, 'The Early Victorian City in England and America', in James R. Ward, ed., *European Settlement and Development in North America* (Folkestone, 1978), 170–89.

WARDLAW, RALPH, *Lectures on Female Prostitution* (Glasgow, 1842).

WARE, HELEN RUTH ELIZABETH, 'The Recruitment, Regulation and Role of Prostitution in Britain from the Middle of the Nineteenth Century to the Present Day', University of London, Ph.D. thesis (1969).

WARE, WILLIAM, *Sketches of European Capitals* (Boston, Mass., 1851).

WARWICK, FRANCES, COUNTESS OF, *Life's Ebb and Flow* (London, 1929).

WAUGH, EDWIN, *Sketches of Lancashire Life and Localities* (London, 1855).

—— *Home-Life of the Lancashire Factory Folk during the Cotton Famine* (London, 1867).

WEIR, DAVID R., 'Rather Now than Late: Celibacy and Age of Marriage in English Cohort Fertility, 1541–1871', *Journal of Family History*, 9 (1984), 340–54.

WEIR, WILLIAM, 'Some Features of London Life of Last Century', in Charles Knight, ed., *London*, ii (London, 1842), 345–68; 'St Giles Past and Present', ibid. 257–72.

WELLS, H. G., *Ann Veronica* (London, 1909).

—— *The New Machiavelli* (London, 1911).

WELLS, ROBERT V., 'Family History and Demographic Transition', *Journal of Social History*, 9 (1975), 1–19.

WELTON, THOMAS A., *Observations upon Population Statistics* (Liverpool, 1869).

WENDEBORN, GEBHARDT FRIEDRICH, *A View of England* (London, 1791).

WEST, ALGERNON, 'Some Changes in Social Life during the Queen's Reign', *Nineteenth Century*, 41 (1897), 639–55.

WEST, CHARLES, *An Inquiry into the Pathological Importance of Ulceration of the Os Uteri* (London, 1854).

—— *Lectures on the Diseases of Women* (London, 1856).

WEY, FRANCIS, *Les Anglais chez eux* (Paris, 1856).

WEYDEN, ERNST, *Sanger-fahrt des Kolner, Manner–Gesang–Vereins nach London* (Cologne, 1854).

WEYLAND, JOHN, *The Principles of Population and Production* (London, 1816).

WHARTON JONES, T., 'Report on the Ovum of Man and the Mammifera', *British and Foreign Medical Review*, 16 (1843), 513–57.

WHEATON, NATHANIEL S., *A Journal of a Residence during Several Months in London* (Hartford, 1830).

WHEELER, JAMES, *Manchester: Its Political, Social and Commercial History* (London, 1836).

WHITE, JOSHUA E., *Letters on England* (Philadelphia, 1816).

WHITE, RICHARD GRANT, *England without and within* (Boston, Mass., 1881).

WHITEHEAD, JAMES, *On the Causes and Treatment of Abortion and Sterility* (London, 1847).

WHITEING, RICHARD, *My Harvest* (London, 1915).

WIENER, MARTIN J., *Reconstructing the Criminal* (Cambridge, 1990).

WIKOFF, HENRY, *The Reminiscences of an Idler* (London, 1880).

WILLIAMS, MONTAGU STEPHEN, *Leaves of a Life* (London, 1890).

WILSON, C., 'Natural Fertility in Pre-industrial England, 1600–1799', *PS* 38 (1984), 225–40.

WILSON, JAMES, *Lectures on the Structure and Physiology of the Male Urinary and Genital Organs* (London, 1821).

WILSON, JOHN, 'Balance of the Food and Numbers of Animated Nature', *Blackwoods*, 28 (1830), 109–35.

—— 'Mr Sadler and the Edinburgh Reviewer. . .', *Blackwoods*, 29 (1831), 392–428.

WILSON, MARRIS, 'Contributions to the Physiology, Pathology, and Treatment of Spermatorrhoea', *Lancet* 1856(2), 215–17, 300–2, 482–4, 643–4.

WOHL, ANTHONY S., 'The Housing of the Working-Classes in London 1815–1914', in S. D. Chapman, ed., *The History of Working Class Housing* (Newton Abbot, 1971) 15–54.

—— *The Eternal Slum* (London, 1977).

WOOD, CLIVE, and SUITTERS, BERYL, *The Fight for Acceptance* (Aylesbury, 1970).

WOOD, HENRY ('An American Lady'), *Change for the American Notes* (London, 1843).

WOODRUFF, WILLIAM, *The Rise of the British Rubber Industry* (Liverpool, 1958).

WOODS, R. I., 'Social Class Fertility Variations in the Decline of Marital Fertility in Late Nineteenth-Century London', *Geografiska Annaler*, 66B

(1984), 29–38.

—— 'Approaches to the Fertility Transition in Victorian England', *PS* 41 (1987), 283–311.

—— and HINDE, P. R. A., 'Nuptiality and Age of Marriage in Nineteenth-Century England', *Journal of Family History*, 10 (1985), 119–44.

—— and SMITH, C. W., 'The Decline of Marital Fertility in the Late Nineteenth Century: The Case of England and Wales', *PS* 37 (1983), 207–25.

WOOLCOCK, HELEN R., *Rights of Passage* (London, 1986).

'A Working Man', *Scenes from My Life* (London, 1858).

WORSLEY, HENRY, *Juvenile Depravity* (London, 1849).

WORSNOP, JUDITH, 'A Reevaluation of "The Problem of Surplus Women" in 19th-Century England', *Women's Studies International Forum*, 12 (1990), 21–31.

WRIGHT, GEORGE, 'Statistics of the Parish of St George the Martyr, Southwark', *JSSL* 3 (1840), 50–71.

WRIGHT, THOMAS, *Some Habits and Customs of the Working Classes* (London, 1867).

—— *The Great Unwashed* (London, 1868).

—— *Our New Masters* (London, 1873).

WRIGLEY, E. A., and SCHOFIELD, R. S., *The Population History of England 1541–1871* (Cambridge, 1989).

WROTH, WARWICK WILLIAM, *The London Pleasure Gardens of the Eighteenth Century* (London, 1896).

YATES, EDMUND HODGSON, *Edmund Yates: His Recollections and Experiences* (London, 1884).

YEOMAN, T. H., *Debility and Irritability Induced by Spermatorrhoea* (London, 1854).

Yokel's Preceptor (London, *c*.1855).

YOUNG, GAVIN, *Observations on the Law of Population* (London, 1832).

YOUNG, ROBERT, *The Second Report and Address of the Philanthropic Society* (London, 1789).

YULE, G. UDNY, 'On the Changes in the Marriage- and Birth-rates during the Past Half Century . . .', *JSSL* 69 (1906), 88–147.

—— *The Fall of the Birth-rate* (Cambridge, 1920).

Periodicals

Analytical Review, Anti-Jacobin, Belgravia, Bentley's Miscellany, Biograph and Review, Blackwoods, Bow Bells, British Controversialist, British Critic, British and Foreign Medico-Chirurgical Review, British Gynecological Journal, British Medical Journal, British Quarterly, Cassell's Illustrated Family Paper, Coal Hole Companion, Cobbett's Twopenny Trash, Crim-Con Gazette, Dublin Quarterly Journal of Medical Science, Dublin University Magazine, Eclectic Review, Economist, Edinburgh Medical and Surgical Journal, Edinburgh Monthly Review, Exquisite, Female's Friend, Foreign Quarterly Review, Frasers Magazine, Halfpenny Journal, Household Journal, Household Words, Imperial Review, Intellectual Repository, Investigator, Isis, Journal of Education, Journal of Psychological Medicine, Journal of

Social History, JSSL, Key, Lancet, Leader, Liverpool Critic, Liverpool Weekly Post, Livesey's Moral Reformer, London Journal, London Magazine, London Medical and Surgical Journal, London Medical Gazette, London Medical Review, London Reader, London Review, London Saturday Journal, London Society, London Weekly Magazine, Magdalen's Friend, Medical Adviser, Medical Press and Circular, Medical Times, Medical Times and Gazette, Medico-Chirurgical Review, Medico-Chirurgical Transactions, Meliora, Monthly Review, Moral Reformer, Morning Chronicle, NAPSS, National, National Reformer, New Monthly Magazine, New Scientist, New Statesman, North British Review, Paul Pry, People's Journal, Political Register, Population and Development Review, Porcupine, Quarterly Review, Rambler, Reasoner, Sanitary Review and Journal of Public Health, Saturday Review, Scourge, Taits, Temple Bar, The Times, Times Literary Supplement, TNAPSS, Town, VPNL, Westminster Review.

Index

OXFORD

MORE OXFORD PAPERBACKS

This book is just one of nearly 1000 Oxford Paperbacks currently in print. If you would like details of other Oxford Paperbacks, including titles in the World's Classics, Oxford Reference, Oxford Books, OPUS, Past Masters, Oxford Authors, and Oxford Shakespeare series, please write to:

UK and Europe: Oxford Paperbacks Publicity Manager, Arts and Reference Publicity Department, Oxford University Press, Walton Street, Oxford OX2 6DP.

Customers in UK and Europe will find Oxford Paperbacks available in all good bookshops. But in case of difficulty please send orders to the Cash-with-Order Department, Oxford University Press Distribution Services, Saxon Way West, Corby, Northants NN18 9ES. Tel: 0536 741519; Fax: 0536 746337. Please send a cheque for the total cost of the books, plus £1.75 postage and packing for orders under £20; £2.75 for orders over £20. Customers outside the UK should add 10% of the cost of the books for postage and packing.

USA: Oxford Paperbacks Marketing Manager, Oxford University Press, Inc., 200 Madison Avenue, New York, N.Y. 10016.

Canada: Trade Department, Oxford University Press, 70 Wynford Drive, Don Mills, Ontario M3C 1J9.

Australia: Trade Marketing Manager, Oxford University Press, G.P.O. Box 2784Y, Melbourne 3001, Victoria.

South Africa: Oxford University Press, P.O. Box 1141, Cape Town 8000.

HISTORY IN OXFORD PAPERBACKS

THE STRUGGLE FOR
THE MASTERY OF EUROPE 1848–1918

A. J. P. Taylor

The fall of Metternich in the revolutions of 1848 heralded an era of unprecedented nationalism in Europe, culminating in the collapse of the Hapsburg, Romanov, and Hohenzollern dynasties at the end of the First World War. In the intervening seventy years the boundaries of Europe changed dramatically from those established at Vienna in 1815. Cavour championed the cause of *Risorgimento* in Italy; Bismarck's three wars brought about the unification of Germany; Serbia and Bulgaria gained their independence courtesy of the decline of Turkey—'the sick man of Europe'; while the great powers scrambled for places in the sun in Africa. However, with America's entry into the war and President Wilson's adherence to idealistic internationalist principles, Europe ceased to be the centre of the world, although its problems, still primarily revolving around nationalist aspirations, were to smash the Treaty of Versailles and plunge the world into war once more.

A. J. P. Taylor has drawn the material for his account of this turbulent period from the many volumes of diplomatic documents which have been published in the five major European languages. By using vivid language and forceful characterization, he has produced a book that is as much a work of literature as a contribution to scientific history.

'One of the glories of twentieth-century writing.'
Observer

HISTORY IN OXFORD PAPERBACKS
TUDOR ENGLAND
John Guy

Tudor England is a compelling account of political and religious developments from the advent of the Tudors in the 1460s to the death of Elizabeth I in 1603.

Following Henry VII's capture of the Crown at Bosworth in 1485, Tudor England witnessed far-reaching changes in government and the Reformation of the Church under Henry VIII, Edward VI, Mary, and Elizabeth; that story is enriched here with character studies of the monarchs and politicians that bring to life their personalities as well as their policies.

Authoritative, clearly argued, and crisply written, this comprehensive book will be indispensable to anyone interested in the Tudor Age.

'lucid, scholarly, remarkably accomplished . . . an excellent overview' *Sunday Times*

'the first comprehensive history of Tudor England for more than thirty years' Patrick Collinson, *Observer*

OXFORD REFERENCE

THE CONCISE OXFORD COMPANION
TO ENGLISH LITERATURE

*Edited by Margaret Drabble and
Jenny Stringer*

Based on the immensely popular fifth edition of the
Oxford Companion to English Literature this is an
indispensable, compact guide to the central matter
of English literature.

There are more than 5,000 entries on the lives
and works of authors, poets, playwrights, essayists,
philosophers, and historians; plot summaries of
novels and plays; literary movements; fictional
characters; legends; theatres; periodicals; and much
more.

The book's sharpened focus on the English literature of the British Isles makes it especially convenient to use, but there is still generous coverage of
the literature of other countries and of other disci-
plines which have influenced or been influenced by
English literature.

From reviews of *The Oxford Companion to
English Literature*:

'a book which one turns to with constant pleasure
. . . a book with much style and little prejudice' Iain
Gilchrist, *TLS*

'it is quite difficult to imagine, in this genre, a more
useful publication' Frank Kermode, *London Review of Books*

'incarnates a living sense of tradition . . . sensitive
not to fashion merely but to the spirit of the age'
Christopher Ricks, *Sunday Times*